The Languages
& Literatures of Africa

KU-525-424

The Languages
& Literatures of Africa

The Sands of Babel

ALAIN RICARD

Research Professor,
Centre National de la
Recherche Scientifique, Paris

Translated from the French by
Naomi Morgan

 CENTRE NATIONAL
DE LA RECHERCHE
SCIENTIFIQUE

James Currey
OXFORD
Africa World Press
TRENTON, NJ
David Philip
CAPE TOWN

James Currey Ltd
73 Botley Rd
Oxford OX2 0BS

Africa World Press, Inc.
PO Box 1892
Trenton NJ 08607

David Philip Publishers
an imprint of New Africa Books (Pty) Ltd
99 Garfield Road
Claremont 7700, Cape Town

© Alain Ricard 2004
First published 2004

Ouvrage publié avec le concours du Ministère
français chargé de la culture – Centre national du livre
Original edition in French, published 1995
Littératures d'Afrique noire: des langues aux livres
CNRS Editions and Karthala (Paris)

1 2 3 4 5 08 07 06 05 04

British Library Cataloguing in Publication Data
Ricard, Alain
    The languages & literatures of Africa : the sands of Babel
    1. African literature - History and criticism
    I. Title II. Centre national de la recherche scientifique
    809.8'967

ISBN 0-85255-581-4 (James Currey paper)
        0-85255-582-2 (James Currey cloth)

Typeset in 9/11 pt Melior by Long House Publishing Services, Cumbria, UK
Printed in the United States of America

Contents

List of Maps

Preface

I started this book in Nairobi over a decade ago: a first version of it was published in France in 1995. This is a revised and expanded translation of the original book. The first text was written with the French and Francophone reader in mind. I argued that there was no general book in French on the literatures of Africa and that the French tendency to separate Ethiopia from the rest of the continent, or South Africa from her southern neighbours had no justification in scholarship. If I excluded from my investigation the five Northern Arabic-speaking states, as well as Sudan, it was merely because of my lack of linguistic competence. The French version dealt with Africa south of the Sahel, her neighbouring islands, and the literature produced in these countries.

The main objective of the book was to study what I call the linguistic consciousness in the literatures of Africa. I was struck by the fact that many writers claimed that writing in a foreign language was no problem, even natural for them. The question was even felt to be irrelevant. For me, however, as a former student of the Nouveau Roman (New Novel), language was always problematic. A diglossic situation merely brought to the fore a pervasive feature of literary creation.

One never writes as one speaks; different sets of conventions operate; the study of literature, whether history of literature or philology, is the study of the different forms these conventions take. Denial of the problematic nature of the relationship with the adopted literary language is a feature of what that expert in literary consciousness, Harald Weinrich, calls 'linguistik der lüge' [lying]: excessive denial implies recognition. This has been especially true in the case of Francophone writers and has taken many forms, from Mongo Beti's assertive assurance to Senghor's nebulous theories on negritude. These attitudes met with enormous Gallic-chauvinist pleasure and propagated a mystical view of literary creation that has hindered generations of readers, scholars and would-be writers.

I was fortunate to come across the works and ideas of Wole Soyinka at the beginning of my studies, more than thirty years ago. They cleared my mind of all kinds of preconceptions and false ideas about Africa and made me focus on the relationship between the writer and his own environment (Nigeria), on the variety of tongues spoken and used there, and on the fantastic poetic resource they represented. From the translation of the Yoruba novel *Ogboju Ode ninu Igbo Irunmale*, to the 'rotten' English spoken by the side of *The Road*, the first books I read by Wole Soyinka depicted, questioned and reinvented the African language situation in a brilliant and convincing manner. His works were also poetic statements – whether translations, plays, other works of art – all crafted with talent. He supplied new forms that would set new terms of reference for the years to come: this was my feeling when I first read him in the late 'sixties and still is. For Soyinka, language was indeed problematic, a permanent challenge, whatever the language. His works demonstrated that he was up to that challenge.

Ngugi wa Thiong'o achieved the same epistemological break when he started to write in Gikuyu. Suddenly the transparency of Karen Blixen's Kenya becomes opaque: Kenya is a country where people speak languages the Baroness did not understand. All Kenyans do not speak English: those who do, ride in downtown elevators and do not live down River Road nor in Kibera. Ngugi questioned the language he used, wrote essays on his efforts and problems in trying to write what he spoke. This is never easy: I was told that students from Mombasa fail the Kiswahili exams more often than those Kenyans who do not live in a Kiswahili environment. Those who speak Kiswahili do not necessarily write it correctly. The standard form is an arbitrary but necessary imposition. Ngugi wrote with great honesty and great depth. He kept encouraging others to follow him and today he heads a centre to promote translation. One of the constant themes of my book is that translation is the key analytic exercise of the linguistic consciousness and that too few translations exist of African literary works. Kenyan bookshops offer many world classics as well as African literary works such as Soyinka's in Kiswahili, but this is not enough. It took fifty years to translate *Indyohesha Birayi* [The flavour enhancer of potatoes, ie: the pig!] from Kinyarwanda into French. Yet the Kinyarwanda version is familiar in book form to all Rwandans....

A century of African thought was set down in written form, quite often by home-grown intellectuals from the grassroots, born and raised far away from any Western metropolis. Their efforts deserve our interest: the recent English translation of a Kerewe novel – now a Kiswahili classic, *Myombekere na Bibi Bugonoka*, is a landmark and a remarkable achievement in African publishing. But I recognize the local differences in Africa. No single formula holds true for the linguistic situation in Côte d'Ivoire, Zimbabwe, Tanzania and the Democratic Republic of Congo (former Zaïre). A creative use of language is built on an awareness of the dynamism of speech communities as well as on a willingness to experiment freely. This applies to those writers I call the 'go-betweens', who have been models of a creative use of language and translation. As Moradewun Adejunmobi so aptly put it in relation to J.J. Rabearivelo, 'translation [was used] as a creative tool'.

This book starts with a critical examination of theories and notions about Africa and her languages. One cannot separate theories about literature from theories about language. The low intellectual estimation accorded to African languages is the product of ignorance and has had a profound impact on research in the oral tradition as well as on African literatures written in African languages. This book attempts to make room for all these. We have, thanks to translations, access to monographic studies (Daniel Kunene) and scholarly studies (Gérard), plus a large body of literature with many important works. The present emphasis on multiculturalism does not translate easily into research on multilingualism. Such research is essential. As Karin Barber comments:

> In Africa and India, English, and writing in English, co-exists with other languages and writings, and is deployed by specific strata of the population for specific

purposes. The relationships between them cannot be reduced to simple assertions about colonial domination, assimilation, appropriation or mimicry.

What goes on in the English texts can only be understood if the full presence of texts in indigenous languages is acknowledged – not as a shadowy, vaguely-delineated, value-laden 'oral heritage' in the background, but as a modern, mainstream, hetero-geneous, hybrid and changing mode of discourse, created and recreated daily by the majority of the population. (Barber, 1995)

Research priority is given to Francophone or Anglophone literature. Too often mediocre works in these languages are subjected to an avalanche of critical readings while important works in African languages are left untouched and ignored by students. Without them Africa cannot be understood. Dozens of theses are written on Shaka in Francophone literature studies while no biography of Mofolo, one of Africa's greatest novelist, is on the market.

My conception of linguistic consciousness comes from Harald Weinrich. As a Romance language specialist he reflected on the different linguistic attitudes of the French compared to the Spaniards. He gave historical context to ideas about precision and clarity of language, relating them to conscious, even political, efforts to promote a language. No language has these virtues full-blown: each one must be refined – precisely what is undertaken now by the Institute of Kiswahili Research.

The French version of this book was reissued in 1998. While partially rewriting and translating the book for an English-speaking audience, I kept in constant dialogue with friends and colleagues in the Anglophone world. This led to important changes in chapters 1 and 5, which were almost entirely rewritten. I also adapted the examples to a different audience and enlarged the coverage of languages I knew, benefiting enormously from the rise of Kiswahili scholarship in Kenya and Tanzania.

More than a decade after the liberation of South Africa from a part of her past, I believe that the future of Africa does not compel us to forget all of her languages. Ngugi has set an example and provides a very powerful and con-vincing pragmatic model: he calls not only for translation, but for exchange! A linguistic community has to agree on a written version of its language. This is an exercise in democracy: reaching a consensus on an orthography is often as difficult as reaching a consensus on a constitution. A decision cannot come from the top but has to be accepted and appropriated by the linguistic community in a practical way that takes its whole history into consideration. A writing system is also a cultural monument.

I completed this introduction while lecturing at the Kigali Institute of Educa-tion. Rwanda will become a trilingual country with two official languages, French and English, and one national language, Kinyarwanda. As of today, very few translations from Kinyarwanda exist, either in French or in English. Rwanda's silence was also our refusal to listen, to pay attention to what was being said. Rwandans have to talk to each other and to talk to the rest of the world: this is the only way to heal.

Kigali – Nairobi

Acknowledgements

Special thanks are due to colleagues and friends who answered my questions and with whom I kept in constant dialogue: Simon Amegbleame, Karin Barber, Elena Bertoncini, Sory Camara, Phyllis Clark-Taoua, Virginia Coulon, Jean Derive, Daniel Delas, Clémentine Faïk-Nzuji, Graham Furniss, Larry Hyman, Abiola Irele, Bernth Lindfors, Alamin Mazrui, Bernard Mouralis, Mwatha Ngalasso, Kole Omotoso, Femi Osofisan, János Riesz, Jean-Norbert Vignonde, Chris Swanepoel, Henry Tourneux, Flora Veit-Wild, Senouvo Zinsou. Thanks also to Eric Audinet, Robert Ageneau, Walter Bgoya, Henry Chakava, Hans Zell, all enterprising publishers.

To Lynn Taylor for her advice, to Naomi Morgan for her comments and her translation, to my wife for her support.

1

The Classification & Ranking of African Languages

ON CONCEPTS & MISCONCEPTIONS

Background to the Debate

Pride in Africa's diversity has long been counterbalanced by its people's desire for unity and a profound longing to discover the roots of a Pan-African community. In *Nations nègres et culture* (1955), the late Senegalese scholar, Cheikh Anta Diop suggested that the origins of such cultural unity were to be found in Egypt. In an article, 'The Semitic Impact on Black Africa, Arab and Jewish Influences' (1984), an alternative theory was raised by the Kenyan scholar, Ali Mazrui, widening the debate by proposing that Africa's contemporary culture was the result of a triple heritage (autochthonous, Semitic and Western).

Both Cheikh Anta Diop and Ali Mazrui are influential African writers and intellectuals whose works provide important material for those readers interested in Africa's intellectual history; at the same time they each have idiosyncratic features. Cheikh Anta Diop was translated into English only recently, while Ali Mazrui is still almost unknown in France and in Francophone Africa. None of his books have been translated into French. In style their respective books could not be more in contrast. A militant student in his day, Cheikh Anta Diop grew up in an anti-colonialist, Marxist environment, while the nuanced thinking of Mazrui, a professor of political science, probably grows out of his deep knowledge of Swahili culture. These two original thinkers provide the main elements of contrast for a theory of African identity, a necessary basis for an African history of literature. The completion in 1981 of UNESCO's *General History of Africa* (subsequently translated into French and more recently (2000) into Kiswahili) provided a wider arena for debate on this theme and offers a number of tentative conclusions.

The idea of an African or even a Pan-African unity, which was central in the minds of the anti-colonialist intellectuals and provided the source of cultural and political nationalism, is now being replaced by the notion of '*métissage*'. An important compatriot of Diop, Léopold Sédar Senghor, has also written several books on this theme, which he considers to be a positive development, and which, according to Soyinka in *The Burden of Memory* (1999), seeks to find a 'prophetic resonance in the politics of post-apartheid South Africa'. The often dogmatic prophets of the campaign for 'unity' are being replaced by newer voices promoting a multicultural Africa.

This is not to suggest that the battle is over. To quote one example, the Congo-Brazzaville historian, Théophile Obenga, continues to promulgate Cheikh Anta Diop's ideas and argues that the Bantu cultures are the key to the theory of a unified identity. The Afro-centrist camp supporting Egypt's central position in relation to Greece somewhat muddles the Diop thesis, but nonetheless comes out of the same corner: if Athena was black, it was because

Egypt was black. The argument is also relevant to so-called racial categories expressed in terms of 'black' and 'white' as this relates to cultural history, and will be addressed at a later stage.

The nineteenth-century approach to the realities of culture and language was characterized by an obsession with rank. Its systematic, hierarchical classification bears the mark of evolutionism. Earlier biblical monogenism, proclaiming the common descent of all men from Adam and Eve, prevented classifications of this nature (although it did not deter Christians from enslaving their black brothers, who 'scientifically' justified their behaviour). Nineteenth-century scientific racism arrived at the very moment Africa found itself divided. The aspect of this racism of special relevance here is that of language – a contribution from French researchers, especially from the comparative philologist, Ernest Renan, as illustrated by the following quotation from Tzvetan Todorov:

> Linguistic races are the product of philology alone, but these products are physical races nonetheless.... Far from jettisoning the concept of race, Renan's work gives it a new footing, since it is with Renan (and certain of his contemporaries) that the terms Aryan and Semite cease to designate language families and begin to apply to races, that is to human beings. (Todorov, 1993:144)

All men may be equal, but their languages are different; some languages are better and more sophisticated than others. The first basis for this theory was Lepsius's three categories of language groups according to the names of Noah's sons (Shem, Ham and Japheth), which Renan took to its logical extreme. The Indo-European or Japhetic languages were the sophisticated languages of dis-criminating minds; Semitic languages were the (as yet unrefined) expression of Oriental creative confusion; while Hamitic languages were the rough instruments of a primitive people. The endless list of contradictions in the theory's draft version did not deter Carl Meinhof (1912, 1936), the foremost Africanist linguist of the 1920s, from supporting its thesis.

On Tones & Noun Classes

Linguistic diversity, or what Mazrui calls the *Power of Babel* (1998), to quote from the title of his recent book, is plain to see/hear in Africa. The builders of that biblical tower must have been sent to Africa, judging from the more than 1,500 languages spoken on the continent. A small country like Togo has 54 languages, while Nigeria boasts 252 languages for a hundred million people. Although its population is five times smaller, Cameroon has the same number of languages. Language atlas makers have worked hard to quantify the seemingly endless diversity of language: languages as typologically different as Chinese from English are known to co-exist, testifying to a variety of African migration patterns in many areas. Numerous unexplored and undocumented areas of African archaeology and history, such as Igbo Ukwu or Meroe, are still to be added to the list. Areas such as Southern Africa, where Bantu languages are closely related and quite often mutually comprehensible, are more homogeneous than those of the Gulf of Benin. Our assessment of this extra-ordinary variety thus has to be measured, for it is only one side of the coin. The other is multilingualism and demographic size. The known homogeneous language communities often have more speakers than many European language communities: there are more than twenty million Yoruba speakers, and the same number applies to Igbo. In Western Europe, Greek and Hungarian have never obtained similar scores. Shona speakers, like their Zulu counterparts, amount to more than ten million. The vernacular languages of 'great expansion' (Ngalasso, 1985) such as Kiswahili in East Africa, are spreading to reach new speakers on a daily basis. The picture that emerges focuses on the inter-comprehension, the similarities, mutual understanding and inter-African communication at all levels of society without the use of a European language. Our intention is not to deny the importance of these new Afro-Western languages. Africa's intellectual elite, as well as a large segment of the middle class (where there is one) have appropriated French, English and Portuguese, languages that are in Africa to stay. They do not, however, tell the whole story, and may obscure other linguistic dynamics operating in the literary and cultural field.

One of the main problems of African languages is their poor image. They have been misrepresented, poorly understood and described in a very negative way. Their position at the bottom of the evolutionary scale has already been mentioned and has played an important role in discouraging and misleading researchers. Although linguists have sought to improve this negative image, it still casts a lingering shadow over the language conceptions of writers, readers, teachers and intellectuals who have difficulty understanding the specific problems of these languages when faced with the so-called 'culture of the book', which is after all what creative writing is all about (for the time being and probably for a few decades to come).

Tone, Pitch, Intonation & Print

> In any case, whatever the contents, their (verbal) relationship is evident from their common lexical stock and by a set of structural features, none of which are present in all the languages, but several of which (such as the distinctive use of pitch, or the distribution of nouns in classes) are widespread. (Manessy, 1981)

Tone is often confused with intonation: a simple method of distinguishing between the two is to remember that pitch (tone) affects the meaning of words while intonation affects the meaning of the sentence. In many languages, the number of minimal pairs (words distinguished exclusively by pitch) is very high and poses a problem as far as spelling and lexicology are concerned. This is a basic problem when it comes to a written or publishable text, and thus impacts on a modern cultural assessment of such a language.

Most African languages are tone languages: all Nigerian languages are tone languages except Fula, which is spoken by five million people and is considered such an exceptional case that it has had enormous influence on the Hamitic theorists. The analysis of tone languages is an ongoing process. As an initial approach, we can differentiate between languages containing a large number of words distinguished by tone, unmodified by the placing of the word within the sentence, and languages where fewer words are distinguished by tones, but these words are modified by their position within the sentence; in other words, syntactical instead of lexical dependence.

In languages belonging to the first (lexical) type, words are modified by tone alone, irrespective of their position within the sentence; in languages of the second (syntactical) type, words are also distinguished by tone, but these lexical tones change according to the position of the words within the sentence. Such a distinction can be useful. The notation of phenomena beyond the syllabic level (which would be called intonation in ordinary speech) is particularly difficult, even if fewer words are identified in this way. In certain languages tones do not occupy a central semantic position: a foreigner can speak Hausa, omit the tones, and still make himself understood. The same cannot be said of Yoruba or even of Igbo: tone differences distinguish a great number of Yoruba words and form the basis of many syntactic Igbo constructions.

The problem is how to indicate the tonal differences in question. For languages with a greater number of minimal pairs (words distinguished exclusively by tone), the solution could be to indicate all the tones. It should be the case in Yoruba, but publishers resent the constraint and native speakers do not insist on its use. They often seem to assume that only native speakers would be bold enough to read a book in their language. As mentioned above, there is no simple way of giving a graphic indication of intonation. As a student during the 'seventies I attended seminars on Igbo tonology. More than 30 years later, the debate rages on and the spelling issue is still being discussed.

Almost all African languages are written according to the Latin alphabet. Despite the invention of various writing systems (Dalby, 1986), the only successful alphabet as far as book publishing is concerned, has been the Latin one, although manuscripts have also been written in the Arabic alphabet. Unfortunately, alphabets are ill-suited to the graphic rendering of tone languages. The Arabic alphabet uses a method that simplifies the question quite dramatically: when no vowels are indicated, the tone marks on the words, reduced to a bare, consonantal skeleton, are rendered useless. Even the writer has difficulty re-reading himself: the vocalization of a text in an African language, written in Arabic script (Ajami) is a rather haphazard enterprise and is certainly not the solution for the transcription of most African languages. Amadou Hampâté Bâ, a traditionalist Islamic scholar, has often remarked how difficult it is to re-read a text written in Ajami script.

An alphabet like Latin, which marks vowels, is more adequate, up to a certain point. Vowel notation provides two parameters: the point of articulation and the aperture. It does not indicate voice pitch, and it is precisely pitch that is pertinent in a tone language. Therefore one has to include diacritics to indicate pitch, since nobody will consider printing in staves. Often, this is done in addition to other diacritic signs indicating aperture, such as an open *o* versus a closed *o* in Yoruba, indicated by an underwritten dot (ọ), or accents in the case of the French e (è é ê, etc.). When more dots are added to these accents, the syllable image being produced becomes rather confusing. This is the case in Vietnamese, but in Africa it would seem that printers recoil from such a task. Unless the writing is done along musical lines, it is impossible to prevent the proliferation of accents and diacritical signs that generate a rather blurred syllable image. Personally, I do not find the use of numbers to indicate pitch a great improvement, despite the positive views of the linguists concerned.

The problem can of course be solved by choosing an entirely different route. Ideograms do not aspire to the coherent analysis of the problem of sound representation; they choose another path, which also contains a (hidden) phonetic component (De Francis, 1989) and which does not present itself in a systematic way. Systems of pictographic and ideographic representation such as hieroglyphs and Chinese ideograms would probably have been more appropriate for the notation of African languages, because the tricky question of sound notation is not tackled in any analytical way. Ideographic representation thus would have solved a problem that had not been addressed directly but now confronts African languages – sound representation.

The 'African chapter in the history of writing' (Raum, 1943) is the study of ways to retain and retrieve information by graphic means:

> When Livingstone entered the country of the Lunda he observed that all the trees along his route bore incisions, which are said to have resembled faces reminiscent of Egyptian pictures. (Raum, 1943:5)

Even if they are not pictographs (and why shouldn't they be?), sign incisions engraved on trees and coloured dots on sticks perform some of the functions of writing by reminding us of the words, spells and prayers of those who inscribed them.

> Symbols are cultural creations that derive their meaning from rituals and cults, intense moments that punctuate the life of their users. In most cases, the body is marked, and objects are carved and modelled for the same purpose. Scarifications are thus messages sent to the ages.... (Faïk-Nzuji, 1992:122)

What Raum calls 'crystallizing and registering thought processes' (Raum, 1943: 183) is thus accomplished :

> Graphic and coloured symbols are used by African people ... and serve three main purposes: the perpetuation of expressions of emotional states and volitional tendencies in inscriptions which bear a magical, and sometimes religious, significance; the regulation of social relations by supplying distinguishing marks for private and clan property and by affording a medium of communication between individuals; finally, graphic symbols serve to record the shape, name and number of objects as well as subjects of negotiations and thus act as instruments of intellectual processes.... (Raum, 1943:187)

Africa is the continent with the largest number of recorded rock art paintings: from mountain ranges like the Drakensberg and the Matopos in Southern Africa to the Saharan Aïr, the continent seems to have been populated by crowds of painters eager to record, to pray, or to celebrate. A recent book by Emmanuel Anati, director of UNESCO's World Archive of Rock Art (WARA), *L'art rupestre dans le monde*, is based on an extensive survey of several million pictures and engravings, and attempts to demonstrate that this is indeed a kind of writing that provides us with a universal code. For Anati, some pictograms are ideograms and point to a universal code of graphic expression. Africa is full of inscriptions of what the Angolan writer Luandino Vieira terms 'illiterate writing'. Paintings and engravings encode stories and rituals and belong to the field of writing, if we adopt De Francis's 'inclusivist' position expressed in his book, *Visible Speech, The Diverse Oneness of Written Languages* (1989). This Chinese language scholar offers two useful distinctions that have quite practical bearings on the analysis of writing in Africa. He divides students of graphic systems into two camps, inclusivist and exclusivist, using their definition of writing as a discriminating criterion:

> Partial writing is a system of graphic symbols that can be used to convey only some thought. Full writing is a system of graphic symbols that can be used to convey any and all thought. Inclusivists believe that both partial and full writing should be called writing; exclusivists believe that only full writing deserves this label. (De Francis, 1989:5)

As a humanist anthropologist, I believe in the suggestive and aesthetic power of partial writing, but as a literary historian, I need to deal with full writing, as the remainder of my argument will show.

In her book *Symbolisme graphique d'Afrique noire* (1992), Clémentine Faïk-Nzuji attempts a semiological analysis of the representational code of different groups, an avenue that was explored in 1951 by G. Dieterlen and Geneviève Calame-Griaule. Dogon graphic symbolism has been the subject of several further studies. It is indeed of the utmost importance, as its symbols are closely related to speech. Produced within particular speech communities, they require interpretation by these same communities. They perform one of writing's essential functions, recording information and allowing its retrieval. This is done in a specialized way, with no allowance for any kind of message. The symbols may be described as partial writing, as recognized by the 'inclusivist' position. However, many writing systems suffer from similar constraints.

It is a well-known fact that graphic symbolism fulfils different functions, magical as well as numerical. Certain systems, such as the Nsibidi script (Dalby, 1986), have been perfected in a particular way. Some objects elicit a verbal response or encapsulate a text. The systematic use of objects can function similarly to that of writing. To prevent confusing these approaches, it is essential to reiterate the propositions in question. These pictograms have been in use for centuries. According to David Dalby, the graphic symbolism of Egyptian ideograms probably belongs to symbolic repertoires previously in use in Africa, whether on rock, wood or skin. The Egyptian writing system is, of course, an example of *full* (as opposed to *partial*) writing, capable of recording any thoughts, as well as constituting a literature that was actually in use in an existing society.

> Some fundamental rules have been identified which would allow us to classify Meroitic among Northern Sudanese languages (which includes Nubian, but so far removed, chronologically, that comparative study will not be of much help). (Priese, in Wildung, 1996:253)

In dynastic times (25–15th centuries BC), the Kush kingdom and its capital, Kerma, were at the centre of an ancient Nubian empire and of Egyptian–African relations. Although the Egyptian inscriptions were found in Meroe, the Kush kingdom between the First or Second cataract and the confluence of the White and the Blue Nile (Priese, in Wildung, 1996:207), the kingdom that succeeded it had its own written language. It was a truly African language, related to the

Thomas Mofolo.
Portrait drawn by
Fredéric Christol, 1907

Photograph of Thomas
Mofolo, from the same period

Sol Plaatje
c. 1899

Herbert Dhlomo,
painted by G.M. Pemba

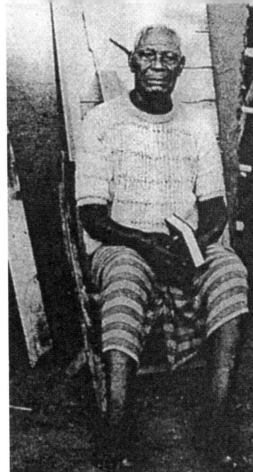

The poet Ntsikana

Aniceti Kitereza (© W. Bgoya)

Félix Couchoro
1900–1968
(© A. Ricard)

The street in Ouidah,
Benin, where Félix
Couchoro lived
(© A. Ricard)

Amos Tutuola at home in Ibadan, 1989 (© G. Lenoir)

Léopold Sédar
Senghor at the
French Academy,
1983

Amadou
Hampâté Bâ
(© Hélène Eckman
collection)

Chinua Achebe, CBC Radio International, Toronto, recording 'Letter to Nigeria', 22 June 1985 (© CBC Radio)

Wole Soyinka, 1989, sitting in the school in Aké where he spent his childhood
(© G. Lenoir)

Ngugi wa Thiong'o
(© George Hallett)

Nuruddin Farah, 2001
(© P. Matsas)

Femi Osofisan, 1989
(© G. Lenoir)

Ahmadou Kourouma, 1987
(© G. Lenoir)

Hubert Ogunde on stage with one actress-wife, 1960

Hubert Ogunde thinking aloud in a Yoruba photo-play

Yoruba theatre comes to town, Zaria, 1972

Comedy actors of
Concert Party,
Lomé, 1975
(© A. Ricard)

Werewere Liking,
1986 (© W. Liking)

Véronique Tadjo
(© V. Tadjo)

Clémentine Faïk-Nzuji,
1982
(© C. Faïk-Nzuji)

Sory Camara, 1993
(© G. Lenoir)

Senouvo Agbota Zinsou,
Lomé, 1985
(© G. Lenoir)

Ebrahim Hussein,
Dar es Salaam, 1997
(© A. Ricard)

languages that are still spoken in the area, and consisting of a selection of Demotic Egyptian hieroglyphs. However, it also contains a fascinating mystery: the vowels and consonants are known to us, but we are unable to organize the discourse, almost as though the written image was too far removed from an actual language. Admittedly, many African languages have been written according to rather inadequate systems. Meroe may have been the first in the series, which may explain its current opacity.

Once these alphabetic inadequacies become apparent, one sees the need for the highly tonal, largely monosyllabic West African coastal languages to invent their own writing system, while, on the other hand, the Bantu class and tone languages would certainly be reduced to bare, consonantal skeletons in the Egyptian writing system. In other words, a different representational approach is needed for these languages, one in which symbolic representation is accompanied by phonemic analysis. Transcribing vowels according to their length and aperture is already a difficult process: how does one transcribe pitch within a phonemic (or alphabetic) system? Inspired by exceptionally strong feelings of national consciousness, the Vietnamese succeeded in this undertaking, thus proving that writing systems (and linguistic questions in general) do not only pose technical problems, but need to be politically and historically contextualized. Achieving a balance between phonemic and other kinds of representation (symbolic, pictographic) within a system is a historical process: a writing system does not exist in isolation from society. For instance, a seemingly cumbersome and inefficient system such as the hieroglyphs had special advantages for its place of use.

> The major criticism is that the Egyptians, evidently lacking in imagination, failed to take what is deemed to be the obvious step: simply to use their uniconsonantal signs in the manner of an alphabet, abandoning the other types of signs. Such criticism, which is based essentially on the assumed superiority of alphabetic script over all others, is quite misplaced. It not only overrates the efficiency of alphabetic systems, it also undervalues the merits of others. The Egyptian system has the disadvantage of containing a relatively large number of signs. In compensation however, its mixed orthography creates visually distinctive word patterns that actually enhance legibility.... (Davies, 1987:35)

Over the past centuries, Egyptian, Berber, Nubian and Ge'ez were the only African languages to have developed their own writing systems, thus creating a literature and a community of writers and readers. Only the Ethiopian syllabary (whether in Ge'ez or in Amharic) is still in practical use in Africa today. Other African languages borrowed Arabic or Roman scripts. During the last two centuries, the invention of specific syllabaries (such as the Vai syllabary in the Mande area) was prompted by intensive cultural contact with Islam, but remained local without producing a literature (Dalby, 1970). Despite the late arrival of these new script inventors, they should be remembered as graphic artists rather than as writers. The Bamun sultan, Njoya, was the only inventor of a syllabary used for writing original historical works:

> In 1910 or 1911, Njoya and his courtiers began to compile the history of the Bamun kingdom. The writing and editing took many years and was finally completed in 1931. (Geary, 1994:16)

Unfortunately, the development of this original creation was interrupted by the destruction of his printing shop during the French colonization process (Konka, 1983). Until the nineteenth century, Arabic was probably Africa's most commonly used written language. We know that it was written in Timbuktu during the fifteenth century and that Arabic literature still exists in West Africa today.

In a sense, Africa's plastic creativity itself solves the problem of representation. Many groups inscribe their genealogy and their praises on objects, masks and bodies. Some symbolic systems started to function as graphic and creative systems and not only as repositories of ancestral lore. This is the case for the Nsibidi script from Calabar in Eastern Nigeria. However, its use has been restricted, since its symbols were reserved for Ekpe masks and have never produced a large number of texts. Once Egyptian creativity became extinct, no other African graphic system was successful beyond its own area of creation. Tone thus poses the complex problem of reducing sound to sign: much remains to be done as far as its analysis and representation are concerned.

Understanding Noun Classes

It is easier to transcribe the other specific feature of African languages – the wide diffusion of noun classes. These have a unifying instead of a distinguishing function. Tones are spread across the lexicons of closely related languages, while many similarities exist amongst the lexicons of closely related *class* languages, such as those of the Southern Bantu. In other words, knowledge of an Ewe tone has no bearing on the tone of the same word in closely related, structurally similar and geographically close languages such as Yoruba or Fanti, while knowledge of a word's class-prefix in Kiswahili provides many hints about the use of the same prefix in Luganda, Kinyarwanda or Zulu. Classes allow us to group lexical items into large, homogeneous sets; knowledge of one class language contributes greatly to the learning of other such languages.

Each noun belongs to a class, or rather to two classes, one singular and one plural. All elements depending on the name have to be marked according to class agreement. Thus, in Kiswahili, which has eighteen classes, a word's use commands a string of affixes throughout the sentence. These affixes are attached to the verbal stem (or root). Being linked to temporal marks and to eventual dependents, they agglutinate in a strict order around the verbal stem. While nominal roots belong to different classes, verbal roots, in the infinitive, all belong to the same class and produce their own string of affixes. Meinhof gives the following example in his analysis of Kiswahili:

> *kile kisu kikuu kimevikata vile vidole vya mtoto mdogo:* the old knife has cut the little child's fingers. Here we must notice first that the prefixes *ki-, vi-* and *m-* mark the three substantives *kisu* knife, *vidole* fingers and *mtoto*, child as belonging to different categories or classes. *Ki* and *m-* mean nothing by themselves, but only indicate that the one word denotes a tool, the other a human being. (Meinhof, 1915:90)

Roots are not modified, but are surrounded by affixes that specify their syntactic role as well as their root links. The absence (or modification) of root flexion produces a rather peculiar result: with minimal knowledge of lexical and root meanings, and none at all of class agreements, a non-native speaker (such as a European) can make himself more or less understood. In this regard, Kiswahili is not only an exceptionally regular language, but also a deceptive one. Many people (especially white settlers in the former colonial East Africa) think they speak some Kiswahili because they can put together a series of nominal stems that are recognized by native speakers. With only five vowels, Kiswahili has a vocalic system that is closest to Italian. It has no semantic tones and its word order is similar to that of many European languages. Thus, simplified varieties of the language (called *Kisetla*, derived from *settler*) were responsible for spreading the wrong, simplistic idea amongst Europeans that Kiswahili was a poor, simple language. Its major difficulty is of course the noun class system, but even if the agreements are omitted, the speaker will be more or less vaguely understood. If tones are forgotten when speaking Yoruba or Ewe, listeners will not have the slightest idea of what is being said; language reputations are made or lost by this kind of empirical observation! Moreover, class agreement is marked by vocalic or syllabic affixes that can easily be represented graphically. Thus, it is much easier to produce a graphic representation of a class language such as Kiswahili or Zulu, than that of a tone language such as Yoruba or Ewe, using the Latin or any other alphabet. It follows logically that it is rather difficult to learn a tone language by using books, since the text's graphic representation mostly carries only a skeleton of the phonic material without indicating segmental or supra-segmental tones. In book-based educational systems, it is easy to print class languages, but printing tone languages is more complex. It is true that many class languages are also tone languages, but the pitch levels are usually less efficient lexically. Kiswahili is certainly an exception, since it is a non-tonal class language. It represents almost the exact opposite of Yoruba: the monosyllabic, highly tonal classless West African language is far removed from the non-tonal polysyllabic East African language. Kiswahili is the mother tongue of a small group of coastal people in East Africa and is used as a vernacular by fifty million people on the East African mainland. Most people who speak the language do not recognize themselves as members of a Swahili tribe: they are not Waswahili. On the other hand, Yoruba is only spoken by the Yoruba, who lay claim to a common origin in Ile Ife, the town that, according to them, is the cradle of humanity. To use Mazrui's useful distinction (Mazrui, 1998:18), Kiswahili is an ecumenical language (not 'race'- or 'tribe'-bound), while Yoruba is a communalist language, defining the community who speak it as their mother tongue. However, these two very different languages are both present in school systems, have access to reasonably good metalinguistic tools such as dictionaries, and are probably very good candidates for surviving as printed African languages of the twenty-first century, a challenge that few languages, unfortunately, may be able to meet. It took a long time to analyse and to properly understand the unity of class languages of Central and Southern Africa and to group them into a single family.

Some Historical Language Analyses

From the fifteenth century onwards, various links were established between Europe and the coastal kingdoms of West Africa. The Catholic missionaries believed that Africa could be converted by drawing the coastal kings to the church. The Jesuits thought that they could accomplish in the Congo what seemed to be succeeding in China. But the Bantu world, like that of China, was far removed from the Christian world of the Middle East. Bantu religions still had to be understood and their languages mastered in order to translate the Bible. The same task had to be undertaken in China. From the mid-seventeenth century onwards, the class system of the Bantu languages was correctly analysed, and there was some understanding of semantic tone. Several grammar books and dictionaries were published at that time on the Congolese languages, but a coherent and general exposition of the principle governing Bantu languages did not appear until Boyce's *Grammar of the Kaffir Language*, published by the Wesleyan Mission in Grahamstown in 1834.

> The most striking peculiarity of the Kaffir and Sechuana family of languages is the Euphonic or Alliteral concord. With the exception of a few terminations in the cases of the noun, and tenses of the verb, the whole business of declension, conjugation, etc, is effected by prefixes and by changes which take place in the initial letters or syllables of words subject to grammatical government; now as these changes, in addition to the precision they communicate to the language, also promote its euphony ... they have been termed the Euphonic or Alliteral concord. In the languages spoken in Congo, Angola, and Loango the same peculiarity was noticed by some Romish missionaries in the sixteenth and seventeenth centuries, though they profess to regard it as an unaccountable philological vagary defying all rule.... (Boyce, 1834: xiii–xiv)

Similar descriptions paved the way for a synthesis. In 1857, the term Bantu was used for the first time by W. Bleek, to group African class languages together. At the end of the nineteenth century, the first comparative Bantu languages grammar book was published by another German scholar, Carl Meinhof. The group's unity had been established, creating the possibility of reconstructing the original Bantu prototype, the UrBantu, which would throw some light on the migrations of black people: a highly controversial topic, especially in Southern Africa. While describing and grouping these languages, Meinhof also put forward certain blatant prejudices regarding black people. For example, he asserted that their languages were considered inferior to those of the Hamitic peoples. As previously mentioned briefly, the latter category was created according to Lepsius's theory of the three language branches named after Noah's three sons: Japhetic (Indo-European), Semitic (Arabic, Phoenician, Hebrew, Ge'ez) and Hamitic (North African languages). For Meinhof, the presence of grammatical gender in Hamitic languages made them superior to the Bantu languages spoken by black people. Civilization would travel from Northern to Southern Africa, from the tall, light-skinned pastoral peoples speaking languages with grammatical genders to the short, dark agriculturalists speaking class languages.

The gender language issue is also important because of its effect on the first literary collection of San stories. While working on his Bantu classification, Bleek was writing 'Reynard the Fox'. He correlated the presence of gender in Hottentot and Bushmen languages with that of animal stories for which the 'Reynard' cycle served as a model.

> But we may well ask why is it that, so far as we know, the Kaffir (Bantu) imagination seems not at all inclined to the formation of this class of fictitious tales, though they

have otherwise a prolific Native literature of a more or less legendary character. This contrast to what we find among the Hottentots appears not to be accidental, but merely a natural consequence of that difference of structure which distinguished these two classes of languages embracing respectively the dialects of the Hottentots on the one hand and those of the Kaffirs and their kindred nations on the other; in the former (the Hottentot) as in all sex-denoting languages, the grammatical divisions of the nouns into genders which do not tally exactly with any distinction observed in nature, has been brought into a certain reference to the difference of sex; and on that account this distinction of sex seems in some way to extend even to inanimate beings whereby a tendency to the personification of impersonal objects is produced, which in itself is likely to lead the mind towards ascribing reason and other attributes to irrational beings. (Bleek, 1864: xx–xxi)

Because they had gender and were capable of imagining animal stories, Hottentot people were supposed to be intellectually superior to Bantu people. Surprisingly, discussions on the scarcity of animal stories among the Bantu continued until the end of the century. Few stories were found until Jacottet (1899) finally dispelled these racist notions.

There is a clear evolutionary outline that ranks languages from isolating (monosyllabic, 'Sudanese' languages) languages to inflective European languages, with the agglutinative (Bantu) languages in the middle. Gerhardt gives Meinhof credit for 'scrupulous observation and careful description of sounds' (1995:167), but is rightly critical of the older Meinhof's efforts to generalize when it comes to a language hierarchy: 'Inflecting languages were for him the languages of the white race, of creators of religion and philosophy' (Gerhardt, 1995:167). Meinhof regarded class languages as a representation of the more developed stage of agglutinating languages, a precursor of gender languages, the end of the road to reason or 'inflexion' for Africans.

Class languages function in a mechanical way. In Bantu languages, according to Meinhof, this grammatical relation seemed to have been taken to a point of mechanical absurdity. He felt that the dominant African races had relegated the 'musical accent' to a position of secondary importance to make room for stress, which was also frequent in European languages (Meinhof, 1936:40). Most of these derogatory comments can be found in his 1936 book on inflected languages. They are typical of a common epistemological fallacy, that of confusing or conflating languages, cultures and so-called races or physical types.

> Meinhof went back to Lepsius's classification in including Hausa and Hottentot in the Hamitic family, but went beyond it by adding Fula (a West-Atlantic Niger-Congo language). But more important than the exact membership of the family was the fact that Meinhof endowed his family with racial characteristics, both physical and psychological. From that point on Hamitic ceased to be an arbitrary name for a group of non-Semitic languages with Semitic-like features, and became the name used for the languages spoken by a specific racial ethnic group, the Hamites, presumed to be fundamentally different from the 'Negroes of Africa'. (Newman, 1980:9)

This type of evolutionary outline led to absurdly racist conclusions, with tragic consequences:

> There can be no doubt that this Sudan negro is physically very different from the white race, and it is equally certain that the Hamite shows striking resemblances to

the Arab and the Europeans.... The Hamite as a cattle breeder and warrior has reached a higher social stage than the Sudan negro who is still in the hoe stage of agriculture .... These light coloured herdsmen drove back, subjugated and in many cases absorbed the dark race. Thus there arose mixed races, of whom the Bantu are the most important; and sometimes as in Ruanda, the component element of the people can still be clearly distinguished.... (Meinhof, 1915:96)

From Dualism to Unity

The opposition between gender and class languages (with Fula, a class and gender language spoken by Hamitic-looking, light-skinned people occupying the middle ground) would be subverted by the discovery of languages that were analogous to Fula, but spoken by peoples who had none of the Hamitic features. The fact that the Fula were almost Middle-Eastern looking was very important in this classification. The emergence of a new Sudanic language category provided the grounds for a new classification in which the reductionist dualism of the Hamitic theory was no longer valid. Between 1950 and 1960, a new classification of African languages was established, based on the works of Delafosse, Westermann, and Homburger. The simplistic dualism of Hamitic theory was a thing of the past. However, the newly-found unity of African languages raised questions about its source:

> Pharaonic Egyptian, Coptic, and as yet undeciphered Meroitic are the African languages with the longest written history. This is Black Africa's linguistic and cultural foundation.... (Obenga, 1980:69)

There is no longer a need for the Hamites to civilize Africa: Egypt was the centre of civilization because it had assimilated all African cultures and restored what it had taken from the rest of the continent. The debate on Afrocentricity will not be pursued here: it is a fundamental epistemological discussion that focuses on the interpretation of data produced by textual and iconographic material provided by Egyptologists. The second volume of UNESCO's *General History of Africa* (Mokhtar, 1981:59–78, annex to Chapter 1) contains a well-balanced assessment of the thesis on how ancient Egypt was populated. Cheikh Anta Diop was the leading exponent of this theory, as we have already mentioned, and his work has been truly seminal. But his undertaking must be considered within the context of the intellectual atmosphere of the 'fifties, marked by anti-colonial student movements in Paris. Although Diop's thesis was rejected by the Sorbonne, it was published soon after (in 1955) in book form by *Présence Africaine*. At this time, the author was the general secretary of the African Student Union and advocated the creation of a federal African state, for which his thesis would serve as an intellectual bedrock. In the 1979 re-issue of his first book, the author summarized all the ideas he had launched a quarter of a century earlier and which have since become common property: African independence; the African origin of humanity; the black core of Egyptian civilization; the linguistic link between Egypt and Africa. Civilization started in Africa, in Egypt, and its promoters were Africans. At the same time, Louis Leakey's discovery of the *Zinjanthropus* in the Olduvai gorge in Tanganyika, seemed to provide yet another argument in support of this idea, although at least a million years separated it from the Nile civilization. Cheikh Anta Diop produced a single narrative, which collapsed archaeological and paleo-anthropological data and created cultural continuity: it gave many Africans a proud sense of belonging and was heuristically fecund. This is no small achievement.

Elaborating on Cheikh Anta Diop's work, his disciple Théophile Obenga has stated that, from its Egyptian cradle, culture and civilization were diffused to the whole of Africa, thanks to Bantu peoples.

> This thesis postulates the teaching of Egyptian humanities everywhere in Africa, to strengthen African historical consciousness as well as to revive Pharaonic civilization thanks to the support of a living community.... Pharaonic heritage belongs in totality, from its origin to the end of foreign dynasties, to the Black African cultural universe, by its dwellings, its race, and the tongue of Ancient Egyptian, creators of Pharaonic civilization. (Obenga, 1988:8)

Théophile Obenga is right: the reintegration of Egyptian antiquities and humanities within an African pedagogy, aimed at promoting a new and positive image of African cultures, lies at the core of Cheikh Anta Diop's thinking. In his Reith lecture series (1980), Ali Mazrui commented rather sadly on the fact that Africa, the place of human origin and of the first great civilization's development, has become the world's poorest area. In his works, Cheikh Anta Diop drew the energy from this memory of past grandeur to project himself into a bright future. He had a global vision of culture. His 'practical' plan for a new, federal African state included fourteen topics ranging from 'the consciousness of our historical unity' and necessary linguistic unification, to the establishment of 'technical institutes necessary for a modern State, in physics, chemistry, atomic energy, electronics, and aeronautics'. (Diop, 1979: 120)

The theme of unity is central to his idea of mythical character, in the sense that a myth can be a dynamic and positive stimulus for working towards change and towards what he would have called progress. This political movement would lead to the establishment of a new federal state, uniting all African nations with Egypt as their common origin.

The theory that underlies his thinking, that of the blackness of Egyptian civilization, may be interpreted as a direct refutation of Hamitic mythology.

> One can wonder by what strange operation Hamites have become white under the pen of specialists to the point of becoming the white races (fictitious), postulated under the most minute cultural manifestation of the black world. The failure of all these attempts, despite the great scientific efforts put behind them is not the smallest of proofs showing that it is indeed difficult to steal from the black people the role of first guide of humanity on the road to civilization, accepted as obvious by all ancient philosophers and historians.... (Diop, 1979:279)

Diop's need for political and scientific struggle is understandable, and easy to empathize with. However, in his proclaimed desire to destroy racist science, Diop himself fell into a few dangerous traps: perhaps he destroyed some of his argument's power to convince by trying to prove too much. For instance, he comments on the observations of one of the first Egyptologists, Count Volney, who mentioned the 'Negroid' character of Ancient Egypt in his writings. Many ancient writers and historians had noticed the import of a black component into Egyptian civilization. In the nineteenth century Egyptologists vehemently refused to accept this black incursion into Egypt. Likewise, Cheikh Anta Diop goes right back to Volney for a more exact picture, and to refute the 'Hamitic' arguments. He first addresses the problem by using visual data from clay vessels, followed by a study of Ancient Egyptian, which is compared to Diop's own language, Wolof. Diop's originality and strength lay in his revolutionary hypothesis and all his efforts to demonstrate it; it has a profoundly heuristic character, focussing on neglected areas of scientific discourse and bringing to light unfounded assumptions based on racial prejudices. He demonstrates the African character of Nubian civilization, the latter serving as a bridge between Egypt and the rest of Africa. As this is of some importance to Diop, his hypotheses in this area are especially prolific; he brought new impetus to Meroitic studies, in particular. Present-day research on Meroitic writing and African languages may still contribute to the deciphering of this as yet unknown language.

Despite admiring the heuristic nature of his work, one ought to maintain a certain scepticism (if not complete opposition) to some of his hypotheses, particularly as regards comparative methodology. Diop's use of the race concept is not acceptable, for example. He uses this 'category' as a central determinant of culture, but it is practically constructed from skin colour. We know that ethnic or language groups are not constituted by skin colour types, and the persistent use of skin colour as a criterion of classification leads only to aberrations. A methodology that consists of comparing potteries and assessing 'race' according to physical features, must be considered dubious, as it belongs to what could euphemistically be called a naïve vision of race. His methodology of linguistic comparison is also fraught with many problems, reviewed by Maurice Houis (1980) in a well-known paper. Cheikh Anta Diop compared Ancient Egyptian to modern Wolof. He knew Ancient Egyptian from books and grammars, and Wolof because he spoke it: this is already a strange asymmetry, since he did not provide the linguistic system for his analysis of Wolof. He never explained the system by which his spoken language organizes the production of meaning; he never produced a grammatical description that could be a valid basis of comparison with the grammars of Ancient Egyptian. He provided lists of words and inventories without any systematic analysis (Houis, 1980:23). In short, according to Houis, Diop's work suffers from a basic flaw: linguistic underdevelopment on a theoretical and methodological level. This does not invalidate the comments made here on the heuristic fecundity of his vision, but shows that he continued to work within the epistemological paradigm of historical philology that produced, among many strange inventions, the so-called Hamite civilizing forces in Africa. What is needed, now, is a different epistemological paradigm.

In the meantime, we have yet to resolve the question whether all African languages have to belong to the same group in order to refute the supposed Hamite–Bantu duality. But why base such a unity in Egypt? Why even postulate such a rigid genetic scheme? Why not face the future with a pluralistic Africa? The mystique of unity is the exact counterpoint of the dualistic, racist thesis that for so long insisted on the fragmentation and dispersion of African cultures, in turn leading to a hierarchy of cultures, with those of the Bantu always placed on the lower rung. The mystique of unity gives a powerful impetus to action; it is the fuel of pan-Africanism; but in Diop's case the accepted definition of unity is subtly blended with a more problematic, Egyptian origin of this unity.

Diop's theses are still all too rarely challenged by African scholars, principally because his political stature, scholarly output and prophetic vision continue to command respect. The critical question remains potent in the field of African humanities, in what Obenga calls the presence of 'Pharaonic culture in today's Africa'. During the Nobel Symposium in praise of Wole Soyinka held in Lagos in 1988, the following declaration was raised for discussion and adoption:

> The Conference pays tribute to the late Professor Cheikh Anta Diop, and expresses profound gratitude for his historic contributions through his studies of Egyptology resulting in the recovery of the achievements of Ancient Africa.... That African writers and critics should return to ancient Egyptian texts, appropriate them, translate them into various African languages and make them available to African people; and that those texts officially be given a place in the teaching of literature in African schools and universities.... (Private communication, AR)

The proposal was not accepted. It was, in fact, barely discussed. In present-day Africa, the Egyptian presence is more of a political emblem than a living, cultural reality. It is precisely because there is no living memory of Pharaonic culture that such desperate efforts are being made to keep it going and they are doomed to fail. A culture does not arise out of conference proposals. African humanities have to include Diop as the writer of a mythical history, the way Michelet wrote about France; 'ancient Egyptian texts' are yet to be appropriated. Diop's special contribution was to draw attention to a neglected area of African history, an historical task that he realized with brilliance. However, one cannot fill a gap of several thousand years by using obsolete methodologies. The pressing problem is to classify African languages and to establish scientific relationships between them while avoiding two particular errors: the mystique of unity stemming from a common origin, and the obsessional hierarchies of dualistic racist thinking.

An Open Vision: the Triple Heritage

Mention has already been made of Mazrui's triple heritage thesis, deriving from the notion of Africa as a 'cultural bazaar', a place of exchanges, mixtures and *métissages*. In this sense, Africa is similar to the rest of the world, the only difference being that African cultures have long been ignored and despised. No complete map of Africa was drawn before 1884, the date of the Berlin Conference, during which the European powers divided the continent amongst themselves. The three elements of the triple heritage are the autochthonous element, the Semitic and Judeo-Christian element and the Western Graeco-Latin element. As an example, Ali Mazrui applies his grid to two African countries, Ethiopia and Nigeria:

> The best embodiment of the ancient triple heritage in contemporary Africa (indigenous, Semitic, Graeco-Roman) is Ethiopia. The best embodiment of the modern triple

heritage (indigenous, Islamic and Western) is Nigeria. The whole cultural history of Africa is captured in the transition from the triple ancient personality of Ethiopia to the triple modern personality of Nigeria. In population Ethiopia is probably the second largest country south of the Sahara. Nigeria is indeed the largest. Culturally probably the two countries tell the whole story. (Mazrui, 1984:3)

Ethiopia's story did not start as tradition holds, with an invasion from the Arabian peninsula of the so-called Sabean culture, whose queen, Sheba, was to become so famous. Ethiopia's population is a very ancient one – even without going back as far as the fossilized remains of 'Lucy' – and invaders discovered people speaking Cushitic languages, which still account for most of the languages in contemporary Ethiopia, from Somali to Oromo.

Highland Ethiopia during the last millennium BC saw a gradual influx of Semitic-speaking peoples across the Red Sea from southern Arabia. The new arrivals may be assumed to have encountered a settled, agricultural, Cushitic-speaking population who had perhaps, although this cannot yet be proven, already learned techniques of copper-working through contacts with the Nile Valley. (Phillipson, 1985:158)

The Ge'ez language probably resulted from an encounter between the Semitic tongues and the Cushitic substratum. The invaders were called Sabean, and the part they allegedly played during the first years of the Ethiopian dynasty can be described as follows: Menelik I is supposed to have been born of the union between Solomon and the Queen of Sheba. The introduction of Christianity into Ethiopia during the first centuries of the Christian era increased contacts with the north and with Egypt (the home of the Ethiopian patriarch), thus providing a solid basis for the third element of this heritage, Hellenistic Christianity.

By the first century AD Aksum, some fifty km south west of Yeha developed as the capital of an extensive state, in which there was a fusion of indigenous Ethiopian and South Arabian cultural elements. Through its port of Adulis on the Red Sea coast, Aksum was in trade contact with the Roman empire, exporting ivory and skins in exchange for imported manufactured luxury goods. Ge'ez – basically Semitic but with a strong Cushitic element – seems to have been the general language of Aksum, but Greek was also in use for commercial purposes. Coins were struck at Aksum, and on the earlier issues the king's name and titles were given in Greek. In the fourth century Aksumite power seems to have reached its peak. It was at this time that King Ezana is believed to have conquered Meroe. It was also in Ezana's reign that Christianity became the state religion of Aksum: on his later coins the crescent and disc of the moon god are replaced by the cross.... (Phillipson, 1985:160)

Today, Ethiopia must come to terms with the difficult coexistence of Muslims and Christians from the same Semitic branch (at least in the northern part of the country), while the country has chosen in the recent past to modernize by taking the socialist route. Ethiopia is now an Orthodox, former socialist country (and has been so for more than a generation, which explains the measure of social upheaval), but it is also firmly rooted in Africa through the desire of its last emperor to host the OAU's headquarters, thus incarnating the difficult synthesis between the three elements of this triple heritage.

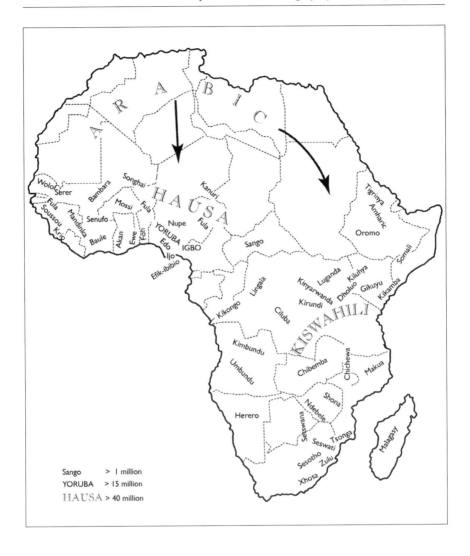

Map 1 *Main African languages in expansion (adapted from* Verkehrs und Nationalsprachen in Africa, *Akademie-Verlag: Berlin, 1985)*

While Ethiopia attempts to retrace the official version of its history back through the mists of time (or expresses the desire to do so, at least), Nigeria is a twentieth-century creation. And yet, the winding Niger has been the home of great African civilizations: that of Nok in the north, followed by Ife and Benin, (exempt from Western influence – less so in Benin, maybe), and not forgetting the enigmatic Igbo Ukwu tombs in the east. During the greater part of the nineteenth century, this continuity of autochthonous civilizations was obscured first by Islamic expansion and then by the arrival of European colonialism. Today, along with Lebanon and Ethiopia, Nigeria is one of the countries where some of the largest Christian and Muslim communities co-exist. Although Nigeria's cultures and languages resisted the double invasion of the last century, they were obviously marked by it.

Hausa is heard on the radio throughout the north, especially on BBC broadcasts. Its religious vocabulary is borrowed from Arabic, while it now uses the Latin spelling that replaced Arabic spelling all over Africa when African languages like Kiswahili or Somali had to be printed on a large scale. The contemporary Nigerian personality has been noticeably influenced by the triple heritage of its peoples' autochthonous traditions, the Islamic influence and the Western contribution (particularly that of the English language).

Ali Mazrui's deceptively simple thesis is an appealing one: it postulates cultural diversity, a sort of 'cultural fair', which must be organized into a coherent system, also taking historical evolution into account. No single factor is promoted to the rank of ultimate explanation. On the contrary, contemporary African culture is constituted by the relations between the three components of this heritage. The quest for 'authentic' autochthonous cultures has greatly occupied nationalist intellectuals; Cheikh Anta Diop's rather unconvincing solution has been well reviewed in previous pages. The most lasting effect of efforts dating from the 'seventies, marked by a 'recourse' to authenticity, was the ban on Christian first names and the return to indigenous names – a positive step(?) but not a huge one. What is more, transforming the search for autochthonous cultural elements into a quest for origins is as vain as it is futile. Cultural 'essence' does not exist. African culture, like that of other continents, is the result of a series of contributions. The chief value of Ali Mazrui's theory is his positive consideration of cultural pluralism and the value he attributes to the various contributions.

Whether one considers the Hamites or the Egyptians, the absence of a central determining factor is manifest in Joseph Greenberg's works on linguistic classification, (published in 1953 and re-edited in 1963). His proposed method of classification is founded (to use Gabriel Manessy's terms) on 'the consideration of obvious lexical resemblances between languages that are sufficiently diverse and numerous for loan probabilities and the risk of fortuitous convergence to be remote' (1981:3). The author no longer makes use of the philological method, dear to the Neo-Grammarian Bantuists of the nineteenth century, which rests upon the 'laws' of historical phonetics – a foundation providing all the more reason to treat their results with caution, considering that the written archives of Indo-European philology that gave rise to these laws were absent in Africa. Thus Greenberg (1963) is induced into classifying African languages into four large groups (the italicized languages are those often referred to in the text):

Congo-Kordofanian	Niger-Congo *West-Atlantic (Fula, Wolof)* *Mande (Mandinka)* *Voltaic (Kabiye)* *Kwa (Akan, Ewe, Igbo, Yoruba)* Kordofanian
Nilo-Saharan	Songhai Saharan Chari-Nile (Acoli, Luo) Fur
Afro-Asian	Berber Semitic (Ge'ez, Amharic) Egyptian Tchadic (Hausa) Cushitic (Oromo, Somali)
Khoisan	Hottentot/Khoi; Bushman/San

This classification is in direct conflict with Hamite-Bantu dualism (the Hamitic languages disappear as a category) and the myth of the Egyptian origin of Negro-African languages, which is given no particular place here. Théophile Obenga rightly concluded:

> The scholarly establishment of Negro-Egyptian has many meanings. Firstly, that is to say fundamentally, that of Hamito-Semitic's non-existence as a genealogical, linguistic family, renamed Afro-Asian by Greenberg and which is as yet still rejected by many specialists. (Obenga, 1980:69)

Although the classification has been rejected, the theoretical issue still remains. To dispute Greenberg means to choose another history, one that differs from Théophile Obenga's so-called new history, since this (as shown in our critical analysis of Cheikh Anta Diop's linguistics) is partially outdated, at least as far as methodology is concerned. To accept Greenberg's classification as a working hypothesis is to postulate a frame of reference that invites falsification, because its construction method is entirely explicit, laying down the data used in its constitution. We are faced with two epistemologies: on the one hand, an historicist epistemology that, on the pretext of correcting the errors of nineteenth-century racist evolutionism, goes to the opposite extreme in search of historical confirmation of the unity thesis; and on the other hand, an epistemology that may be called neo-positivist and that considers classification as an empirical exercise. Therefore it searches for a method that is principally adapted to oral data, instead of tacking philological methods (derived from research on written documents) onto material where these documents are lacking. The method begs certain questions: practising historical phonetics in the absence of written documents comes close to working magic!

It seems that certain subtle affinities exist between the notion of a culture that developed from a triple heritage and the classification of African languages into four groups that lie open to reassessment. African history and culture are no longer directly perceived in terms of symbolic issues, but in terms of a 'cultural fair'. Colonial racism and pan-African nationalism are incapable of accounting for the plurality of languages and cultures that cannot be reduced to simplistic outlines. During the 'sixties, without daring to say so, those of us involved surreptitiously took leave of the infernal *tête-à-tête* between the colonialist, racist residues and the vaguely totalitarian attempts at cultural nationalism. At the time, I attempted its illustration in a work on two writers, Wole Soyinka and LeRoi Jones – both beacons, each in his own way, of their generation (*Theatre and Nationalism*, English edition, 1983). Today we should have the willpower to declare that, now that apartheid has ended, we are abandoning colonial and anti-colonial epistemologies for good.

Everywhere, Africa's inscriptions are beckoning to us: these 'illiterate writings' (Trigo, 1981) never cease to pose endless questions. Of all the continents, Africa houses the greatest number of rock paintings and speaks the most languages. What are the profound, obscure links between these two facts? It may be that the paintings were not executed by the ancestors of those speaking today's languages, but how do we know that? Africa is covered with incisions and inscriptions, the continent is certainly not a blank page. The difficulty lies in turning these many pages and all these inscriptions into a text that speaks about the past to our contemporaries, and that gives meaning to these signs, so that the future can be faced with confidence. In other words, it lies in succeeding more convincingly than Cheikh Anta Diop in what he proposed, and yet did not ultimately achieve.

The notion of a triple heritage can be particularly useful when analysing languages and literatures and may serve as the golden thread of our study. The autochthonous heritage is that of the oral tradition. The Semitic heritage is that of the manuscript cultures, such as Arabic or Ge'ez, as well as that of the languages and literatures that developed from a synthesis between an autochtonous substratum and a strong Semitic influence, such as the Swahili or Hausa language and culture. Lastly, the Graeco-Latin heritage is that of Christianity and of the European version of Western civilization, which expanded the use of a few important European languages and simultaneously developed new African languages. Contrary to Islam, Christianity first tried to translate the founding text and to speak the language of the local people. Modern African and European literature result from this encounter.

The presence of these three cultural elements (autochthonous, Islamic and Western) is obvious in the case of a new cultural object, represented by an extensive lingua franca. Swahili stock and lexical roots are largely of Bantu origin, as is, obviously, the system of nominal classes that characterizes Bantu languages. However, almost 40 per cent of the Swahili vocabulary and especially its conceptual vocabulary (religious, literary or philosophical) is of Arabic origin – although not exclusively: the word for the National Assembly is *Bunge*, a Bantu word, while the word for Republic is *Jamhuri*, an Arabic word. The word indicating socialism – *ujamaa*, (the Bantu prefix *u* has been added) – indicates the category of collective, abstract words from the Arabic word *jamaa* (family). For centuries, Kiswahili was written according to the Arabic alphabet. Manuscript collections can be found all along the Indian ocean coastline. However, since the end of the nineteenth century, under the influence of Christian missionaries, Kiswahili has been written according to the Latin alphabet. This new influence was superimposed on that of the Arabs whose encounter with the Bantu on the shores of the Indian Ocean gave birth to the most important African language of our time. A similar process can be observed in Somali: to a great extent, this Cushitic language was influenced by Arabic and borrowed an important part of its vocabulary from it. From the end of the nineteenth century onwards, the Arabic alphabet was used for writing in Somali, although the output was not huge. The adoption of the Latin alphabet, less than forty years ago, was one of ex-president Syad Barre's first revolutionary measures. Socialism and the Latin alphabet were supposed to lead Somali into a new era: but Syad Barre was deposed, and socialism collapsed. The Romanized Somali spelling, which helped many a student to learn to read, is probably all that will remain.

It is important to think about Africa in terms of plurality and not just in terms of unity. It is also crucial to free oneself, on the one hand, from dualistic patterns that only serve to organize fossilized cultures into a hierarchy, and on the other, from theories that are obsessed with myths of origin and verge on totalitarianism. The compatriot of Cheikh Anta Diop, Léopold Sédar Senghor, clearly expressed this necessity of being open to others in a beautiful expression: 'where giver and receiver meet'. Senghor, who hails from the coast and from the ports, like Ali Mazrui, is well aware that culture means exchange. Ali Mazrui hails from that great Indian Ocean port, Mombasa, which is Africa's gateway to the Great Lakes. It is surely no coincidence: a port is a market, a fair, a cultural bazaar; a creative Africa is one that trades, just like Mombasa.

2 Tradition & Orality

The vague, old phrase, 'the oral tradition', comes from the tiresome equation – Africa equals oral tradition versus Europe equals modernity and the written word – and must be replaced by a more nuanced vision of relations between North and South, or between cultures dispensing different means of expression. But we should not delude ourselves: dualistic clichés carry a lot of weight and have established themselves as a vital form of common sense, or, in other words, an important source of inaccuracies.

To start with, I would like to examine the pertinence of the equation. Although the formula 'tradition = orality' is a simplistic form of algebra, it is nevertheless widely accepted. Once I have demonstrated that oral literature does not equal that to which it is so often reduced, I will attempt to formulate a more precise definition, based on the notion of oral style borrowed from Marcel Jousse and appropriated by Maurice Houis, together with the idea of performance, stemming notably from the research of Dell Hymes, which Geneviève Calame-Griaule examined in the new introduction to *Ethnologie et langage* (1987).

The discourse of oral literature possesses certain prominent indicators: either internal, by means of the type of prosodic traits found in oral poetry, or external, that is to say in generic terms, since in every language and culture it is possible to slot a certain number of discourses into cultural and semantic categories that double up as literary genres. This possibility was illustrated by Pierre Smith with regard to Kinyarwandan prose (Smith, 1975). However, every African who proceeds to speak cannot be said to produce oral literature! Words leave their mark on social and linguistic frameworks, and are organized around prosodic and/or generic frameworks so as to be a truly oral art, that is to say an oral literature. I would like to retain this term, despite its inherent contra-diction, because the notion of criticism and critical metalanguage that occupies us here would be difficult to separate from that of the written word and thus from literature. Any form of art is contingent on poetics, any performance calls for systems of implicit rules that the researcher must bring to the fore. The task of both the historian and the literary sociologist is precisely to show its logic, to construct its organization, while indicating its presence in all languages and cultures. Abiola Irele (1989) expressed this well when he said that the West was not differentiated by rationality as such, but by the logic of rationality. This, to us, would seem impossible to separate from alphabetical writing, as demonstrated by Jack Goody (1993) on the basis of research done by Eric Havelock (1976).

My attempt at defining oral art will be followed by a presentation of the work of those African researchers who have posed the problem of an oral poetics. Why focus exclusively on African researchers? The question deserves an answer, if our aim is truly to reflect on literature in all its aspects. Numerous researchers and writers have considered their own language at a time when they were elaborating works in other languages. Reflections on the oral literary forms of their respective languages often accompanied the creative process. These poets – Kagame, Rabearivelo, Daniel Kunene, Mazizi Kunene, J. P. Clark-Bekederemo, and many others – seem to present key examples for any discussion on the practice of literature in Africa. Their cases have not been well studied, due to the simplistic dichotomies opposing the oral and the written word, mentioned above. This is all the more unfortunate because these poet/researchers were able to undertake the production of a new type of African literature.

Within the scope of this book, the problem of oral art is considered inseparable from that of the discourse on orality. It is up to us to dismantle the articulations of this discourse and to understand its construction from performances and texts, especially for the way in which it is offered to us as a representation of oral art. We have to discover the rules of the game, the keys to the translation, the generic logic behind it. These theoretical reflections on oral art are primarily of a poetic nature. As such, they can nourish activities of a theoretical as well as a practical nature, as in literary creation. There are still too few African specialists in oral literatures. Too often, the new generation of writers who come from the educated, urban sector of the independence era tend to neglect oral creations, often considered as products of the 'bush'. The absence of any active interest that ought to have manifested itself in fieldwork, instead of vain laudatory incantations, explains the lack of conceptual instruments to place these oral productions in proper context. Too often, the (at times excellent) French adaptations of oral productions are considered satisfactory restitutions, while in fact they stem from a completely different approach. Some attempts, like that of J. P. Clark who dedicated more than fifteen years' work to the collection and translation of the most significant Ijo epic, *Ozidi*, are unique in their genre. What is more – particularly in the Francophone domain – oral literature has fallen foul of an ethnological vision that attached too much importance to the texts' social functions. The outstanding research done by Geneviève Calame-Griaule stresses the status of the word in society, but dilutes oral art as part of social speech. In the end, the structural analyses of tales has also led to too much emphasis being placed on semantic mechanisms at the expense of expressive devices and of the works themselves. We have very few works and comparative analysis of the various oral genres at our disposal; the few we have deal with only a few African societies and languages. As languages and societies change on a daily basis, this gap becomes increasingly difficult to bridge.

In this chapter I shall try to present a general picture of the oral literature produced in languages such as Yoruba or Mandinka. For example, it is obvious that Yoruba intellectuals, artists and especially writers are particularly language-sensitive when it comes to the study of Yoruba oral art forms; such a state of affairs can only contribute to enriching their writing. Wole Soyinka, a writer, but also a theorist of literature and drama, can thus refer to almost a century of linguistic and literary analyses of Yoruba verbal, oral and written art.

Nothing equivalent exists in Francophone Africa, except for G. Hulstaert's (1972) work on the Mongo, which does not seem to have had any effect on contemporary literature.

The scarcity of research on African poetics in the Francophone domain – with the notable exception of Madagascar – is doubtless a major cause of the disappearance of Francophone poetry in Africa. Poetic reflection is an entity, whether it concerns oral or written literature, in an African or a European language, and its weakness in one domain affects all others. The introductory question to this chapter provides the material for my final comments: does orality equal tradition? Is tradition always of an oral nature? Contemporary orality, associated with songs or with urban theatre, has little to do with tradition as depicted by its appointed supporters. This new orality often articulates secret, veiled or startling breaches with the old days. Tradition thus emerges as what it usually is: a textual (and therefore ideological) product, often entrusted to written texts, held dear by traditionalists in West African societies, who are mostly the well-read Muslims. Orality is a textual product that can be transmitted, diffused; how does it relate to theatre? How can one apply the kind of intertextuality that seems essential for understanding these oral practices? There is a special kind of orality that has freed itself from tradition, or rather, that is trying to free itself from it: it is this orality that we must try to comprehend, as it is a specific practice, in so far it relates to poetic devices – prosodic, but also compositional – and in so far as these devices are part of the poet's verbal art. Some are obviously peculiar to the oral poet, but reflections on theory should encompass not only oral production, but its transcriptions, translations and adaptations. There is no such thing as pure orality. We cannot avoid the discourse on what is oral, but let us at least try to break through the theoretical armour and get to the heart of the matter.

Pseudo-oral Literature

For more than a century, from Bérenger-Féraud's (1885) *Recueil de contes populaires de la Sénégambie* [Tales from Senegal and Gambia] to those from Equilbecq (1913) or Roland Colin (1957) via Cendrars, the publication of an entire series of collections provided us with 'samples' of African literature in French. The virtual absence of any research on the poetry in these collections is amazing, as though researchers – more often than not administrators or enlightened amateurs – themselves reduced the literature of Africa to 'tales'. Madagascar is included in our field of investigation, principally to record the unique case of Jean Paulhan, who took a great interest in Malagasy poetry. Why has no other French writer bothered to analyse Zulu or Basotho poetry? Moreover, one of the first studies on poetry in an African language was based on that second ethnic group: the Protestant missionary Eugène Casalis's essay on the Setswana (sic) language, published in 1841, included quite a detailed chapter on its poetry. What a pity that no other missionary was interested in pursuing research on this aspect of African oral art!

Tales restore the image of an Africa seen from 'within'. Despite the structural complexity they involve, they offer an uncomplicated, even infantile, 'African' mentality, which fitted in with the previous century's dominant ideas about the African continent. It is impossible to separate the fate of these animal tales from the European representation of Africa that cannot be labelled as anything other than racist. In 1882, the president of the Geographical Society in all seriousness asked the explorer Alfred Bardey (later to become Rimbaud's patron, he relates this incident in his memoirs, 1981), if he had seen men with tails. Such people, if they existed, could not produce texts that were more complex than tales, or maybe proverbs, a literature that was basically functional, far removed from the more sophisticated literary works of our own cultures. The entry for 'Negro' in that bastion of common sense, the Pierre Larousse dictionary, contains the following statement:

> It is an indisputable fact that the Negro brain is smaller, lighter and less voluminous than that of the White species, which is sufficient proof of the White species' superiority over its Black counterpart. But does this intellectual superiority give Whites the right to reduce the inferior race to slavery? No, a thousand times no! Their intellectual inferiority obliges us to protect them. (*Grand Dictionnaire universel du XIXe siècle*)

To this day, an abundant production of collected tales continues to sustain a naïvely simplistic (although benevolent) vision of Africa and its literature. Colonial literature also provided readers' interest in Africa with food for thought. As Mohammadou Kane correctly pointed out:

> Both literatures (colonial and African) had the same objective in the eyes of the French public: to give an account of Africa. It was logical that the African's testimony from within would, of necessity, prevail. (Kane, 1981:279)

Birago Diop

Collected tales, adapted by the French, were followed by works written by Africans and presenting a traditional and oral Africa from 'within'. The well-deserved success of Birago Diop's *Tales of Amadou Koumba* is based on these elements and on an obvious misunderstanding regarding the nature of oral literature. The author tells us that he heard the tales from the *griot* [travelling bard], from Amadou Koumba's mouth, and he takes the trouble to pay him a moving tribute. That is all very well, but according to Mohammadou Kane, who dedicated an essay to this book,

> Birago Diop makes use of a foreign language which has its own spirit.... The problem is obvious: yet as Birago does not limit himself to his role as a translator or transcriptor, and as he never fails to demonstrate his concern to provide a faithful illustration of the specific nature of the African soul, he has managed to go to every length to give a faithful translation of his people's genius. (Kane, 1981:93)

Mohammadou Kane poses a fundamental problem, which he dismisses almost immediately, continuing as though it had never been mentioned. His memorable essay on Birago Diop's book encouraged the appropriation by the Francophone literary corpus of a work that was supposed to restore the oral tradition to its former glory. His gesture had founding status: Birago Diop's talent equalled that of Mohammadou Kane's, in fact; the writer's excellence was matched by the perspicacity of the critic who cleverly avoided the problem of the connection between orality and original language. Mohammadou Kane's position was of lasting importance: his 1967 book was republished in 1981. In his capacity as university professor in Dakar, he had influence on the new literature syllabi of the African high schools and universities from the 'seventies onwards. His viewpoint provided a platform for a lot of research and dozens of theses. What is truly remarkable is the way his judgement systematically avoids the language question, which is something of a paradox in a study on orality. The critic's own logic is not at issue. It just so happens that what he considers to be the most perfect form of appropriation of African orality is in fact an extraordinary travesty, the consequences of which are still being felt today. In fact, Kane tells us that

> Birago Diop once again finds himself in the position of a traditional storyteller [because] he is supplied with the material: he can draw from his cultural heritage with both hands.

Later, he provides the following tautological observation: 'A traditional tale is oral, that says it all' (Kane, 1981:97). And yet, Kane's presentation does not take Birago Diop's personal contribution into account at all. Diop used French to adapt and recreate the texts he had heard on his rounds as a veterinarian in Senegal and in the former Sudan. As a great lover of classical literature, he was able to recapture the conciseness and the sense of reminiscence of a La Fontaine or a La Bruyère. In fact, some of his texts are not tales, but short novellas, the success of which has endured until the present day. A tale that comes to mind is that of *Sarzan*, an infantry sergeant who loses his mind on his return to his native land. The text, which was adapted for both the theatre and the cinema, was quite well-known. Another is *Mor Lam's Bone*, which was adapted for the theatre in 1982 by Malik Bowens and the Peter Brook Company in a production that highlighted its accurate characterizations and the author's powers of observation of a famine.

Birago Diop is an admirable writer, but he is by no measure a storyteller in the traditional sense. He does not write fireside tales any more than Perrault does. Mohammadou Kane only gets to tackle the question of the shift from the source language (Wolof, Bambara?) to the written language (French) in the last few pages of his work, and very briefly at that. There is no discussion anywhere of the question of stylistic *calques* and technical procedures, peculiar to oral style, that may be found in these texts. All in all, the tales become paradigms of a tradition that, we know, is also oral, but no methodological consequence is drawn from this fact. Traditional literature requires a contents analysis that will demonstrate its moral, pedagogical and 'cultural' (i.e. functional) value within the framework of a school or university project. Cross-fading can thus take place between the oral, African text and the written, French text. All the production operations of the new text are erased. And the birth of traditional oral literature takes place inside a book!

D.T. Niane

The same misunderstanding occurred in the case of another fascinating work, this time by Djibril Tamsir Niane, entitled *Sundiata or the Mandinka epic*, first published in 1960. Today, one marvels at the nonsensical interpretations given to this text. It arrived at just the right moment to complete the picture of an oral tradition that laid great emphasis on tales, as shown above. When independence was granted to Mali in 1960, a modicum of hero worship was not out of place, and Sundiata Keita, the great Malian king, fitted the bill. D.T. Niane modestly claims: 'This book is actually the work of an obscure *griot* from Djeliba Koro village in Guinea's Siguiri district. I owe him everything'; and further on:

> This book is therefore the result of my first contact with the most authentic Mandinka traditionalists.... I am only the translator, I owe everything to the Fadema, Djeliba Koro and Keyla masters and particularly to Djeli Mamdou Kouyaté, from the village of Djeliba Koro. (Niane, 1960:5)

Is he indebted to a *griot*, or to several traditionalists? It is a question worth asking, not with the intention of impugning D.T. Niane, whose authority as an historian and talent as a writer are undoubted. The *Sundiata* text is only an epic in the literary sense. It involves recreating an epic, constructing a synthetic text from other texts produced by *griots* and traditionalists, as well as from historical data. The author is inviting Africans to *'come and listen to the words of the griots who teach wisdom and history'*, on condition that the words of these *griots* be adapted to a considerable extent, because where would one hear a version of the Sundiata directly from the *griot*'s mouth, in his own words, with an annotated translation provided for the reader? Where is such a text to be found? It has often been said that French ethnography, preoccupied as it is with 'speech and language', did not provide any textual version of this legend in the original language before the remarkable work of Youssouf Cissé and Wa Kamissoko (1988), whereas a great many French versions, adaptations and commentaries have appeared: M. Delafosse (1909 and 1913), J. Vidal (1924), Charles Monteil (1929), Mambi Sidibé (1937), P. Humblot (1951) and D.T. Niane (1960) – according to the incomplete list supplied by R. Pageard (1961:52). Massa Makan Diabaté produced at least three new adaptations: *Kala Kata* (1970); *L'aigle et l'épervier* (1975) [The eagle and the sparrow-hawk], *Le Lion à l'arc* (1986) [The lion and the bow], not forgetting Camara Laye's *The Guardian of the Word* (1978). To summarize: we have numerous French texts and adaptations over an extended period of time, all preoccupied with historical information or epic evocation, but precious little about the original language, the circumstances in which these texts were recited, or about what the epic 'means'.

The success of D.T. Niane's text exemplifies the fact that the project of adaptation is considered to be entirely legitimate. Sundiata becomes a literary hero and is no longer the subject of an epic. With this status transition from oral text subject to hero of a literary creation, oral literature is left behind, in the same way as Shaka, a subject of Zulu panegyrics, retires from oral literature when he becomes the subject of Mofolo's novel in Sesotho, despite the insertion of extracts from the Shaka panegyrics, collected from Zulu bards. The problem is not whether D.T. Niane's *Sundiata* is historical or not: historically speaking, it should in fact be the closest, seeing as Niane applied himself to the adaptation of the various conflicting versions in order to create his character. It is simply a matter of highlighting the distance between the Sundiata rooted in orality and the Sundiata portrayed in oral texts. The Mandinka text, edited according to minimal scholarly norms, with the names of the actors, recording circumstances, linguistic annotations and literary commentaries, only came to be published in 1975. *Sundiata: Three Mandinka Versions* (Innes, 1975) meets all the requirements. There is one disparity between D.T. Niane's text and the one presented by Gordon Innes that I would like to point out: the role of the supernatural. Robert Pageard observed with great accuracy that in the published form of Mandinka epic, 'in Niane's retransmitted narrative, much greater importance is given to weapons than in the regular versions, where a lot of emphasis is put on the two rivals' magical powers' (Pageard, 1961:66). As a result, much greater magical powers are granted to the protagonists (Sundiata and Sumanguru) in the three texts collected by Innes than can be found in Niane's narrative. In this way, they remain faithful to the marvellous universe of heroic oral narrative comparable to the Fula *Sillamaka et Poullori* (Seydou, 1972) or the Ijo *Ozidi Saga* (Clark, 1977).

The central question is the *intention* of the adapter or transcriber. If the aim is to create a 'committed' literary work in French to provide younger generations with a flattering image of their past, weaponry must occupy a key position. If, instead, the aim is to provide a faithful description of the functioning and organization of an oral text, as well as the conditions in which the reciting took place, the custodians of the oral tradition must have precedence over the publisher, and what we read from that may be quite different from the French adaptation. It is thus only fair to point out, as Robert Pageard does with regard to D.T. Niane, that 'his translation is a work of art, greatly superior to previous attempts on the same subject. He joins the ranks of the best African storytellers; one is reminded of Birago Diop's most inspired works.' (Pageard, 1961:69) That is all very well, but where does it leave orality? In this case, it disappears from view, hidden by a brilliant adaptation. The tradition becomes acceptable, as long as it is in French! We have to remind ourselves that when these texts were produced during the 'sixties, French was still the official language in this part of West Africa. I recall debates towards the end of the decade, when simply referring to the concept of 'French as a second language' earned the unlucky speaker a reprimand from the French government's official representative. African tradition *had* to be expressed in French; texts by B. Diop and D.T. Niane suggested that this appropriation was indeed possible. No mention was made of the cost in terms of editing; nor, most importantly, was it mentioned that what they were supposed to promote was obscured in the process. This elegantly disguised 'tradition' proceeded to erase all traces of the eloquence, roughness and truth contained in speech. In the field of literary studies, appeals for the preservation of traditional, oral literature were tantamount to the promotion of ersatz – works that, although rooted in tradition, could never be considered as its true representation.

What is Oral Literature Exactly?

First, oral literature is another language that has to be translated; second, it is another means of communication that has to be reconstructed. Although there is nothing original in this statement, it is surprising just how often its principles are still disregarded. Jean Derive's seminal 1975 work on the Ngbaka tales takes stock of the question in terms of literary studies and provides an answer to the problems posed but not resolved by Mohammadou Kane: 'The foreign reader who thinks that written works will provide an authentic equivalent of what is considered as traditional oral literature in sub-Saharan Africa, is probably mistaken.' Jean Derive also commented on the fact that Birago Diop, Bernard Dadié and Djibril Tamsir Niane were all 'moulded by French culture' (1975:41) and even by classical literary culture. Derive rejected D.T. Niane's claim to authenticity in the preface to *Sundiata*, and rightly so.

> Adolescents who have received a certain amount of schooling and who will later play an important role in their country's cultural politics, do sometimes continue to maintain close ties with African literature, but for the most part their only opportunity to encounter its traditional aspect is through re-creations in European languages by writers who are themselves immersed in Western culture. (1975:84)

Unfortunately, these lines, written almost thirty years ago are still just as relevant: anthologies consisting of translated texts (edited according to the norms of scientific textual criticism) and free (or even emancipated) adaptations that obscure the originals, are still being published today. As Jean Derive once said, we still have 'a simplistic idea of African literature, produced by superficial anthologies' (1975: 83). The situation is unchanged.

But what is oral literature? How can its language be distinguished from daily speech? The question is simple, but crucial, and requires answers based on solid linguistic knowledge. The discourse of French linguistics must be completed, enhanced, by a discourse on the linguistics of African languages. All too often, people think the question has been answered before even being taken on board. One cannot simplify the task by just bypassing transcriptions or critical editions and/or by avoiding the issue of how the graphic reduction of the oral text could solve the problem of how to identify the stylistic forms that distinguish that discourse (in captured form) from daily speech. Dealing with this last point is the only way to broach the issue of its 'literariness'. There is obviously a high price to pay for embarking on this field of research, and it is easy to understand it is preferable to hold forth about French adaptations while paying tribute to an orality that is as idealized as it is misunderstood. As an art, verbal art survives on forms; it is important to identify these forms *within* the oral discourse and eventually to reflect on their transposition into written discourse. The critical and pedagogical enterprise is certainly of a textual nature; the question is knowing which text we are talking about and how it was produced.

Jean-Émile Mbot's (1975) knowledge of biblical exegesis resulted in a work on oral literature that sets out the right approach. He clearly illustrates that the oral text, which will of necessity be made available to the public in written form, is the result of a series of textual interventions made up of social relations: those between informants – poets or storytellers – and transcribers, between transcribers and translators, between translators and publishers. Any one of these roles can be filled by different people, which only complicates the issue further. It is also possible for one person to play all the parts, thus taking charge of the lot: transcription, translation and publication. Different types of logic are illustrated by these three operations: which spelling should one choose? Is there a standard spelling? How does one deal with the dialectal features? Is it better to translate word for word, or remain faithful to the spirit of the text? Should there be explanations of the cultural references, of the elements resulting from the texts' representational context, the public interventions, the storyteller or poet's hesitations or even his mistakes? In its written form, the text is thus the result of a whole series of transactions, all of which are situated in different scholarly and social domains. Transcription is located in the linguistic field, including linguistic politics and especially the link between dialects and the standard language. Translation is located in the literary field, as indicated by the issue of connotative capacity of translation figures and the generic shaping of the text by the insertion of a whole network of indices. Translating a tale also means introducing a text into a literary tradition that, in French, means Perrault. Lastly, the publication of the written version of an oral text also means specifying the exact circumstances of the performance: where and how was the tale told? Did the storyteller or the poet use gesture? How did the public react? The text bears the mark of something like stage directions, and the choice of these is also the result of a series of compromises between the often contradictory demands of readability in its written form and the accuracy of the performance's manifold dimensions. However, the main element is still the priority of oral style indications and the stylistic forms of the original transcription. This is where literature is shaped, and where the inevitable path that the text must follow is to be found. Echoing Roman Jakobson, Jean Derive calls this the 'aesthetic function' of language, expressed in recognizable, repeatable, classifiable forms, those rhetorical procedures that are the basis of oral literature.

The rediscovery of the works of Marcel Jousse – another biblical scholar – resulted in an important theoretical step forward in the study of oral style. For Jousse, rhythm was essential in the memorization process, hence its presence in oral literatures, where it contributes to utterance memorization. Claude Hagège comments as follows:

> Oral style has recourse to different techniques of gestural and articulatory symbolism that ensure surprising mnemonic effectiveness, such as refrains, release syllables, appeals, recurring names, inductive expressions, a profusion of virtual synonyms, assonances, rhymes, alliterations and other phonic and semantic echoes, lexical and grammatical parallelisms, paired meanings, the establishment of rhythm through gestures and mouth movements. To control these manifestations, the general technique is one of repetition. (1985:85)

In the first place, orality involves the phonic reality – breathing, panting, cries – of the human voice that becomes incantation, imploration, invocation and abuse. Each of these forms corresponds to a rhythm and a particular intonation that is recognized in every language and culture. This phonic reality is shaped around a central rhythmic concept that is also found in prosody, as well as that of repetition, applicable to the fields of vocabulary and syntax, notably using formulae. The latter are defined by M. Parry as 'a group of words which is regularly employed under the same metrical conditions to express a given essential idea' (Parry in Duggan, 1975:4). Gordon Innes comments on his translation of *Sundiata*:

> In the speech mode, the *griot* tells the story in his own words. The material in the recitation mode consists of formulae and formulaic expressions, resembling in this respect the Yugoslav epic material discussed by Lord (1960).... (1975:15)

The text is thus woven with 'word groups regularly used' in order to recall certain ideas. Any transcribed oral text, whether it is *Sillamaka et Poullori* or *Ozidi*, displays these same characteristics. The narrative production depends on the repetition of these formulae for its development. Although they are also found in the translation of the oral text, they mostly disappear from the adaptations. In the case of an oral text like *Sundiata* – narrated? recited? sung? declaimed? by a *griot* – it is essential to understand that the inner traits of metric, lexical and semantic repetition are introduced into a broader form that gives unity to the narrative, from Sundiata's birth to his victory over Sumanguru. The narrative unfolds by means of three vocalization modes, each with its own formal characteristics.

Speech mode, which most often has recourse to formulae, is distinguished from normal speech by the voice's pitch, which is slightly higher than in conversational mode. Narrative mode pitches the voice even higher and employs strong nominalization, as it declares the genealogies of the *griot*'s patrons and of the heroes whose brave deeds he narrates in panegyric form. This mode, sometimes called *eulogy* or praise proverb, is composed of a combination of a phonic form and a specific semantic content, as in the case of the previously mentioned mode. The third mode, the vocal version, is accompanied by the *kora* or the *balafon*. These short songs of no more than two lines are generally in a fixed form: they recall the extraordinary events in the hero's life. These three modes are to be found in the transcription/translation of another Mandinka epic narrative attributed to a *griot* by the name of Kambili. Oral narrative does indeed possess an overall structure somewhat in the Aristotelian sense, as well as a prosodic texture distinguishing it from daily speech. The continuous link with music, an essential element in the *griot*'s performance, would be enough to convince us of this, but we should also identify the pertinent stylistic traits. The alternation between these modes also constitutes a rhythm, possibly the type alluded to by Christiane Seydou when commenting on *Sillamaka and Poullori*, the Fula epic: 'Besides the rhythm of the diction, another broader, fuller rhythm orchestrates the narrative's entire composition'. (1972:56) The repetition technique is not limited to the 'formulae' borrowed from Albert Lord; it also includes 'motifs', those action sequences found in the oral folklore of all countries worldwide that have been gathered into the universal repertory of tales.

The work of Denise Paulme (1977) provides an excellent application of this type of approach to West African tales. Sundiata, the child who has been pinned to the ground, takes up the motif of the lame child. There are also more markedly West African motifs, when Sundiata cuts off a piece of his own flesh to feed the famished *griot*. The most common motif is surely Sumanguru's revelation of the secret to Sundiata's sister, who won his favour. This is a new version of the Delilah story in which Samson loses his strength when its secret becomes known. The motif of the secret of 'the sole weakness' as well as that of 'the sole deadly weapon' can be found in numerous literatures. The question arising from this brief summary of some techniques used in *Sundiata* is to what extent can a certain text serve as a general basis for historical knowledge. As Gordon Innes warned us earlier, his intentions were of a literary and not an historical kind:

Hence in the case of the Sundiata epic, which contains so many common motifs, one might ask what, if anything, is based on historical facts. I must confess that in the absence of any independent historical documentation to confirm the existence of Sundiata, I must say I would be inclined to doubt that there had ever been a historical Sundiata at all. (Innes, 1975:26)

Such clarity leads to a different reading of D.T. Niane's work and allows us, in any case, to measure the distance that separates his adapted version from the one provided by oral tradition fifteen years later. One cannot help but wonder why research methodology on orality, which was revolutionized by Albert Lord's *The Singer of Tales* (published in 1960, the same year as D.T. Niane's *Sundiata)*, did not influence research on African orality sooner, to the extent that a number of formal problems went unnoticed for want of true textual work on original transcriptions. Robert Pageard's previously quoted article, which appeared in *Présence africaine* in 1961 and raised historical questions about· Niane's text, provides food for thought: when 700 years have elapsed, how is one supposed to discuss historical points on the strength of an oral text alone? However, the article is not solely dedicated to that issue; it attempts to bring it together with archaeological information and other elements collected by Arab chroniclers. The undertaking is legitimate, but it must not lead to the oral tradition being adapted to the demands of historical criticism. The oral text is repetitive and often incoherent, it is true – in one of the three versions collected by Gordon Innes, Mange Yura is Sumanguru's sister and in another, the lover of Sundiata's sister. In one version, the Mandinka people ask Sumanguru for assistance against Sundiata; in another, Sumanguru sends his *griot* to ask Sundiata to return to the country. However, the two texts end similarly: Sundiata's sister learns the secret of Sumanguru's vulnerability: he can only be wounded by an arrowhead made from a white cock's spur. And so he is felled by Sundiata after a narrative where, as we have seen, the role distribution varies according to the *griot* recounting the epic. There are too many similarities between the episodes of heroic narration (from the birth of the disabled Sundiata through his exile to the final discovery of the secret of his adversary's weakness), and a number of other heroic narratives studied by Maurice Bowra or covered by Pierre Smith in his *Le récit populaire au Rwanda* (1975) for such a tale to serve as a basis for historical knowledge.

One cannot have it both ways: D.T. Niane's *Sundiata* is a product of historical research rather than a transcription of an oral text with all its banal structures, repetitions and the inevitable incoherence of verbal virtuosity. And yet this text is a true epic, which was still being told up to twenty years ago, portraying heroes who had lived more than seven centuries ago. It is impossible not to be moved by such a recitation. How can one not take pleasure in it, show no interest for the techniques that still make it come alive and that revive the basic creative mode and transmission of oral texts? The methodical work of Innes on *Sundiata* and of Derive on the Ngbaka tales invites us to deconstruct this adapted orality. In both cases we are far removed from Birago Diop and Djibril Tamsir Niane.

There is thus an oral style that forms the basis of what some people call an 'orature', but that we will persist in calling 'oral literature' so as to maintain a dialogue with matters of general literature. Oral literature has its own stylistic techniques, its own forms, which presuppose working with the original texts.

A critical, historical and aesthetic discourse on orality that fails to take this into account will disqualify itself. As illustrated above, the publication of a certain amount of research had to happen first during the 'seventies before this problem could be tackled in aesthetic and not merely in ethnological terms. The debate on the subject of 'literariness' that raged amongst French university critics during that period finds an African response here: there are oral texts that approach literature either by their inner form, or by their narrative circumstances. Narratives of the *Sundiata* type, such as *Sillamaka* or *Ozidi* (to which I have dedicated several pages below), seem particularly interesting to me; far more interesting than the tales, to tell the truth, because they display a variety of formal resources. These vary from an almost conversational style to a fully fixed style of traditional song, exhausting all the poetic resources of the narrative mode, as Gordon Innes calls it, or the laudatory 'sapiential' mode, as it is termed by Charles Bird. This verbal continuum, produced in the uninterrupted torrent of the unfolding heroic narrative, demands sudden diction changes and carries the listener away to a marvellous universe where wisdom, praise and song are mixed. It is both a genre in itself and a generic mixture of many cultures: the Gabonese *mvet* comes from the same blend.

In 1970, the heroic narrative was at the centre of a controversy raised by Ruth Finnegan: she actually maintained that sub-Saharan Africa had no epic. If her definition of an epic is based on criteria from the *Iliad* or the *Aeneid*, she may be right: African texts are shorter and are not written in verse. However, we consider these heroic narratives, these songs about heroes, to be true epics.

> That view (that a heroic song must necessarily be in verse) has been categorically expressed by Bowra, Parry and Lord, and verse appears to be one major criterion on which Finnegan denies that the epic as an African art form exists in Africa.... I urge that, as far as oral performance is concerned, some of our present understanding of the nature of verse should be re-examined. It may well be as Lord has observed, that 'prose would be the easiest and most natural way to tell a story'. But prose placed in the rather complex musical and histrionic environment such as we can see of *Mwindo* and *Ozidi* is not simply prose. It is prose propelled by the force of music, and the aesthetic results are bound to be different from those of an unaccompanied narration. The story thus told is a song, and its poetry consists more in the fervid process of making than in any qualities we may recognize when the hands are resting and the voice is still. (Okpewho, 1979:65–6)

These few lines provide a good summary of the problem of characterizing oral style: heroic narratives are connected to complex rhythmic modalities that cannot be summed up by fixed metric and prosodic patterns. And yet, oral discourse is a truly artistic form and should be recognized as such. For example, our difficulties in transcribing African music are part of the same problematic: neither musicality nor rhythm is determined by our recording and retention capacities. Christiane Seydou addressed this question in *Sillamaka et Poullori*; her fair, cautious observations on rhythm were quoted above. The heroic narrative should thus be given prime position in African oral literature. 'The epic can be considered as being eminently oral, because it is a genre where language cannot do without the voice' (1972:52). The study of oral literature has suffered from its marginalized position when compared to the success of its adaptations and the lack of knowledge of the stylistic techniques inherent not only to orality, but to African orality, which does not entertain the same relations with fixed prosodic and metric forms as in a written culture. Moreover, the attention to tales and to forms of apparently simple contents (which I find excessive for the reasons indicated above) resulted in the establishment of a diminished image of African literature.

Considerable efforts have been made to remedy this state of affairs, particularly within the framework of three literary collections: the Oxford Library of African Literature, the African Classics series and the SELAF (French Society for Linguistic and Anthropological Studies) library. These publications display the same serious-mindedness as the Guillaume Budé series for the classical humanities. It is an attempt to save Africa's literary heritage before it is too late. While the Oxford series specializes in oral literature, 'Classiques africains' have prioritized the publication of manuscript texts (especially Fula); SELAF seeks to promote new norms of scholarly, critical editions, notably by insisting on an original language edition.

Now that the specific nature of the oral text has been more clearly defined, I would like to deal with a few questions pertaining to our readings of this type of text. Erudition aside, what is the relevance of these forms of expression for today's Africa and its literature?

The Poets' Orality

I have attempted to demonstrate that reflections on oral poetics have suffered from an excessively functional conception of literature: the tales portray the 'African soul' and incidentally represent the mysterious oral phenomenon while epic narratives provide historical information. Speech is entirely socialized; little room is left for the poetic function of language referred to by Jean Derive. The aforementioned collections suffered from this type of insufficient literary analysis (apart from a few exceptions such as the work of Christiane Seydou).

However, this approach led to another version of appropriation of the oral literary heritage through the observations made by critics such as Birago Diop and D.T. Niane: this consisted of restoring the texts' own phonic materiality, translating, annotating and providing commentaries to illustrate their value and literary interest. Some African writers became not much more than adapters, translators of original texts attempting to render the spirit and the letter of a text in an African language as faithfully as possible. This type of reflection focusses on the position of orality within a group culture and thus, in part, on the connections between different modes of expression. An almost complete picture of the oral literature of certain ethnic groups, such as the Yoruba, were thus obtained. It is a success story one finds rarely, and one may surmise that contemporary written Yoruba literature will somehow be influenced by this unique achievement. It can be no coincidence that Yoruba oral literature is one of the best known on the continent, that Yoruba researchers are responsible for much of the best work on oral literature and that a Yoruba writer received the first Nobel Prize for Literature ever awarded to an African. I will attempt to show that theoretical knowledge of orality also has practical use and that it can serve as a catalyst for other literary works.

Will the African poet imitate his early twentieth-century Irish counterparts and go in search of his people's popular – that is, oral – poetry, with the same enthusiasm, so as to translate it? Will he lend an ear to this authentic type of speech? Africa's literary history gives us only a few examples of a similar approach to literature. Although Senghor tells us that he translated a few Serer poems, he remains rather discreet about the subject, providing no theory on this conception of the relation between literature and the oral tradition. Few poets have made the effort actually to translate the oral poetry of their people. A few remarkable, little known examples should be mentioned: Vilakazi's (1946) research on Zulu literature, and the literary historian and poet, Daniel Kunene's (1971) study on heroic Basotho poetry. His work earned him the deserved praises of Albert Lord:

> Professor Daniel Kunene, in his *Heroic Poetry of the Basotho* (1971) has written a detailed and sensitive account of his subject. Kunene does not follow the formulaic and thematic type of analysis associated with Milman Parry, although he is well acquainted with it, but makes his own kind of investigation. This is perhaps as well, because the heroic poetry with which he is dealing is not narrative in our sense of the word, but eulogistic; it is praise poetry of a kind common, I believe, in Africa. Kunene's work adds a new dimension to the study of oral literature which is most welcome. (Lord, in Duggan, 1975:5)

J. Nketia & others

Amongst other similar studies, we might also mention the work of J. Nketia (himself a musician and an Akan poet) on the dirge, also called a threnody (1955). His approach has not been followed up by other researchers, however. Nketia looks at the dirge from a musical standpoint, as its basic artistic form; he is thus on solid ground. The threnody is a traditional form of expression emanating from the individual human spirit and recreated in the appropriate context. It is a traditional form of expression that people learn to make use of because society looks for such formal responses in ceremonies such as funeral rites. There is a large degree of interdependence between linguistic and literary traits; they both share a common sociological background and situational context. Both provide identical verbal techniques; the problem of meaning, a major issue in the threnody, is also identical. In addition, there are common means of expression, the particular musical form related to weeping, the gestures and other corporal movements with which grieving is expressed.

In many cases, decades were needed to gather the texts published in these collections: Isaac Schapera wrote down the Tswana poems from 1930 to 1950; Gordon Innes recorded the *Sundiata* at the beginning of the 'sixties, only publishing it fifteen years later; John Pepper Clark spent almost fifteen years of his life recording, transcribing, translating and annotating the saga of *Ozidi*, the cultural hero of his people, the Ijo from the Niger delta. Speech that reaches us from the mists of time is as patient as the publishers of oral literature, who know that scientifically transcribed texts cannot touch as many readers as the adaptations. The texts will remain objects of scholarship without a wide circulation. Reading them is not an easy task, even when the translation is a faithful and a flowing one.

Poets & the Texts

Too few poets have occupied themselves with translating their people's texts; too few have taken the trouble to listen to the bards, the *griots*, the poets and the storytellers, in order to transcribe and translate their texts. The Malagasy poet Jean-Joseph Rabearivelo collected, transcribed and translated a few *hain-tenys*, thus following in the footsteps of Jean Paulhan (1938). We have seen that L.S. Senghor translated a few Serer poems and dedicated a study to these texts. Unfortunately, the complete version of the study was not reproduced in the volumes of *Libertés*, neither were his many general reflections on the rhythms of Bantu poetry, less useful in a precise study of the poetics of an African language (1964). Another writer who has dedicated a large part of his activities to poetry in his mother tongue is Antoine-Roger Bolamba, one of the first Zaïrian poets. His translation of two Mongo poems published in *Esanzo* (1956) elicited the following observation from Albert Gérard:

> One notes an appreciable difference between the texts belonging to Bolamba's oeuvre and the two poems that he translated from Mongo; in the latter, no free verse, no cosmic images; the two short, gnomic poems each illustrate a moral truth in an elliptic style. (1966: 287)

It is noteworthy that this example is about Mongo: G. Hulstaert and A. de Rop's research on this Zaïrian language produced the most complete study of its oral literature to date. Does one detect a correlation between the African poet's discreet interest in and respect for his own language and the European linguist's research, an all too rare occurrence in African literature in French?

It is true that the illustrious Alexis Kagame was well-placed to do the same as Bolamba, but he did not follow it up, being busy in another field. Kagame's oeuvre has yet to be evaluated. It is possible that in future the historian will make way for the writer and the poet; it is to be hoped that the former role will not always overshadow the latter's importance for African literature.

> After having enrolled for theology in 1935, he [Kagame] was authorized to spend his holidays recording the recollections of the bards living on the outskirts of Kabgayi, who were compensated by the rector for travelling to and fro.... From 1937 onwards, he separated out and analysed his country's three great genres of traditional poetry.... As a Kinyarwandese poet, he did much to communicate to a Francophone public the beauties and the subtleties of traditional Rwandese poetry. His translations illustrate his artistry in moulding French to the genius of the Rwandese language. In this sense he was an inventor. His contribution as a translator and a poet rests on the collection and transcription of oral texts. He contributed to the systematic undertaking of collecting oral traditions, which was of course followed by creation in Kinyarwanda, and then by translations into French of these texts – an all too rare occurrence in 'Francophone' countries. The true thread of tradition unwinds in Kagame's oeuvre, which he does not try to pass off as an adaptation, as something that it is not. Rwandese poetry, notably dynastic poetry, is part of an order of society and it is imperative that it should be preserved and collected accurately. This he did, and it provided him, as a young priest, with a decisive impulse for his literary work. (Vidal, 1987:5)

Investment of this kind in the language and culture of one's people is a rare occurrence and its true value has not been not appreciated. Mazizi Kunene also followed in Kagame's footsteps: he started by collecting and analysing Zulu poetry before composing his own works in Zulu and translating them into English, thereby producing an English version of his own Zulu poem on Shaka.

Other poets have also reflected on their people's oral tradition and have written essays on poetics; one thinks in particular of Clémentine Faïk-Nzuji, the first poetess, a linguist and the author of a fascinating work on the *kasala* song, a laudatory heroic genre of Baluba origin, a 'free poem made up of names'. Here one rediscovers a feature already found in the *Sundiata* epic, within the panegyric proverb mode: the strong impact of nominalization. Faïk-Nzuji (1974) poses poetic questions about poetic texts: this should be an obvious task, but it is in fact quite unusual. Most researchers prefer to ask historical, anthropological or even strictly linguistic questions.

The *kasala* is not a closed genre: it is the work of true poets, known for the quality of their improvisations:

> The *kasala* is composed of more or less set verse, but the eulogist knows which verses to choose at a specific moment, after which sentence to pause, which gesture should accompany which words and which accent to give to the melody'. (Faïk-Nzuji, 1974:49)

Faïk-Nzuji also contributed a work on proverbs and another on riddles. She exemplifies the situation of the African writer who is first and foremost concerned with questions about literary technique and who asks herself the essential question on literariness: what formal properties turn an ordinary oral discourse into a poetic discourse? Do such qualities even exist?

Other writers have dedicated an important part of their oeuvre to the study of their own tradition. A.C. Jordan provided us with an general essay on Xhosa literature, entitled *Towards an African Literature: the Emergence of Literary Form in Xhosa* (1973), putting a lot of emphasis on oral poetry and containing numerous comparative observations:

> In general, Bantu traditional poetry has much in common with Hebrew poetry. There is no metre in the classical sense, but there is marked rhythm achieved, inter alia, by means of balance of thoughts. (1973:17)

A.C. Jordan left some remarkable English translations of Xhosa narratives, in which the writer devoted much space to oral tradition; he reflected on the situation of the first Xhosa writers who 'had no written tradition to guide them'. We will come back to his example and to his oeuvre, which is at the root of Xhosa written prose.

Amadou Hampâté Bâ is another essential figure in the field of orality; however, it must be noted that the number of his studies on orality are relatively few, and are limited to Fula texts about initiation, which he himself transcribed, translated and edited with the help of foreign specialists. He gives small space to the literary analysis of these productions, the narrator of which is none other than the editor, which eliminates much of the textual asperity that the reader encounters in other translations from oral literature. The value of Amadou Hampâté Bâ's works lies in his reflection on oral ambiguity, rather than in his oral, textual production.

J. P. Clark-Bekederemo

As stated above, few poets have devoted sufficient time and effort to oral poetry. Kofi Awoonor (1974) translated the poems of an Ewe oral poet called Apaloo; unfortunately, he did not take the trouble to transcribe the original poems, thus considerably reducing the importance of his work. Ultimately, it is the major work of the Nigerian poet and dramatist J.P. Clark, *The Ozidi Saga* (1977), that provides the most influential attempt at doing justice to Africa's oral creation, reflecting as it does on links with written literature and attempting to relate it to audio-visual media, which certain superficial minds may view as a new form of orality. 'Oral literature needs translations more than commentaries': J.P. Clark responded to this call and spent fifteen years restoring the saga of Ozidi, the Ijo mythical hero. Fully aware of the urgency of the task, he started collecting saga texts from the 'sixties onwards, either from individual narrators that met in towns (notably in Ibadan and Lagos, where many Ijo had settled), or in village squares where the saga was not only still narrated, but also acted out, mimed and danced. In 1964, he recorded one version of the saga and produced a 45-minute film. In 1966, he took *Ozidi* to the stage, writing a five-act play that can be considered an adaptation of the saga. However, the objective remained transcribing and translating the saga's complete text, which was a substantial undertaking: its recitation alone would take seven evening performances of four hours each. In this way, J.P. Clark was able to collect three different saga versions, produced by three narrators. What is more, he could compare the texts to the (week-long) performance on which his film was based. Instead of synthesizing three versions into one text, he chose what he thought was the best version. Although the episodic structure was similar in the three narrative cycles, two of the narrators were not up to their task: one forgot the episodes while the other provided the outline or the synopsis of events, but was unable to find the words that would put meat on the bones.

> It's the first time that an author has used a traditional text as the basis for three major artistic productions exploiting different forms. The tale of Ozidi is still told in Ijo country and was recorded by artists like Sonny Okosun, the Nigerian musician on his record entitled *Ozidi*. (Ikiddeh, 1982:63)

Ozidi is the Ijo cultural hero. Like the heroes celebrating the Gabonese *mvet*, he is part of the Ijo culture that has developed around Ogbu village.

> The saga of Ozidi has become the proud property of all Ijo-speaking people in the Niger delta of Nigeria. Told in seven nights to dance, music, mime and ritual, it begins with the treason and treachery committed by a group of war-lords in the city-state of Orua against the brothers Temugedege, who is king, and Ozidi, the leading general of the state. (Clark, 1977:xx)

From the point of view of memorization alone, restoring a lengthy prose text such as a saga is a great exploit. The way myth unfolds into ritual should delight anthropologists. In a way, the reciting takes stock of all the festival elements (narrator, assistants, village choir, singers, dancers). A 45-minute film that had to limit itself to presenting an action framework could only give a simplistic rendition of this festive atmosphere. The to-ing and fro-ing between narrative and drama is handled smoothly: admittedly, none of the gestural or spectacular elements are present, but there is a text. 'Unlike most Ijo festivals and religious occasions, *The Ozidi Saga* observes no distinctions of age, sex, season, and place' (Clark, 1977:xxxii). Several locutory modes are used during the reciting: the panegyric mode, with recurring laudatory epithets addressed to the hero, consisting of a liberal share of juxtaposed nouns; the 'shout' mode, similar to cries of joy or pain, equivalent to the ululation of Muslim women from the Maghreb; and lastly, a mode defined by its contents, that consists of recalling past events, and possibly involves spectator intervention. Although this is not poetry in the prosodic sense of the word, particular forms of oral delivery are recognizable, unmistakeably revealing an aesthetic intention in the chain of speech. Special care was taken to record spectator intervention and the narrator's hesitations or even mistakes, which makes *Ozidi* a fascinating and exciting textual object.

J.P. Clark succeeded in rendering the characteristic roughness of the oral version. The text recreates the reciting conditions for the reader; it has not been smoothed out by the elegance of a Birago Diop or by the accuracy of a Djibril Tamsir Niane. On the contrary, the transcriber-translator, the author in question, takes mischievous pleasure in indicating borrowings from English as well as anachronisms that never fail to annoy the purists looking for 'authentic' orality. The link between narrator and sponsor, the author J.P. Clark Bekederemo, the grandson of Bekederemo, a famous Delta personality whose name Clark adopted, is also recorded in the reciting. Similarly, the local context of the utterance becomes apparent, that of Mokola and Dube, the Ibadan markets where the Ijo merchants gather together. An often recurring figure is that of the narrative being called to order; the praise song is used for parodic ends. The text bears the mark of the location and of the time of utterance. Sometimes, the narrator's fatigue makes itself felt; during the last few pages, he has difficulty hiding his exhaustion. These difficulties multiply until at last he cannot hide how worn out he is; he is in such a hurry to get it over with! Throughout his narrative he depends on a certain number of formulae. Ozidi's anger, which is a type of possession, is compared to 'the stampede of those daemons' coming from his bowels (Clark, 1977:187). The loanwords obey certain rules: the songs are in Urhobo or in Edo, while the magic formulae are in Igbo. In addition to this language mix, one of the pleasures of the narrative lies in the

> recourse among narrators, especially ones resident in cities outside the tribe, to a frame of reference in which, like Amos Tutuola, mythical personages and objects are seen in contemporary technological terms. The flight of a witch is likened to an aeroplane, a tall champion is compared to an electric pole, and time is measured out by aid of clocks and weeks. (Clark, 1977:xxvii)

Sory Camara

In the Francophone domain, the works of Sory Camara come closest to that of J.P. Clark. Camara devoted more than twenty years of his life to the collection and translation of the Mandinka oral tradition. His approach was that not only of an ethnologist, but also of a writer. His thesis on the *griots*, entitled *Gens de la parole* (Word People) was justifiably awarded sub-Saharan Africa's Grand

Prix for literature in 1976. Beyond its ethnological thesis, the work also contains numerous well-translated texts, constituting virtually a small anthology of Mandinka literature. Camara's most recent book, *Les Vergers de l'aube* (2001) continues this literary exploration. There are several aspects to his work. To start with it is a sociology of producers of *griot* texts, followed by a typology of the various poetic genres presented, and lastly a general reflection on Mandinka creative traditions, coupled with hermeneutic considerations on the meaning of the texts presented to the reader.

In Mandinka society – that of early-twentieth-century Upper Guinea, soon the familiar object of Sory Camara's investigations – the *griot* is mediator *par excellence*. In this very specific sense, the *griot*'s art is committed to the life of his community and its social conflicts. *Griots* are men who are not quite men, because they don't wage war: they are closer to captives than to other men. They participate in female activities such as singing and playing musical instruments. It is exactly this ambiguity that confers on them the status of mediator, and by implication considerable 'spiritual power' and skill as an arbiter. Speech is performed not by but through the *griot*:

> The communication established between the repressed or suppressed content of the spectators' personality and the character played by the *griot* at that moment is a silent and unconscious one. The show he provides is instrumental in purifying the nobles of their impulses and unworthy emotions. (Camara, 1975:158)

The *griots* are in effect everyone's jocular older relative, a role that places them at the heart of society. Although their speech is intensely socialized, yet at the same time it defines them as a group of specialists. Sory Camara's work does not draw on a reductionist conception of orality, according to which all oral productions would be filed under the *tale* label, as in the French adaptations reviewed above. His analyses are supported by his own translation of a number of texts, of which a transcription was provided in *Gens de la parole* (1975). His work enables us to understand the different levels of Mandinka textual production. The *griots* compose poems, some of which may be presented in translated form (such as, for example, a poem on General de Gaulle) for set occasions. Sometimes, these texts achieve a measure of notoriety and become part of an oral heritage that is known and sung by everyone. Sory Camara also provides examples of a female repertoire. These texts are presented in the form of satirical poems, proverbs or even epigrams that are recounted by the *griots*. As in the case of the *Sundiata*, the griots also transmit the oral tradition and partially compose epic narratives in which, for lack of a written form, Mandinka history may be heard.

Other Literary Forms in Mandinka

However, Mandinka oral literature is not limited to these few genres. It consists of two other very important categories that Sory Camara deals with in some detail: first, the *tali*, which are wrongly considered to form the bulk of the output. Referred to as 'tales', they have become a hotchpotch of Mandinka orality. *Tali* are nocturnal words:

They can be distinguished from very ancient words by their simpler narrative organization. One cannot deal with very ancient words and with the *tali* in the same fashion. In a way, the latter are part of a more spatial order while the former belong to a more temporal order. Very ancient words deal with human beings' complex evolution; the *tali* are situated in a given era and deal with case studies. (Camara, 1982:11)

Although the *tali* may be narrated by anyone, the speech specialists or *griots* will obviously give a better account of them and are capable of provoking a livelier response from the public than an amateur storyteller.

Second, there are the ancient words of the initiation texts, of which only the masters of the word, the *somo* or initiators, hold knowledge: in this case, stricter rules are applied to the reciting process than in the categories that have been dealt with above. Mandinka knowledge of the esoteric is communicated through these texts: Souleymane Cissé's film *Yeelen* provides a remarkable iconographic equivalent of these narratives on the birth of light. At times, certain *griots* will sing texts that are distinguished by not being in the domain of public speech. Thus, collective, public texts that are known to all are opposed to esoteric texts, in the same way that the public speech specialists, the *griots*, are distinct from the masters of initiation speech. As in the case of producers, oral tradition reveals a stratification of genres – here, we are quite far removed from the vision provided by the tales of (Birago Diop's) Amadou Koumba.

Sory Camara does not restrict himself to producer-type sociology and generic typology; he undertakes a hermeneutics of esoteric narratives whose extreme originality needs to be emphasized. The ancient initiation texts are myths for which he provides a French edition in *Parole très anciennes* (1982). He reflects on the particular nature of the knowledge contained in them. To him, it is clear that the frequent allusions to masks and to dual personalities are the means through which knowledge and criticism may be communicated to the universe: knowledge would not be possible without this dramatic art of duality. The mechanics of it are represented by an interior world that is connected to the description of an exterior world. Such is the proper mode of mythical know-ledge: 'the reinterpretation of everyday things from within'. In order to under-stand the links between tradition and orality, it is essential to get acquainted with the richness and depth of Sory Camara's research, which is the product of lengthy investigations. His translations and his abilities as an interpreter and a writer are unrivalled in French: he serves the Mandinka cause very well.

The Yoruba Tradition

The Yoruba are fortunate to have had a multitude of active researchers and specialists from the beginning of the twentieth century onwards, thus providing a picture of their literature seldom equalled in Africa. Like the Mandinka, they represent one of West Africa's most important language com-munities, which is now twenty million speakers strong, mostly concentrated south of the Niger in Western Nigeria. Unlike the Mandinka, the Yoruba population is concentrated in cities that have existed from the nineteenth century and remained within the framework of a strict hierarchy of social structures controlled by 'kings' or *oba*. Books in Yoruba have been published for more than a century. It has an indigenous tradition for the study of language and literature, which is unique in an African culture. The Yoruba themselves have produced an entire body of knowledge on Yoruba orality that is today without rival in any African language.

Certain phenomena have attracted researchers more than others, starting with the oral corpus of texts devoted to divination. These diverse texts are organized as an entity; their variety, number and the wealth of their historical contents have inspired numerous research projects. Several volumes devoted to these collections have been published: in 1943, B. Maupoil published a study on geomancy, the *fa* from the Slave Coast. P. Verger followed in his footsteps by publishing a number of textual excerpts in French from the *fa* corpus that were familiar to him as an initiated *fa* priest (Verger, 1965, 1972). In 1969, William Bascom provided the first general collection of these texts and, above all, a theoretical analysis of the functioning of this mantic art. Before 1970, except for a few locally published brochures by Yoruba intellectuals, no studies regarding this discipline were published by the country's own writers. Wande Abimbola's oeuvre filled the gap, notably with two essential works: *Sixteen Great Poems of Ifa* (1975) and *Ifa, An Exposition of Ifa Literary Corpus* (1976).

By comparison with previous research, the originality of this latter work lies in its exclusive preoccupation with the study of texts associated with divisions of the *fa*, which number 256. Each division, every chapter, bears a name and is associated with a divination figure. The principal chapters, numbering 16, each contain a motto; the *fa* priest recites this before proceeding with reciting the poems associated with the chapter in question. The divinatory transaction is therefore above all a linguistic operation: words that the client entrusts to palm nuts; words that the priest detaches from the immense *fa* corpus. The corpus is vast because the number of sub-chapters (the *ese*) associated with each *odu* is unlimited, or rather, is limited only by the priest's abilities. It is thought that every *ese* consists of 600 associated texts; in the majority of cases, the short pieces consist only of a few verses, but sometimes an *Ifa* poem may contain a larger number. These poems are known as *Ifa Nlanla*: the great Ifa poems.

Wande Abimbola, who anthologized these poems, also studies the rhythmic phenomena, wordplay, onomatopoeias, repetitions, and other figures such as metaphors – in fact, everything that contributes to transforming the *fa* discourse into a poetic discourse (he also provides appropriate examples). Transmitted from Yoruba origins – we should not forget that the Yoruba consider the city of Ile-Ife to be the cradle of humanity – this tradition probably spread from this centre to a large part of the coast, which offers rather similar divinatory systems:

> From Ife knowledge of divination and art spread to other parts of West Africa where the cultures concerned fashioned the knowledge to suit their own cultural, linguistic and philosophical requirements. The case for Art has been made quite often, but that of divination literature has not received sufficient attention. (Abimbola, 1975:38)

The *fa* certainly constitutes a corpus of poems, but it is not the only one in Yoruba oral literature:

> The main distinguishable genres of Yoruba spoken Art are the *iyere Ifa* of the diviner-priests; the *ìjálá* of the hunters; the *ewì* or *èsà* or *oɡ̀béré* of the entertainer-masqueraders

... the *rárà* of the itinerant minstrels, the *oríkì jáàntìrere* of the mothers and grand-mothers; the *ọfò* and *ògèdé* of the medicine men ... Each genre has its distinctive style of vocalization or technique of vocal performance. Yoruba traditional poetry in general is best classified not so much by the themes as by the stylistic devices employed in recitals. (Babalola, 1968: 23)

Adeboye Babalola, quoted above, wrote an original study on hunters' poems, *The content and form of Yoruba Ijala* (1968) in which he poses the question of rhythm in Yoruba poetry. He claims to have found a metric regularity in hunters' poems and extends this discovery to the remainder of Yoruba poetic creation and specifically to *fa* poetry, in which he rediscovers the conclusions of Wande Abimbola, another inventor of Yoruba metrics:

Each line as a rhythm unit consists of unstressed and/or stressed syllables. There are usually not more than six stressed syllables per line in all parts. The line unit is not very difficult to establish in *ẹsẹ Ifá*. Each line has a significant breath pause at its end.... (Abimbola, 1976:65)

The debate on the true nature of Yoruba poetry is of particular interest to me: everyone is sensitive to the poetic virtues of the texts in question, but Yoruba scholars who grew up in a classical Anglo-Saxon culture (despite wishes to the contrary) are determined to rediscover regular metres, as though that would finally assure them that they are in fact dealing with poetry.

The mechanical application of the rhythmic patterns of European languages to a language like Yoruba with its formidable tonal or musical complexity will be unproductive. It is unthinkable that poetry must always be squeezed into the iron collar of fixed metrics, just as it is unthinkable that poetry must necessarily rhyme. In these texts, formal unities can be identified, even if they are difficult to typify, but that gives us no right to tack European models onto them.

Babalola's assertion that there is a metre based on the difference between stressed and unstressed syllables as in Abimbola, for *ẹsẹ ífá*, is debatable. The occurrence of the physiological feature of stress is not regular or predictable in the Yoruba language. Its prominence, on which he bases his analysis, is not so evident. And even when it does appear, it is the individual performer or poet that imposes it on the words he intends to emphasize. It is a subjective element. (Olatunji, 1984:60)

Each formal unit is characterized by various prosodic, syntactic or even lexico-semantic traits:

One can conclude that there are several factors that create rhythm in Yoruba poetry. Syntactic and sense parallelism, tone patterning, the pause and line length are but some of these factors and the way they are combined and coordinated varies from one type to another. (Olatunji, 1984:64)

The quest for poetic invariants (such as metre) can only lead researchers astray. Olatunji's research put the efforts of Babalola and Abimbola in their right perspective. What remains is to provide a systematic description of the functioning of many Yoruba poetry genres. For example, the *oriki* is one of the great genres of Yoruba poetry, and has survived through contemporary songs that take up the litanies of laudatory epithets using *Fuji* rhythms. As Olatunji

correctly says, 'there is not a lot of narrative in the *oriki*' (1982:83), characterized as it is by a strong impact of nominal sentences and many loanwords
from relations terminology, unified by frequent references to the *oriki* theme,
i.e. the person whose praises are being sung. The *oriki* is a language situation
as well as a poetic genre; it includes all the aforementioned traits, but maintains
great fluidity of content and structure. 'Thus a performance of *oriki* appears
fluid and fragmented, strings of interchangeable utterances which can appear
in variable order and which often seem unconnected.' (Barber, 1989:18)

It is an intensely socialized genre, as shown by its use in popular music.

> An *oríkì* is fluid in its structure. The praise units constituting minimum themes in the
> *oríkì* can be variously ordered, or some left out in different versions. It is the basic
> meaning or content of the units that matters because their wording often varies from
> one version to another. This variability in the number, sequence and wording of the
> units has an implication for *oríkì*. What we are given as the *oríkì* of a subject needs to
> be seen as a performance which could have left out some praise units or added others.
> A poet can therefore suit his choices and elaboration of the units to the occasion.... In
> a situation where the poet does not have enough time at his disposal, e.g. when the
> audience is restive or wants something other than lineage *oríkì*, or under the temporal
> limitations of radio/television programmes and cultural shows, he may no be able to
> touch or elaborate upon some praise units. In addition the poet may have forgotten
> some of them. This fact accounts for the comprehensiveness and length, or otherwise,
> of the various *oríkì* collections that we have. (Olatunji, 1984:106–7)

Conclusions

I hope the above-mentioned examples have shown that much remains to be
done in order to understand the functioning of oral literary creation to enable
us to reach an in-depth understanding of its creative mechanisms. It should be
agreed that orality ought not to be confused with tradition; on the one hand, it
cannot be excluded from contemporary creation; on the other, it cannot pass as
the exclusive vehicle of tradition. New oral genres are being created, such as
popular theatre in West Africa, while other, older genres are being taken over
by new groups in unusual situations. One such is the labour union poetry
found in South Africa, based on the model of traditional praise singing, the
Zulu *isibongo* or Sotho *thoko*.

What is more, the very modes of production of the oral text, whether
concerning the use of formulae or of repeatable sequences (which Jean Derive
calls kits), belong to what we would call intertextuality in written production:

> By using preliminary motifs within the same genre, as in the case of distinct genres,
> it was possible to compose works that were different every time. The emphasis which
> is placed on similar compositional techniques enables one to highlight the way in that
> intertextuality functions in popular oral culture and determines the process of literary
> creation. Analysing the modalities according to which this phenomenon occurs can
> probably revive studies in literary creation in a very fruitful way. (Derive, 1990:226)

This circularity of mutually echoing texts, based on one another or contra-
dicting one another, is in fact the way any literature functions, whether its

vector or mode of composition be oral or written. The inexhaustible productivity of language that is imprinted on previous utterances or *déjà dit*, and formalized by ethical and aesthetic intentions, is surely the mark of verbal art. This intertextuality also involves a mix or even a linguistic *métissage*, where oral production may feature within the research framework of contemporary writing, as in the case of the 'naïve' Amos Tutuola, the 'logothete' Luandino Vieira (Trigo 1981), or with the defenders of 'Creolity' (Bernabé, Chamoiseau and Confiant, 1993).

How does this intertextuality function? Will a single subject (such as tradition) or the authority of lineage be maintained, or will different points of view be respected, thus truly restoring the polyphony of social reality? It is impossible to give a simple answer to this question. Certain oral genres (such as sacred writings) function decisively: Wande Abimbola's *fa* is a case in point. Others depict the fluidity of social life and echo its polyphony, like the *oriki* studied by Karin Barber (1991). How can this liberated speech be perpetuated and developed? Will orality provide the resources for the successful completion of such a project? I doubt it, as I will try to show in my analysis of narrative fiction in the last chapter of this book.

3 The Manuscript Heritage

The storyteller's voice is succeeded – or accompanied – by a voice endlessly reading and rereading the manuscript, while awaiting the coming of that instrument of wider distribution, the book. A manuscript is still part of the universe of the voice, which explains its centuries-old coexistence with orality. In Africa, the book, a contribution from Christian Westerners, was supported by Latin alphabet systems that were very effective as far as their extraordinary sign economy was concerned. At the same time, however, they were too elliptical for certain languages, such as the tone languages (as we have attempted to illustrate in the first chapter). The manuscript culture is the domain of scribes and readers who ensure the safekeeping and cautious circulation of texts written in a type of language that necessitates specialist deciphering. The various spellings are all of Semitic origin, whether it is the Arab alphabet or the Ge'ez syllabary, which was developed from a consonantal alphabet.

Ethiopia & Sub-Saharan Africa

Why do we discuss the Islamization of Western Africa without first dealing with the Christianization of Eastern Africa, and particularly Ethiopia? Once again, disciplinary divisions and intellectual traditions encourage researchers to maintain completely outmoded categories. Ali Mazrui showed us the way; for the Kenyan scholar, the frontier with Ethiopia did not indicate the separation of two worlds. Certainly, Ethiopia has a separate history, but there is no need to detach it from the rest of Africa. Instead of Asianizing Ethiopia, it might be more appropriate to Africanize Arabia, as Ali Mazrui suggested. Ethiopia is singled out because of its age-old Christianization process and continuous church tradition. But the human settlements in this region date from ancient times. The Sabean invaders from Arabia did not find virgin lands, but peoples speaking Cushitic languages, which even today are the most widely spoken in Ethiopia and in the Horn of Africa.

Ge'ez, the most important of the known Ethiopian languages, was used to write the first inscriptions dating from the third or fourth century AD. It is a Semitic language with traces of a local Cushitic substratum. As such, it attracted the attention of the Semitic Studies tradition, which considered itself completely separate from African Studies, as it was engaged in an Aryan *tête-à-tête* with only marginal interest in Africa. In France, well-known Semitic specialists such as Marcel Cohen grew interested in Ge'ez and later in Amharic, but their perspectives and methods were quite different from those of Africanist linguists, who almost never work from written documents. Ethiopian studies also form part of Patristic Studies: the church fathers were often

Map 2 *Towns & regions of Ethiopia*

translated into Ge'ez and in some cases the Ethiopian text is the only one known to have been written by these authors. The theology of the Orthodox Church is thus of great historical interest. Everything, it seemed, came together to isolate Ethiopian studies and to separate it from African studies. And yet, one need only consider the cultural situation to realize that a vital continuity exists between Ethiopia and its African neighbours to the south and to the west. The importance of the Cushitic substratum has already been mentioned; another point of interest is that the Oromo, a Cushitic people of more than ten million individuals, must certainly be Ethiopia's second largest ethnic group today.

In addition, Ethiopian Christianity ensured the survival of certain practices adopted from pre-Christian religions. The Gondar *Zar* cult is one of possession, found in a number of African regions, including the Hausa, despite Islam. One must not be deceived by the official version of Ethiopia's history: Solomonic mythology, which crowned the emperor as the descendant of Solomon and thus legitimized claims from the Amhara on the Shoan plateau to rule the entire country, must be deconstructed to make room for the history of other (notably Cushitic) groups. It is true that the prevailing historical factor was the hegemony of the central kingdom in regions that had been unified by Christianity (at least in the northern part of the country). As is the case elsewhere in Africa, Islam and the various native religions have often coexisted under these new powers, which were strengthened by the new religion. All these reasons argue in favour of a common reading of Ethiopia's history and that of sub-Saharan Africa.

In addition, it is significant that various publications devoted to African literatures have adopted a similar viewpoint, especially Albert Gérard's *Four African Literatures* (1971). It was an intriguing novelty to be writing about Amharic, Zulu, Xhosa and Sesotho literatures at the same time. In this study, Albert Gérard demonstrated that the problems of an Amharic literary history could easily be compared to those of literatures in other African languages. His argument was very convincing, but it did not lead to new research in the field of Francophone studies. For too long, Ethiopian studies in France have been the domain of Semitic and Patristic Studies specialists, archaeologists and palaeontologists. There are tentative signs of a revival in Jacques Bureau's *Éthiopie, un drame impérial et rouge* (1987) and Alain Rouaud's (1991) biography of Afä Wärq.

Moreover, from the beginning of the twentieth century until the Italian invasion of 1936, Ethiopia's elite spoke French and was educated in the French secondary school of Addis Ababa. Whether one refers to Marcel Cohen, Cardinal Tisserand or the results of the Griaule mission, French scholarly research on Ethiopia represents quite a respectable tradition. Unfortunately, this entire intellectual effort to all effects disappeared after the Second World War, and today the members of the Ethiopian elite speak English. One could even advance the idea that, officially, Ethiopia speaks and writes English more than Tanzania, which values the Kiswahili language as cementing its national unity, while the widespread contestation of Amharan hegemony is to the advantage of the English. The stagnation of Ethiopian Studies in France explains why there is still no Amharic–French reference dictionary and why the Ethiopian production of the past fifty years is still more or less unknown, despite some recent interest (Rouaud, 1991). If Ethiopian works are not generally mentioned in publications on African literatures, it is because (as in the case of the Islamic-Arabic production to be discussed in the following chapters), they pose problems of definition, apart from those of access to texts or translations. It is the same problem mentioned in Chapter 1: the nature of African humanities. As in the case of Pharaonic literature, these texts have remained isolated and have not inspired new generations of students and thinkers outside Ethiopia. Access to these texts has to be guaranteed, interpretation models have to be proposed, and in the last instance they have to be fitted into a global conception of analysis of African literary production. Only these new exchanges will secure their status as classics in the sense of texts that are used to nurture a lively culture of learning, not only to satisfy scholarly curiosity.

Reintroducing Ethiopian works into the field of African literary production poses different types of problems. Our conception of literature is not similar to that of the Ethiopian Middle Ages, as is the case in the Ge'ez and Arabic domains. The major genres are as follows: (in the field of religion) theological treatises, hymnal and didactic poetry and the lives of the saints; (in the secular field) the chronicles of great kingly deeds and sometimes love poetry. Several genres are conspicuous by their absence: chronicles are the only narratives on the list, and there is no dramatic literature. In a general sense, it can be suggested that what constitutes our defining feature of literature – setting down a subject in writing that will leave its mark on language and history – is absent from these works where the subject of utterance is often an institutional one, whether an ecclesial or Islamic tradition, or the royal authority. The text is the instrument of an intention that overtakes the subject of utterance; within our conception of literature, a text is the product of a personal writing experience, and a signature is inscribed in language as well as history. This dimension is very difficult to perceive in the texts we are about to present. But it could be that this makes us victims of a reductionist literary vision. After all, our personal subjects of utterance also serve as a vehicle for traditions and institutions. As for the theologians, the chroniclers, the Ge'ez or Arab poets, surely it is our responsibility to learn to read them and to understand how they were able to leave their mark on language and history within a strictly defined framework. The modern, individualist conception of literature should not lead us to deny the original in the literary practice of past centuries and cultures, where all aspects of life were invested with the sacred. Orientalists know this, but much too often Africanists do not.

Ge'ez Literature

Ethiopia is the only sub-Saharan African country to have produced literature without a break from the first centuries of the Christian era until the present day. Nowadays, it is certainly not easy to obtain texts written in Ge'ez, as they are scattered between journals and patristic, theological, or church history collections, or other literary anthologies (Cerulli, 1961). However, it would be a mistake to think that the entire Ge'ez production is confined to religious literature. One of its most striking features is that an important part consists of translations: mostly from Greek, but also from Arabic and Coptic. A number of texts translated into Ge'ez during the first centuries of the Christian era were thus preserved in northern Ethiopian monasteries. One is reminded that the Ge'ez Old Testament contains 81 books, while the Catholic version contains only 45 and the Protestant version 39. Several books that Catholics consider to be apocryphal were accepted by the Ethiopians while certain books, such as that of Enoch, exist only in Ge'ez.

Ethiopian monasticism started developing in the Aksum period and the *Lives* of the monks was one of the first genres to be practised: the *Lives of Saint Paul the Hermit* and of *Saint Anthony* were translated from the Greek while, according to Bureau (1987), Ethiopian monasticism originated with the *Rules of Saint Pakome*. The collection of Ethiopian *Lives of the Saints* makes up a large proportion of the Eastern Christendom's *Golden Legend*, which continued to be read and to serve as a model of composition within the Ethiopian Church. Ge'ez has remained the liturgical church language, as Latin was in the Catholic Church in former times.

The Aksum kingdom (third to eighth centuries) marks the era when Ge'ez was established as a literary language. The period between the end of the Aksum kingdom and the fourteenth century is defined as Ethiopian history's Dark Ages by official historiography. At that point, power fell into the hands of the Cushites, the Agaw, whose reign was like a blot on the well-regulated succession of Solomonian dynasties listed in the fourteenth-century *Kebra-Negast* (The Glory of the Kings), a collection of legends and history pertaining to the Sabean dynasties. To this present day, it constitutes one of Ethiopia's historical, poetic and literary monuments. *Kebra-Negast* consists of four parts: the first deals with the encounter between Solomon and the Queen of Sheba and the fruit of their union, Menelik I, the founder of the Ethiopian dynasty. The second part recounts the return to Aksum of the Ark of the Covenant, brought back from Jerusalem by the same Menelik. The third consists of the genealogy of all the kings who succeeded him; the fourth evokes Ethiopia's redemptive mission (Bureau, 1987:87).

The exceptional development of hymnal and religious poetry in the fourteenth century marks the beginning of the Ge'ez literary apogee. The *Synaxaron*, a translation from Coptic, is supplemented with poems on specifically Ethiopian saints. During the same period, panegyric poems in honour of King Amda Seyon I were written in a language that is not exactly Ge'ez, but probably old Amharic, although the dating of these texts is the subject of controversy: the language, whether the poems date from the fourteenth or sixteenth century, is identical. Furthermore, the texts could still be understood by the twentieth-century reader. It might be more logical to assume that they were nineteenth-century compositions.

Apogee of religious works

Zara Yakob's fifteenth-century reign was a period of particular splendour: a number of lives of the monks were composed, as well as the *Lives of the Kings* of the Ethiopian dynasty, including the Zagwe or Agaw kings (Tigrayan and not Amharic kings). Of special interest is a *Life of Lalibela*, the king who bequeathed his name to the capital. Here he strove to decorate his city with magnificent, time-defying monolithic churches that continue to awe visitors with the elegance of their construction. *Lives* of the monastery founders were written in which heavenly visions were combined with descriptions of supernatural encounters. The *qene*, a poem form that is typical of Ge'ez artistry, dates from the reign of Alexander (1478–1494); mastering the *qene* 'is the mark of a truly well-read person' (Bureau, 1987:156).

The sixteenth century was characterized by internal theological struggles and wars between Muslims and Christians. To resist the Islamic and imperial Ottoman expansionism that was overcoming them, the Ethiopians appealed for help to the Portuguese, who provided military assistance as well as Jesuit missionaries. The Jesuits proceeded to compose texts in Amharic, which became the popular language from this period onwards. The wrath of the Coptic clergy as well as of the emperor rained down on them: towards the end of the century, the Jesuits were driven out and all their texts burnt. Another notable collection from this period, including several types of poems used in the liturgy, is entitled *Treasures of the Faith*.

One of the 'most beautiful works in Ethiopian literature' dates from the first half of the sixteenth century (Cerulli, 1961:199). *The Interpretation of Divinity* has survived thanks to a manuscript that is kept in the French National Library, and of which E. Cerulli furnished a published version. It is in fact a treatise on the Michaelite heretics, who denied that man could know God through his own efforts. The poem's emotional quality and elevated tone make it one of Ethiopia's literary gems (Cerulli, 1958).

Another typical Ge'ez poem from this period (according to some) is the *melke*, although similar poems have been discovered in hagiographical Scandinavian literature (Pedersten, 1989). It is a type of blazon, in the form of a litany: a series of nominal phrases enumerate the different body parts of the male or female saint, leaving nothing unpraised. This enumerative fascination reveals a tendency found in a number of panegyric poem genres in the rest of Africa, but is applied here to the veneration of a holy person.

A recent publication of Ethiopian philosophers drew attention to the significance of Ethiopian output during the seventeenth century (Mudimbe, 1988:201). The *Treatise of Zära Ya'acob* is divided into 25 chapters: variously on the life of the author, the eternity of God, the division between believers, the meaning of faith and prayer, the laws of God and men, marriage and the nature of knowledge. The central themes of another work, the *Treatise of Walda Heyrat*, are creation, knowledge, faith, the nature of the soul, the law and judgement, social life, etcetera. Scholars were aware of these works and their originality of thought, but wrongly attributed them to an Italian Capuchin, while Claude Sumner, as quoted by Valentin Mudimbe, made it his task to establish their Ethiopian origin as well as the convergence of their argumentation with the *Discourse of Method*, 'within a common rationalistic approach' (Mudimbe, 1988:202). These texts, which are opposed to any kind of revelation, cannot be termed Christian, yet their rationality leads to a kind of abstract theism. Whatever the opposition to revelations of any type, the light of reason is nevertheless a penetration of the divine in this world (Sumner, in Mudimbe, 1988:203). According to Sumner, the common characteristic in these various treatises is what he calls the notion of centrality, 'which characterizes all Ethiopian thought' and emphasizes the debate's moral importance. Mudimbe has observed that the re-reading of these texts signals a 'remarkable instance of regional, cultural authority regarding creativity' (Mudimbe, 1988:203).

Richard Pankhurst (1962) has provided a statistical table of the literary genres present in the manuscript collections to which he has had access. The greater part, more than half at least, was composed of religious works, translations from the Bible, and liturgical and ritual dictates. A not inconsiderable proportion, in the region of one tenth, was made up of the *Lives of the Saints*, while in certain collections, such as that of the French National Library, poetry (the *melke*) accounted for one fifth. Regrettably, scholars paid less attention to the 'magical' manuscripts, 'magical rolls' and manuscripts on popular medicine, which were sometimes viewed with a certain suspicion by monks and the clergy. However, they reveal the existence of a sophisticated popular culture that existed alongside the official one. These texts are now in the process of being republished, an undertaking that will change our vision of the Ge'ez culture and that may bring it closer to other African cultures.

Printing was only introduced to Ethiopia by the nineteenth-century Protestant missions. In 1824, the British and Foreign Bible Society published the first, bilingual edition of the Gospels in Ge'ez and in Amharic. Amharic literature gradually replaced Ge'ez literature in all its secular uses. From the nineteenth century until the present day, the only Ge'ez experts and practitioners are the Ethiopian clergy. In the seminaries, the future priest, the *abba*, is initiated into the practice of *qene* poetry, thus ensuring that new collections are still being produced. At present Ge'ez is used only in rare works on grammar and theology.

> Despite the profound changes which have occurred, particularly in recent years in the political and economic systems of Ethiopia, as well as in many other spheres, literature and writing in the Ge'ez language have remained important elements in one of the oldest cultures and civilizations of Africa. (Ferenc, in Andrzejewski, 1985:291)

The extraordinary originality of this cultural development should not lead to a separate examination of these productions, but rather encourage researchers to fit them into the cultural history of the Horn of Africa and the Sudan, in comparative studies, following Mudimbe's example. On several occasions, we have observed the significance of the 'indigenous' Cushitic element in Ethiopian history; it is certain that this theme will be increasingly present as Ethiopia distances itself from the aftermath of feudalism and the totalitarian mirages that still profoundly mark its contemporary history. Mengistu did not descend from the Sheban Queen, even if he would have liked to delude people into believing so!

Amharic Literature

Ge'ez production is inseparable from the manuscript culture; it cannot be detached from the voices of the *abba,* articulating poems and reading narratives. Ge'ez belongs to a universe where the voice is truth, where the breath of the spirit is also that of the voice. In the past, Ge'ez was never – and never will be in the future – the language of massive book production. Manuscripts will be produced and distributed directly; the copyist will be replaced by the photocopying machine, skipping the typesetting phase.

Amharic was first situated on the fringe of the manuscript culture: it was the language of the people, not of the scribes. The blossoming of the Shoan monarchy was responsible for imposing it on the entire country; its development coincides with the centralization of royal power and the introduction of the printing press. The new Amharic literature also produced new genres, such as travel writing and even novels. Although clearly distinguishable from Ge'ez manuscript culture, we have to deal with each one successively, because Amharic is closely linked to Ge'ez. Ge'ez not only provided Amharic with a syllabary, but also an entire religious tradition.

As mentioned before, royal hymns from the seventeenth century were written in a language that was not Ge'ez but might have been old Amharic. Doubts were expressed about the authenticity of these hymns; however, if Amharic could become the language of the Shoan state in the nineteenth century it means that it was spoken in Shoa and Godjam and may even have provided a written form as well, by means of a Ge'ez syllabary. The central variety, that of the Shoan region of which Addis Ababa is the capital, became the standard. It is this variety that was used to compose two *Chronicles of Emperor Tewodros* (1856), thus breaking with the tradition of previous emperors and *de facto* instituting Amharic as the official language thenceforth.

> These two chronicles, written in a lively style that often reminds the reader of spoken language, teeming with picturesque details, are in contrast to today's lengthy, moralizing discourses. (Comba, 1958:125)

The linguistic unification of the Amharan plateaux and the rest of the empire around the Shoan dialect goes hand in hand with the Ethiopian state's consolidation around Amharan royalty. Under the influence of Menelik II, the Shoan royalty imposed its hegemony on the entire region and opened the country to foreign influence. Printing houses started appearing in Ethiopia: 1887 saw the publication of John Bunyan's *Pilgrim's Progress* in translation. This edition greatly influenced the new Amharic literature, which was receptive to the confident, industrious and concerned piety of this ascetic, moralizing traveller. The journey was translated into several other African languages in the early stages of their printing production and often affected the languages in question: to the Protestant missionaries, going the route of pilgrimage and austerity seemed the surest way to free the new Christianized elite from paganism and ignorance!

Rare works from the end of the nineteenth century were printed on missionary presses, especially those of the Swedish Protestant church. But these missions had settled on the fringe of the empire, while everything was happening in the centre of it: in 1911, Makonnen II installed the first printing press in Addis Ababa. In 1917, a writer by the name of Heruy Selassie became director of the Imperial Printing Works. These institutions would play an important role in the development of Amharic literature: their proximity to the corridors of power enabled their imposition of the dominant Shoan dialect over Amharic and of Amharic over the other languages of the empire, which were even transcribed into Amharic letters. It is significant that Heruy Selassie, the director of the Imperial Printing Works and one of the first writers, published a *Catalogue of Ge'ez and Amharic Manuscripts*. This marked the end of an era: literature was slipping from the hands of the monks and the copyists and falling onto the desks of journalists, politicians and teachers.

Another consequence of opening up the country to the outside world was that young Ethiopians were sent overseas to complete their education. On returning home, they became the true creators of a new Amharic literature. Their texts expressed the need to transform a feudal country into a state closely resembling the European model. None of these figures became revolutionaries, but it is obvious that, speaking from experience acquired during their travels and overseas training, their individual statements could no longer be restricted to trotting out the 'glory of the kings' or the 'golden legend' of the Ethiopian monks.

Modern Ethiopian writers

The Ethiopian creator of the novelistic genre was Afä Wärq. In 1887, at the age of 19, he was sent to Italy as a tutor to teach Amharic. He then composed a series of didactic and fictional works that marked the true beginning of modern Amharic literature. At the same time, a young Zanzibari was describing his first European travels in Kiswahili, thus also inaugurating a new era in Swahili literature: from now on, the subject would speak in his own name. Afä Wärq composed an *Amharic Grammar Book*, followed by an *Italian-Amharic Dictionary*, before publishing the first Amharic novel in 1908: *Lebb Wällåd Tarik* [A story from the heart], 'one of the first novels of African literature', as Alain Rouaud (1982a) rightly stated. Several editions of the novel, including schoolbooks, were published – in Amharic – the title was even used to describe the novelistic genre itself.

This 'story from the heart' tells of the tribulations of a Christian general and his two children, made prisoners by a pagan king. After many trials and tribulations, related to the cross-dressing of the general's daughter who is courted by the king, all is well that ends well: the pagan king is converted and marries Tobya, the general's daughter, while Tobya's twin brother marries the king's sister. 'The novel ends in two poems, or rather, in two love songs' (Fusella, 1984:17). Afä Wärq, the first Ethiopian novelist, was also the first grammarian and the first modern intellectual, 'a harsh critic of his country's backward customs and an admirer of Menelik, who had favoured Ethiopia's modernization' (Fusella, 1984: xx). Another of his works, partly written in French, a *Traveller's Guide to Abyssinia* (Rome, 1908) bears little resemblance to our contemporary notion of a 'guide'. It is a conversation between a European traveller and an Abyssinian, providing us with an 'uncompromising description of Ethiopia as it was at the time' (Fusella, 1984: 185). One notes with regret that none of Afä Wärq's works have been published in France, although some of his works were actually written in French. His novel has not been translated into French, either; it has, however, been translated into English, and an abridged version has appeared in Italian. The recent publication of his biography is good news, as it signals a revival of Ethiopian studies in French (Rouaud, 1991).

The second Amharic writer of note is Heruy Walda Selassie. He also travelled to Europe. Soon after, he was given an official post in the imperial administration, which was in the process of modernizing under the influence of Ras Tafari, the future emperor Haile Selassie. We have seen that when Heruy Selassie was appointed administrator of Addis Ababa in 1917, he was also put in charge of the government's printing works. His literary oeuvre is first and foremost of an historical nature: a *History of the Reign of Yohannes IV* and the *Catalogue of Ge'ez and Amharic Manuscripts* mentioned above. His oeuvre is not restricted to these relatively traditional genres: he also wrote a whole series of little essays on the customs of his time, containing reflections of a political and philosophical nature and revealing his desire to modernize the country. For example, one of Heruy's 'tales' is full of admonishment, encouraging young people to free themselves from the practice of precocious marriages and to renounce wearing amulets for protection against the evil geniuses or *Zar*. His 'modernism is of the indirect kind' (Tedeschi, in Fusella, 1984:82). He clearly distinguishes himself from his contemporary, Afä Wärq, who, according to Tedeschi,

> openly admired the West and considered that Ethiopia's salvation could only come from a speedy adoption of the values of Western civilization. Heruy's modernism in contrast depended on the future emperor Tafari's reformism and was contained within this same movement. (He) [Heruy] considered that Ethiopia could limit itself to selecting certain principles and practices from Europe, injecting them slowly and cautiously into the body of Ethiopian society (Tedeschi, in Fusella, 1984:86).

Afä Wärq and Heruy Walda Selassie are the first names in Amharic literature we need to remember. They wrote for a new public who had received a Western-type education in the international schools that had opened their doors in Addis Ababa in the 'twenties (particularly the French school, which would become the Franco-Ethiopian *lycée*). The war against Italy, the massacre of the Ethiopian elite and the country's occupation after liberation caused a break in Amharic productivity. These tragedies strengthened the country's patriotic sentiments and its cohesion around the Emperor, who took advantage by increasing Amharan hegemony, thus provoking the Eritrean rebellion at the beginning of the 'sixties. In May 1991, the rebellion ended with the occupation of Addis Ababa by the different movements opposed to Mengistu's regime and with the acceptance of Eritrean independence a few years later.

New authors are making themselves known: Makonnen Indalkachew, who was also the empire's Prime Minister for a time, wrote an autobiography that contains a description of traditional customs. He also produced a number of novels and plays dealing with moral and philosophical problems.

In 1950, Germaccaw Takla Hawaryat published his great novel, *Araya*, in Asmara.... It is a real book, its format reminds one of a schoolbook: 17 x 23,5 cm. It is larger than Afä Wärq's novel, and thicker as well. (Tubiana, in Fusella, 1984: 124)

It is indeed a proper, lengthy novel, which was prescribed in schools for many years, and not one of those 'brochures' on sale everywhere in Addis Ababa and in other big African cities: 'For the specialists of African literatures, this sort of reading material is characteristic of what is called market literature' (Tubiana, in Fusella, 1984:124). Translations from the classics of world literature (Shakespeare, Molière, Tolstoy, and Pushkin, whose grandfather was Ethiopian!) were published during the same decade. New genres such as literary theatre were developed too: a play by Kebede Michael, entitled *Hannibal*, was staged at the 1966 Dakar festival, and a play by Menghistu Lemma, *The Marriage of Unequals*, translated from Amharic into English by the author in 1970, was an open critique of the feudal concept of arranged marriages.

The 1974 revolution did not result in the end of literature: socialist realism, took the place of honour and adapted effortlessly to extolling Ethiopian history and denouncing feudalist flaws; unfortunately, literature made do with trotting out the same themes. Who dare say the *samizdat* era never reached Ethiopia! The fall of the Marxist regime may result in a liberation of speech; but what will the language of this liberation be? Will the rejection of Amharan domination (of which Mengistu's regime, which was probably held in greater contempt for its brutality than the feudalism of past times, represented the final 'flowering') lead to the rejection of Amharic, in favour of English? English has *de facto* become the language of the Ethiopian elite: those seeking to escape imperial censorship as well as those fleeing the Mengistu regime. Today, a significant part of Ethiopian literature exists in English, which is also the language of higher education at the University of Addis Ababa. The fate of Amharic is probably one of the many cultural stakes in the reconstruction of a country that woke up from an imperial dream to find itself in a Communist nightmare.

From Writings in Arabic to Arabic Spelling

According to Salvatore Tedeschi, the presence of writers and of literary activities was already noted in the Timbuktu of the fifteenth and sixteenth centuries. Writing was truly a means of communication and of expression, as testified by two works that were transcribed and translated at the beginning of the twentieth century and are known as *Tarikh es Sudan* and *Tarikh el Fettach*, two chronicles written in Arabic that may be the oldest known books of West African literature.

> Thus, I witnessed the ruin and collapse of historical science [knowledge] and saw its gold and small change disappear. And so, as this science [knowledge] is rich in gems and fertile in its teachings, as it acquaints man with his fatherland, his ancestors, his annals, the names of heroes and their biography, I sought divine assistance and undertook to write down everything I could gather about the Sudanese princes of the Songhai race, to recount their adventures, their history, their feats and their battles. To that I added the history of Timbuktu, the founding of this city, the princes who reigned there, the scholars and saints who lived there and even more, continuing my narrative up to the time when the Ahmediyan, Hashemite and Abbasid dynasty ceased to rule in the red city of Marrakech. After having begged for the assistance of God, whose aid suffices and who provides the best support, I began in the following terms.... (*Tarikh es Sudan*, 1911:3)

These are the first lines of a text that is not unique of its kind: significant Arab manuscript collections have been found in Nigeria and in Ghana and their transcription and translation have enabled us to retrace the principal features of pre-nineteenth-century Arab literature in West Africa. Amar Samb was the first to provide an exhaustive account of its production in the country that is now called Senegal (1972). All the listed works have been heavily influenced by the classical tradition, and yet they are original works to which the following observation applies:

> The average Ghanaian student knows something about H.G. Wells or Arnold Bennett, but probably knows nothing about their contemporary, Al Hajj Umar ibn Bakr al Salghavi. And yet the works of Al Hajj Umar are at least as important for an understanding of Ghana's recent social history as those of H.G. Wells and Bennett are to the social history of England. (Hodgkin, 1966:443)

Knowledge of the Arabic language was never widespread, but it allowed the production of a significant literature in African languages, transcribed in an Arabic alphabet and called 'Ajami'. The works of Usman Dan Fodio are written in Arabic, but also in Hausa and Fula.

To promote enlightened and realistic proselytism, a certain number of thinkers and masters devoted themselves to the task of providing the masses with access to new information that they hoped would be adopted by all. To this end, they added to their own output in Arabic with a parallel, complementary one in Fula. One such example is the prolific activity of Dan Fodio, whose works in Arabic, Fula and Hausa run into hundreds, as well as the considerable achievements of the Fouta Djallon and Massina poets, Tierno Allidou Ndiang, Tierno Diawo Pellel, Allidou Mohammadou, Yero Massina and Mohammadou Toukourou (Seydou, 1973:178).

Indeed, the abundant literary creations in Fula, listed in the 'general bibliography of the Fula world' prepared by Seydou (1977), led to the publication of numerous texts in the *Classiques africains* series (notably the two collections of *Poésies peules de l'Adamawa* [Fula poetry from the Adamawa], translated and published by P.F. Lacroix in 1965, and the collection entitled *La Femme, la vache, la foi* [Woman, cow and faith], translated and published in 1966 by Alfa Ibrahim Sow. All this nurtured the work of one of Africa's most original writers, who will be known as one of the century's great exponents of linguistic ingenuity, Amadou Hampâté Bâ. The scattered, stateless Fulani nation despairs of developing a standardized version of their language, considering the plan to do so was agreed at the Bamako conference thirty years ago (1966), within the context of the Mandinka and Fula Project initiated by the Francophone Cultural and Technical Cooperation Agency (1983). Today, it is often collectors and transcribers rather than authors who write books in this language; they are seldom published locally (cf. Fagerberg-Diallo, 1995). Hausa finds itself in a totally different situation, as its literature is probably the most dynamic and the most original of the literatures stemming directly from West Africa's Islamic tradition.

Hausa Literature

As is the case of Kiswahili, the wide diffusion of the Hausa language is a recent phenomenon. The first known texts probably date from the end of the seventeenth century and are written in Arabic characters. The great movement brought about by the holy war, which ensured the power of the Islamic dynasties in northern Nigeria, dates from the beginning of the nineteenth century. Under the leadership of Usman Dan Fodio, the Fulani took control of the region. Dan Fodio was a well-read philosopher, poet and theologian, not just a warlord. Several texts, written in Arabic, Fula and Hausa, are attributed to him. Although Arab–Hausa bilingualism continued, it declined in favour of Hausa during the course of the nineteenth century. Hausa literature had already acquired its dominant traits, which were spread across religious and didactic poetry and historical chronicles. These texts are obviously in written form and not from the oral tradition, which contains a greater number of genres. Following the canons of Arabic metrics, Hausa written poetry is often didactic in nature, centred on moral questions illuminated by the light of Islam. It can be grouped into four genres:

> *begen Annabi*, or the praises of the Prophet
> *wa'azi*, teachings and sermons
> *tauhidi*, Muslim theology
> *fikihu*, Muslim law (Zima, in Klima, 1976:167)

Graham Furniss (1991) poses the question why Hausa poetry should still be read, when its preoccupations and precepts seem so far removed from the contemporary reader. His answer is based on a particular notion of poetry that is current in the Arab world: poetry is a space of debate about values and the practical conception of life, using the forms of Arabic poetics. It is certainly not the place for a personal expression that creates and masters its own form: there is no endeavour to innovate or to fantasize.

The preservation of social structures produced a very interesting phenomenon: in the course of the twentieth century, many poets continued to use Arabic letters. Because of its social impact and political importance, this type of writing has continued until the present day.

However, historians have discerned an evolution towards more secular themes. At the beginning of the twentieth century, Aliyu Dan Sidi, the emir of Zaria, who was deposed by Lugard, governor of the protectorate of Northern Nigeria, and exiled to Lokoja, wrote *Mu sha Falada* (Poem of abundance), only published in 1957. It is very difficult to distinguish Hausa poetry from singing and to draw a distinction between a strictly literary (and thus also didactic and religious) tradition – Jihadist – and an oral tradition with more varied genres and its many texts circulating in written form. The simplest division would be between sung oral poetry (songs), and written poetry (poetry). The important genres of popular poetry (poetry that is not the work of well-read clerics) include panegyrics and satire; they are often treated in a way that is far removed from the canons of Islamic tradition. The *bori* possession cult is present in this type of popular poetry with its modes of composition that are independent of Arabic poetry. The influence of this activity on sophisticated poetry is obvious and contributes to its renewal. A religious poet by the name of Aliyu Namangi, the author of a *Wakar Imfiraji* [Religious poem] in eight volumes (1972), deals with themes that are not limited to the Islamic tradition, but are aimed at all readers, thanks to what P. Zima calls his 'humour and realistic attitude toward life' (Zima, in Klima, 1976:169). All sorts of poetry, sometimes in Arabic type and at other times in Latin lettering, have been produced from Gaskiya printing presses, providing clear evidence of a new attitude towards the Islamic tradition, which we shall reconsider later, after discussing the prose production.

The Hausa prose tradition

One could contend that no Hausa prose tradition existed before the end of the nineteenth century. Prose texts using the Ajami Arab spelling are rare indeed and one wonders whether these texts were written down directly or transcribed from oral literature. Nineteenth-century correspondence and other historical texts were first published by F. Edgar (1911), but the entire field still needs further exploration, especially the incomplete listings of manuscript collections that exist outside the Hausa region, particularly in Ghana. The missionary activity of S.W. Koelle, the author of the *Polyglotta Africana*, stands as the first example of comparative research on African languages, and is equally noteworthy as far as Hausa is concerned. In 1859 Koelle translated the *Second Book of the Pentateuch* and provided an anthology (in translation) of his earlier collected texts (1885). By 1932 the translation of the Bible had been completed: missionary activity north of Nigeria was being slowed down by lack of support from the colonial administration, and thus turned its attention to the region's non-Hausa-speaking pagan minorities, such as the Gbari.

In 1930, to promote modern education and provide the administration with much needed clerks and executives, the colonial government created the Bureau of Translation, later renamed as the Bureau of Literature. Its function was to produce Hausa texts by using a Romanized spelling called *boko* (from the English word 'book', which, as we have seen, incidentally sounds like the Hausa word *boko* or trickery). Vincent Monteil (1980) provides an excellent description of this undertaking and its consequences. While the poetic field was entirely occupied by didactic and religious poetry cast in Arabic metrics, the new spelling called for new forms of writing and this led to the birth of novelistic fiction, of which the first titles are the following:

Shaihu Umar (1933)
Gandoki (1934)
Ruwan Bagaja (1935) [The water that worked miracles]
Magaana Jari Ce (1938) [Speech is a capital]

The first of these books, *Shaihu Umar*, was immensely successful; it was adapted for theatre and cinema, translated into English, and continually republished in Hausa. The author (Abubakar Tafawa Balewa, the future Prime minister of Nigeria who was assassinated in 1966) recounts the adventures of a young boy, born in Borno (which was raided by the emir's horsemen), educated at court, and sent to Libya, where his intellectual talents worked wonders. He returned to his own country where he became a scholar and a respected, well-read member of society. It is, in fact, an exaltation of Islam's civilizing mission within the context of slavery. The author's lack of critical distance makes it a hard read for a contemporary mind.

Gandoki is the story of a braggart, defeated by the English, who goes to seek his fortune elsewhere and undertakes amazing journeys before returning to his own country; *Ruwan Bagaja* and *Magana Jari Ce* make ample use of oral literature. It is quite remarkable that none of the works of fiction from this period hesitate about using supernatural elements: there is an absolute proliferation of flying carpets and talismans, as if the new prose found its source of inspiration in narratives in the mode of famous tales from Arabic literature, such as *The Arabian Nights*.

A Hausa newspaper entitled *Gaskiya Ta Fi Kwabo* was created in 1939; its columns would contribute to the development of Hausa journalistic writing. Post-war political activities provided the expansion for the creation of new genres. The period is dominated by the personality of Aminu Kano: in 1965 he published a romanticized narrative of his travels in Europe, *Motsi Ya Fi Zama*; he wrote numerous plays and became known as a committed poet, along with Saadu Zungur (Abdulkadir, 1974), another reformer of Northern feudal society.

Public cultural developments
The 'fifties also saw the creation of the Northern Region Literature Agency (NORLA), which strongly influenced the development of Hausa literature. Besides prose texts (plays or novels), it published the work of poets who had played an important part in the evolution of ideas in the north of the country. Poetry has always been of central importance in Hausa literature, but the genre has also evolved: the poets began to produce texts in a Romanized form as well as in Ajami. Their idea of society was reformist in nature; their opinions were energetically relayed by the Northern Elements Progressive Union (NEPU) party. The poems of Muazu Hadeja, Mudi Sipikin and especially Saadu Zungur attest to this change in attitude (Furniss, 1985).

Poetry continues to be a public practice: it is read in public or on the radio and published in newspapers. It is a collective activity, as demonstrated by Graham Furniss in his research on Hikima, Kano's poetic circle, created on Mudi Sipikin's initiative. The poets in this group came from different types of professions: some were butchers while others were airport managers. Their texts are a continuation of a well-known, although modified tradition, while retaining its essence: that is to say, poetry is more a place of ethical debate than of aesthetic innovation.

Furniss also illustrated the political consequences of this situation: that poetry reflects certain values. Within the context of a radicalization of the political debate, as was the case in Nigeria during the 'eighties, the classical, almost incantatory denunciations of corrupt times can produce an immediate and very precise echo, especially where poets start embellishing their rhetoric with the names of current targets of criticism, and publish their texts in a local press, in the familiar way that this ritualized genre has always functioned (Furniss, 1989:6).

After NORLA's demise in 1959, Hausa literature was mostly characterized by numerous reprints. In 1967, the Gaskiya Corporation, which published newspapers, created the NNPC (Northern Nigeria Publishing Corporation) in partnership with Macmillan, an initiative that relaunched Hausa writing. The 'seventies were relatively productive years: the development of education in the North created a demand for texts that publishers tried to accommodate. Oxford University Press published transcriptions from oral literature, but also poetry from the Hikima circle; Longman and Nelson also added to their Hausa catalogues.

The chief initiative, however, came from the Kano State government, which set up the Triumph Publishing Company, bringing out two Hausa newspapers, one of which was written in Ajami. Offset printing made it possible for the writer to bypass typography, as photocopying a manuscript could be achieved directly. In 1980 the Federal government launched a competition to replenish the stock of available Hausa texts of fiction. The seven winning books were published in *Nigeria Magazine*. The list contains several novels that differ in tone from that of widely distributed texts such as *Gandoki* or *Shaihu Umar*. The fictional universe is no longer peopled with genies or haunted by warning dreams, where fountains work miracles and everyone lives happily ever after. We now find ourselves in the country of *Turmin Danya*, [the iron man] (Katsina, 1982), in the contemporary world of Northern Nigeria, a land peopled with greedy merchants, corrupt policemen and venal politicians.

Alhaji Gabatari was a robust man; his skin was so black that it seemed to shimmer; he smoked, but took care of his teeth, which also seemed to shine; at 37, he was still a young man, but wealth had already endowed him with a respectable measure of portliness.... He was the obligatory point of passage for access to the customs officers, so as to come to some arrangement about passing the goods without hassles. If he was not part of the plan, everything went wrong; goods got lost, and sometimes the contractors found themselves in prison.... He had friends amongst the aristocrats, and if anyone had problems with the law, he took it upon himself to put things right. When he passed the cup, everyone drank, however bitter the beverage! (Katsina, in Furniss, 1991:11)

These are new themes, which show that fiction is moving closer now to journalistic writing and political poetry. In other words, the fiction writer no longer has disdain for his link with reality and the ethical stakes involved. The creation of new forms such as the detective novel also brings the reader back to contemporary reality. In *Karshen Alewa Kasa* [The Dregs of Society] (Gagare, 1982), groups of demobilized soldiers start working for themselves.

Poetry too is being renewed, for one of the texts appearing in 1980 was a volume of love poetry: a genre surprisingly absent from tradition whereas, on the continent's eastern coast, Islam created an entire tradition of amorous verse.

Today, Hausa writing is confronted by new challenges. It is worth noting that the long-established habit of writing poetry in Arabic form, helped preserve a special relationship with older, classic Hausa (notably Jihadist) literature and with Arabic literature in general, which provided its metrical forms. In this area, Islam still constitutes the aesthetic and political language of reference.

Within this language (which makes the study of contemporary Hausa literature so interesting), a struggle has developed between conservatives and reformists: the works of Saadu Zungur, Mudi Sipikin and their followers in the Hikima circle make this clear. Islam did not always go hand in glove with the great feudal lords; on the contrary, it could adapt to or even benefit from the progressive republicanism of certain elements emanating from the leftist parties in the North, one of which seized power in Kano at the beginning of the second Republic in 1980.

Poetry can serve as a medium for social criticism; it can contribute to the struggle against corruption; it can invoke Islam's democratic values when confronting the corrupt 'haves' from the North. Indeed, the language of social progress is one of the key aspects in contemporary Hausa literature, particularly when the ties with the Arabic written form have not been severed and when, from the start, the author's Arabist-Islamicist convictions are clearly demonstrated by the use of the Ajami written form. But it is obvious that social criticism cannot be formulated solely by means of poetic forms, however new and original they are. This must be taken into consideration when creating new literary genres such as the novel or drama (Beik, 1984). The inquiry of the Zaria University theatre company (Etherton, 1982) into political conscious-ness by staging issues of social reality and conflict, has shown that theatre can be a debating place for everyday problems such as the home or the children – topics that are bypassed in other genres restricted by their public ethos, whether in the context of Islamic tradition or that of contemporary social criticism (Kofoworola & Lateef, 1987).

The future for Hausa

One component that adds to the dynamic, expanding, adaptive nature of Hausa culture is in my view the strength of its moral discourse – the fact that discussion and argument about what is right and what is wrong is the stuff of public discussion and at the heart of the thinking and creative output of so many writers of prose and of poetry. To the ear of an outsider like myself, more used to the refracted values of the advertiser's symbols and the encoded morality of novels, plays and contem-porary discussion of politics and current affairs, the language of much modern Hausa poetry evokes memories of the Victorian tract or the revivalist preacher (Furniss, 1996:214).

What is more, there is a dialogue or even a debate between the two written traditions of Hausa production, which represent two world views. The secular vision of the Romanized form contrasts with the Arabic form, the Islamic character of which is revealed in numerous ways. It is evident that these two conceptions are not antithetical, and that it is imperative that the dialogue between the two schools should continue. It is an important debate because the development of Hausa literature beyond its linguistic community in large measure depends upon it. It is obvious to many people that Hausa, which is spoken and understood by more than half the population, is Nigeria's main language; it has the most native speakers and continues to be the lingua franca of most Nigerians. Hausa circulates in written form thanks to its Romanized spelling, which requires no knowledge of Arabic and has no special link with Islam. The relative timidity of its output must obviously be compared to the new vitality of Ajami productivity: Hausa would probably circulate even more easily if it were perceived as a secular language, as is the case with Kiswahili today. Hausa has not yet reached this point; some would even prefer it to take the opposite route. For them, 'Romanization' comes close to being an imperialist, Christian plot. That might have been true in the 'thirties, but times have changed! Unlike Kiswahili, Hausa is first and foremost the language of speakers who identify with the *name* of their spoken tongue. It is not the official language of any country, but could become one if, like Kiswahili, it were no longer perceived as a vehicle of Islamic thought, but rather of a certain type of African modernity and Nigerian nationalism that is promulgated, for example, though the BBC's Hausa service. The Bureau of Literature uses the Kano variety as a basis for its translations, while the Kano dialect has become the Hausa lingua franca (Furniss, 1986a). This practical consensus should enable the language to be endowed with the necessary lexicographical instruments. Although there is at yet no atlas of Hausa dialects, a unilingual dictionary of standard Hausa is in preparation. In addition, a French–Hausa dictionary (by B. Caron and A.H. Amana) was published in 1997 and Paul Newman's *The Hausa Language, an Encyclopaedic Reference Grammar*, came out in 2002.

Kiswahili Literature

Writing the history of Kiswahili literature presents a certain number of specific difficulties. Although some research has been done, few researchers present a coherent thesis. There are several reasons why: it is a well-known fact that the Indian Ocean's written tradition is very ancient – archaic. Islam reached Kilwa on the Kismayo coast more than ten centuries ago and Arabic manuscripts started circulating shortly after. During the process of text-based Islamization, the encounter between Arab and coastal peoples gave birth to a 'creole' language that became Kiswahili, thus following the path of other great, modern languages (Whiteley, 1969). How does one date the birth of a language? The first oral texts? Glottochronology is no great help; one could retain the name that dominates the oral tradition of those who speak and consider themselves Swahili, Fumo Lyongo (thirteenth century). This glorious past speaks to us through the narratives orally transmitted in Lamu. In his book, *Swahili Origins*, James de Vere Allen (1993) outlined a new and surprising view of the subject that John Middleton (who wrote the introduction and edited this posthumous text), found very convincing despite its novelty and its rather makeshift methodology (due largely to the fact that the author worked outside of any academic institution of historians and/or archaeologists). What is at issue is the opposition between this people's African and Arabic character. The struggle was fought in literature and linguistics and the cause was heard: Swahili is a Bantu language and part of its texts have no relation to Arabic literature, especially the epic of Fumo Lyongo. De Vere Allen's original exegesis of this text supports his hypothesis of the existence of a continental Swahili entity, the Shungwaya phenomenon, which, for several centuries, was the centre of Swahili culture. This explains the (numerous) incoherencies of East African history, dominated for too long by British Arabophile prejudices. Thus, there is a Swahili heroic oral tradition parallel to coastal Arabic literature. Kiswahili, written in Arabic form, came into being contemporaneously, and this literature translated and adapted epic Arabic texts, for example the epic of the battle of Uhud:

> *Utenzi wa vita vya Uhud*. It was written during the lifetime of the Prophet, but the author of the Swahili version is anonymous. Most of the verses were remembered and passed on orally from generation to generation, no doubt undergoing some changes in the process. (Chum, 1962:v)

Although similar texts may be read as narratives of African peoples' defeat by the Arabs (Mulokozi and Kahigi, 1979) they belong to the history of language and literature. They were abundantly published and glossed, particularly the Fumo Lyongo epic, which was transcribed and published in the course of the twentieth century. Sayyid Abdallah Nassir (1720–1820) composed *Al Inkishafi* (1972), [*The Soul's Awakening*], a long sapiential poem (see p. 33 above) in assonant stanzas of four lines. Continually in print to the present day, this text expresses the religious preoccupations of Swahili poetry. Along with *Mwana Kupona* and the *utenzi 'wa Kiyama'* of the Resurrection, translated into French by Charles Sacleux to complement his Swahili–French dictionary, these four texts signify the four essential components of Swahili literature: the epic (*Fumo Lyongo*), Islamic wisdom (*Al Inkishafi*), practical life from the female viewpoint (*Mwana Kupona*) and lastly, considerations on the end of the world, 'an account of the general judgment, of the condemnation of the damned, with the impressive description of their torments' (Sacleux, 1939:1093) in an eschatological vein (*utenzi 'wa Kiyama'*).

These lengthy texts are called *tenzi* in Kiswahili and constitute a particularly important corpus of this language's literature. They often exist in manuscript form, although the more interesting examples were transcribed into a Romanized version. They are composed in forms borrowed from Arabic metrics, in quatrains of 8-feet lines, of which the last line retains the same rhyme from beginning to end, while the other three lines rhyme amongst themselves (and differently) in each quatrain. Originally, this was probably a 16-syllable line that, today, has been separated into two hemistiches by a voice-pause creating a new rhyme, while only the rhyme of the second line was of some importance (Karama and Khan, 1980).

Other *tenzi* are linked to historical events and were the object of some controversy regarding their mode of publication: for example, those epics composed at the time of the German conquest: *Utenzi wa vita vya Maji-maji,* was published in Germany during the 'thirties without any indication of the circumstances of its composition, but republished by Wilfred Whiteley just before independence.

> Whiteley relies completely on Lorenz's edition and like Lorenz suppresses the evidence that this is a coerced text. This information may not have been of interest to German readers in the 1930's, but would have been of great concern to East African readers in the late 1950's. (Bierksteter, 1996: 199–200)

Ann Bierksteter describes this type of publication as a 'neo-colonialist marginalization', because we are deprived of the political context – the colonial war – in which the text was composed. The various deficiencies that distort our comprehension of Swahili literature are once again highlighted here.

A critical re-reading of the historiography calls into question the research of J. Knappert, the author of numerous anthologies and several publications of 'anonymous' texts, which were in fact collected from poets who were active along the Indian Ocean coast during the 'fifties. Poetry was blossoming, but its creators, hidden behind the collectors, had no identity. Islam was everywhere, but the Muslims, especially those of Bantu origin, were mute! Thus the image was created of a Swahili culture and literature that belonged exclusively to the oriental universe of the Arabo-Islamic world, entirely derived from 'non-classical Arabic literature from the Islamic shores of the Hadhrami and the Persian Gulf' (Harries, 1962:x). The critical re-reading process undertaken by researchers such as I. Noor Shariff or Alamin Mazrui changed this (mis)representation by providing it with an historical and political context. Moreover, Mulokozi and Kahigi's philological research tried to widen the very notion of poetry and not to confine it to what was inherited or adapted from Arabo-Islamic models, notably the *tenzi*. It would be absurd to deny the latter's importance, but it should be mentioned that they correspond to only one part of the Swahili world.

From the *tenzi* probably derive the *mashairi*, non-narrative, shorter poems reflecting all aspects of Swahili social and cultural life, and notably relations between men and women.

> For *mashairi* literature is essentially gnomic, and the work of the poet is to express the common feeling and humour in the best idiom his skill can devise. (Abdulaziz, 1979:66)

They engage with general ideas about societal behaviour, defining the ethics of relationships and sociable ways. Mombasa poetry has maintained this tradition, which, for the last few decades, was represented by a poet such as Ahmad Nassir bin Juma Bhalo (1966), while A. Sheikh Nakhbany had greater pedagogical and political ambitions, as demonstrated by two translated texts, *Sambo ya kiwandeo* (1979) and *Umbuji wa Mnazi* (1995). The speakers of dialects from the coast and the islands, from Lamu to Mombasa and Zanzibar, certainly have a clear awareness of the regular nature of Swahili prosody. And yet, the first *mashairi* must be distinguished from the *mavugo* poems in free verse in which it is impossible to discover either metric or prosodic constraint, although they were certainly considered as poems as well. What is more, in the context of Swahili prosody there is a term – *guni* – that refers to breaching traditional rules, whether intentional or not.

> The Swahili poets who defend rhyme and metre are not defending anything essential, other than Arabic influence, even though they do so against their will, sometimes in the name of Africanness. Swahili poetry is not characterized by rhyme and metre, which merely indicates an Arabic or Persian origin.... (Mulokozi & Kahigi, 1979: 10)

Before the 'fifties and the publication of Amri Abedi's research, there was no treatise available in which the whole collection of rules could be found, although the writers (whether their works were written in Arabic form, or in Romanized form as is the case today) were thoroughly familiar with the rules of poetic art. It is noteworthy that Swahili poetics, which originated in Arabic poetics, could not apply all the rules of its model with equal success because of the different nature of the languages, particularly as far as vowel quantity is concerned. A number of rules from Arabic poetics presuppose the alternation of long and short vowels, which is not the case in Kiswahili, where all the vowels have the same quantity. This creates quite a difference between Kiswahili and the languages influenced by Arabic, such as Hausa, in which the adaptation of Arabic poetic rules was facilitated by the presence of long and short vowels, as demonstrated brilliantly by Joseph Greenberg (1949). Today the situation has undergone some changes: the philological (and thus political) stakes of the 'sixties have been modified. Abdilatif Abdala, who is considered 'the best contemporary Swahili poet' for his collection of poems entitled *Sauti ya Dhiki* (1973) continues to use classical forms. The drive for innovation, represented by the free verse form at the birth of the new Tanzanian literature, has been partially overtaken by other considerations, notably poetry's role in society, in Kenya as well as in Tanzania. Formulae such as the very rhythmical free verse used by Ebrahim Hussein in *Jogoo Kijijini* (1976) seem to offer a more elegant means to overcome a 'divide' that really does not separate the Ancients and the Moderns, the Kenyans and the Tanzanians, any more, even less so the Coastal inhabitants (Lamu, Mombasa) and the Continentals, or the island and Coastal people. The endless distinctions are disappearing in the face of the need to understand and revitalize the teaching of Swahili literature. Otherwise, it will not expand or even survive. The publication of the first, general teaching manual of Swahili literature in Kiswahili testifies to this new perspective on the role of literature in today's society (Njogu, 1999).

A special poet

The most famous nineteenth-century Swahili poet, and probably the first to escape the consensual anonymity of 'tradition', is Muyaka, who was born in Mombasa and lived during the era when the governors of Mombasa, the Mazrui, succeeded in freeing themselves from the tutelage of the Sultan of Oman. The city's new-found independence gave birth to a flourishing culture celebrated in its poetry. It expresses patriotism for the town of Mombasa: 'It is a place full of shields, lances, bows and arrows, and long swords, The dead are dead and gone!' (Abdulaziz, 1979: 147)

The wars between Lamu and Pate, between the subjects of Oman and the tributaries of Mombasa – another division – provided the opportunity to compose numerous occasional poems until, in 1836, the Omani once again became the masters of the town, putting an end to the period of independence maintained by its governors. Muyaka would never cease preaching resistance; he satirized the town elders who surrendered – or sold out to – the Omani from Zanzibar, where the Sultan had transferred his capital: 'Man does not feel sorry at the beginning; remorse always comes in the end ... the destroyer of the motherland is the son of the soil himself ...' (Abdulaziz, 1979:152).

Muyaka's output is not limited to themes of war and politics. He dwells on many other subjects: he pokes fun at an unfaithful mistress (1979:175); regrets his past youth (1979:177); deplores his repulsive looks (1979:181). Friends, love, illness and disappointments are the themes of the poems translated and published by Abdulaziz. They illustrate the talents of Muyaka, who was able to make a personal voice heard in poetry that, as we have seen, was previously dedicated to epic or religious themes.

The use of ancient poetic forms is still maintained on the Kenyan coast and especially in Mombasa. A different evolution took place in Tanzania: the national political debate in Tanganyika took place in Kiswahili, and *Mwalimu* ('teacher') Nyerere's commitment to Kiswahili was an essential element in developing poetic expression. The newspapers published poems, and continue to do so; these texts obey – or not, as the case may be – the canons of Arabic poetry, in which poetic practice was a popular verbal art form. An intensive survey such as that undertaken by Mulokozi and Sengo (1996) enables us to identify dozens of poets who are still active.

Shaaban Robert

As Swahili gradually became the national language, poetry became a national genre. M. Mulokozi is quite right to mention the fact that the first poets to free themselves from canonical Arabic forms were published in Swahili newspapers. Shaaban Robert's career is typical of the new national role attributed to poetry. Today, his name stands for the beginnings of Kiswahili literature written in Romanized characters, thus more or less graphically detached from the Arabo-Islamic context. Robert had a modest career in the administration of the British territory. Born in Tanga, a coastal town halfway between Mombasa and Dar es Salaam, he was not an ethnic Swahili: his Yao father came from a group of Southern Tanzanian traders, but his mother spoke Kiswahili and the language became his own. He knew Arabic, but started writing poems in Kiswahili in the 'thirties, which he submitted to newspapers. A Muslim himself, he translated the poems of Omar Khayyam (from English), which shows that his idea of faith was an open one, judging by Wole Soyinka who considered Omar Khayyam as the 'Patron Saint of agnostics'.

Shaaban Robert wrote the story of his life, which consisted of administrative transfers, and the difficulties he encountered in publishing his first volume. During the Second World War, he wrote a *utenzi* against Hitler, praising Allied efforts. His poetry is very varied, obliging us to consider his work as a type of moral or even political essay, rather than a lyrical effusion.

> In Shaaban Robert's social and philosophical search, based on abstract ethic and civilising principles; his humanitarian outlook, tending towards some fusion of Muslim and Christian doctrines; his own personality and abilities – all are catalysts for the evocation and evolution of the common good. The heroes of his works,

Karama, Itubora, Ayubu, Adili are characters who are ready to make sacrifices for the well-being of their people'. (Zhukov, 1998:186)

Shaaban constantly composed poems and reflected at length on their status, which he defines as follows:

> Poetry is the art of rhyming, which distinguishes songs, poems (i.e. of the more cultured kind) and heroic verse. Beside being the art of rhyming, poetry expresses lucidity and preciseness of style. You may ask: What is a song, a poem or an heroic verse narrative? A song is a small poem; a poem is a big song and heroic verse is the peak of poetry ... (Robert in Harries, 1962:273)

Robert's 'personal anthology', *Pambo la lugha*, published in 1947, contains poems on a great variety of subjects: the war, obviously, but also family and social life and questions of language. The titles are eloquent: *maisha* (life), *imani* (faith), *rangi zetu* (our colours), *ua* (the flower), *Hitler*, *haki* (justice) and *Kiswahili*. His writings were republished many times during his lifetime thanks to his position as the President of the East African Kiswahili Committee in charge of standardizing the language in East Africa. 'Sheikh Shaaban was the undisputed Poet Laureate of the Swahili language, and a pioneer in the development of this language,' as Knappert wrote in a special edition published after the poet's death (1962: x). For Robert, 'Kiswahili was a unifying force in East Africa,' which was also the title of the last speech he gave in Kampala in 1961. The truth of this statement is evident in Tanzania and seems to be gaining support in Kenya as well. His activities as a poet and a 'language militant' are complemented by his novelistic works in which he expresses the political and social problems of East Africa in allegorical form. His oeuvre is large and varied; aside from its numerous printings it is present in all examination syllabi and on all prescribed reading lists for the study of contemporary Kiswahili. Highlights are: *Pambo la lugha* (1947, 1966) [Flowers of rhetoric], *Insha ya Mashairi* (1967c) [Essays and poems], composed in traditional forms; and political fiction (*Kusadikika*, 1951, *Kufikirika*, 1967), narratives whose titles are the names of imaginary countries in which the supernatural context provides the background for discussions on the nature of government at the sultan's court (*Kusadikika* takes place in heaven ...). Last, he reveals something of his life, his career, his disappointments and his successes in a brief autobiography that is essential reading, and also explains why he wrote it in two parts: *Maisha yangu* na *Baada ya Miaka Hamsini* (1991a) [Autobiography, and, Fifty Years Later]. He also contributed to the genre of biography through his story of Zanzibar's most famous female singer, Siti Binti Saad (*Wasifu wa Siti Binti Saad*, 1967a) [The life of Siti Binti Saad]. It is true that the reader discovers precious little about the singer's life, but does pick up an impressive knowledge of the virtues she practised!

Shaaban Robert was truly at the crossroads of several worlds. Although born on the coast, he was not a coastal Swahili; although an African poet and a militant nationalist, he was also a colonial civil servant; he invented the Swahili novel, but wrote texts in which he borrowed from Arabic narrative; although an apostle of Kiswahili, he nevertheless defended rhyme in poetry, which is the hallmark of the Arabic presence in the language; although a poet and a novelist, he was above all an essayist whose chief preoccupation was to find the most appropriate form to express the new ethical conflicts provoked by the transformation of the colonial world.

His first novel, *Adili na Nduguze* (1951) [Adili and his brother] imitates the intrigue and moralizing of a tale from the *Arabian Nights*, 'Abdallah Bin Fadil'. However, it is difficult to say whether he was directly inspired by this text, although he knew Arabic.

> Shaaban's treatment of it places him within the Kiswahili oral tradition, not only in his treatment of the safari story, his characterization, and his use of the episodic structure, but also in his conception of man as an ethical being determined by his choice of good and evil. (Mbughuni, 1978:95)

Kusadikika (1951) has a sub-title that stretches credibility, 'a country somewhere in heaven'. The king gives audience to ministers and the populace and in this way the principles of good government are debated. We find the same theme in *Kufikirika*, a novel published in 1967, but which is dated 1946. This text is 'an education in political consciousness' (Mbughuni, 1978:112); the hero, Utubusara, succeeds in convincing the sultan of the inanity of his politics, which were on the verge of leading to human sacrifice. There are numerous tests, for history is not made without a struggle; the sultan pays homage to Utubora in the following terms at the end of the novel:

> I am glad to see a man who brought so much to my house and to my country for 16 years, first by your prophecies, which are engraved in Kufikirika's memory, second, by your teachings and last by the fine way in which you took care of my son.... (Robert, 1967:47–8)

The theme of human sacrifice in this quotation alludes to the world wars in which many Africans also perished.

Poets such as Mathias Mnyampala (1917–1969), who was also a Mgogo – the Wagogo are a group from central Tanganyika – placed Swahili poetry in the service of the socialist ideal by using the traditional quatrain form, as Muyaka would have done. These poets have dedicated themselves to the propagation of *ujamaa* ideals (Ndulute, 1985). Curiously, Mnyampala also wrote an historical essay in Kiswahili on Gogo history. What is more, he gave new life to a traditional form of poetry in dialogue form, the *ngonjera*, which found an appropriate theme in the debates surrounding ways of putting *ujamaa* into practice: this gave birth to the genre (*ngonjera*) responsible for translating the Arusha declaration (socialist Tanzania's plan of action) into verse. The school of thought that tends to turn versification into the criterion for poetry was demolished by the young generation of Swahili writers after 1970. Why retreat into Arabic metrical and prosodic forms? Nothing in the Bantu tradition – and Kiswahili is certainly a Bantu language – calls for stilted versification or rhyme! In his collection entitled *Kichomi* (1987) [Suffering], Euphrase Kezilahabi (1944 –) attempts to create Swahili free verse that draws on traditional metres while obeying no rhythm but its own:

Halafu wakati
Ujao utafika
Makubwa madogo
Mazuri mabaya.

[A time will come
When I will bring different fruits
Large and small
Pretty and ugly.]
(Kezilahabi, in Bertoncini, 1987:26)

Even though it is sometimes contested, the poetic tradition has ensured the unity of Swahili literature over the past ten centuries. The language has evolved, the dialects are very different and in fact it is difficult to read nineteenth-century poetry (that of Muyaka for example), in an edition that is not annotated. And yet this is a living tradition that has been transmitted from manuscripts to today's printed books. Swahili poetry, that is created to be sung rather than read, is also very much alive in today's newspapers and in *taraab* songs, a type of musical theatre that has dominated cultural life in Zanzibar as well as along a large part of the Swahili coast. The essential theme is love: it had already been Muyaka's central theme. Thus even the fixed forms are perpetuated by means of song, while the free verse forms have some difficulty getting accepted.

The prose question is similarly problematic. Narrative poetry or *tenzi* has already been discussed, but there is also a narrative prose to be found in the old chronicles of the coastal towns, such as Pate for example. A theological-juridical type of literature was produced during the nineteenth century and is still to be found in manuscript form to the present day. There are other forms of prose, however, such as narratives and tales. They abound in the oral tradition: did they originate in Arabic to be appropriated by Swahili speech, sometimes transcribed and translated? The narratives of Fumo Lyongo, the Swahili mythical hero from the thirteenth century, may be the first known oral narratives. In 1870, an Anglican bishop, Steere, published a dictionary as well as a volume of transcriptions of oral texts. Our aim, however, is not to provide an inventory of fictional prose. There are many debates on the typology of narrative genres. Classification difficulties are explained by the ambiguity of the position of Kiswahili, which has numerous dialects; a regional language, standardized in only one country, it sometimes has difficulties imposing its views. Old Swahili oral literature is coastal in nature; it is strongly influenced by Arabic-Islamic and Persian literature. Instead of a collection of traditional Bantu texts, one finds in it a collection of narratives influenced by Arabic-Persian Islamic literature.

> In the field of prose, fiction did not always have a strong standing. It is not surprising that my research into the nineteenth century only produced a meagre harvest. Words abound to describe the various forms; some have been borrowed from Arabic, such as *hadith* or *riwaya*; other, rarer terms, referring to certain types of tales, come from Bantu languages: *ngano*, for example (Rollins, 1983).

Modern writing, characterized by the subject's attempts to make his mark on history and on language, probably dates from the first Kiswahili texts (Bertoncini, 1989) signed by authors relating their (previously unpublished) personal experiences, like that of the young boy (called Salim Abukar) who travelled to Russia and, following the example of his Ethiopian contemporaries, narrated his discovery of Europe; and, especially, the narrative of an unparalleled historical experience, that of the slave trader Tippo Tip who, although outside the hierarchies of lineage and religion, set himself up for several decades during the second half of the nineteenth century as East Africa's most important potentate. Living in retirement in Zanzibar, he decided to set down his life story on paper.

> Tippo Tip, who was living the life of a rich landlord on the isle of cloves, was convinced by his German friend to write the story of his eventful life. As he mastered Swahili better than he did Arabic, Tippo Tip wrote his autobiography in Swahili with the use of Arabic characters. Brode transliterated this text and translated it into Arabic. He completed the task on the 19th September 1901. (Bontinck, 1974:9)

Tippo Tip was an adventurous but cruel man, a lucid observer of men and notably of his great rival, H.M. Stanley, whose glory was as much the result of his exploits in the field as of his great tales, which must have incited Tippo Tip to follow his example. All those who came into contact with him towards the end of his life agree that Tippo Tip was a fascinating character, perhaps one would even say a 'gentleman'. As one of his promoters puts it, 'Tippo Tip is the only one of his category who is capable of transcending prejudice' (Bontinck, 1974:306). His fame, which was due in part to his cruel exploits,

> carried the tales of his actions far and wide, transforming them into an epic and turning him into a sort of hero who was celebrated by all the black bards of Eastern Africa. (Bontinck, 1974:309)

This autobiographical text has particular value as a document covering Tippo Tip's business dealings and travels. He also mentions his encounters with Livingstone and Stanley; the latter he graces with the following caustic remark: 'I have never known another European or any other creature who could lie like that man' (Bontinck, 1974: xxx).

A new type of Swahili prose was born with this exceptional character, a prose that is neither didactic nor apologetic, narrated in the first person and with nothing to prove except to express a certain truth on paper. Tippo Tip is not worried about creating a work of art, but rather about leaving behind a reliable testimony – creating a true oeuvre, in a sense. His work, which has been translated into German, English and French, is an historical document of prime importance, but it is also a linguistic and literary document: how many African autobiographies existed at the time? Tippo Tip, who was born in Zanzibar in 1837, is well and truly an African: he spoke better Kiswahili than Arabic, his translator tells us – that criterion determines identity along these shores.

At the beginning of the nineteenth century, Kiswahili's destiny as a standard language had not yet been determined. Tippo Tip wrote his text in Arabic characters at a time when there was no dictionary or spelling source. Once the International Swahili Committee had been put in place in the 'thirties the language was made the object of a development plan.

The first Swahili writer to use the standardized language was, as we have seen, Shaaban Robert (1909–62). This master of the language, word-spinning prose writer and industrious poet freed Swahili literature from its coastal and Zanzibari context, while with Tippo Tip and other examples of travel writing it had already distanced itself from its Islamic context.

In the wake of Shaaban Robert and with the proclamation of Kiswahili as Tanzania's national language, new possibilities were created for writers and especially for young people who were desirous to contribute to the edification of the *ujamaa*, but were also conscious of the difficulties of the task. To delve into yet another category of writing, one must not forget 'entertainment' literature, which has continued in Zanzibar with the detective novels of Mohammed Saïd Abdullah (*Mzimu wa Watu wa Kale*, 1960) [The ancestral forest]. After the 1964 revolution, a more committed literature was born in novelistic form. One notable author was Adam Shafi Adam, whose novel *Kasri ya Mwinyi Fuad* (1978) was translated into French (1986). In another of his novels, 'Lord Fuad in his palace' (a literal translation of the title), the lord in question lives on the island of Zanzibar during the last years of Arab feudalism. This lazy, brutal alcoholic manhandles his old nurse, fondles the servant girls and does not see the approaching revolution, which will change the town but not in fact the countryside. Unfortunately, the socialist realism of this text is not the best introduction to Swahili literature, although it does provide precious information on Zanzibar's intellectual climate after the 1964 revolution.

A new generation?

At the end of the 'sixties, a new generation of writers came to the fore with the creation of the University of Dar es Salaam and the priority given to Kiswahili, which became Tanzania's official language. The novelist Kezilahabi stands out in this group: he tries to use the novel as a means of philosophical enquiry and not as an instrument of propaganda or of pure distraction. His writings earned him a reputation as an avant-gardist and 'existentialist' literary figure. *Rosa Mistika* (1971, 1981a), with its eponymous central figure, a tormented young girl, is a novel set against the backdrop of the post-colonial cultural conflict and the continuing struggles between the old and the new generation, as defined by Kezilahabi's own words in a personal interview. Another title, *Dunia uwanja wa fujo* (1981b) [The world is a field of chaos] pretty well summarizes the author's rather sombre vision of life. It deals with 'villagization' problems – with population displacements and an individual's dilemma when faced with this upheaval, which can often destroy a person, all in the name of progress. The work of the new intellectual generation is characterized by a preoccupation with socialist problems of social reconstruction, rather than with writing to mobilize popular energies.

A novel such as Ndyanao Balisidya's *Shida* (1975) also bears a title that could best be translated by a loanword from African French: *la conjoncture*, the experience of young people transplanted from a rural community to city life. As in the novels of Kezilahabi, the principal characters here are young people and especially girls. Rural exodus, urban misery, social and political crisis are the substance of this novel, which is truly representative of the critical tone adopted by Tanzanian literature during the second half of the 'seventies.

As a national language, Kiswahili has contributed to the unification of a country where no local literatures were able to develop. In this sense it seems very significant that an unpublished, lengthy novel (600 pages) written in Kikerewe during the 'forties was translated into Kiswahili (*Bwana Myombekere na Bibi Bugonoka*, 1980) ten years later by the author, Aniceti Kitereza (1896–1981). It was published in Dar es Salaam and finally translated into German in

1991 and into French in 1997. Unlike that of the younger Shaaban Robert, the author's mother tongue was not Kiswahili; he was a teacher working for the Catholic missions, which had a long and active history in the region of the Ukerewe islands on Lake Victoria (Hartwig, 1972). This bulky novel relates the amorous *peripeteia* of Bugonoka and Myombekere. At first rejected for her sterility, Bugonoka is taken back by her love-sick husband and bears him a child after she is treated by a healer. We follow the daily lives of the characters on the Ukerewe Islands – Bugonoka will bear another child – from the cradle to the grave. The author excels in hunting scenes; he is sharp-witted and highly cultured, and his novel, first translated into French in an abridged but unpublished version by Simard (1945) followed later by the complete version in 1999, offers an original panorama of rural life through the tales of an inseparable married couple. It is one of the first 'conjugal epics' produced in African literature. Its lively, didactic subject matter does not lapse into proselytism: Bugonoka's son takes several wives, while his father remains true to the wife he almost lost. The *apologia* for Christianity succeeds through the realistic goodness and open-mindedness of its characters.

The long period of silence imposed by Zanzibar's authoritarian regime – Tanzania is a federal republic and the Zanzibari government was autonomous to a large extent – ended in the 'eighties. 'Lord Fuad in his palace' made way for other issues relevant to the future of the revolution and life on the islands. The first name to mention is that of Mohammed Suleiman (1945–) alias M.S Mohammed, the author of *Kiu* (1972) [Thirst], *Nyota ya Rehema* (1976) [The Star of Rehema] and a collection of tales, *Kicheko cha ushindi* (1978) [A triumphant laugh].

Saïd A. Mohamed (1947–) is not only a professor and a critic, but also a poet, dramatist and novelist, the author of *Dunia Mti mkavu* (1980) [The world is a dry tree], which has often been reprinted and recommended as a text in Tanzania. He paints a picture of the difficult life of Zanzibar's proletariat in prose that is influenced by the techniques of the modern narrative (Bertoncini, 1989:246). Currently, a unique, original and almost unnoticed phenomenon has taken place in sub-Saharan Africa: writers expressing themselves in English in an 'Anglophone' country have virtually disappeared from the map! In 1985, of the 84 members of the Association of Tanzanian Writers, only five were still writing in English, while Tanzanian intellectuals in exile became the chroniclers (in English) of their country's history: Vassanji or Gurnah wrote in Canada or in Great Britain about a disappearing world, and remained on the fringe of Tanzania's literary history. A new literature has been created in Kiswahili, one that is seldom translated and is virtually unknown outside the country, despite the interest of the work of someone such as dramatist Ebrahim Hussein. This trend symbolizes Tanzania's political and ideological trajectory – one of a country that has renounced socialism and that at least had the lucidity and merit not to try to impose it by violent means.

Ebrahim Hussein was first known as a poet who rejected Arabic and European models (Abdulaziz, 1979: 104), and later mostly as a dramatist after the success of a play entitled *Kinjeketile* (1969). The hero of this piece, which takes place during the Maji-maji revolt against German occupation, is Kinjeketile, a charismatic leader but at the same time a man riddled with doubts about the future and the effectiveness of the magic water that is supposed to make his troops invulnerable. Written in beautiful Kiswahili, the play was and remains very successful. It avoids the over-simplification that so often marks political theatre. Kinjeketile is not just a warlord; he is also a man in doubt and this brings him closer to us.

At the same time, Hussein wrote short comedies such as *Wakati ukuta* (1970) [The time wall], published in *Michezo ya kuigiza*, which evokes the generation gap in Dar es Salaam's lower-middle classes. *Mashetani* (1971) [The demons] portrays the troubled conscience of the socialist state's new elite. In this ambitious and successful work, possession becomes the metaphor for Westernization, thus allowing the dramatic discourse to operate in reality as well as in an imaginary world. It expresses young intellectuals' (already noticeable) disarray confronting the contradictions between their autochthonous cultural heritage, Western lifestyle models and official socialism.

Doubts about political action and the Tanzanian regime implicit in the action of *Kinjeketile* are openly expressed in *Arusi* (1980) [The marriage], one of Hussein's most beautiful plays, but also the one that has been least understood. In a village on the Kenyan coast, the women find themselves alone: once married, the men leave for Arabia to seek their fortunes, while the more idealistic ones go to Tanzania to build a socialist country. Kahinja is one of the latter, but he returns home disappointed and guilty, having stolen money from his village's *ujamaa* coffer – not a very socialist act but one that he nevertheless justifies by the need for compensation after all the free labour he has given to the community. Here the theme is the break with past idealism.

Ebrahim Hussein's last work, *Kwenye ukingo wa Thim* (1988a) [On the shores of Thim] was inspired by a news item that became a major political event in Kenya: the Otieno case. Amongst the Luo tribe, a wife cannot choose where to bury her husband and Mrs Otieno, the widow of a famous lawyer, had to accept handing over her husband's corpse to his clan, against her wishes. In Hussein's play, the action is played out amongst the educated middle class – lawyers, students – and reveals the persistence of sectarian or even chauvinistic cultural attitudes.

For many, Hussein the political dramatist has gone astray in his criticism of socialism and tribalism. To many of us, this does not seem to be the case: the criticism contained in *Arusi* is directed at individual destinies and concrete problems without proposing any other model of social organization. He denounces an authentic crisis that the government pretended not to notice: the failure of 'villagization', regrouping peasants into new, purpose-built villages. He criticizes the Tanzanian mode of socialism at least as a mode of economic organization. As for his last play, which appeared ten years after the previous one, it shows the persistence of ethnic prejudices despite the high level of education. Is Hussein pessimistic? Certainly, but he still believes in literature and in our opinion incarnates the perfect model of the writer who has remained true to the quest for an authentic, personal way of expressing himself, far removed from institutional cant. But even in Julius Nyerere's benevolent and disorganized socialist country, this type of behaviour has the effect of isolating and marginalizing an author. Hussein is no political or linguistic militant: his only aim is to illustrate the development of an autonomous writing culture in Kiswahili, which needs space so as not to be stifled. His much-misunderstood oeuvre is often considered futile, even reactionary, whereas it represents an (admittedly bitter) quest for what is essential.

Conclusion

The remaining paradox is, however, that the Tanzanian regime's greatest success is the 'Swahilization' of teaching and culture. No other African state has succeeded in a similar (and voluntary) process of Africanization. But even this victory is turning against Hussein: inside the country, no-one wants to hear what he expresses so well in Kiswahili, and few people understand him beyond its borders. Had he written in English, he would probably have been famous throughout the world. He thus seems to be the victim of his loyalty to Kiswahili and of *ujamaa*'s only success story, which can only increase his bitterness.

4 Books & the Latin Alphabet in West Africa

During the first half of the twentieth century, the Latin alphabet was disseminated through a great many new languages. It was also widely used to transcribe and publish books in African languages that had for centuries past been written in the Arabic alphabet. Kiswahili was one such case, followed by Hausa and the most recent example, Somali.

In fact, it was not just a case of cutting the 'umbilical cord' linking Swahili or Hausa literature to Islam – the basis of literacy education in regions where these languages were spoken – but also of developing a complete technical vocabulary, independent of Islam, capable of articulating the colonizer's world and of developing the chosen languages for the promulgation of Western civilization.

The widespread application of the Latin alphabet was obviously not limited to languages already written in the Arabic alphabet. It is a known fact that from the seventeenth century onwards missionaries had written Kikongo (Bontinck, 1978) or Ewe (Labouret & Rivet, 1929) in the Latin alphabet. In the nineteenth century, Protestant missionaries translated the Bible into dozens of new languages (Coldham, 1966). These attempts were directed at linguistic communities of varying importance and served the project of evangelization, rather than any desire to educate the masses or to develop literacy. In other words, any dialectal variety was of interest to the linguist and the educator (in theory anyway): thus, Togo contains a Mina transcription from Anecho, alongside an Ewe transcription from Lomé as well as a Fon transcription from Ouidah, all produced in a coastal strip less than 100 km long and with a population of barely a million inhabitants. Three different transcriptions, a literary debut, some translations from the Bible – whereas for Westermann (1907) all this is lumped together in one language. The question is, who decides? On whose authority is a standard to be imposed? Probably the colonial power, but it was not the same one in Dahomey and Togo, just as even the missionary confessions are different in Togo: in Anecho, the Anglo-Saxon Methodists evangelize, while in Lomé, the German Evangelical and Catholic churches officiate. Multiple transcriptions from the African languages in question are indeed an obstacle to the project of expanding education and literacy, as the following examples will fully demonstrate.

Now, at the beginning of the twenty-first century, there are few languages in Africa with a significant written production (a bibliography consisting of a few hundred titles at least) covering the full range of genres, from religion, grammar, fiction, written poetry, to scientific texts or technical manuals. These languages have been nurtured; they have been the subject of research aimed at not only the completion, but also the standardization of vocabulary in various branches of science as well as other human interests. The result has been the normalization of language into a cultural object, easily manipulated by

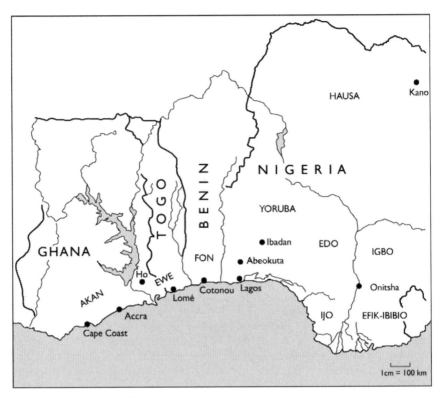

Map 3 *Languages of the Benin Coast*

institutions such as the educational establishment of the modern state whose first concern is instrumental rationality. As a result it was possible to prescribe texts and to set examinations in these languages in the certainty that the markers and the candidates could refer to the same corpus of terms, all approved by a recognized authority. Although these issues may appear futile or unnecessarily bureaucratic, they lie at the root of the development of African languages and establish the basic conditions for these to develop into modern entities – as has happened, say, for Hebrew or Italian. The number of African languages operating at this level is considerably fewer than those demarcated in language atlases; it is the same small number in which, at the present time, one may write a secondary school certificate in Anglophone Africa or a *baccalauréat* in the Francophone areas. In other terms, these are the places where African languages have gained official educational status, as in Ethiopia or Madagascar, or where French *baccalauréat* sessions are organized with the option of one of the national languages. The list, based on a UNESCO document (Ngalasso, 1985) and on the most recent source of reference (Mann & Dalby, 1987) reads as follows:

West Africa   Yoruba, Igbo, Hausa, Akan, Ewe
East Africa   Kiswahili, Amharic, *Arabic*

| South Africa | Sesotho, Zulu, Xhosa, *Venda, Tsonga, Sepedi, Setswana, Seswati,* Shona, *Ndebele, Chichewa, Chibemba* |
| African islands | Malagasy |

I will provide a survey of the current political and cultural issues for each of the languages on the list, including an appraisal of the principal genres, with the exception of the languages listed in italics. Obviously, I do not intend to be exhaustive. In this respect, the works of Albert Gérard (1971, 1981) are as detailed as can be expected when the principal sources are translations and critical articles. I have used the same method and have endeavoured to refer to the same sources, although from a different angle. Also, in the case of Yoruba and Kiswahili, I have often had direct textual access. Lastly, I was able to converse personally with many of the quoted writers. After some twenty years, hindsight helps to reveal the main tendencies of these literatures and allows one to evaluate the distance between what was planned and what was eventually achieved, between the rhetoric and the created works. It also provides a view of the sort of solid foundations that may serve as a basis for other literatures in the African languages in the twenty-first century. Studying Nigerian languages other than Hausa will enable us to define a framework for study; the parallel and yet dissimilar fortunes of the Yoruba and Igbo languages also help us to determine the importance of the choice of spellings, which will come up throughout this survey.

Yoruba Literature

As regards the local teaching of African languages, it would be incorrect to summarize the colonial situation as a contest between French hostility and English acceptance. An effective Anglomania did exist, and in fact still does. To take Nigeria as an example, only the first two years of schooling took place in the local languages (if grammar books were available) while the rest of school education was completed in English. The cult was not the language of Descartes, but rather that of Shakespeare and Lugard! Even in Nigeria, the promotion of African languages was a battle waged by cultural nationalists and not just a peculiarity of colonial politics.

In Nigeria, the official 1981 document that defines federal education policy, declares on p. 9:

> The Government considers it to be in the interest of national unity that each child should be encouraged to learn one of three major languages other than his own mother tongue. In this connection the Government considers the three major languages in Nigeria to be Hausa, Ibo and Yoruba.

To this end, the high school syllabi offer courses in these Nigerian languages. The aim is to succeed in obtaining the West African School Certificate (WASC), the (Anglophone) West African qualification that gives access to university after a very tough selection process. The candidate's entire university career depends on getting an A or advanced-level WASC (WAEC, 1985). It is obvious that the best pupils will not choose subjects not included in the A-level options syllabus, which thus reduces the development possibilities of the subjects concerned (Federal Ministry, 1985).

For the Nigerian languages, the 1983 WASC programme, which is valid from Gambia to Nigeria and includes Liberia, Sierra Leone and Ghana, differentiates between ordinary and advanced level. Four Ghanaian languages and five Nigerian languages (including the three main languages) belong to the first category. The second category contains only two Ghanaian languages and the three main Nigerian languages. In comparison with the 'sixties, this is a new development. For a long time, Yoruba educators insisted on the possibility of studying a Nigerian language at the WASC advanced level, but their demand was only satisfied around the mid-'seventies. This victory made it possible to continue recruiting quality students: Ibadan University only produced its first Yoruba graduate in 1969. Today, the teaching of the Yoruba language and literature *in Yoruba*, which originated in Ibadan, is ensured in the three universities in the western part of the country. Yoruba has thus become a vehicle for higher education; entire classes of graduates and teachers can teach one of the advanced-level WASC subjects in high school.

The Nigerian languages were accorded no official status in the 1951 organization of the Nigerian system of education; in that sense they fared no better than African languages in their Francophone neighbouring countries. M. Awoniyi, the author of a study spanning twenty-five years of Yoruba teaching, could still correctly observe in 1978 that African languages were not compulsory anywhere in Nigeria, except during the first two years of school, and in fact mostly during the first year, for want of anything better, as English was introduced as a subject in the second year and thereafter became the sole vehicle of teaching.

Nevertheless, the situation of Yoruba improved considerably during that same period. The right to be presented as a WASC advanced-level option did not have mere symbolic value. While English was a compulsory subject at ordinary level, it is noteworthy that wherever Yoruba was offered as an option between 1960 and 1969, two out of three students chose to take it.

This encouragement of Yoruba was the achievement of a group of contemporary intellectuals who may quite rightly be called cultural nationalists. It is true that their work drew on a long tradition of language studies, led by the Yoruba themselves. Samuel Crowther, a Yoruba whose name was actually Ajayi, wrote the first grammar book and the first dictionary, which was published in London in 1852. During the 1875 conference in Lagos, agreement was reached on standard Yoruba spelling rules. Admittedly, more than a century later, certain problems continue, but these are minor in comparison with what has been accomplished: to convert century-old spelling rules to a reference form for printers is no small achievement (Ade Ajayi, 1966).

Crucial problems were posed and partly resolved: tones are seldom indicated, which still causes some confusion. The variety of reference is based on the Oyo dialect, but dialectal variations have an effect on the tonal structures, giving rise to possible misinterpretations. By disregarding tones when writing, one implies that the community of speakers is an homogeneous one, capable of completing the spelling score and of tonalizing the Yoruba language without the help of diacritic signs. To have international impact (for reasons of national prestige) non-speakers should not have to face too many difficulties when deciphering printed texts. This is also a problem for Yoruba speakers themselves, as observed by D.O. Fagunwa (1903–1963), whom we will meet again at a later stage in his role as a novelist, but who also taught the language at a primary level for quite some time:

> Few as these tone marks are, experience in secondary schools, teacher training colleges, and from the hundreds of manuscripts handled by me as the Education officer in charge of production in our office has shown that 90% of Yoruba readers and a good number of writers hardly ever master them. (Fagunwa, 1958:7)

Although the debate on issues of spelling rages on, it has not held up the production of a large number of texts. The same Fagunwa observed that:

> After a child has reached primary VI, he may leave the school and enter either the Secondary Modern or the Secondary Grammar School. In the Secondary Modern School, his interest in reading vernacular literature is very weak, because as a rule he is not expected to offer this for any examination. This is a period during which special attention is necessary. The vernacular books to be used must be very interesting. At present we have no Yoruba books on Academic subjects and what is chiefly derived from reading is pleasure. Here a novel written in good language must be used. There is always something fascinating in a novel. You start reading it and you want to see the end of what you read. (Fagunwa, 1958:7)

There is no better way to describe the stimulus that drives writers in general and Yoruba novelists in particular: to retain the faithful readership of the language. The overlap of language teachers and writers is obviously specific to situations of linguistic dominance where the preservation and illustration of the language must go hand in hand. Yoruba language teaching was thus followed by the development of printed Yoruba literature, but only partly so, because we know how old the written language is.

For the past twenty-odd years, the two movements have been intimately linked. In 1968, the current president of the Society for Yoruba Studies, A. Bamgbose, formulated this fact very clearly during a seminar in Ife: 'Any Yoruba course must be built around a core of language and literature, and at no time should students be required to abandon either ...' (Bamgbose, 1982:2) In this case, the functionalist point of view is in perfect agreement with the pedagogical objectives: 'Literature is nothing but a creative use of language and ... all literary statements proceed from a knowledge of the texts' (Bamgbose, 1976:2). He thus defines the need to implement a living tradition. The WASC programme is wholly contained in the principles defined in 1968. It distinguishes between traditional literature (collected and published oral texts) and modern literature (texts that have been authored by an historically individualized subject) by the signatory of the text. Many subdivisions can be found within these two large categories. Traditional literature is divided into prose collections of tales and proverbs and praise poetry: *oriki, ijala, ofo, rara*. In modern literature, the distinctions are between prose (including novels, notably those of Fagunwa or Akin Isola, 1988), written poetry and theatre: in the 1983 programme, there is the noteworthy inclusion of a transcription of Duro Ladipo's (1931–1975) (initially oral) productions.

Every year, pupils enrolling for the WASC's A-level Yoruba have to answer the questions on the prescribed authors in Yoruba. According to the official recommendations, the emphasis is on the pupil's ability to write and to analyse literature in that language, and not on translation. Such a point of view is quite healthy, but it has the inconvenience, in our (unimportant!) opinion – of discouraging translators by depriving them of a market, and of condemning researchers, including myself, who have only a theoretical knowledge of Yoruba, to an incomplete knowledge of the texts involved. A few recent texts have been translated, however, some of which are in manuscript form. Further comments are based on the following four texts: a translation by Wole Soyinka (1968) of D.O. Fagunwa's first novel, *Ogboju Ode ninu Igbo Irunmale* (1938, *The Forest of a Thousand Demons*); an unpublished translation deposited at SOAS of a second Fagunwa novel, *Adiitu Olodumare* [The Mysterious Plan of the Almighty]; R. G. Armstrong's translation of Duro Ladipo's play *Oba Ko So* (1972, The King Did not Hang) commissioned by Ibadan University's Institute of African Studies; and lastly, an unpublished translation into French of Akin Isola's play, *Efunsetan Aniwura* (1970).

Thus, the non-Yoruba scholar can get a general idea of a literary production that is quite original, well integrated into the school fabric, and that guarantees an African authenticity that one finds it difficult to question.

D.O. Fagunwa's *Ogboju Ode ninu Igbo Irunmale* was the second novel to be published in Yoruba (the first being I.B. Thomas's novelette, *Itan Emi Segilola*, 1930). Published in 1938 by a missionary press, it was reprinted by Nelson and became successful during the 'fifties. Wole Soyinka's 1968 translation made it accessible to all readers who understand English. However, I prefer taking my example from the author's own translation of *Adiitu Olodumare* (1961), at which time Fagunwa had not yet donned the rich robes of an author translated by a Nobel Prize winner.

The book is dedicated to Chief the Honourable Obafeni Awolowo who, at the time of publication, was Prime Minister of Nigeria's Western Region. The preface tells us that the book is aimed 'at young men and young girls capable of reading with a certain degree of judgement. It is also written to be used in schools with my previous books.' Although the author targets a school-going public, it should not be inferred that the text makes for boring, juvenile reading. Although Fagunwa's novels are all the same, he always manages to surprise the reader. He masters the technique of episodic narration that is so typical of oriental tales very well. In *Adiitu Olodumare*, after recounting the sorrows of the hero's childhood, the author livens up his narrative with an exchange of letters between Adiitu and his beloved Iyunade. The rich Adiitu's efforts to seduce Iyunade, who is as talkative on paper as she is in conversation, make up a well-conducted and funny little epistolary novel. Adiitu achieves his aims; the two heroes' marriage is a chance to celebrate in the company of storytellers and masked dancers.

> For seven days people streamed into Emidunjuyo compound to listen to the stories and dissertations on human character. You have heard what happened in three days: you will hear the rest in a separate book. There is no space to continue the account. (Fagunwa, 1961:148)

With a great deal of psychological finesse, Fagunwa makes eloquent use of the storyteller's techniques. His world is a fantasy universe; the forests and villages are populated with monsters and demons; but in his last novel, *Adiitu Olodumare*, a slight change in the imaginary setting becomes apparent. The characters draw up their last will and testament, speculate on the property market and live in a contemporary, urban world. Admittedly, the novel has not lost its sense of morality: the injunction directed at the reader of his first novel, twenty years previously, must not be forgotten:

> Even if you are educated, even if you become a doctor twelve times over, a lawyer sixteen times over; when you become thirteen types of Bishop and wear twenty clerical stoles at once, never condemn your father. Observe several sons of the black races who are brilliant in their scholarship, who have studied in the white man's cities, but who adopt the entire land of the Yoruba as the parent who gave them birth, who love their land with a great love so that many wear the clothes of their land, *agbada* and *buba*, love to be photographed in the clothes of their grandfathers; while others wear the outfit of the Ogboni to show that they submit themselves to the country of Nigeria.... (Fagunwa, 1968:105)

The nationalist, Yoruba discourse is just below the surface; a superficial reading of these texts should not lead us to see Yoruba and the Nigerian cultures under construction as opposed to each other. One could talk about the contribution of tribalism to nationalism (Sklar, 1960): for a traditionalist there are no Yoruba, but only Egba, Ijebu, Oyo, etcetera. Fagunwa's extensive use of the Yoruba concept only has meaning within a political framework that focuses on Nigeria's new statehood. Fagunwa's conception of Yoruba literature corresponds to this present situation, which is one of national construction and not about the expression of a minority. Its place in national (that is, state) school politics is thus guaranteed. According to Karin Barber (1983:14), there is a 'constant tendency in Fagunwa to move away from the immediate narrative situation to more general themes' (Barber, 1983:14): Fagunwa, pedagogue and school inspector, could not always abandon the habits that came with his job.

His position as promoter of fantasy fiction and as dedicated pedagogue, has been taken up by a new generation of writers. The WASC's 1984–86 list of prescribed books still includes a Fagunwa novel, making it the king of classics, but also a novel by Akin Isola. Isola, a professor in Ife and a shrewd critic, is probably the best representative of a new generation, who care about the literary genre and about renewing its themes. He writes plays that have often been added to the prescribed titles list. He deals with the different aspects of Duro Ladipo's neo-traditionalism, including a play called *Oba Ko So* (1972). It relates the death of Shango, the Oyo king and founder of a cult. Instead of returning to a mythical past and to the 'operatic' grandeur so typical of Ladipo's hero worship, Akin Isola writes historical dramas in which he tackles questions posed by the participation of ordinary people in history. In another piece, *Efunsetan Aniwura*, the eponymous heroine tells the story of the president of Ibadan's market women during the pre-colonial era. She was a woman of remarkable energy and cruelty who, after savagely putting many of her slaves to death, was finally reduced to slavery herself and driven to suicide by a band of Ibadan notables. In Isola's world, the chiefs are not always men, and they are not always right. The play was a great success: four editions were published in 1970 and in 1980; in 1982, it was adapted for the screen in Nigeria and translated into French.

Isola's world is no longer one of fantasy like that of Fagunwa, or of myth, like that of Ladipo. It is an historical world, richly populated with many characters, but not excluding ordinary people. It probably corresponds to the rise of a new audience – all the students who choose Yoruba for their various exams and who come to further their studies at university.

A new, realistic type of prose is beginning to appear: its setting is the city and its model is the detective novel.

> Oladejo Okediji writes the tough type of detective novel, while Kola Akinlade writes the tender. There is a lot of violence in Okediji's novel but just one elusive murderer in each of Akinlade's novels. (Isola, 1988: 82)

A typical Okediji title, *Aja Lo Leru* (1969) [Credit to Whom Credit is Due] portrays a former policeman, Lapade, who has retired to the country but is recalled for further investigations where his experience works wonders. Meanwhile Akinlade's professional detective approaches an investigation as one would the solution to an enigma, as in *Owo Eje* (1976) [Love of money]. Readers who appreciate the beauty of the Yoruba language and particularly its poetry will be sensitive to the enigmatic quality of the writing:

> The critic who reads through Yoruba novels will be struck by the amount of poetry incorporated into many of them. Although the Yoruba novelist knows that prose is the language of the novel, he finds it difficult to overlook the special attention the Yoruba pays to poetry in everyday life. (Isola, 1988: 83)

The novelist thus adapts the oral poetry forms to his purpose. A critical, two-volume edition in Yoruba of the poetry of Adebayo Faleti, the most important contemporary Yoruba poet, has been published with great care by Olatunde Olatunji (1982a), accompanied by a critical edition of his poems in English (Olatunji, 1982b). This scholar has also provided us with a study of a new Yoruba poet, Femi Fatoba, who makes use of familiar, everyday words, but steers clear of the structural parallelisms and rhetoric that have been identified as Yoruba poetry, as the following comments suggest: 'Is his poetry *ewi alakowe* (literate people's poetry), the pejorative nomenclature for early transliteration of English hymns?' 'Each poem is like a divination verse' and 'Fatoba seems to have borrowed from Yoruba oral poetry the art of multi-dimensional communication' (Olatunji in Owolabi, 1996:337).

So: it is clear that Yoruba writers have their own society, congresses and reviews; they publish books that appear on the prescribed book list for exams; thus, they are read. But their books are seldom translated. Ironically, there are not only Yoruba studies in the Yoruba language, but there also exists an English literary criticism on Yoruba literature. In 1974, A. Bamgbose dedicated a monograph to Fagunwa: a model of clarity that is considered the classic text for this author. The publications list of Ife University's Department of African Languages and Literatures includes articles signed by various specialists referred to in this publication. The intellectual production in and on Yoruba prompted Albert Gérard to say that 'nowhere have historical study and critical evaluation of the literature in the local language been pursued with as much zest and efficiency as among the Yoruba intelligentsia' (Gérard, 1981:258).

Igbo Literature

The Igbo are Nigeria's third most numerous ethnic group (after the Hausa and the Yoruba), but the development of their literary production was very unusual.

At the beginning of the 'sixties, the list of literary works published in Igbo was brief: there were no anthologies of poems, no plays and only three novels. The fact that the main reference work on African language literatures (Gérard, 1981) makes no mention of it, says everything. However, in 1986, Chukwuma Azuonye, a professor of Igbo literature at the University of Nigeria in Nsukka, listed 70 novels, 25 dramatic works, and 11 anthologies of poetry in the language. In addition, there are at present two reviews dedicated to the literary study of Igbo; today, we have studies summarizing all the literary genres. It is thus possible to measure the remarkable impetus that has invigorated Igbo writing in the years since the civil war (Azuonye, 1992).

'That cultural renaissance which from the beginning has been an essential aspect of African Nationalism, by and large bypassed Igboland.' (Afigbo, 1975:82) This relevant observation from one of the great Igbo historians lays the foundation of our reflections. The system of indirect government put in place by British colonizers, supported by the Yoruba kingdoms and the Hausa emirates, kept a number of the old social structures alive, thus avoiding the collapse that Igbo culture suffered, which only had units of lineage, regrouped in independent villages, to keep it going. All of this is well known: political fragmentation did not allow for the maintenance of social structures, clearing the way for an acculturation that was more thorough in Igboland than in the remainder of Nigeria. The Igbo spoke English and were not interested in their own language. They gave up their traditional dress: they were Anglophone Nigerians in suits and jackets: such was the cliché in circulation at the time. In such a context, the cause of the Igbo language, its teaching, its literary practice, seemed to have little chance of evoking any positive response.

The Igbo language had existed in written form for more than a century, but saw the development of its written practice impeded, even thwarted by conflicts between the missionaries of different faiths who were unable to agree on a standard spelling or a dialect of reference. Once again, Afigbo gives us an accurate assessment of the situation:

> It could be argued that the crisis of the Igbo language is attributable to the virulence of the conflict between the Catholics and Protestants in the land, a factor which was absent from the Yoruba mission field. There the CMS (Church Missionary Society) had a free hand, with inestimable advantage to the Yoruba language. In Northern Nigeria, the Administration tried to contain the activities of the Christian missions, while encouraging traditional Koranic education and using Hausa as its second administrative language, entirely to its benefit. (Afigbo, 1975:80)

The first (Anglican) missionaries in fact settled in Onitsha, which was already one of the biggest West African markets, as well as the largest Igbo market. Consequently, they started translating the Bible into Igbo using the Onitsha dialect as a reference, for it had the advantage of being almost a lingua franca. At the beginning of the twentieth century, archdeacon Dennis who, judging by the consequences of his initiative, was probably ill-inspired by the Holy Ghost, undertook and completed an unabridged translation of the Bible into a 'synthetic' Igbo made up of five dialects. This translation became the standard text, although no Igbo speaker was satisfied with it, because of its markedly artificial character. In 1939, a team of linguistic experts led by Ida Ward started from scratch and suggested using the two dialects of central

Igboland (Owerri and Umuahia) as references, based on her extensive field research. This became Central Igbo, which was promoted to the rank of standard dialect and then to the official examination norm, without any consensus on the part of native speakers to support the innovation. In fact, these recommendations were to create strong opposition from the Northern speakers (today's Anambra State) and from Onitsha, whose dialect could still be designated an effective lingua franca. At the time of independence, confusion reigned; people had to wait until the end of the civil war for the adoption of a new standard Igbo, resulting from a compromise between Onitsha's lingua franca, widespread in the cities, and Central Igbo. In 1972, this solution was finally worked through and adopted, after the first 1961 agreement by the Standardization Committee of the Society for the Promotion of Igbo Language and Culture (SPILC) which acted as the linguistic authority. This rather uneasy compromise still annoys certain quarters, with the result that a quasi-artificial dividing line separates the Imo speakers (from Owerri state, home of the Central Igbo dialect and core of standard Igbo), from the Anambra speakers, who often find the standard too 'Imo'. As soon as authorities attempt to define a norm, as soon as a school or a language policy is put in place, debates on the dialects of reference flare up again.

Issues about dialect and spelling are obviously linked; the immediate, practical consequences are that, for lack of any agreement on spelling, editors hesitate to publish any texts. The small number of Igbo titles published before 1961 bears witness to this. Although the dialects clearly present certain phonological differences, the spelling convention is always rather far removed from phonological analysis. Spelling precision will always be a matter for debate, but the competition between different spellings creates an intolerable situation that is likely to distract people from studying the language. Fortified by their lead position, the Anglicans had developed their own spelling system. Ida Ward's survey led to the recommendation of a different version, immediately adopted by the Catholics in an effort to regain ground lost to the Anglicans. This injurious competition continued for several decades, and adds to our appreciation of the publishers' reluctance to promote Igbo literature. Official Igbo spelling was only laid down by the Onwu Commission in 1961, the year after independence. It was the point of departure for publications in Igbo. Unfortunately, the civil war, which started soon afterwards, interrupted the development of this new writing practice. A revival of Igbo creativity only arose in the 'seventies, demonstrated by the sudden increase of literary publications in the language.

However, Igbo literature got off to a good start: as early as 1933, the Prize for Literatures in African Languages, created by the International African Institute, had been awarded to Pita Nwana (1900–1940?), a carpenter by trade and the author of *Omenuko*, its subtitle translating as 'The man who acts in times of crisis', a fictionalized biography of an assistant chief called Igwegbe Odum de Ndizuogo. Published in the two competing spelling systems, the book was very successful amongst the Igbo, who considered it their classic novel. It tells the story of how Omenuko successfully puts right a commercial deal that is compromised by the inadvertent sale of some of his own fellow-countrymen (without their knowledge) to slave merchants. The guilt he bears for this shady exploit haunts him for the rest of his life; the novel recounts his redemption.

The tension between his schemes and tricks (which would have made him a good 'picaro', if he had given full rein to his fantasy) and his repentance, provides the novel with an ethical dimension that probably explains its unwavering success over the past sixty years.

One of the key points in the development of Igbo studies and Igbo literary production, was the extensive research into their own language by Nigerian linguists. The age of local scholars and polygraphs, those 'language militants' who have contributed much to the knowledge and dissemination of the language, but who lack the training that alone ensures scientifically sound theories, has been followed by the age of 'real' linguists. They too have been 'militants', but they have tried to take into account the demands of modern pedagogy while in pursuit of maximum dissemination of the Igbo language.

Igbo Language and Culture (1975) is a good illustration of this transition, being a collaboration between a scholar (F.C. Ogbalu) and a linguist (E.N. Emenanjo): at the time of writing, Emenanjo is a professor in Port Harcourt, after completing his thesis at the University of Ibadan. Ogbalu teaches at the Alvan Ikoku College of Education, which specializes in the training of Igbo high-school teachers. We have seen that the Igbo in general did not actively participate in the cultural renaissance along with the other Nigerian ethnic groups; it reached them much later. Two reviews dedicated to 'the defence and illustration' of Igbo language and culture appeared in the early 'eighties: *Nka,* published in Owerri, and *Uwa ndi Igbo,* published by Chukwamu Azuonye in Nsukka. Almost half a century after the emergence of Nwana, the novel is now at last an active genre, thanks to Uchenna Tony Ubesie, whose strength lies in combining an innovative approach to style with realism in his selection of themes, according to Ernest Emenyonu (1988a:37). This rebirth is also a reconstruction: the war destroyed what remained of the traditional habitat and now radio and television are everywhere. The written, now-standardized language has become the refuge of perceived traditional values. It also serves as a space of conflict between lecturers and artists. To teachers, the necessity for a graphic norm and a dialect of reference seems obvious. Similarly, terminology development commissions are concerned about enriching the language, enabling it to give an account of modern world realities.

What role should artists play in this enrichment of the language? The question has been raised through dispute between Chinua Achebe and E.N. Emenanjo. Behind the debate about choosing between the standard (Owerri, enriched by modern, urban Igbo) and Northern (Anambra state) varieties, the issue is that of a lexical production cut off from the language's dialectal roots, and left to canting professional 'communicators' and the philistinism of academic professors. As the writer (Achebe, 1984) quite rightly declares, it is not the university lecturers' role to censure artists. Yes, but it is the lecturers' responsibility to propose norms and methods of producing terminology, the pedagogue rightly replies (Emenanjo, 1984). They both agree that the future of the language will be determined in the schools; pupils should not be given texts to study whose only virtue is that they are written in the standard language. Such is Achebe's implicit accusation, made with the authority of an inter-nationally recognized writer, and we understand his concern. His rebellion is a reminder of a few essential literary truths: literature cannot prosper when deprived of contact with the outside world. Exchanges and translations are necessary. It is not a healthy situation when lecturers are the only critics and often the only writers, addressing a captive public of their own pupils. The Igbo literary milieu is a constricted one, controlled by a few linguists writing texts that they then add to the recommended reading list, for their own greater benefit and probably to the detriment of the literary language. This may gradually weaken, leaving a reading public who can hardly distinguish between their Igbo literary and school experiences. A few other African languages (Yoruba, Ewe, Akan) display a somewhat similar situation, but not so keenly. The likely explanation is the Igbo people's need to accomplish in ten years what their neighbours did in fifty, in a context made even harder by the moral and physical destructions of civil war. It is easy to see how defending a language can become the primary objective as well as a matter of considerable affective, intellectual and material investment.

Akan Literature

The Yoruba and Igbo examples may be very different in nature, but both are dynamic illustrations of writing development in African languages. In Ghana, Akan and Ewe follow the same historical pattern of development, but seem unable to impose themselves in the context of a national language programme.

Dotted with Portuguese, Danish, Dutch and English forts, the shores of the Gold Coast bear testimony to encounters between Europeans and Africans over more than five centuries: the Portuguese built their first fort in El Mina in 1482. The principal attractions of this beautiful, rocky coastline were gold and slaves. The Asante hinterland was not penetrated until the mid-nineteenth century; Kumasi's capture and sack by English troops took place later, in 1897. The coast's inhabitants had time therefore to dialogue with Europe and to form a mixed culture, out of which the first creations were the many Fanti hymns. In 1868, the coastal principalities formed a confederation that saw the development of an intellectual milieu around the Cape Coast at the beginning of the twentieth century, right in the vanguard of the West-African intelligentsia. J. Mensah-Sarbah (1864–1910), J.E. Casely-Hayford (1866–1930) and James Aggrey (1875–1927) expressed themselves in the English language. However, in *Ethiopia Unbound* (1911), the hero's ambition is to found a university where chairs for African languages will be created:

> Then I should like to see professorships for the study of the Fanti, Hausa and Yoruba languages. The idea may seem odd upon the first view. But if you are inclined to regard it thus, I can only point to the examples of Ireland and Denmark, who have found the vehicle of a national language much the safest and most natural way of national conservancy and evolution. (Casely-Hayford, 1911:195)

His intention is all the more commendable since (according to what one of his admirers has revealed) J.E. Casely-Hayford could not even write his own name correctly in Fanti! (Ofosu-Appiah, 1975:3) The foundation of the Vernacular Literature Bureau in 1951, transformed into the Bureau of Ghana Languages in 1957, did not lead to a significant literary output (Bureau of Ghana Languages, 1967). The reason is that Fanti is only one of the Twi dialects; also, the question of a spelling reference has not been settled (Birnie,

1969). The region's traditional centre is the Asante country around the capital, Kumasi, where the palace of the Asante king, the *asantehene*, is situated. The dialect there is Asante-Twi. However, the most significant corpus is in Akwapem-Twi, the language of the Twi region closest to the coast, which has not succeeded in imposing itself as the standard dialect.

> Certain Asante-Twi speakers were especially opposed to such a choice. One may well wonder whether the pre-colonial life and existence of the so called Asante Empire did not create a tendency to use a sort of local 'oral standard' based on the prestige dialect of the Asante areas, as the core of that social and ethnical unit. (Zima, 1976:157)

Johann Gottlieb Christaller published the *Gospels* (1859) and a grammar (1875) in Akropong, in Akwapem country. From then onwards, the need for a standard spelling seemed to demand solution. Christaller noted that the differences between Twi and Fanti were few:

> The tribes of the Gold Coast need a common literary language and the matter must be considered from a practical point of view. The Akan (Twi) and Fante dialects do not differ so much: half a million Fantes could easily unite with three million Akans. (Christaller, 1875, in Andoh-Kumi, 1985:93)

More than a century later, the issue still needs to be addressed:

> Akan is spoken by 40% of Ghana's population as mother tongue and by a further 15% as a second language or lingua franca. In all about 55% of the population has a command of it.... But when one goes to the schools and colleges one would not normally find any such subject as Akan on the time-table. It is the same situation in the publishing houses. One would more likely find Fante and Twi (Asante or Akwapem). These dialects of Akan are taught separately.... Speakers or readers of Twi claim that they find it difficult to read Fante books and vice versa. As a result many non-natives have always considered Twi and Fante as different languages. (Andoh-Kumi, 1985:2)

The question marks and manifold spellings (three for a single language: Akwapem-Twi, Asante-Twi, Fanti-Twi) are a source of concern for publishers and of confusion for teachers and pupils, besides intimidating writers. A standard spelling was unanimously accepted only in 1981, but the recommendations were still not immediately implemented (Andoh-Kumi, 1985:93). This hesitancy probably explains why no writer from the Akan literary milieu has succeeded in making his mark. Cultural nationalists were disappointed by the absence of a clear commitment (Verlet, 1986) in favour of African languages by the government of Kwame Nkrumah who did, however, Africanize the name of the first decolonized state of sub-Saharan Africa: the Gold Coast became Ghana.

> Unfortunately, nationalism in Ghana led to the stressing of all the other aspects of Ghanaian culture, except language study. So, with the coming of independence, less attention was paid to Ghanaian languages than was done during the colonial era. My translation of the Odyssey into Twi seemed to be wasted effort and the publishers found themselves holding nearly 10 000 copies in London, which they could not sell from 1957 till 1967.... (Ofosu Appiah, 1976a:v)

Literature in the Ghanaian languages does, however, have a long history. First steps in Fanti-Twi were marked by the 1875 translation into Fanti of the

Pilgrim's Progress, but most works were written in the Akwapem dialect. J.B. Danquah (1895–1965), a lawyer and a distinguished politician, Nkrumah's fellow traveller and later adversary, wrote plays in Akwapem (*Nyankonsem*, 1941) and in English (*The Third Woman*, 1943). He exemplifies the intellectual elite's possible bilingualism or rather digraphy (creative writing in two languages), which, unfortunately, remained theoretical. The influence of missionary shows, and the spirited style of the popular theatre concert parties that sprang up in the Fanti country in 1930, probably explain the number of plays.

> Works by Tolstoy, Shakespeare, Homer and Chaucer have also been translated.... The section headed novels (a few of which may be termed novelettes by some students of literature) represents a more recent genre in Akan publications, the majority of novels having been published by the Vernacular Literature Bureau and its successor, the Ghana Bureau of Languages. (Warren, 1976:xxiii)

Bediako, a novel written in Akwapem-Twi (1962) and translated into English by the author, Victor Amarteifio (1965), was republished recently (1983). The English translation is twice as long as the original and includes extremely boring digressions that are absent from the Akan version. The book tells the story of Bediako who repudiates his wife, steals from his employer, is abandoned by his second wife and is eventually condemned for a crime he did not commit. In prison, he is converted to Christianity. When he is about to be hanged, a timely power failure jams the trapdoor of the gallows, which allows a letter proving his innocence to reach the prosecutor. The novel is recounted in a narrative style aimed at young people. The author uses letters, court case transcriptions and different types of set expressions. He also sends his hero on a visit to the Akropong missionary station, as is to be expected from a work written in Awakpem-Twi.

Asante-Twi literature was founded by Joseph Nketia (1921) who published the first spelling rules in 1955. This internationally renowned musicologist and former director of the University of Ghana's Institute for African Studies, who authored a thesis on Akan funeral chants (1955), also writes poetry and novels in his own language (*Anwonsem*, 1952) and collects examples of oral tradition, particularly talking drum poetry (*Ayan*, 1974). The encouragement given to this literature was maintained within the framework of the Bureau of Ghana Languages (Birnie, 1969). The attempt to further enrich the Twi language in its Asante form has also involved translations from the Greek classics. Plato's *Apology of Socrates* (1976) and Sophocles' *Antigone* (1976) were translated by L.H. Ofosu-Appiah.

> Too much time is being spent on the linguistics of Ghanaian languages by learned men who cannot write in those languages! But I feel that the establishment of a special Training College for Ghanaian languages will be worthwhile only if Ghanaian scholars can write in Ghanaian languages.... (Ofosu-Appiah 1976b:5)

Ultimately, the issue is about providing Twi with a metalanguage, not only in philosophy, but also in mathematics and in linguistics, failing which studying and teaching the language cannot be continued beyond secondary school. Developing the language implies standardization constraints that apply not only to spelling and to a practical lexicon, but also to a *conceptual* lexicon on which the scientific community of speakers must reach consensus.

Despite the quality of nineteenth-century Fanti language studies, which created a language with a literary corpus comparable to Sesotho or Yoruba, there has been no flowering of texts in the twentieth century. Unfortunately, the circumstances of this state of affairs are similar to those that, in the case of Igbo, prevailed until the 'sixties: the multiple spellings and uncertainties about the standard language have discouraged the efforts of the many enlightened Ghanaian intellectuals.

The flourishing intellectual life on the shores of the Gold Coast at the turn of the century was unparalleled elsewhere in Africa; it did not lead to a conclusive enhancement of African language production. As in the case of Sol Plaatje (who will be discussed in another chapter), nationalist, cosmopolitan intellectuals demanding black rights in Europe, inspired by the example of Booker T. Washington or W.E.B. Du Bois, tried to touch the hearts of the European or American public by using English. It is still very surprising that a literature in African languages did not develop more extensively on the Gold Coast and later in Ghana; the high literacy rate and written knowledge of African languages, promulgated by the missionary schools, did not succeed in producing a new generation of writers once the technical problems pertaining to translation had been solved. Contrary to the example of the Igbo renewal, no Akan renewal occurred.

Ewe Literature

Like the Fanti coast, the Ewe or Slave Coast (according to the previous geographical terminology), a contact zone for European and African slave traders, was the setting of early attempts to transcribe African languages. The *Doctrina christiana*, a doctrinal treatise by minor Capuchin friars, which appeared in 1658 and was rediscovered in Madrid in 1909, is a study of the Arda language, 'an idiom that is very close to Fon or Dahomean and to the Ewe of Lome, although it differs from these two languages' (Labouret & Rivet, 1929:36). The vocabulary of the coastal dialects was enriched by hundreds of words borrowed from Portuguese. Contrary to Labouret's opinion, Dietrich Westermann's research found general acceptance for the idea of the coastal zone's linguistic unity, whether the language was called 'Ewe' or 'Gbe' (Duthie, 1981).

The disputes between different missionary creeds regarding transcriptions did not prevent the dissemination of a standard language based on interior Ewe, standardized by B. Schlegel from the Bremen missionary group around the middle of the nineteenth century. By the beginning of the twentieth century (1907), Westermann (1875–1956) had provided an Ewe grammar book, soon followed by a dictionary (1910) that is still authoritative. This missionary evangelist, who had been trained at the Basel missionary station, acquired extensive experience in the field of African languages. After teaching in Togo in 1900, he became professor of Ewe at the University of Berlin in 1910 and was the undisputed master of African linguistics during the first half of the twentieth century (Möhlig in Riesz & Ricard, 1991:67–82). Westermann's contribution to Ewe studies was invaluable. According to him, there was only one language, Ewe, between the Volta and the Oueme, between the Asante and the Yoruba, among the Ewe and the Fon. When he established this linguistic geography, the greater part of the territory, with the exception of Dahomey, was a German colony. This changed after the First World War, when Ewe country found itself divided into four distinct entities: Dahomey, a French colony (still Ewephone in the south, if we accept Westermann's analysis), Togo territory (under French mandate), the territory of British Togoland (under British mandate) and the Togoland coast, which belonged to the Gold Coast colony. It soon became apparent that Westermann's eastern Ewe, Fon, could not be reduced to the status of an Ewe dialect and that its development would follow its own logic. During the colonization process, French missionaries' interest in the local language met with hostility from the colonial administration. In 1975, the revolutionary regime accorded it a rather artificial promotion to the rank of national language, which failed because of a dearth of books. Luckily, that was not the case in central Ewe. It became a reference dialect, shared by the two mandate territories, and from 1957 onwards between the two states of Togo and Ghana. The Ewe, an influential Gold Coast minority, could have been a majority in Togo: in 1956, history decided otherwise when voters chose to be annexed to Ghana, thus cutting the language community into two equal parts. The Togolese capital, Lomé, an Ewephone city, was deprived of its hinterland, which remained confined to an inaccessible corner, far from the centres of power and cultural production.

These administrative and political divisions worked to the detriment of Ewe production, by multiplying the obstacles impeding the circulation of works and preventing a single educational policy that would do for Ewe what it had done for Yoruba, in the context of a voluntarist educational policy. This is all the more of a failure since the first Ewe literary text to be largely disseminated was the work of a minister from Ho (a Togolese city under British mandate), Ferdinand Kwasi Fiawoo (1891–1969), *Toko Atolia* (1937). It is noteworthy that this text was the first play in an African language to be translated into a European language: German (in 1937) and English (*The Fifth Landing Stage*, 1943). The title refers to the fate reserved for criminals, to be buried in the sands of the lagoon – the same fate awaits the play's hero, Agbebada, a likeable lout and an inveterate charmer who, like his friend Kumasi, is in love with Fudjikomele. He leaves it to Kumasi to free the beauty from the hands of slave merchants, staying behind in the village where he is accused of seduction and condemned after an unfavourable ordeal. Fortunately, his friend Kumasi, who has returned in the nick of time, will pull him from the sands, which would have suffocated him gradually. He thanks God for his lucky star and goes east, keeping a low profile. It is a well-conducted play; Fiawoo's regard for Aristotelian rules, quoted in the introduction, at least has the advantage of consolidating the action and avoiding digressions. F.K. Fiawoo also wrote *Tuinese*, which was performed in 1945; unfortunately, the play's manuscript was destroyed in a fire in 1953, along with all the author's papers. A new bilingual edition was only published in Germany much later, in 1973. The text reveals the author's effort to cast regular Ewe poetry into pentameter metrics. Moreover, regular sonnets inaugurate the different scenes. Lastly, the author, who dedicates a large part of his introduction to considerations on Ewe poetry, is keen to respect classical unities. Fiawoo's influence can be judged by the number and the quality of other plays authored in Ewe: B. Setsoafia, a translator of Shakespeare, wrote a satiric comedy entitled *Mede Ablotsidela* (1968),

[I married an upstart]. Closer to home, thanks to the Bureau of Ghanaian Languages, who took over from the missionary publishers, several more plays were published. These Ghanaian works had difficulty breaking into the Togolese market where, until recently, the Ewe language was not widely taught at high school level.

Another Gold Coast Ewe, S. Obianim (1921–1982) wrote a novel, *Amegbetoa* (published in 1949) that was soon recognized as a major work and became an Ewe literary classic, judging by its almost inevitable presence in examination questions and by Ewe reference to it in daily life. Fortunately the text can be read in French translation, *Amegbetoa ou les aventures d'Agbezuge* (1990), but no translation exists in any other European language. The hero, who is grappling with a series of misfortunes that would defeat most people, embodies Christian virtues with a constancy that develops into heroism, with no thought for proselytizing. The suffering of this Christ-like figure (*Amegbetoa,* 1990:8) has redemptive value. We are a long way from Fagunwa's adventurous hunter or Nwana's 'picaresque' chief. However, none of the novel's characters are expressly religious and there is no complacent display of good intentions. The author harmoniously unites novelistic action and pedagogical purpose.

In Togo, tentative steps to publish in Ewe are taking place. Gratification of national self-esteem are not enough to constitute a policy; Togo still lacks the means to develop the teaching of Ewe. Moreover, the policy of linguistic egalitarianism in force during the Eyadema era actually favoured the other national language, Kabiye, blocking any form of Ewe progress in the name of a requisite equal treatment of the two languages, while there were many Ewe projects to be developed. In Ghana, the crisis in the 'seventies and painful adjustments of the 'eighties almost destroyed locally produced literature, whether Akan or Ewe – both were held up by scarcity in the supply of paper.

How will Ghana's economic stabilization influence the orientation of its education policies? Will truly regional collaboration between Togo and Ghana be an advantage to Ewe literature, freed at last from border constraints? One may hope as much for an African literature that was formerly able to produce valuable works in spite of its language community's light demographic weight.

5 Books & the Languages of East and Southern Africa

In East Africa, Kiswahili has become the dominant language not only in Tanzania, but also in Kenya, and Uganda may one day follow. Its progress is relegating other African languages to that of minority, local, or even 'tribal' status, considered good enough for primary school, but not for serious, literary writing ... except for Ngugi, whose reputation is already well-established. As far as production in African languages is concerned, vast grey areas remain in Rwanda and Burundi, despite the daily use of the two national languages. Each has produced only a small literature. In the former Central African Federation uniting the two Rhodesias and Nyasaland, which is now divided into the states of Malawi, Zambia and Zimbabwe, the situation is somewhat different. There are dominant languages in each of these countries: Chichewa in Malawi, Chibemba in Zambia and Shona in Zimbabwe. Literary output in each of these languages is fairly recent: the example of Shona in Zimbabwe serves to illustrate the problems created by a production destined for a school-attending readership in small states where no well-defined language policy exists.

And then there is the 'South African miracle' (Apronti, in Birnie, 1969:18) as it was described by the Ghanaian intellectual a few decades ago during a conference on the teaching of African languages in Ghana: that is to say, the South African languages' rich literary production. Its history is complex and one which is in the midst of radical transformation. I will attempt to present the history of each of this country's great languages, all of which boast a written output spanning at least a century. I shall also indicate the principal changes taking place.

Gikuyu Literature

The history of Gikuyu literature is dominated by the decision of Ngugi wa Thiong'o (1938), formerly James Ngugi, to write in his mother tongue. Before the 'seventies, there were very few Gikuyu texts: for the most part, the latter consisted of pamphlets or works belonging to the 'market literature' category (Pugliese, 1994a). The latter consisted mainly of political or religious brochures sold very cheaply by the author editors, the exception being Gaakara wa Wanjau (1920–2001), 'the most creative of those Kenyans then writing in Gikuyu' (Ngugi, 1986:71). At the beginning of the Mau Mau movement, wa Wanjau was responsible for a number of political and religious pamphlets, which earned him several years behind bars. His reputation was made by a short fictional essay entitled *I Want You to Kill Me* (Pugliese, 1994a:15) published in 1951. In December 1966, he launched the *Atiriri* series, containing several short stories, moral essays and practical information (Bennett,

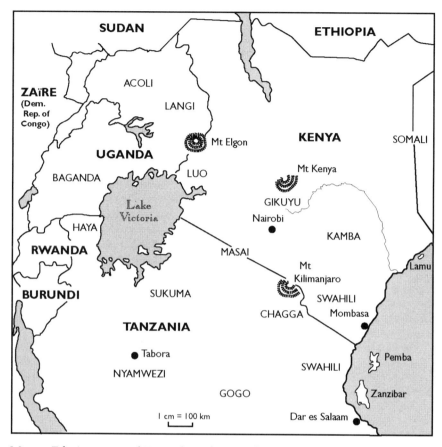

Map 4 *Ethnic groups of East Africa discussed in the text*

1983). He admits that 'ethical teachings' and 'Gikuyu customs' constitute the essential aspects of his writing. At the beginning of the 'eighties, probably with Ngugi's help, Gaakara produced an account of his years in gaol, entitled *Mwandiki wa Mau Mau Ithaamirio-ini* (1983) [A Mau Mau writer in prison]. In 1984, this text received the Noma Award 'with the help of Kenyan exiles' (Pugliese, 1994a:83) and was immediately translated into English. 'Unfortunately,' according to Pugliese, exile 'interest in Gaakara's work attracted the attention of the Kenya police, more that that of an international audience...' (1994a:83). It also brought some of the contradictions within literary production in African languages to the fore. Gaakara was a grassroots intellectual who had grown up in the countryside, close to his readers; he was no academic and did not seem to be radical enough for Kenyan academics:

> In spite of the Gikuyu academics' intention to present Gaakara as a radical 'Mau Mau' fighter, in his speech at the prize awarding ceremony, Gaakara explained that he had been detained by the colonial government because he was a strong supporter of Mzee Jomo Kenyatta, the leader of the Mau Mau. (Pugliese, 1994b:182)

The translation of his diary was transformed and edited to make it sound more radical than the original: Cristiana Pugliese provides several convincing examples of these distortions, such as the elimination of all terms of respect towards Jomo Kenyatta:

> On the whole the editor and the translator of Gaakara's diary transposed the writer's vivid language in clumsy and rhetorical Marxist idiom, thus completely distorting his ideology and spoiling his style. (Pugliese, 1994b:186)

A literature in an African language is also one that is alive; organic intellectuals are not elite cosmopolitan intellectuals. Such conflicts should enable us to distance ourselves from the notion of the homogeneous, consensual language community that is too often the misconception arrived at through a lack of in-depth, critical reading.

Ngugi insists that his novel, *Caitaani Mutharabaini* (1982a, 1982b) [*Devil on the Cross*] was the first novel of that length published in Gikuyu, a language 'which did not have a significant tradition of novel or fiction writing' (Ngugi, 1986:74). While this statement inspires hope, it does not mitigate one's concerns for the future. Indeed, the only increase in the Gikuyu literature corpus seems to come from Ngugi's own productions: *Ngaahika Ndeenda* (1980) [*I Will Marry When I Want* (1982)], and several children's books: *Njamba Nene na Mbaathi-i-Mathagu* [Njamba Nene and the Flying Bus], and *Bathitoora ya Njamba Nene* (1982) [Njambe Nene's Pistol].

There is no bibliography of Gikuyu literature at present. The other Kenyan languages (Kikamba, Kiluhya and Dholuo) are being demoted because of the constant progress of Kiswahili and, of course, of English during the 'eighties. Writers like David Maillu, who writes in Kikamba but is known for his novels in English, and Adenath Bole Osaga, who writes in Dholuo as well as authoring English books for children, also provide short school texts in their mother tongues. Acoli literature, which seemed to flourish during the 'fifties with Okot p'Bitek, seems to have become extinct, as is apparently the case for Luganda. Only the Swahili writers are producing texts for universities and the general public, as they can count on an educated and, moreover, bilingual readership whose cultural expectations direct them to a universal literature.

Shona Literature

In Zimbabwe, which, as Southern Rhodesia was the other jewel in the crown of the British Empire beside Kenya, two principal groups make up the African population: the Shona, who represent almost three quarters of the present ten million inhabitants; and the Ndebele, who are of Zulu origin and make up most of the remaining quarter, along with a minority of 100,000 whites. The Gospel according to St Matthew was translated into Ndebele as early as 1884; the four Gospels were translated into Shona in 1907. There was, however, no noteworthy literary development during the first half of the twentieth century. As Ndebele was considered a Zulu dialect, it was not taught in the Western part of the country (where it was replaced by Zulu) until 1958. This explains the meagre literary corpus existing in Ndebele today. Since independence in 1980, two decades of its promotion have attempted to remedy this state of affairs (Veit-Wild, 1992a).

Map 5   *Spatial distribution of the principal languages of South Africa*

The development of the main language, Shona, has also been rather slow. Few English books were published in Rhodesia. Disputes over Shona dialects further reduced the potential school market. History was well on the way to getting stuck at what had been defined by the vagaries of the missionary enterprise:

> I do not believe in the historical reality of dialect zones, any more than I believe in the historical reality of sub-Shona tribalism. In my view, prior to the development of written Shona dialects there was a situation in which a single, common language was spoken over a very wide area. (Ranger, 1985:14)

The great East African historian's observations are also true for a large part of the continent and can guide us in our analyses. In Zimbabwe, dialect and spelling differences were no obstacle to communication, only to the dissemination of literature. The creation of a Bureau of Literature at the beginning of the 'fifties resulted in rapid literary growth (Kahari, 1990a:2). In an effort to end the dialectalization of spelling, the Shona spelling committee, which was established in 1954, proposed a certain number of modifications and simplifications. In 1964, the committee finally came to the conclusion that dialectal forms could be used, on condition that the spelling be standard. The number of volumes published under the aegis of the Bureau increased from 45,000 in 1966 to 124,000 in 1970 and to more than 200,000 in 1980, according to Kahari's figures (1982). Although the number of authors grew, their quality did not improve, once again according to Kahari, himself author of two studies in English (1972, 1975) on the principal Shona authors, Patrick Chakaipa (1932–)

and Paul Chidyausiku (1927–). Shona studies are being developed at secondary school level and demand greater sophistication regarding critical analysis, as the language of its expression is English and not Shona (there is no dictionary of reference concepts available.) This situation is not peculiar to Shona: one recalls Ofosu-Appiah's laments about researchers writing essays on the Twi language without actually writing in it. Similarly, the most significant work on Fagunwa, published in English in 1974, was that of A. Bamgbose, and a recent study of literary criticism on the principal Yoruba poet, Adebayo Faleti (Olatunji, 1982b), was also published in English. The question about the meta-language of criticism is posed in many languages and has probably only been solved in Kiswahili and in Amharic. However, the development of Shona calls for an act of will, to put together a monolingual dictionary and to procure works of reference. Almost twenty years after Zimbabwe became independent, the matter has still not been resolved.

Zimbabwe's literature was influenced by three very different periods: from 1953 to 1963, the Federation of the Rhodesias and Nyasaland, known as the Central African Federation, advocated a partnership policy between Africans and Europeans that could serve as a 'counter-model' to apartheid. From 1964 to 1980, the white minority's regime of 'unilateral' independence gradually found itself in a cul-de-sac, opposed by a guerrilla movement inside its borders and by a blockade outside. Finally, after 1980 the socialist Zimbabwean regime with its strong Christian influence began to serve as a model for a reformed South Africa where blacks and whites will be able to live on equal terms. During the 'nineties, the continuation of Mugabe's autocratic regime cast doubts on the 'model' quality of this example.

Thus, it is understandable that *Feso* (Mutswairo, 1956), a novel about the victory of a Shona hero from former times over the 'White Sword' despot, is read as an allegorical satire on Rhodesia's political situation. The book, which was prescribed reading for schools at the beginning of the 'sixties, was removed from the list in 1964. Translated into English in 1974, it became symbolic of Zimbabwe's black struggle against white domination and one of the few overtly political novels in Shona literature. Although originally written in the Zezuru dialect, it was claimed as a Shona novel, thus signalling the pre-eminence of the capital's dialect and symbolizing a growing cultural homogeneity. 'It is not without reason that more books are written with a Zezuru flavour' (Kahari, 1972:8).

An analysis of the titles published up to 1972 reveals a large proportion of maxims or well-intentioned advice intended for young readers, mostly pupils: Patrick Chakaipa's *Rubo Ibofu* (1961) [Love is blind], Paul Chidyausiku's *Nyadzi Dzinokunda Rufu* (1962) [Shame is worse than death]; and E. Ribeiro's *Muchadura* (1967) [You will confess your sins] are typical. This moralistic tendency discourages students, who are easily bored by this type of reading matter (Kahari, 1972:19). In fact, most of the authors are teachers, and two of the best-read authors, Ribeiro and Chakaipa, are priests; the latter was Archbishop of Harare during the 'eighties. All of these writers have been influenced by the Bible, by Bunyan and fortunately, at times, by Shakespeare. An in-depth study of the Shona novel's development up to 1984 listed 95 novels, including, of course, an impressive number of texts published in the early 'eighties (Kahari, 1990a). It is quite clear, as observed by Emmanuel

Chiwome, that 'the formative years of the Shona novel were crucial to its development' (1996:156)

The constraints peculiar to the period 1964–1980 in Southern Rhodesia – an authoritarian, racist regime where censorship was ever-vigilant – may explain the lack of variety as regards theme. The emergence of new writers from different horizons, such as Charles Mungoshi (1947–) in the 'seventies, or Chenjerai Hove (1950–) in the 'eighties, is a noteworthy development. Mungoshi wrote *Makunun'unu* (1970) [Heart-breaking thoughts] and *Ndiko Kupindana Kwamazuva* (1975) [With the passing of time], in Shona, while *Waiting for the Rain* (1981) was written in English. He also wrote a Shona play, *Inongova Njakenjake* (1980) [Every man for himself], which celebrated its fourteenth edition in 1989. Shona literature is dominated by student problems and boy/girl relationships in an urban environment. Last but not least, Mungoshi translated Ngugi's novel, *Grain of Wheat* (1967), into Shona as *Tsanga Yembeu* (1987). This is a remarkable achievement, especially taking into account the novel's length. Mungoshi's work is also remarkable for his efforts to break away from older modes of narrative representation and is truly 'avant-garde' in experimenting with the existentialist idiom and the experience of social alienation. He is an exception: 'Shona fiction in Rhodesia was part of the literature of colonial politicization. After the attainment of Independence, the same fiction became the foundation of nationalist de-politicization' (Chiwome, 1996:154). This antithesis lies behind Marechera's angry derision:

> In Zimbabwe we have two indigenous languages, ChiShona and Sindebele. Who wants us to keep writing these ShitShona and ShitNdebele languages, this missionary chickenshit? Who else but the imperialists? (Caute 1986 in Veit-Wild, 1992b:307)

These languages and their literatures are part of Zimbabwe's heritage. The country's fictional and critical writing tradition (the latter in English, not surprisingly!) is an asset to further development and will enable writers to break away from the situation denounced by Dambudzo Marechera, so that they may aspire to what he defines as poetry:

> An attempt by the individual to become invisible, but with a kind of invisibility which illuminates things from within as well as from without. That sort of poetry you can't really find in Africa and if you do it is always denounced as being 'bourgeois' (Marechera, 1992:209–10).

The difficulties that Shona written poetry faces in establishing itself between the dualistic thrust 'of European cultural chauvinism and African nationalism' (Chiwome, 1996:139) testify to the same struggle for artistic liberation.

Today, writing in two different languages (as in the case of the Kenyan, Ngugi) has become one of the original aspects of Zimbabwean literature and of Shona writers: Chenjerai Hove, the author of an admirable English narrative, *Bones* (1988) and winner of the 1989 Noma Award, is also a Shona novelist and poet who wrote *Masimba Avanhu* (1986) [Power to the people]. S. Mutswairo, a pioneer of Shona literature, also wrote an historical novel in English (*Mapondera*, 1983). Changes in South Africa will have certain consequences for Zimbabwe: will Zulu once again be taught in that country? What does the future hold for this original type of literature? Future South African decisions on language policy may provide some answers to these questions. English will remain an international language, but how will the African languages be taught? In Zimbabwe, the end of the political conflict in the region may allow the teaching of Shona to develop without hidden agendas.

Xhosa Literature

In the eastern Cape Province, the Scottish missions were active amongst the Nguni groups or Kaffirs [sic] as they were called at the time. Later, they were followed by the Paris Evangelical Missions, who were invited to Lesotho by King Moshoeshoe. The Cape Nguni (the Xhosa) in the south and the Basotho in the north, sheltered by the Drakensberg, were neighbours of the Zulu under Shaka. Between 1818 and 1838, the region was ravaged by this martial nation composed of distinct clans, whose formal independence ended only in 1887 with the incorporation of Zululand into the province of Natal. It comes as no surprise that missionary activity could not be developed in Zululand before the end of the wars set in motion by Shaka. This happened in 1840, on the death of Shaka's successor. Delayed contact with Europeans increased divisions between the Cape Nguni (the Xhosa) and the Natal Nguni (the Zulus), resulting in the codification of two different languages where, ideally, their common origin should have resulted in a unified conception. Although Xhosa and Zulu are two closely related languages, they have now been equipped with different spellings and lexicological instruments.

In many respects, Xhosa literature occupies the prime position. Between 1818 and 1820, Ntsikana, a 'Kaffir' bard who had converted to Christianity, composed a hymn that was immediately translated into English and that is still sung today. It is one of the first texts composed and signed by an African poet:

> The fact that his Hymn of Praise is the first literary composition ever to be assigned to individual formulation – thus constituting a bridge between the traditional and the post-traditional period – is of great significance. But even more important than this is the fact that, through his influence, a few young disciples were introduced to the arts of reading and writing, and that, inspired by his exemplary life and teaching, these men became the harbingers of the dawn of literacy amongst the indigenous peoples of Southern Africa. (Jordan, 1973:50–51)

The context was a favourable one: the Glasgow Missionary Society was established at Lovedale; a grammar book was published in 1825; from 1823 onwards, the Lovedale Mission's printing press published the first primers or 'Xhosa reading sheets', the forerunners of the *Lovedale Kaffir Readers* that were still in existence a century later (C.M. Doke, 1936).

The study of the 'Kaffir' language (Xhosa) made rapid progress on such solid foundations: 1846 saw the publication of an English–Xhosa dictionary, while the Bible was translated in 1857. At the same time, they were recruiting native priests. Tiyo Soga (1829–1871), the son of one of Ntsikana's disciples, was ordained in Great Britain, worked on the translation of the Bible, and took an active part in the development of a native press to which he contributed regularly. For instance, we read the following in the first issue of *Isepa le-Ndaba Zasekaya*, published in Xhosa in 1862 (in a translation by James Ranisi Jolobe):

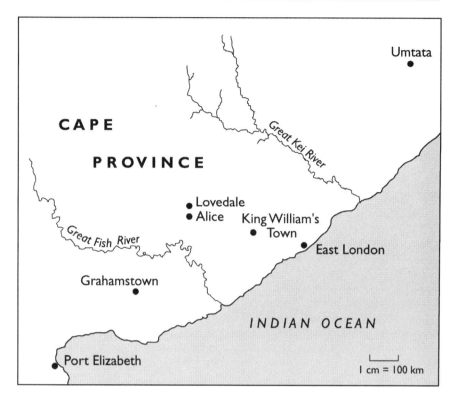

Map 6 *Main Xhosa-speaking areas in the Eastern Cape*

> We Xhosas are a race which enjoys conversation.... So I anticipate great happiness
> from the publication of this newspaper. We shall be having a visitor who will
> converse with us very agreeably. Where are our fellow tribesman? Sound the horn
> and invite our people to swarm around him. Say to them, 'Here you are! You lovers
> of conversation.' One advantage we shall reap with the coming of this journal is
> that we will be confident that the people now will get the truth about the affairs of
> the nation. As people who are always hungry for news often we find ourselves
> dupes of deceivers under the guise of relating genuine facts. (Soga, in Williams,
> 1983:151–2)

He also produced a translation (which was considered excellent) of the
Pilgrim's Progress (1867).

> The seed which Ntsikana planted had flourished through the efforts of men like Tiyo
> Soga, son of one of Ntsikana's converts, and Christianity was well and truly planted
> among the Xhosa as an African religion brought not by missionaries but by
> Ntsikana.... (Peires, 1981:74)

The influence of Soga's translation and the desire to create Christian poetry
are also evident in W. Gqoba's two great didactic poems: 'Discussion between a

Pagan and a Christian', and the 'Great Discussion on Education'. Moreover, as Albert Gérard (1971:37) observes, Gqoba was not only interested in matters pertaining to the Xhosa, but also wrote a *History of the Peoples of the North-East* illustrating the emergence of an African consciousness. It is not within our scope to relate the history of South Africa's black movement. Suffice it to say that at the beginning of the twentieth century, Xhosa intellectual activity around Lovedale and in King William's Town (where the first African weekly was published) was being deployed for the recognition of native rights. In 1916, this struggle would lead to the foundation of the first native college – the first university – for Africans, in Fort Hare, right next to Alice and Lovedale. The journalist and educator, J.T. Jabavu (1859–1921) whose son, Davidson Tengo Jabavu (1885–1959) would be the institution's first professor of Bantu languages, and J.T. Bokwe (1855–1922), Ntsikana's biographer (1904), were the pioneers of this struggle.

Oral tradition provides no appropriate models for expressing the radical change introduced by Christianity and colonization. Hymnal poetry admittedly derives from the traditional panegyric, the *isibongo*, but does not lend itself to the expression of personal questions. Samuel Mqhayi (1871–1945) arrived as a pupil in Lovedale, where he started his teaching career in 1891. He later became a journalist in East London, where Jabavu recognized his talents as a poet. He was rewarded by being employed in the Xhosa Bible revision committee and by participating in the codification of the Xhosa language on the basis of norms already in force in the Cape Province. Mqhayi is considered the century's greatest Xhosa author, as much for his biographical activity (he wrote Bokwe's biography in 1923) as for his talents as a poet and a novelist. He maintained the *imbongi* tradition, as he was capable of improvising on the praises of chiefs and notables. According to S. K. Matthews:

> In his ordinary conversation he was never careless in the use of his language. In his extempore praises of Chiefs and other notabilities he always proved himself a master of the telling and memorable phrase. In his writing he exploited to the full the ample potentialities of the Xhosa language for idiomatic expression and for giving vent to the wide range of human emotions (Kunene & Kirsch, 1967:28)

In 1943, a collection of his Xhosa poems appeared as part of the Bantu Treasure series. Mqhayi is known for his utopian novel entitled *UDon Jadu* (1929), which throws an interesting light on the future of South African society imagined by one of the most enlightened spirits of his time. The author tells the story of a fictional country, Mnandi, which becomes part of the Union of South Africa. The Union disintegrates and becomes a trust territory of Great Britain, which allows it to develop in a harmonious way under the presidency of Don Jadu, whose name is also the title of the book.

> There is neither racialism nor isolationism in Mnandi. Immigration is encouraged and experts of all races and shades of colour come from the four corners of the earth to make a permanent home there. There is full social, economic and political equality. Women are free to go into Parliament, but the sensible women of Mnandi decline this offer on the grounds that there is enough work for them to do at their homes. Education is compulsory, Xhosa is the first language but English is such an important second language that no one who is not strictly bilingual may hold an

office of State.... *UDon Jadu* makes very interesting and thought-provoking reading. It is true that in constructing a 'bridge' between our present South Africa and his utopia, the author idealizes away a few hard facts but its soul is right.... (A.C. Jordan, 1973:110–11)

Mqhayi is considered to be the first *imbongi* (traditional, improvising, oral poet) who successfully introduced the techniques of oral composition into written literature. He was the first to exploit the possibilities of the printing press without betraying the spirit of oral poetry. For Jeff Opland, an expert in the field, 'Mqhayi was committed to writing original poetry in style and purpose hardly distinguishable from the oral poetry of the traditional imbongi' (Opland, 1983:94). In contrast to Mqhayi's work, the texts of J.J.R. Jolobe (1902–76) can be situated within a purely literary framework. Jolobe, who was a 1926 Fort Hare graduate and the author of novelettes published in Lovedale, is a sophisticated poet who no longer finds himself within the tradition of panegyric poetry, a chain of laudatory epithets and bold and concrete images, which, strung together, constitute the *isibongo*. He is a narrative as well as a lyrical poet: *Umyezo* (1936) [The orchard], the second volume in the Bantu Treasure series, contains some freely and diversely inspired pieces on the theme of the shepherd, the death of a child and the river. In 1946, the author published his own translation of four of his poems, *Poems of an African*, including 'Thuthula', a narrative poem situated in an historical past. He pursued his work as a poet and an essayist until the 'sixties and greatly influenced younger generations by showing that poetry could be a personal and even intimate mode of expression, and that there was as much room for thematic as for stylistic innovation in Xhosa poetry.

In fact, Xhosa literature cannot be reduced to the evocation of eastern Cape Province pastures and the celebration of a traditional society, even a Christianized one. The Xhosa are also leaving the land; their horizon will become the urban world of the mining towns. G. Sinxo (1902–62), Mqhayi's son-in-law, author of the constantly re-edited *UNomsa* (1922), and a Johannesburg journalist and educator, published a collection of short stories that describe urban life without complacency, *Isakhono Somfazi Namanie Amabalana* (1956) [A woman's address and other stories]. In 1936, while a senior lecturer in English at the United Bantu School, A.C. Jordan wrote a novel entitled *Ingqumbo Yeminyanya* (1940) [*The Wrath of the Ancestors*] that critically describes tribalism and is considered by many to be the greatest Xhosa novel. The author's own translation appeared posthumously in Lovedale in 1980. He tells of the tensions between the Mpondomise and the Mfengu (two Xhosa clans), between traditional and Western customs, between those who went to school and the others. He retraces the ascension of the young Zwelinsima, a Fort Hare University graduate and son of a chief, who has progressive ideas and becomes the chief of the Mpondomise; he tells us of the disastrous consequences when Zwelinsima's wife kills the sacred serpent of the Mpondomise, in whom the spirit of the ancestors was supposed to reside.

After the passing of the apartheid laws and the Bantu Education Act of 1953, the era of the pioneers was followed by that of the academics rebelling against the barriers being erected around their ethnic group and prompting them to emigrate: A.C. Jordan, Daniel Kunene and several Fort Hare graduates left the country, having found no job opportunities in the White universities where they were no longer welcome. Xhosa literary production continued, but in a different form. What is particularly original is the pursuit of *isibongo* production, in the vein of Mqhayi's pioneering successes. Oral poets with the gift of *bonga*, the talent of improvised composition, practise their art through direct contact with the cultural and social life of the Xhosa world, and sometimes publish their works in book form. Jeff Opland devoted a fascinating book to this phenomenon, and particularly to the study of four poets: Mqhayi, (who serves as a model), Sipho Mangindi Burns-Ncamashe, Melikaya Mbutuma and David Livingstone Phakamile Yali-Manisi. As Ncamashe so aptly puts it:

> When I do bonga – and not writing – the words come spontaneously. It makes some difference when I sit down to write, because then I read over it and have time to think and revise. (Opland, 1983:98)

Two volumes of his poems have been published: *Masibaliselane* (1961) and *Izibongo ZakwaSesile* (1979). Mbutuma published a text entitled *Isife Somzi* (1977); in 1952, Yali-Manisi published his first collection of poems, *Izibongo zeenkosi zamaXhosa*, before producing several other texts towards the end of the 'seventies (Yali-Manisi, 1977). He is first and foremost an oral improviser, who does not disdain to exploit the notoriety and legitimacy conferred on an author by the production of a book. The term 'oral poet' certainly does not have the meaning of a travelling African poet and musician (the French *griot*) or a hired praise singer. Jeff Opland's account of a poem that Manisi improvised during a 1974 ceremony at the University of Fort Hare, in which he does not hesitate to address the problems of the time, reads as follows:

> Transkei is small, confined to the eastern portion of the Cape Province ... the heroes of the nation lie buried below Table Mountain on Robben Island where they died as prisoners of the whites; all will be well again, the time to reclaim the hidden stick of pride will have arrived, when all the country down to Cape Town is in black hands and when reparation is made for the national heroes who died in exile and were not accorded traditional burial on ancestral land. This settlement will not come through armed struggle but through inspired leadership that will bring the Xhosa to the destiny prophesied by Ntsikana.... (Opland, 1983:114)

The poem is not a call for violence. On the contrary, it is in line with the tradition started by the first Xhosa poet and it does so without making any concessions, clearly showing the strength of an identity supported by popular tradition, capable of fuelling literary practice to the present day. The *isibongo* is a living genre: in 1820 it celebrated Christ; in 1990, it celebrates Nelson Mandela's return to Umtata, the town of his birth in the Transkei (Kashula, 1991:17).

Sotho Literature

The Xhosa live on the coastal plains, sheltered by mountains; the Basotho and the Tswana herds graze on the high plateaux of that southern savannah, the veldt.

The main Basotho or Bechuana branch can be subdivided into two principal branches. In Western Bechuanaland and in the Western Transvaal and the Orange colony, we find the Bechuanas as such ... In the eastern part of the Western Transvaal and in Lesotho or Basotholand we find the Basotho branch. These are divided in turn into Northern and Southern Basotho, or Basotho as such, for which our mission is responsible. (Livre d'Or, 1912:673)

Around 1833, Moshoeshoe, the chief of the Bamokotedi Bakwena clan, invited the missionaries from the Paris Evangelical Mission Society to establish a station on his land (Perrot, 1963). Moshoeshoe reigned for almost forty years and the station prospered under his protection. E. Casalis and T. Arbousset were amongst the first young missionaries to share his destiny. In Moshoeshoe's company, Arbousset would travel across the mountain kingdom and provide us with a very detailed description in his *Relation d'un voyage d'exploration au nord-est de la colonie du Cap de Bonne-Espérance* (1842), followed by the *Missionary Excursion*, which was only published in English in 1991 and in French in 2000. The first printing press arrived in Lesotho in 1841; in 1845, the young missionaries produced a translation of the New Testament, while 1872 saw the publication of *The Pilgrim's Progress*.

E. Casalis' contribution was the *Études sur la langue sechuana, précédées d'une introduction sur l'origine et les progrès de la mission chez les Bassoutos* (1841). The third part of this interesting text is dedicated to Basotho poetry and is probably one of the first critical essays on African literature in any language. General reflections on poems that 'offer no methodical arrangement of feet and bars', not to mention rhyme, but 'can be distinguished from ordinary discourse by the use of elevated sentiments, metaphors and ellipsis and by a turn of phrase that can be lively or energetic, melancholy or naïve, characteristic of the language used to express passion' (Casalis, 1841:42), are followed by a selection of panegyrics in translation, but not in transcription, which is rather a pity.

> Young warrior, as light-footed as the giraffe, Ratakane's companion, it is up to you to find the paths followed by the herds; I have turned them away from the paths they were used to; today they are leaping along the paths leading to my hut. The white heifer is as beautiful and as fertile as Orion; she is as beautiful and as fertile as Orion....
>
> The name of the humble cow, which our best French writers were not able to ennoble, occupies a place in Setswana poetry that is as elevated as the words sceptre, crown in Boileau and Racine's poetry. (Casalis, 1841:54–6)

Each text is followed by analytical commentary of the poem's highlights. In the panegyric of Goloane, one of Moshoeshoe's bravest officers, surprising images abound: 'the coat made of spider webs' (the warriors who died in battle wore woollen coats); the 'shield shines like a red-hot coal' (it is covered with shiny copper plates reflecting the sun's rays).

These few samples of panegyric poetry are followed by hunting songs, or poetic pieces inspired by animals: the antelope, 'longing for cool streams'; the gnu 'with its blazing tail', the 'Baroas' bullock'; the wild boar, 'master of the green gardens' (Casalis, 1841:77–9). The charm of these translations, exuding the spontaneity of fresh discoveries, has remained intact even 150 years after publication. Casalis gave us what can be considered as the foundation of performance anthropology from his own experiences of Sotho praise singers:

The hero of the piece is nearly always the author. Upon returning from combat, he purifies himself in a nearby river, then he goes to put down, religiously in the depths of his dwelling, his lance and his shield. His friends surround him and demand of him the recitation of his exploits. He recounts them with emphasis, the heat of sentiment leading him on; his expression becomes poetic. The memory of the young takes hold of the most striking parts: they are repeated to the delighted author, who ponders over them, and connects them in his mind during leisure hours; at the end of two or three months, these children know these praises perfectly, which are thereafter declaimed at the solemn celebrations of the tribe. (Coplan, 1994: 48)

Few texts translated that early from an African language have retained this quality. Casalis successfully identified the genre that dominates this type of literature: the panegyric, the chief's praises, generally composed by the person concerned (which today is becoming increasingly rare). As a chief with a sense of humour nostalgically put it, like the cows, they are now praised by others. (Damane & Sanders, 1974:18)

This type of poetry dominated nineteenth-century Basotho oral production at a time when the kingdom was victorious in defending its independence. Panegyric poetry (which has been collected and published by scholars and folklore specialists since the end of the nineteenth century) became the foundation of Sotho poetry, constituting its first written accounts. The classical study devoted to these texts, *Heroic Poetry of the Basotho* (Kunene, 1971), draws on the 1921 collection made by Z.D. Mangoaela. *Lithoko, Sotho Praise Poems* (Damane & Sanders, 1974) is also based on the Mangoaela collection, as well as on the works of G. Lerotholi, who self-published *Lithoko tsa Morena emoholo Seeiso Griffith* [Panegyrics of Headman Seeiso Griffith], (1940, edition revised in 1962), and *Lithoko tsa Motlotlehi Moshoeshoe II* (1964) [Praises of His Majesty Moshoeshoe II]. Finally, a number of *lithoko* have never been put down on paper, but were transmitted orally for many years and collected by the authors (Damane & Sanders, 1974:viii). The different spelling used in Lesotho (*lithoko*) and in South Africa (*dithoko*) must be mentioned in passing, giving some idea of the differentiating pandemic that affects the spelling of Southern African languages!

Collectors like Mangoaela, A. Sekese (see below) or Lerotholi made it possible to introduce others to ancient poetry. They put together a classical tradition that can serve as a basis for the definition of a new type of poetry – using a certain number of techniques from oral poetry, the epic themes of which will be replaced by the expression of personal sentiments, by 'descriptions' and 'emotions' and a lyrical sensibility (as opposed to the essentially laudatory tone of the *lithoko*). In this vein, it is worth remembering the name of K.E. Ntsane and his two works: '*Musa-pelo* (1946) [Heart's remedy] and *Mmusa-pelo, Book 2* (1961). There were also attempts at experimenting with rhyme, with limited success, as in the case of other Bantu languages.

While initial rhyme is a natural property of the languages, *inter alia* on account of an extensive concordial system underlying their sentence formation, end-rhyme is made difficult by various factors. Thus most words end on vowel, with the final syllable often only a whisper. The penultimate syllable has a longer duration than those in its immediate vicinity, while the phrase as such carries various prosodic features, among which is syllabic tone. If not handled with care, these factors may disturb correspondence of sound and coherence of rhythm, causing discord, even bathos. (Swanepoel, 1988:446)

The same author also alerts us to the birth of a literary, panegyric genre, the *thoholetso* (Swanepoel, 1988:449). The system of recruiting migrant workers for the Kimberley and Rand mines favoured the development of a new genre: miner chants, or *difela*. They tell of the journey, of the long months of work and solitude, the sexual misery, while evoking family and the native land with sadness and nostalgia. The literary poems are organized according to stanzas, although the poems born of oral recitals are presented without typographic breaks. Poems collected in book form may contain more than a thousand verses. The *difela*, although springing from the same genius as the *dithoko*, are less dramatic and are in fact closer to songs. Some of them are recited with concertina accompaniment (Swanepoel, 1988:447).

Chris Swanepoel has also explored narrative Sesotho poetry (Swanepoel, 1997). He studies J. Moiloa's *Thesela Ngwana Mmatmokgatjhane* [Smasher, child of Mmamokgatsjhane, meaning Moshoeshoe], which he considers to be an 'innovative' literary epic couched in praise poem style, or as a true interface between oral and written creativity. His textual analysis testifies to an in-depth use of the available philological resources: *dithoko*, praise poetry, *dithokokiso* (modern – written – poetry) but also references to *mokorotlo* (war songs) and *kodiamalla* (dirges). This dialogic composition (in the sense of weaving several threads of Sotho poetry) is truly 'novel': the question shifts to its polyphonic character. The epic celebrates whereas the novel argues and contrasts from different levels. The renewal of poetry about Moshoeshoe can also be read against the background of the dismantling of apartheid and could possibly be called a novel in the modernist sense.

Living Sotho poetry has kept its oral and popular roots. The chief's praises disappear when the chiefs are no longer worthy of praise and when men have no other option than to go down the mines. The point of crossing from oral to written poetry can thus be clearly detected through the example of poets such as Lerotholi, who probably prefigures the Xhosa poets studied by Opland. The same approach cannot be followed in the case of narrative fiction. E. Jacottet has studied the narrative traditions of the Basotho (1909); A. Sekese published numerous extracts from Basotho historical traditions in the columns of *Leselinyana* (the missionary journal, and the oldest of its kind in Southern Africa).

Thomas Mofolo

However, the real criterion for the success of the missionary educational endeavour could only be the birth of an 'indigenous' literature: in this respect, the emergence of the novel is truly a landmark.

Thomas Mofolo was in fact the first Sotho novelist, but also the first African novelist and the author of the work entitled *Chaka* (1925), which today belongs to world literature. This book dominates Sotho literature and deserves special attention. Many shadowy patches remain, despite the study that Kunene (1989) dedicates to it; they are given here, for in a way they enhance the interest of the subject. Born in 1877, raised in the southern part of the country in the valley of Quomongqomong, 'a valley which had no equal in beauty in the entire

Basotholand' (Mangoaela, in Mofolo, 1940:7), Mofolo had the good chance to have Everett Segoete as his teacher, a man who became one of the most respected and influential leaders of the indigenous church. Mofolo would later describe the valley of his childhood and his teacher in his novel *Pitseng* (1910). He finished his studies in 1899, then found a job as a teacher and later as a secretary at the Mission's print shop, where for a while he worked as a journalist and a proof corrector for *Leselinyana*. An assiduous reader, if we are to believe Mangoaela, he devoured religious works, but also Marie Corelli and Rider Haggard: what is more, he travelled in the rest of Southern Africa, particularly 'amongst the Kaffirs of the province of Natal, whose life and history he learnt to know' (Mangoaela, 1940:9). In 1906, Mofolo, a man with a curious and adventurous spirit, published first in a serialized form then in 1907 as the first novel: *Moeti oa Bochabela: [Traveller to the East]*.

> It is the story of a Mosotho from the days before the missions who, disgusted by the turpitudes of paganism and intrigued by the mysteries of nature, leaves his village and makes his way towards the east in order to find an answer to the questions torturing his soul. Through the greatest privations and through numberless dangers, he reaches the sea, is captured by white smugglers, is taken by them to their country, learns about the Revelation and dies of happiness on the day when, for the first time, he is permitted to approach the Lord's table. (*Livre d'Or*, 1912:508)

Fekisi, the hero, lives in the 'old times, when this land of Africa was still clothed in great darkness, dreadful darkness, in which all the works of darkness were done. It is the days when there was no strong chieftainship, the tribes still ate each other' (Mofolo, 1934:8). He searches for God and, without clearly rejecting the customs of his Sotho ancestors (he eloquently praises his cows!) finds the light of the rising sun on Mount Sion (1934:123). The 'Son of Man' invites him to follow him and Fekisi enters the Holy City where he reigns with God because he has no fear and left his country for the love of God (1934:124). The construction of the narrative and of the dialogues was well done and the proofreader was congratulated on his achievement: 'This story is told with such charm, such colour, such vividness! Its style is pure, its language excellent; it is a masterpiece in our opinion!' (*Livre d'Or*, 1912:508).

A second novel did not see the light of day for reasons that have remained obscure. 1910 saw the publication of a new work, *Pitseng* (its unpublished translation from French reads 'Pitseng, the happy valley'), which goes beyond the bounds of edifying literature and is based on the author's own experiences during his travels through Southern Africa. In the eyes of the missionaries, this third novel contained 'some very strange details on the life, loves and fancies of young, educated Basotho' (*Livre d'Or*, 1912:509). After his first novel, Mofolo consulted the great book of the world: upon leaving the mountains of Lesotho, the author went down to the coast where, like his hero Pakue, he was able to see the new white settlements and the ruins of Shaka's capital in Natal.

> Pakue takes the boat and goes to Port Elizabeth and East London. Most of the goods coming from Europe enter Africa through these two ports. His travel teaches him a lot: in his village the only white man has a shop; here he sees white people working in all areas of life.... In Natal he sees how sugar cane is grown and he goes to the ruins of King Chaka's camp, built with great care. This camp, for those who see it for the first

time, and even though it is only in ruin, makes him want to run away, because one feels it has been built with frightening cruelty. (Mofolo, 1910: 54–6)

The young man also makes observations of a linguistic kind to distinguish the situation in Lesotho from that existing in South Africa:

> The number of white people is fairly big, and thus one can learn English well; it is the language spoken in school. Since children come from the neighbouring tribes it is only in English that they can understand each other.... (Mofolo, 1910: 50)

The success of these two books was incredible: the missionaries could be rightly proud of their pupil. However, Mofolo left the mission in 1910 and his next novel, *Chaka*, only appeared in 1925. The book is mentioned as a manuscript in the 1912 *Livre d'Or* and thirteen more years passed before its publication, sparking a debate amongst the missionaries. Mofolo's defenders and the adversaries of censorship won the case and the book saw the light of day, as described by Albert Gérard (1971). In retrospect, one can wholly understand the Christian educators' point of view: although Mofolo's book certainly criticizes Shaka's cruel megalomania, his picture of the Zulu world is nonetheless one of admiration, already apparent in the description of the visit to Shaka's camp in his previous book. However, Thomas Mofolo himself is not a Zulu: he writes about Shaka as a Mosotho – as a member of a people who knew how to protect themselves against Shaka's incursions, but who might have been their victim had Moshoeshoe not had the prudence to swear allegiance, despite being well protected by the Drakensberg cliffs. Mofolo, a fervent Christian, writes the story of a cruel, powerful and unscrupulous pagan, led by a witchdoctor who urges him to commit a sacrificial murder. Nonetheless, Mofolo cannot prevent his 'admiring contemplation' (Albert Gérard) from coming to the fore for this inventor of a new nation. Consisting of a collection of diverse clans, the Zulus were united around regiments of age classes, and led by a chief who was initially devoid of all customary authority. Mofolo admires the general, the inventor of a new style of fighting that proved invincible during the few decades in which the short Zulu *assegai* or stabbing spear overpowered the adversaries' javelins. The author also admires the builder and the creativity of the man whose name still resounds in the poetry of the Zulu bards. Besides the numerous Zulu borrowings in his text, Mofolo offers the reader an *isibongo* of Shaka in the original language. This text was supposedly communicated to him by Chakijana, Msenteli's son:

> Ferocious one of the armies of Mbelebele
> Who unleashed his fury within the large villages
> So that till dawn the villages were tumbling over each other
> Elephant which, on turning its head devoured the men.
> (Mofolo, translated by Kunene, 1981:119–20)

In the original text (*Ushaka – NguChakijana ka Msenteli*) the praise poem is given in Zulu without a Sesotho translation. This is an interesting collage and quite a powerful intrusion of a Zulu text into a Sotho novel, an example of this new 'greater space for different and dissonant voices, new tongues' that Liz Gunner (2000:1) is calling for and I am also eagerly seeking! The text also testifies to an extraordinary hermeneutic ambiguity. For instance, the French translator, Victor Ellenberger, who contributed so much towards the success of the text, put forward an interpretation that alludes to Shaka as a Hitler. The translation was published in 1940 and was advertised thus by its publisher, Gallimard, in Nazi-occupied France:

> A cruel adventurer, cleverly and with the help of sorcerers, manages to conquer all powers. Identifying his own ambition and his nation's destiny he institutes compulsory military service, reorganizes his country with an iron discipline, focuses all its activity towards war-mongering and, thanks to his own bold tactics, subjugates all his neighbours..... To prevent all misinterpretation, let us specify that all these events took place more than a century ago, among the Pagans of Southern Africa. (Ellenberger, 1940, cited in Ricard, 1997:56)

With such a promotional campaign, the book was eventually prohibited by the Nazis (P. Ellenberger, Victor's son, personal communication to the author), but a valid point had been made. The exaltation of violence can always lead to such interpretations. It is precisely to explore this complex web of contradictions that Senghor, who had fought the Nazis, produced his own tragic *Shaka* in 1956, a decade after the end of the war.

In Mofolo's novel, Chaka is moved by the passion of his own greatness, which is a universal dramatic mechanism. His evil genius, the witchdoctor Issanoussi, suggests that it is his duty to kill and to massacre without mercy (Mofolo, 1981:80). The witchdoctor has understood that power is not Chaka's only ambition, but fame as well, and that if a human sacrifice is needed to reach his goal, Chaka will not hesitate. There is a clear indication that Chaka's power is evil:

> I, Chaka, do not ponder long over a problem. I have decided in favour of the kingship you have just described; I only regret that I do not have any children. I do not know whether the blood of my mother or of my brothers would be suitable; if it is suitable, I shall let you have it so that you may mix those medicines of yours.... Today, Chaka, we are teaching you witchcraft. (Mofolo, translated by Kunene, 1981:101)

Chaka's talents as a war chief, as the creator of a nation, which elicit Mofolo's admiration, are in opposition to his cruelty: he never turns aside from the massacre of all the peoples who are vanquished by him. Thus, after his victory over Zwide, women, children and the aged perish; only the young men are spared, if they choose to join his army (Mofolo, 1981:159).

These horrors, which culminate with the ritual murder of his pregnant wife, come back to haunt him at the end of his life and make him wish for death, which he accepts as deliverance when his half-brothers come to get rid of him. Unlike Fekisi or even Pakue, the heroes of his previous books, Chaka's character is a complex one which, despite his cruelty, cannot be reduced to simple caricature. He is cruel and impulsive, but also calculating and organized. He loves his wife, but does not hesitate to sacrifice her to his ambition. Mofolo makes us share his own contradictory feelings when it comes to his hero's exploits. There is no trace of Christianity in this text, which shows the birth of a hero in the midst of those 'dark ages' from which Fekisi extracted himself. This new hero is not illuminated by a light from the Orient; on the contrary, he is guided by an evil genius; the size and number of his crimes generate a feeling of horror mixed with a fascination that Mofolo must have had difficulty in sharing with his missionary mentors.

Whereas a sizeable amount of Sotho literature, like Xhosa literature, consists of a rather naive apology for rural Christianity and a denunciation of the evils of urban civilization, Mofolo escapes from the control of the institution that produced him by applying himself to a great historical subject. In a sense, the Mission has been betrayed; dare one say, along with Sartre, speaking of Genet, that there is no literature without treason? Sotho literature offers us an extraordinary exception, even more extraordinary when one thinks that Thomas Mofolo wrote nothing else after this triumph: the novel was translated into English in 1931 and Mofolo died in 1947, ruined by the loss of the farm he had acquired in the Union of South Africa, a transaction that was in violation of the Native Land Act of 1913, which reserved most of the good land for whites.

The book's destiny was an equally strange one; the different translations did not focus much attention on the author, who remained in the shadows. The book has been read as the epic of a Zulu bard, while it is the text of a Sotho writer. In a sense, in our conception of the literatures of Africa, it remains a shocking work that escapes from any pre-ordained genres: because it is difficult to categorize, it has ended up in the rag-bag category of oral literature (Chevrier, 1986:212). The motives here are not so hard to grasp: either to ennoble Shaka by making him escape the narrow confines of the literature written in African languages, or else to confer on him the nobility of the oral Africa, far removed from the reveries of a missionary station proofreader. The excision of Mangoaela's 1940 preface from the new 1981 French edition is tantamount to erasing the author's identity. What makes these mistakes and errors even less excusable is the fact that an important collection of studies on Sotho literature exists in French in the form of translations by Victor Ellenberger (the titles in translation are his own), which in themselves constitute an anthology of Sotho literature: E. Segoete, *Monono ke moholi ke muoane* (1912) [Riches are but mist, a simple vapour]; E.Segoete, *Raphekeng* (1915) [Raphekeng, or the life of the ancient Basothos]; J.J. Machobane, *Mahaheng a matso* (1946) [Inside the dark caves]; *Senate, shoeshoe a Moshoeshoe* (1954) [The life of Princess Senate, Flower of Moshoeshoe]; *Mphatlalatsane* (1961) [History of a bull]; and M.P. Motlamele, *Ngaka ea Mosotho* (1937) [The Sotho healer]. *Chaka* also had the rare distinction of being produced in a new English translation, published in 1981. It was decided to do away with the somewhat heavy, biblical style of the 1931 translation to give greater prominence to Mofolo's craft.

Chaka is thus a highlight, in the wake of which other Sotho works have difficulty asserting themselves. Mofolo, who for a short while had been a recruiter for the mines, had shown the Basotho the way: that of exile. In the 'thirties, the gap began to widen between the literature of those who had remained in the country, that still bore the mark of religion and of nature, and the texts of the Basotho of the Union of South Africa with their descriptions of the harsh realities of mining work. The texts translated by Ellenberger belong to the first category while the novels of A.S. Mopeli-Paulus (1913–60) represent the second. As a Mosotho living in the Union of South Africa, he published several volumes of poetry, followed by a short novel, *Liretlo* (1950), dealing with ritual murders. He also co-authored two novels in English, *Blanket Boy's Moon* (1953) and *Turn to the Dark* (1956). In the first of the two books, published outside South Africa, the condition of young Sotho migrants is treated with a rare honesty that touches upon the question of homosexuality and ritual murders, rarely mentioned in other works.

Other notable authors are B.M. Khaketla, S.M. Mofokeng and K.E. Ntsane; the first excels in the novel, the second in essays and novellas, whereas the third is a master of poetry and the essay (Lenake, in Gérard, 1982:93).

Khaketla's novel, *Mosali a Nkholoa* (1960) [The woman who caused trouble for me], is considered to be the masterpiece of the post-Mofolo generation. He describes how chief Mosipo, raised in the Western way, is persuaded by the elders or *induna* to offer a human sacrifice in order to make his business prosper. He is arrested, condemned to death and hanged. When he is about to die, he blames his acts on his wife's superstitions: the novel's structure is curiously similar to that of *Chaka*:

> Both Chaka and Mosito are of royal origin although of lower rank: thus ends the similarity in backgrounds. The two books probe into the lives of individuals; they are psychological studies of Chaka and Mosito. Other characters are used to illuminate the life of the hero.... In both works witchcraft and magic have been effectively used to stimulate suspense and to advance the story.... (Moloi, 1975:33)

Creative writing in Sesotho is still being practised by younger writers who know the language's literary tradition and are ready to face the challenges of a new nation:

> [Nhlanhla] Maake, in a certain respect, could be regarded as a post-apartheid writer of the 'nineties, introducing (and possibly leading) a fifth generation of writers in Sesotho since the introduction of literacy in Lesotho since 1833. Deeply rooted in the political struggle of the late 1980s–early 1990s and in moral considerations of the justness of the cause, *Kweetsa ya pelo ya motho* [The depth of the human heart, or simply the depth of the heart] does not directly allude to the political context within which the narrative is situated, or to the moral considerations of the justness of the cause. But it does capture the riddle of how different characters become their original selves when suffering from the grave consequences – political and moral – of the clash between the forces trying to uphold the unjust system and those trying to overthrow it. (Swanepoel, 1998:144)

The literature of other related languages

Related languages have had a different history. The 'fifties saw the development of a Northern Sotho or *Sepedi* literature, for the exclusive use of the South African Republic's apartheid regime. The case of Setswana is a little different. For a long time, the Tswana clans exploited the advantage of living in the Bechuanaland protectorate (now Botswana), which was formally independent and shielded from the ambitions of the Union and later those of the Republic of South Africa. A literary form of Setswana had existed since the nineteenth century, as mentioned in a biography of R. Moffat, translator of the Bible and founder of the Kuruman Press (Bradlow, 1987).

The great Tswana writer Sol Plaatje wrote in two languages (Couzens, in Plaatje, 1975:1). As the editor-in-chief of a Mafeking newspaper published in Setswana and English, *Koranta ea Bechuana*, and then the editor-in-chief of *Tsala ea Batho*, a Thaba Nchu newspaper, he wrote articles in Setswana as well as books in English, and translated Shakespeare into Setswana (Willan, 1984). However, even though at the present time the language is spoken in Botswana and in the northern provinces of South Africa (Shole, in Gérard, 1982:97), it has produced fewer than a hundred titles, the works of thirty authors which, with the exception of the output of D.P.S. Monyaise (Moilwa, 1983), seem to be exclusively for school use. One of the major handicaps for Setswana diffusion is probably this artificial 'fragmentation' (Mpotokwane, 1990:7), which is particularly evident in the tragi-comic story of Bophuthatswana itself, the now defunct homeland, the poor neighbour of prosperous Botswana, the cousin from across the Limpopo, 'liberated' by the South African army that had put it there in the first place! A literature worthy of the name would first have to deal with these questions, but they were 'obviously' outside the school curricula for which the books published were supposed to provide reading material. That certainly would account for the triviality of many of these texts.

Zulu Literature

Arbousset's transcription of the praises of Dingane, which was completed in 1840, is a monumental panegyric in rhythmic prose – and not 'metrical verse', as the English translator erroneously defined it (Rycroft, 1984) in a too-narrow assessment of this *isibongo's* poetic qualities. It is often mentioned and rarely read, but it is certainly not the scrap of text that Liz Gunner makes it out to be in her otherwise excellent book (*Musho* 1991:8). The poor English translation created a lasting misrepresentation of this work, which was only corrected in 1984 by D. Rycroft, who tried, with some small success, to reconstruct the Zulu almost a hundred and fifty years after the original transcription. Of course, this goes against a well-entrenched prejudice originally expressed by the Rev. Dohne:

> Some have expected to find much poetry among the Zulu-Kafirs [sic], but there is, in fact, none. Poetical language is extremely rare and we meet only a few pieces of prose.... The Zulu nation is more fond of *ukuhlabela*, i.e. singing and engages more in '*ukuvuma amagama ezinkosi*', i.e. singing the praises of the chiefs, than any other kafir tribe. But their capacity in this respect is very limited.... (Dohne, quoted in Jordan, 1973:15–16)

Shaka and his successors, like Dingane, left their mark on Zulu culture. The kingdom he had founded, sandwiched between the English in the provinces of the Cape and Natal and the Boer expansion in the Transvaal, was annexed by the British crown in 1887, while its Lesotho and Swaziland neighbours succeeded in maintaining a protectorate status, which saved them from being incorporated into the Union of South Africa in 1910.

Shaka's wars delayed missionary expansion and at the same time forged an identity characterized by violence. Until the end of the nineteenth century, few written texts have come to light. A grammar written in Norwegian is published in 1850, a dictionary in 1857, and a grammar in English by the press of the American mission of Umsunduzi in 1859. The translation of the New Testament was published in 1865 while 1860 saw the publication of a book prepared by the Anglican bishop, Colenso, *Three native accounts*. Destined for those study-ing Zulu, the book consists of three edited and annotated travel narratives, which as the first literary narratives in Zulu, became minor classics (Doke, 1936). In short, compared to Xhosa literature, Zulu literature starts a generation later.

> A student of Bishop John Colenso, Fuze, wrote the first book to appear in print by any Zulu author: *Abantu abamnyamalapha bavela ngakhona* [Black people: Where they come from]. (Herdeck, 1974:140)

The work was written in the late nineteenth century and only published in 1922. According to the entry in Don Herdeck's dictionary it had a strong influence on later writers through its exaltation of the Zulu nation, the nostalgic memorial of vanishing customs and beliefs of the Zulu, and the growing feeling of a pan-Bantu loyalty.

Later cultural influences

In Natal and Zululand, national consciousness was raised to another level by contact with the message of Christianity, producing the prophetic movement led by Isaiah Shembe. For Shembe, the Zulus were the chosen people and he was the new Messiah of the 'Nazarenes', as his adepts were called. Shembe composed a whole corpus of hymnal poetry, which was published by his disciples in 1940 (Gunner, 1988). At the same time, the struggle against the Native Land Act, the 1913 law that abolished African access to land and deprived them of a large part of their cultivated holdings, mobilized the intellectuals and churchmen of all ethnic groups. The African National Congress (ANC), which was founded at the beginning of the twentieth century, chose a Zulu writer, John L. Dube (1870–1949) as its first president. In a great show of African unity against the (white) Union of South Africa, which was being constituted at the same time, Walter Rubusana, a Xhosa writer, was made the first vice-president and Sol Plaatje, an Anglophone writer and Tswana journalist, the first secretary-general.

John Dube was the first important Zulu writer. A journalist and a pedagogue trained in the United States, he succeeded, in 1901, with American backing, in founding the first institution of technical secondary schooling for black people. This was the Zulu Christian Industrial School of Ohlange, where he hoped to give future African farmers a technical training. When elected president of the ANC in 1912, he led the delegation that went to Great Britain to protest against the Land law (then in preparation). In 1933, he published *Insila Ka Tshaka*, which was later translated into English in 1951 as *Jeqe, Chaka's Servant*. It recounts the adventures of Jeqe, one of Shaka's 'page boys' who is disgusted by the horrors of war and leaves his master, taking refuge with the Tsonga. He marries the king's daughter and learns the secrets of traditional medicine. Having become a famous healer, he ends his career amongst the Swazi who, thanks to his occult knowledge, are able to rout the army of Shaka's successor, Dingane, who is killed in Swaziland in 1840. The book, an historical novel as well as a *Bildungsroman*, had a great influence on African literatures and languages. Like his hero, Dube considered Swaziland to be a 'sort of prototype of the ideal that the Zulu themselves had been unable to materialize ... true to its traditions, while managing to frustrate European imperialism', according to Albert Gérard (Gérard, 1971:216). Although Dube belonged to the generation of Mofolo and Mqhayi, his attitude was different: he was Zulu and knew that meeting whites not only constituted cultural exchange, but a power struggle. He also published his articles in English so as to introduce foreigners to the Zulu world.

> Since the first Zulu novel was published in 1933, must it be compared with the contemporary English novel? Must we look for stream of consciousness technique in Dube's *Insila ka Shaka*? Is *Insila kaShaka* necessarily inferior because it does not employ the stream of consciousness technique? On the other hand, would it be more reasonable to compare the first Zulu novel [i.e. *Insila ka Shaka*] with the first English novel, *Robinson Crusoe*? Could this be plausible despite the fact that *Robinson Crusoe* was written in the eighteenth century and *Insila ka Shaka* in the twentieth century? (Msimang, 1986:37)

To put matters in a true perspective, Msimang refers to Anthony Burgess's comments about the limitations of contemporary English novelists and is thus able to restore some relativistic ground (Msimang, 1986:37).

The practice of writing in two languages clearly distinguished Zulu writers from their Xhosa or Sotho counterparts. Only Plaatje, who was Tswana and was familiar with Boer intentions from the siege of Mafeking (as revealed in his posthumously published diary of the siege, 1989), felt the need to address the British in their own language. A later writer, R.R.R. Dhlomo (1901–1971) published *An African Tragedy* (1928) the first novel written in English (note that Plaatje's *Mhudi*, written in 1916, was only to be published in 1930) Dhlomo's novel deals with the tragic consequences of the massive expropriation sanctioned by the 1913 Land Act. Unable to pay their taxes, reduced to meagre plots on poor land, the Zulus emigrated to the cities. Although they represented eight times the white population of Natal, they were allowed six times less land. Dhlomo later produced a series of historical narratives on the nineteenth-century's great Zulu history personalities: *UDingane ka Senzangakhona* (1936) [Dingane, son of Senzangakhona], *UShaka* (1937), *UMpande ka Senzangakhona* (1938), [Mpande, son of Senzangakhona]. Zulu literary activity was now centred in Johannesburg. A new generation of writers emerged who, like Davidson Tengo Jabavu, made a critical study of their literary and linguistic heritage (Jabavu, 1923, 1943).

S. Nyembezi gave a precise description of the situation in his preface to the English translation of the poems of B.W. Vilakazi (1906–47), whose work dominates Zulu literature: 'When Vilakazi entered the literary field there were no books of published plays or poems written by a Zulu. Only one short novel had appeared in print' (Nyembezi, in Vilakazi, 1973:xviii–xix).

B.W. Vilakazi's achievement

In 1935, Vilakazi published *Inkondlo Ka Zulu* (Zulu chants) followed in 1938 by *Amal'ezulu* [*Zulu Horizons*], which would later be translated and adapted into English verse (1973). In 1946, he wrote a doctoral thesis (which remains unpublished) on the 'Oral and written poetry of the Nguni'. The Zulu-English dictionary to which he had contributed was published posthumously (1948). In 1978 his work was the subject of a doctoral thesis by D.B.Z. Ntuli, who investigated the problems resulting from the encounter between Bantu languages and that other universe outside of tradition. In fact, B.W. Vilakazi may be considered the true descendant of the Zulu *imbongi*, despite the comments of Taylor, who made them in 1935, that 'the background of his thought is not that of the imbongi' (Ntuli, 1984:7). Yet Vilakazi's themes, his way of developing them, as well as his sensitivity, are all very far removed from the Zulu *imbongi* and bring us closer to Western poetry, as the latter critic admits: 'Although Vilakazi's poetry has traditional traces, it is essentially patterned according to Western styles' (Ntuli, 1984:13). For Vilakazi, the mixture of the *isibongo* style and European forms may result in new forms. He thus defends the introduction of rhyme into the *isibongo* with original arguments, an approach that cannot be considered the same as the simplistic mimicry of European poetry. These attempts typically are to be found in the writings of such figures as Mqhayi who, in his later works,

> decided to break entirely with the diction and artistic formlessness of *izibongo* in favour of modern versification. With his limited knowledge of prosody it was only natural that he should not be able to go much further than to discover rhyme – of all the artificial ornaments of Western versification, the most obvious, and yet to the Bantu, the least desirable.... (Jordan, 1973:111)

In fact, all this is perfectly clear to anyone who knows Bantu languages and who has followed the Sesotho example as demonstrated by Swanepoel (1988): on the one hand, the word endings fall on a very limited number of vowels, and, on the other hand, the use of class affixes (which the missionary linguists from the beginning of the nineteenth century called 'euphonic concord', situated at the front of the word) limits the possibilities of rhyme on the last syllable. This euphony creates a 'noise' and suppresses the effect of repetition between sentences, between 'verses' of euphonic elements to which rhyme can ultimately be reduced. Although Vilakazi knew that, he still wanted to use rhyme. He proposed several modifications to the almost crippling drawbacks, described above. To prevent monotony or poverty of possible rhymes at the end of a word, Vilakazi suggested having the rhyme fall on the last two syllables – an original and enriching solution! He also proposed considering different types of clicks as rhymes, irrespective of their position: the physiological mechanisms inherent in their production are similar, and thus also the sound effect. Vilakazi's observations on rhythm results from repetition in the *isibongo*, with the euphonic repetition in verses of an equal number of syllables grouped in free stanzas.

> It is not easy to set a fixed rule on how rhythm is determined in Zulu. We have proposed that we be guided by the position of lengths and pauses. It is the manipulation of these lengths and pauses at desired intervals that results in rhythmic patterns. (Ntuli, 1984:232)

Ntuli's observations remind us of Olatunji's proposals regarding Yoruba prosody: instead of discovering structures analogous to that of European poetry in the Bantu or Yoruba poetic discourse (Babalola, 1968:358), he prefers to innovate. Himself a scholar and a poet, Ntuli is sensitive to the variety and richness of the *isibongo* and tries to give an account of its rhythm and its own movement, as Olatunji did for the *oriki*. The possibility of repeating not only words and syllables, but also tonal supra-segmental structures (going beyond the syllable) gives this poetry a complexity and a variety that is inexplicable if one approaches it as mere 'imitation' of prosodic forms original to European languages. B.W. Vilakazi makes an ambitious attempt to synthesize Zulu and English poetry, without restricting himself to formal considerations. The reading of the English adaptation of his poems is absolutely convincing. Although he fails in trying to rhyme the *isibongo*, if we are to believe D. Ntuli, he succeeds in transporting their style into his free-verse pieces. So it seems if we rely on the adaptations available to the reader. The titles of diverse poems give an overview of the variety of his themes: 'Ode to the Victoria Falls'; 'Come, Iron Monster'; 'Ode to Aggrey'; 'Jubilee'; 'Chaka, Son of Senzanga-khona'; 'The Poet'; 'Tell Me, O You Son of a White Man'; 'The Church Bell'; 'Gold Mine'; 'University Education'. A Catholic, he sings the praises of the missionaries:

> Thus today I sing the praises
> Of sons and daughters
> Who left their homes
> To wander far and wide:
> Who, knotting their bundles, went away
> Never again to return.
>   (1973:67)

Although there are obvious traces of Zulu nationalism in his great and beautiful poem, *Khalani, MaZulu* [Weep you Zulus!], it is there to deplore the wars amongst the Zulus that allowed the whites to plunder the Zulu nation. It is not surprising that a member of the royal family

> Is weeping as wept the Qulusis – when she
> Had learnt that the Zulus' Inkatha –
> Whose promise was peace and advancement –
> Would not even last through the year!
>   (1973:25)

The Qulusis are the clan of Shaka's paternal aunt and the Inkatha is the Zulu national council, symbol of loyalty to the king. But the Inkatha's character has been modified; it has become the guarantee of the convenant between the royal house and the chiefs in Natal and Zululand to supply a fund destined for projects of collective interest. Zulu solidarity is thus jeopardized when the Inkatha finds itself in a precarious situation. Addressing them in a sharp tone, Vilakazi invites the Zulus to dedicate more energy to education than to war: 'Listen to me you ignorant people!' (1973:35) This is the first line of a poem on Shaka: the Zulus should take more pride in education than in war.

> Dear Muse! Impart to me today
> Your knowledge of my people's heritage,
> That I, endowed with power to record it,
> May pass it on to Zulus yet unborn!
>   (1973:34)

The grandeur of the past will only be perpetuated through education. However, Vilakazi does not wrap himself up in Zulu culture, neither does he restrict himself to being nostalgic about a golden age. As a university professor in Johannesburg, he understood all too well that racism was directed towards all black people and that the exaltation of one group at the expense of the others was the best justification for white domination. In his doctoral thesis, submitted in 1946, he analysed not only Zulu poetry, but also that of the Nguni: he was interested in what the Southern Bantu have in common. He studied Zulu and Xhosa literature as though it were one and the same nation. This linguistic choice was also a political stance: some 'unsuccessful efforts have been made in the previous two decades to bolster African unity by fusing Zulu and Xhosa into one single language' (Gérard, 1971:256). Proposals in recent years (Alexander, 1990) show that the question has still not been resolved: Vilakazi's quality contribution to the project of uniting the two languages will be important for a future solution.

Zulu literature today

Zulu literature is certainly far removed from the rich history of Xhosa literature, but in Johannesburg it now occupies an important place thanks to brilliant intellectuals like H.I.E. Dhlomo and B.W. Vilakazi. S. Nyembezi, a former professor of Bantu linguistics at the University of Fort Hare and a collector of traditional poems (1958), has written several novels, notably *Inkinsela Yasemgungundlovu* (1961) [The Notable of Pietermaritzburg], 'a novel on the feats of a criminal in a rural province', to quote from the English cover blurb. In 1987, it was in its eleventh reprint and in its second edition in the new spelling. D. Ntuli, author of a doctoral thesis on Vilakazi, is also a poet of value who expresses himself in free verse. The radicalization of the political struggle forced Mazisi Kunene (1930–), into exile. He is probably the greatest Zulu poet after Vilakazi, and the author of an epic poem in 17 volumes and of a funeral chant entitled *Emperor Shaka, the Great* (1979). Kunene was for a long time treasurer of the ANC in exile and a professor in the United States; he is currently living back in South Africa. He has translated his imposing poem into English and has told me that he collected historical Zulu traditions from his parents. However, he did not limit himself to this ethnographic enterprise, according to the preface of his epic:

> It is regrettable in a way that this book should first appear in translation before it is published in the original.... It is only through the collective efforts of many of my relatives and friends that this has been possible. I was fortunate in having relatives both on my mother's side (Ngcobo family) and my father's side who took great pride in preserving and narrating our national history.... Through these traditions and literary techniques I was able to learn much about the history of Southern Africa. The dramatization and enactment of the important historical episodes added great meaningfulness to the facts of the cultural life.... (Kunene, 1979: xi)

It is certainly regrettable that no Zulu version of the poem has yet been made available, despite the fact that a manuscript copy was deposited at the Humanities Research Centre of the University of Texas archives where I was able to consult it in 1995.

During the apartheid era it was impossible to publish texts in Zulu dealing with the struggle: the new Zulu poets, like Oswald Mtshali, wrote in English. Nevertheless, in the name of all those who remained in the country, Ntuli rightly observes that despite their roles as schoolmasters, which evidently excluded them from directly taking a political position, certain poets found a 'subtle way' to approach 'thorny' subjects (Ntuli in Gérard, 1982:68). Zulu poetry is still alive and well in the country. It is probably also part of the so-called martial 'tradition', often praised by Gatsha Buthelezi, the Zulu leader to whom Mazizi Kunene dedicated his *Shaka!* '... from the 1930s onwards, the Zulu evinced considerable interest in writing and two writers in particular – Vilakazi and R.R.R. Dhlomo – dominated the literary scene between 1930 and 1940' (Nyembezi, in Vilakazi, 1973: xviii–xix).

Not only did the Xhosa and Zulu literatures blossom during the 'thirties, but the period also marked the beginning of literatures in other languages or dialects that had been promoted to the status of official languages by the Republic of South Africa. Although the promotion of Northern Sotho (Sepedi) and Setswana (the Setswana of the missionaries) were probably based on dialectal realities, they also result from the perverse intention to divide an important dialectal ensemble by fragmenting it into as many languages as there are dialects. This was done in the name of an educative policy of 'separate development', which 'congealed' tribal communities into a static identity to the advantage of the white community. Terence Ranger has said all there is to say about this policy, founded as it is on the corruption of the notion of identity:

> Tribal identity is not inevitable, natural, unchanging, given, but a product of human creativity which can be reinvented and redefined to become once again more open, constructive and flexible.... (Ranger, 1985:19)

The Promotion of Bantu Self-Government Act of 1959 had two consequences for the development of African languages:

> Firstly composite committees for Nguni and Sotho were dissolved and each language committee convened separately. The result was the publication by the Department of Bantu Education of separate issues of Terminology and Orthography lists of 1962, – i.e. one for Zulu, one for Xhosa, one for Tswana, etc.; secondly, new languages, Swazi and Ndebele, were reduced to writing.... (Msimang, 1992:5)

These languages would all be coupled to the homelands that were being created at the end of the 'fifties (Ciskei and Transkei: Xhosa; Kwazulu: Zulu; Bophuthatswana: Tswana; Qwaqwa: Sesotho; Gazankulu: Tsonga; Venda: Venda; Lebowa: Sepedi). If we exclude the three national languages of the old British protectorates of Botswana (Setswana), Lesotho (Sesotho) and Swaziland (Seswazi) – states that were theoretically autonomous but in practice almost completely dependant on South Africa – a clear distinction must be made between languages whose development and standardization resulted first and foremost from an appropriation by African intellectuals and artists and those languages where the promotion of schooling and publication was in a sense bestowed and granted new educative responsibilities through the creation of the homelands, those ephemeral substitutes for black South African states that were finally suppressed in 1993.

The development and promotion of Zulu and Xhosa cannot be separated from the awakening of a black political and cultural consciousness in South Africa. The same applies to the parallel, remarkable history of Sesotho and Setswana, or of Seswazi, a language that is closely linked to Zulu. On the contrary, the recent development and promotion of Venda, Tsonga (and to a lesser extent, Sepedi), correspond to the apartheid regime's need to provide distinct languages for the separate entities of the racial South Africa that it planned to construct. Xhosa and Zulu writers were more confident about their cultural legitimacy, and could refer to a prestigious past. Thus it is not surprising that their judgement of the consequences of apartheid at the beginning of the 'eighties was more nuanced than that of their colleagues writing in the other languages. I have already quoted D.B.Z. Ntuli's observations on the subtlety of Zulu poets. To this, he adds the fact that Zulu writers were able to deal with 'essential aspects of the human condition, to the extent that they sustain the comparison with works produced in languages where censorship is absent' (Ntuli, in Gérard, 1982:68). As regards Xhosa, S.C. Satyo points out that during the 'eighties the theme of 'tribalism, racial bias and violence seem to come forward' (Satyo, in Gérard, 1982:88), thus clearly showing Xhosa writers' capacity to take charge of society's problems instead of limiting themselves to 'innocuous' texts produced for use in schools.

For the 'small' language literatures (Tsonga, Venda) the future is much less bright. Critics and historians observe that these languages had an exclusive text-book usage that excluded the problems of the 'real world' of apartheid society under a vigilant censorship (Gérard, 1982:94–116).

The Future of Literatures in African Languages

Our goal has been to write a comprehensive history where the problematic of exchange and dialogue was not systematically repressed or even suppressed. Within this perspective, examples of exchanges between languages and mutual readings that occurred between writers working in the same world but in different languages become relevant.

Mofolo's *Chaka* was written before 1910, but was only published in 1925. Plaatje probably wrote *Mhudi* between these two dates; it was published only in 1930. One book is in Sesotho, the other in English; but Plaatje was also a Tswana writer who could read the closely related Sotho language. If we accept the idea of the possible contact between these two eminent black intellectuals, *Mhudi* can be read as a reaction to *Chaka*: in *Mhudi*, the woman is a peaceful heroine pitted against a brutal male chief. In a sense, Plaatje follows Mofolo's lead: the latter points out that Mzilikazi, who is Mhudi's principal African hero, escaped with all the girls from Chaka's army (Mofolo, 1981:140). What Mzilikazi proposed instead of Chaka's all-male world (warriors on the point of death expressed the desire to admire the body of their chiefs, according to Mofolo), confined to a closed, almost homosexual community of Spartan – or Nazi? – elite warriors, was the possibility of joint escape for boys *and* girls. Plaatje develops this approach by inventing another type of African king, a sort of anti-Chaka, in the person of Moshoeshoe who, it will be recalled, in Mofolo's novel, is a mere background figure who is never introduced to the reader. This king is also inspired by history, much more humane and wiser than the illustrious and sinister Shaka.

The Zulu author H.I.E. Dhlomo (1903–56) wrote an English play about Moshoeshoe that explains the reputation of this original figure. Mofolo's *Moeti oa Bochabela* is also an illustration of the soul's progress, modelled on Shembe's Zulu narratives. Reconstructing the literary history of South Africa is first a matter of circulating between different corpuses, opening up libraries and removing books from their pre-assigned shelves:

> Perhaps the recognition of so many official languages provides the opportunity for expanding their interrelatedness rather than agonizing over their pecking order. Perhaps this new 'official' Babel has a key role to play in an emergent national identity, one that does not glibly collapse histories or gloss over past oppression but allots a greater space for different and dissonant voices, different tongues. (Gunner, 2000:1)

In other words, the exploration of a new space, textually occupied by those authors exploring the frontiers of literacy.

> Translation has also a role to play in pointing up a situation of reciprocity and heteroglossia in South Africa, particularly if it is able to avoid what Gayatri Spivak has called the 'tedious translatese' that so often marks 'the act of wholesale translation in to English' and gives a sense of the 'rhetoricity of the original', the 'rhetorical silence of the original'. (Gunner, 2000:3)

This is a situation reminiscent of what is happening in many other African countries: a literature's development and vitality depend on a variety of circumstances. On the one hand, as illustrated by the case of Nigeria and Tanzania, governmental choices and a clearly defined policy with appropriate means at its disposal constitute the best developmental contexts. This is true only to the extent that a policy officially favouring the national languages does not combine with an authoritarian or even dictatorial regime, which has the effect of rendering creation sterile and intimidating writers, as in the case of Madagascar, Ethiopia or Somalia, in the course of the last three decades. South Africa under apartheid provided another register: in a country where any reference to questions of a social and cultural nature, to society's political organization and the distribution of power was prohibited, writers often had no choice but to keep quiet and slowly drift into irrelevance.

These constraints (or assets, in certain cases) belong to a cultural object – literary language – which has its own history and its own dynamics. Although censorship prevented the development of a Venda (Venda) or Kabiye (Togo) literature, it could not silence Xhosa literature, with its century-old tradition and means of expression allowing for all sorts of guises. Similarly, a policy that favours the development of an African language may find itself considerably handicapped by the absence of a long literary tradition: if, for example, there are no translations, as is unfortunately the case in Igbo; if, except for the Bible, no other text (fiction for example) has been published. That describes the context of Ngugi's Gikuyu writings: his language has no long literary tradition, and creating one is not easy when few texts have been published and when, despite an important market for these books, an authoritarian regime is ever vigilant. An intellectual climate favouring the creation of artistic works must be encouraged, but an atmosphere of liberty will not suffice in the absence of a complete history of literary language to fuel the debate and to produce new works, as in the case of Xhosa, Yoruba and Kiswahili speakers. An endogenous creative momentum is essential. It is lacking in Gikuyu, where in fact it never existed, as shown by the meagre output of works printed in this language; in the case of Ewe it collapsed under the weight of Ghana's economic difficulties and Togo's political authoritarianism.

A double overlay should thus be used to read the present situation: on the one hand, that of official attitudes and practices, including censorship, and on the other, that of the community's linguistic consciousness, which is always a product of history. If the community is not capable of creating its instruments of literary expression on its own – agreeing about the standard language – one may consider that it is in fact abandoning the field to the European languages. How many African language communities have produced unilingual dictionaries and written treatises on metalanguage? Only the Swahili, Yoruba and Amharic speech communities have followed this road. Should one deduce that only these communities will still be publishing texts by the end of the twenty-first century? Turning our attention once again to South Africa, important languages with a prestigious history (such as Xhosa) should receive a decisive boost from the current process of political and cultural liberation. Benefiting from lexical and literary research, they could be turned into modern languages within a radically transformed system of education, instead of being shackled with a restrictive ethnic identity as defined by administration, preventing them from illustrating the common culture and destiny of all the peoples of the region.

The reader requiring more detail may refer to the exhaustive research of Albert Gérard (1981). I hope to have illustrated the possibilities and impediments of the great African languages, those that may continue producing books in the next century. Along with Edouard Glissant, I believe that 'a nation reduced to the oral practice of their own language would be doomed to a cultural death, which is nothing more than the pale reflection of another type of very real agony', so aptly expressed in his *Discours antillais* (1981:316).

If a few general ideas are to be deduced from this survey of literatures in the African languages, it would be that common features drawn from a shared historical destiny can be identified amongst all of these linguistic communities. Biblical influence is evident, as is that of Bunyan, Shakespeare and even Tolstoy, all of whom were translated into several languages.

In formal terms, a number of similarities are evident: poetry is probably the most interesting genre, offering the greatest literary and textual challenges, particularly with the status of oral creation, but it is also the least known by non-native speakers. One can imagine comparing Mqhayi, the Xhosa bard, to Faleti, the Yoruba poet. Both mastered the art of improvised composition, but were also able to present their work in written form. The oral form with its own particular techniques (notably repetitions, parallelisms and formulae) is the matrix of composition. The attempt to transpose the rules of writing that originated in the Western tradition, with its fixed rhymes and metres, did not lead to very convincing results. At a time when fixed forms are being abandoned in the West, it is paradoxical (to say the least) to see African poets trying to impose them on their languages instead of reflecting on the conditions of their own poetry. A.C. Jordan's recommendations resulting from his observations and analyses must not be forgotten; it is probably a lesson that Kezilahabi remembered when composing *Kichomi* in free verse.

Theatre is certainly a new genre, one that is greatly appreciated in schools, which obviously influences the forms and themes of dramatic expression. In Hausa, for example, problems of family and domestic life are analysed in the theatre and nowhere else (Beik, 1984). Original forms (such as Yoruba opera) are being created, which will influence English drama with its successful combination of static staging of panegyric recitation and narrative modes borrowed from biblical dramatizations. In short, it offers a new creation of traditional poetry for the stage. In a genre at the opposite end of the scale, Ebrahim Hussein adopts the idiom of contemporary international drama, creating a Kiswahili theatre of images characterized by a fluidity very far removed from the heavy text-book type compositions steeped in simplistic Aristotelian dramaturgy.

Narrative fiction is in abundance everywhere, although books of more than 200 pages are scarce. This shortness of written narrative breath poses several questions: is it caused by the (imperfectly mastered) limitations inherent in the genre? Does the difficulty lie in writing long prose passages in initially oral languages? To my knowledge, the longest narrative prose text (591 pages) in an African language is the Kiswahili novel *Myombekere*, translated from Kikerewe by the author, Aniceti Kitereza and published by the Tanzania Publishing House in 1980. The question of a novel's length has not as yet attracted much attention from critics, while a lengthy text like Ngugi's Shona-translated novel, *Grains of Wheat*, which runs into more than 400 pages, merits consideration from the point of view of focalization and the problematic transposition of different types of reported speech. I would like to be more familiar with reflections on writing in African languages. Ngugi provides us with a remarkable example in his essay on the conditions of Gikuyu writing; it is an honest, precise analysis of his difficulties in writing his own language in prose. He had no model except for the Bible. Apart from the delicate spelling problem, which can be happily resolved in less 'tonal' languages or in languages where the spelling is not too far removed from phonetics (such as Kiswahili, Hausa or Gikuyu), there are the difficulties of narrative construction and the temporal marking of narrative voices. All these problems can be solved but demand perpetual inventiveness from the author, constituting a considerable impediment to the narrative flow, exactly as described by Njabulo Ndebele (Lindfors, 1986:50). He tried writing in Zulu, but finally chose English so as to add his text to the universe of common references. The idea of facility associated with writing in one's spoken language is a totally simplistic one.

> If I were to write in Zulu now, I think I would have to spend a tremendous amount of intellectual energy trying to master the language for literary purposes. I have simply not used the language very much for that kind of artistic activity. (Ndebele, in Lindfors, 1986:51–2)

The case of French, a language that has not only been refined, but also planed down by centuries of standardization, is an exceptional one, as the French often tend to forget (Weinrich, 1990). Almost everywhere else, there is a gap (and often quite an important one) between spoken and written language. The same applies to African languages. Njabulo Ndebele's choice is to distance himself by writing in English, for which he is rewarded by a greater familiarity with other books and instruments of reference, seeing as there is as yet no unilingual Zulu dictionary. This is a common situation, but also an absurd one, even if it helps to explain why a writer chooses English, French, Portuguese, or other adequately 'developed' languages.

These difficulties and their causes have only recently come into the debate, thus posing a fundamental question about the future of literatures in African literatures.

> Beyond 2000 the African languages will retain at least their present level of importance as regional and/or national languages in fields such as education and communication; even if English becomes the sole official language, or remains the most used national vehicular language which it is at present. (Swanepoel, 1996:24)

It is possible to provide a parallel history of literature in the African languages up to the present day and to write another history, that of African literatures in European languages (Gérard, 1986). Today the question is, for instance, how to merge African-language literature into South African literary history, as suggested by Chris Swanepoel. Through the concept of linguistic consciousness, our whole purpose is to show the extent of such an illusory duality. Linguistic consciousness is, most importantly, the recognition of the coexistence of languages, society's diglossic situation, and the writer's multilingualism. I have indicated the (all too rare) translations of works in African languages as well as the case of 'digraphic' writers (who express themselves in two languages). I will now move forward with a systematic examination of some of the works situated precisely in the field of linguistic consciousness, duality, multiplicity – or even ambiguity.

6 The Go-Betweens
WRITING IN TWO LANGUAGES

The notion of a language go-between is inseparable from the concept of language consciousness. If the writers discussed in this chapter are considered to be such go-betweens, it is precisely because during the first half of the twentieth century, they generally connected a universe where education provided by foreign power structures did not exist (or where it did, touched only a small part of the population), with the other world where it was becoming widespread. They never pretended to be European-born and their attachment to writing in European languages was always problematic. Today, more than half a century later, we tend to forget how painful or even dangerous this way of life could be: the suicide of the Malagasy writer, Jean-Joseph Rabearivelo, who was the most brilliant of the group, serves as a constant reminder. All of the writers of this period were sensitive to the advantages that their people could gain from the new forms of Western education, but they saw no reason why this education could not take place in their own language, or any danger that it would ever make them forget the written and oral tradition of their own language. This utopian view, which had already been imagined by J.E. Casely-Hayford in *Ethiopia Unbound* (1911), a novel that refers to a Fanti-speaking university, was also the driving force behind Tanzania's successes in the literary field.

As my first examples, I have chosen three very different writers. They have one point in common: they are practically the only Francophone writers to have created work in two languages: their own, and French. As a group, they exemplify the different routes available to the writer: Jean-Joseph Rabearivelo wrote in Malagasy and in French. His name is significant in the canon of Malagasy literature. His chosen route was governed only by his faith in, or rather, his quasi-religious belief in the great world literature, the canon of works by the likes of Tagore and Valéry. The second writer I deal with is Alexis Kagame who wrote poems in Kinyarwanda and French: his aim was to Christianize Rwandan oral poetry and record it on paper. His oeuvre is an original attempt to combine poetic virtues and the teachings of the Gospel in Kinyarwanda. Lastly, Amadou Hampâté Bâ, a well-read Muslim and an important member of a respected religious brotherhood. His entire production (in French and Fula) stems from the oral tradition, but also and above all from the teachings of well-read Muslims. He considered himself as an interpreter, but contrary to his two companions above, in digraphy (creative writing in his two languages), he chose not to expatiate on his literary objectives and hid himself behind various scientific projects that fell far short of the importance of his true work. A significant part of the three authors' output was written (if not published), before 1960, during the colonial era. Should it therefore be considered outmoded? On the contrary, I think that the contemporary significance of these works lies in their expression of the authors' interest in specifically linguistic issues. A superficial reading of these texts will focus on the problems of making the transition from an African language (or Malagasy) to French, without revealing that their significance lies in maintaining a certain tension between the original language and French – *without* giving up the struggle and thus benefiting the French language.

This view helps to explain why this type of (continuously digraphical) creation was found only in the Francophone domain. There was a lot of pressure to choose French, in Rwanda and within the Catholic church as well. Artists and intellectuals who were well-equipped to create in their own language, gave in to pressure and produced the works that are of interest to us in this chapter. In Anglophone areas, the situation was less tense: polite interest in local languages and benevolent neglect of African efforts to learn the colonial language resulted either in self-confident works in the English language – fully embraced by the authors in question – or in works in African languages. However, there was rarely an effort in these regions to maintain the kind of fruitful, contentious dialogue that we shall discuss in the rest of this chapter. A comedy such as *The Blinkards* (1915) written in English and in Fanti, seems to have been an exception in the Anglophone literary corpus of the Gold Coast.

What other Anglophone texts display this type of tension between English and the mother tongue? The division between languages is often a social and academic one, a practical separation rather than the expression of a dynamics of linguistic dialogue. Expression in English soon found its appropriate forms in Chinua Achebe's narrative prose and Wole Soyinka's dramatic prose. Chinua Achebe knows how to 'work on' English prose with the palm oil of Igbo proverbs (Lindfors 1973:73), while Wole Soyinka's characters speak to the beat of Yoruba drums. Only the work of Okot p'Bitek (1932–82), which will be analysed later in this chapter, is very precisely related to the original language and fits into the category of a translation from Acoli to English. The previously quoted example of the Zulu poet Mazizi Kunene is probably also the result of similar creative tension. This same tension between mother tongue and European language is found in the actual language of Amos Tutuola's work, whose opaque 'naïvety' has already been mentioned (Chapter 2). Instead of keeping a certain distance from both of his languages, his shameless linguistic confusion results in a prose style deemed outrageous by the standard bearers of linguistic norms and utterly magical by lovers of poetry.

So we have the potential dynamic exchange between languages proposed by Jean-Joseph Rabearivelo; or, a confusion of languages in fusion. The third, worst outcome is a language erased from the atlas to make room for another – which, in many cases, represents the dominant model of an African continent speaking and writing in European languages. There is no literary production in African languages in Lusophone Africa, however, and no apparent exchange occurs between the older and the imposed languages. The only means of Africanizing such writing is by contamination (as in the case of Tutuola), resulting from a conscious effort to restore the plurality of voices (the plurality of linguistic subjects in conversation with one another). That is exactly what Luandino Vieira (Trigo 1981) created on the sands of Babel (as we shall see in the last chapter). Uahenga Xitu, (translated into Portuguese and published in 1979), has followed in Tutuola's footsteps, on that shore.

Jean-Joseph Rabearivelo (1903–37):
Translation as a Creative Principle

Rabearivelo, who descends from a noble family from the Malagasy plateau or *hova*, who lost their fortune with the abolition of slavery, started writing poetry in Malagasy at a very early age. He was able to do so because Madagascar abandoned a more than century-old standardized written language, and because other poets had created an embryonic literary tradition that provided a reference point for him, particularly in terms of genre. Rabearivelo's keen interest in Malagasy poetry inspired him to write a number of articles (Joubert 1991a:33–5): 'Literature and us' (1930), 'Discourse on our poetry' (1927), 'Testimony to Hova poetry', and 'Urgent necessities in art and theatre' (1932). In 1931, his endeavours to promote Malagasy language and culture were rewarded by membership of the Malagasy Academy. He expressed his attachment to the national language and culture on numerous occasions, by composing a *fasana* [threnody] for the Malagasy poetess Esther Razanadrasoa, and by dedicating his last collection of poems to the poet J.H. Rabekoto. Then why did he choose to write in French, and how did he manage it?

Rabearivelo's oeuvre is scattered across the globe: his collections of poems, published in the four corners of the earth, in often inaccurate editions (as demonstrated by Jean-Louis Joubert, 1991b), cover numerous poetic modes. First, there is in him the post-symbolist French poet, followed by the transcriber-translator of oral literature – notably the *Vieilles chansons du pays d'Imerina* (1980) – and lastly, the author of texts that he 'pretends' to have 'transcribed' (sic) from Malagasy and where, paradoxically, his voice is at its most original, possibly most authentic.

> The existence of a large, age-old Malagasy press enabled Malagasy literature to develop .... At the end of the Merina monarchy, there were a dozen periodicals in existence, published in Antananarivo, in numbers that were quite significant. (*Teny Soa*, for example: 3,000 copies in 1875).... Towards the end of the previous century, newspapers started publishing poems and literary texts in prose (tales, fables, short stories). In this way, Malagasy-speaking writers were offered a natural public. (Joubert 1991b: 30)

This vitality facilitated Rabearivelo's task of publishing in reviews: initially in the review founded by the magistrate and poet Pierre Camo entitled *18°, Latitude Sud*, and later in the *Capricorne* review that he himself set up in 1930.

Presques-songes [Near Dreams] and *Traduit de la Nuit* [Translations from the Night], published in French in Antananarivo and Tunis, are presented as 'Hova transcriptions' by the author. The term 'transcribed' catches the eye: poems cannot be *transcribed* into French, only *translated*. An initial explanation was provided in the 1960 publication of Hova versions of the poems, confirming that it was not a case of pure fiction. Rabearivelo himself maintained that the texts were originally written in French; thus, a study of the manuscripts

> enables us to clarify the debate. [In] those of *Near Dreams* [it is] as if Rabearivelo was no longer writing directly in French or Malagasy, but in the perpetual passageway from one language to another.... (Joubert 1991b:67)

In fact, Rabearivelo wrote in French *via* Malagasy, which explains some of the strange turns of phrases as well as the impression of distance created by writing one language through another, seemingly a trans-written language. The recent, bilingual edition (1991) of *Near Dreams* and *Translations from the Night* enables specialists to relate to the Malagasy version and thus to appreciate the author's trans-writing achievements.

> There is something that the Malagasy reader is particularly sensitive to, the fact that a Rabearivelo text inspires an irresistible feeling of having been 'translated'; upon examination, a Malagasy text may seem to have been modelled on a French one, while with Rabearivelo, a work written in French is often merely the reflection of Malagasy visions translated into French words. (Andrianarahinjaka, in Rabearivelo, 1980:10)

It is not a question of determining the original text, the one that serves as the translator's source. For someone like Jean-Joseph Rabearivelo, linguistic *métissage* was a given; it would be impossible to ascertain the original text with any certainty. Rabearivelo's aim was to prove that French can be used in Malagasy genres and in descriptions of Malagasy realities. He wanted to create a new type of poetic writing that echoes the original language, but that can be appreciated for what it is itself. Such an undertaking was way ahead of its time. During the 'twenties, many Francophones considered that writing in French was already a commendable deed for an indigenous writer: why should he take it on himself to innovate and shake up the French language? For the colonists, for the French, such an ambition was inappropriate. For the Malagasy nationalists, on the other hand, the poet's enterprise signalled betrayal: with his thorough knowledge of his country's culture, Rabearivelo should have written in Malagasy. But Rabearivelo had measured the upheaval caused by the emergence of French teaching in Madagascar: he knew that it would change the fate of Malagasy, that this 'interference' – the title of the novel he wrote in 1927, although it was only published in 1988 – was not temporary. Malagasy culture could not remain closed to the outside world, left in the hands of ministers translating the Bible and to scholars singing the praises of the past. Rabearivelo wanted to be a poet of his time: he had read Rimbaud, Verlaine and Whitman, and had translated Valéry into Malagasy. Although he continuously moved backwards and forwards between French and Malagasy, he would never leave his island. He could free himself from the rigid forms of classroom poetics in an attempt to adopt the rhythmic flow of the *hain-teny:*

> Rabearivelo's growing intuition concerning the significance of translation for the postcolonial writer led him to make it the theme of his final collection of poetry, entitled *Traduit de la nuit* [*Translations from the night*]. In addition to the bilingual format of the work, the French Malagasy poems provide images of the many possible ways in which the phenomenon of night can be translated.... Translation in Rabearivelo's writing therefore does not lead back to uncontaminated origins and linguistic states; on the contrary, it substantiates the inevitable linguistic mobility that had in his time become the vocation of the postcolonial writer (Adejunmobi, 1996:177)

His constant preoccupation with poetic reflection, his interest in the situation of the writer from both a theoretical and a practical point of view, together with a vivid awareness of the experience of a colonized person and the condition of a not quite cursed but certainly marginalized poet, infuses Raberarivelo's texts with a depth and emotion that are very rare in African poetry in French. He was and still remains one of the few writers to have established himself at a language crossroads. He renounces neither his ancestors nor his cultural heritage, but he wants to make (passionate) use of all the possibilities offered by French, which he considers to be the type of modernity that will draw him out of his insularity. Mastering French means taking the path towards assimilation; it is the progressive response given to those colonials who doubt the natives' capacity for progress. The rejection of this approach during the anti-colonialist era should not make us forget that, in a world with entirely colonial horizons, assimilation represented a way of maintaining one's dignity. The astonishing thing about Rabearivelo is that he kept his interest in his mother tongue and tried to make the modes of Malagasy expression and thought part of his French oeuvre. He is one of a very small group of writers from the colonial era who never went to France.

The Dahomean writer Félix Couchoro (1900–68) (he only became Togolese in 1940) is a similar case. Despite the difference in talent and means of expression, their work displays numerous similarities, particularly between their two more or less contemporaneous novels: *L'esclave* [The slave] (1929) and Rabearivelo's *L'interférence* (written in 1927). In both cases, the memory of a pre-colonial universe is still very much alive and slavery is a central theme. But while Couchoro (who lacked a literary culture) has recourse to the recipes of the colonial novel to structure his melodrama, Rabearivelo creates a more nuanced work with moments of nostalgia for past royalty, although the author is all too aware of the decrepitude of the institution and its representatives. Neither Couchoro nor Rabearivelo pretends that writing in French is a self-evident solution or unproblematic. Using Couchoro's terminology (1929), one may say that the 'cultivated foreign language' must bend to the genius of 'local idioms'; this was also Rabearivelo's true aim. This linguistic consciousness is character-istic of a generation of writers who studied French and used it as a weapon in their struggle to assimilate. The assimilated person of that era is an intellectual who does not want to lose anything of his own culture but, on the contrary, to promote it, thanks to the new possibilities offered by his very position. The pride of these two writers kept them at a distance from the administration, preventing them from breaking out of the classification of indigenous people and attaining the 'assimilated' category, or even of obtaining French citizenship. But even if proof of their assimilation had been provided, probably the colonial administration would have detected something of a 'subversive bent' in them: at all events, neither escaped his indigenous status. Couchoro was another who never saw France, while the work of both men was a marvellous illustration of a measure of success for the colonial policy of elite Francophonization.

Alexis Kagame (1912–81): Bantuist, Philosopher & Poet

In his own words, Alexis Kagame was not only a priest, but also a writer:

> People are often not aware of the fact that I spent most of my time writing in Kinyar-wanda. In 1966, I finished *La divine pastorale* there, which I had started writing in 1941. I wrote it in Kinyarwanda, for the Banyarwandans. (Kagame, 1967:44)

Ordained as a priest in 1941, Kagame published numerous works and articles over a period of forty years, providing readers with a history of Rwanda that has become indispensable.

> Born in 1912, Kagame entered a small seminary in 1928. He started studying Rwanda's traditional dynastic poetry in 1936. The king sent poets to him and the seminary's rector exempted him from manual labour.... (Vidal, 1991:45)

Listening to and transcribing the declamations of the bards enabled him to collect a vast amount of documents, which were compiled as a collection destined for publication in Kinyarwanda by King Mutara III Ruhadiga.

In neighbouring Democratic Republic of Congo (formerly Zaïre), he was suspected of nurturing ideas of Rwandan expansionism in his historical works and of giving in to 'traditional Rwandan chauvinism' (Kagabo, 1986:36). As an historian, the fact that he wrote for Rwandans in the first place makes his case an original one when compared to other African historians. His aim was to show the Rwandans that they had their own roots and need not have any inferiority complexes. However, his activities as the monarchy's intellectual caused him to be treated with a certain condescension by European researchers who saw him as a resource or a kind of super-informer, rather than a fully-fledged colleague.

Kagame's poetic activities in his native language have seldom been analysed. He often translated his own texts, although a certain number have still not been translated. His choice of a title, considered below, reflects his acute linguistic consciousness of the translation problem:

> The French explanatory title *Le relève goût des pommes de terre*, which may be translated into English as 'The flavour enhancer of potatoes' has been noted with variations. A number of bibliographies have suggested that another French title *L'assaisonnement des pommes de terre* (Flavouring of potatoes, my translation) would be more accurate, because it is argued, '*relève goût*' is not good French.... In the case of Alexis Kagame's *Indyohesha Birayi*, the appropriateness of the title '*relève goût*' is likely to be appreciated by the poet's public of Rwandan readers for whom '*assaisonnement*' (flavouring) would evoke rather the condiments added to meat than the meat (pork) itself.... In linguistic terms the poet strove to find a dynamic equivalence that would render in French the poetic atmosphere and the intentions of the composition in Kinyarwanda. (Nzabatinda, 1999:206)

Although his fields of study are varied, they are linked by a common centre of interest: Rwanda. His diverse activities may be summarily classified as follows:

- A priest's reflections: 'Christian poetry in Central Africa' (1946–47); 'Christianity in Rwandese poetry' (1950) – on the lack of knowledge about Christianity in Africa and in the Bantu culture of the Great Lakes region;
- Poetic activity in Kinyarwanda: *Indyohesha birayi* (1949) [The flavour enhancer of potatoes];
  Isoko y'amajyambere (1949–51) [The source of progress];
  Umulirimbiyi wa nyili-Ibiremwa (1950, 1953) aimed at a practical application of his initial field of study, which resulted in numerous and often unpublished translations;

La divine pastorale [The divine pastoral], a translation of *Umulirimbiyi* (1950, 1952), as well as a reflection on translation and poetics: 'Introduction to the great lyrical genres of the former Rwanda' (1969);

- Historical research: in *Le code des institutions politiques du Rwanda précolonial* (1952b) [A code of pre-colonial Rwanda's political institutions]; *Histoire des armées bovines dans l'ancien Rwanda* (1961) [A history of the regimental cattle herds of old]; and *Les milices du Rwanda précolonial* (1963) [Militia of pre-colonial Rwanda], considered to be a source of authority in his own country, based on his poetry collections;
- Theoretical reflections on the linguistic (and in Kagame's view, philosophical) relations between Bantu peoples) in *Les philosophie bantu-rwandaise de l'être* (1956) [The Bantu-Rwandese philosophy of being]; *Les philosophie bantu comparée* (1976) [Comparative Bantu philosophy], on what could be considered a Bantu conception of the world.

Dynastic poetry, which expresses the filiations legitimizing the position of the dynasty in place, serves as a foundation for his research as a historian. In his own words, his poetic aim is a form of 'Christianization of our regional prose' through the writing of *La divine pastorale*: 'Divine, because its object is God, His nature and His works; pastoral, because the genre is an adaptation of Rwanda's pastoral poetry' (Kagame, 1955a:19). This is truly functional poetry and as such an authentic part of the framework of Rwandan national culture:

> I started writing the poem towards the end of 1940 in order to provide the indigenous mentality, which is inclined towards poetry, with subject-matter susceptible of initiating the Christianization process. (Kagame, 1955a:17)

Alexis Kagame uses his knowledge and his talent to serve this objective. He starts by selecting from the three most important genres (war, dynastic and pastoral) the most appropriate one for what he is trying to accomplish. The tone of the poems can be judged by reading his translations for the names of the *armées bovines* (1961): 'audience drums', 'lyred horns', 'wetting the javelins', 'initiatory cantors', 'leoparded ones'; or the names of the militia (1963), less noble but more evocative in a concrete sense: 'hammerers', 'climbers', 'tumblers', 'mortifiers', 'carvers', 'extinguishers', 'never treacherous ones', 'radiant ones when great acts are announced' and 'rival crushers'. Kagame wants to Christianize this entire martial universe, with an epic inspiration equalling that of his oral precursors. The pastoral genre seems to lend itself best to the grafting of Christianity that Kagame wants to perform on Rwandan culture; he can thus resort to war or praise songs, which provide his *Divine pastorale* with a useful variety of elements. Moreover, the fact that this genre requires a regular rhythm pleases Kagame, who points out that his epic can be sung with 'indigenous' musical accompaniment.

He spent 25 years of his life composing this text, which consists of 150 poems divided according to 18 'nights', 'following the example of the Psalter of the Bible'. This immense work, which is still partially unpublished, can only be compared to Honegger's oratorios or Messiaen's instrumental works, with its union of great compositional skill as shown in the Kinyarwanda text inspired by oral poetry, and the expression of a faith that may seem naïve. Kagame the poet and translator reflected pertinently on his activities:

Our languages are developing within a civilization completely foreign to the doctrinal subtleties that must be taken into consideration in languages that are familiar with the sacred sciences. A few centuries from now, Bantu languages will have reached the same point. Sometimes, this type of operation can have disconcerting results: if one thinks for example of the Lord's Prayer, French-speaking Christians will say 'Let thy kingdom come' while Rwandan Christians will translate this, in all seriousness, as 'let thy drum be heard everywhere...' Up to a certain point, *La divine pastorale* is a documentary poem in the sense that it was translated to provide ethnologists and linguists with the means of bringing Rwanda's soul within their reach. This obviously is germane to the translation; as for the original, the motive governing its composition is already known. (Kagame, 1952a:23)

Kagame's thought

The philosophical status of Kagame's oeuvre raises a lot of questions. Using as his starting point an overlay of classical philosophy, consisting notably of the categories of logic, ontology and ethics, he proceeds to analyse Bantu philosophy. Who are the Bantu? It is a matter of using comparative linguistics as a basis for separating out the linguistic categories in which Bantu languages are organized. Is it possible to reduce this diversity to four fundamental classes, as Kagame did, while most Bantu languages are composed of some twenty classes? Can one go from term to concept, paying little attention to the sign's arbitrary nature, as Mudimbe (1988:150) pertinently observes?

The basic point Kagame expresses is that concepts, and indeed whole world views, precede language. The structure and grammatical rules of language are modelled in agreement with the cosmological ordering of the universe. The modelling of linguistic structure in accordance with philosophy, according to Kagame, was done by the great ancestors – philosophers who were also the sages of the tribe. It is what was formulated by these forefathers that constitutes both the language and the philosophy of the Bantu. It is this premise that drives Kagame into making the comparative study of Bantu philosophy, based on the analysis of linguistic variations, back to its original roots or something approximate thereto. In this sense it can be said that Kagame accepts and applauds Tempel's presentation of African philosophy as a static phenomenon that is impervious to change. (Masolo, 1994:96)

These questions remain and seriously compromise his theoretical project. They should not, however, divert us from the poet's oeuvre, which is unique in its scale and inspiration.

Amadou Hampâté Bâ (1901–91), the Fulani Interpreter

The wide-ranging knowledge of Amadou Hampâté Bâ, historian, poet, theologian, philosopher and novelist, is astonishing. What strikes the reader of a catalogue of his manuscripts, such as the one established by A.I. Sow in 1970, is the number of unpublished texts and the variety of subjects treated by the author. Amadou Hampâté Bâ was producing texts for decades: he collected, transcribed, translated and also wrote directly in French. He accumulated a certain learning, which he undertook to transmit to others.

Millions of people speak Fula, expressing themselves in one of that language's dialects. The Fula language was purposely written down and recorded in manuscripts; Hampâté Bâ tells us that almost every writer had his own spelling; every *marabout* adopted his own alphabetic system for certain phonemes – 'with the result that a composer or a writer who could not remember his own text very well could no longer read it six months later' (Bâ, 1972). This was a highly paradoxical situation: on the one hand, a vast language community consisting of several million people, and on the other, no written standard of reference or adequate instrument to record a literary oeuvre for distribution beyond the regional horizons, in order to reach the greater community of speakers and potentially literate people. Hampâté Bâ wrote in his own language, but nobody will be able to read him if the schools do not learn how to decode his spelling ...

In the preface to the catalogue of the Hampâté Bâ library, A.I. Sow indicates that he has classified the texts of which 'Hampâté Bâ is himself the author or the reporter, and on the other hand texts dictated by other traditional authors, that he took down in writing, in his capacity as a researcher,' (Sow, 1970:7). These distinctions are fundamental: they enable us to distinguish between a scholarly type of practice, that of the researcher, and the type of practice one would call literary or artistic; between a practice where the text is signed by its subject and one where the subject delegates this signature to another authority, to a 'traditional' author or simply to tradition, without further distinctions, or else to 'science'.

A classification of Hampâté Bâ's works includes:

- Historical or theological essays in collaboration or simply co-signed, as in *L'empire peul du Macina* [Macina's Fulani empire] (1962) or the first version of *Tierno Bokar* (1957);
- Transcriptions of oral and Fula texts, accompanied by the French translation with the collaboration of professional researchers: these include *Koumen* (1961), *Kaïdara* (1969), *L'éclat de la grande étoile* (1974) [The brilliance of the big star];
- Translations of Fula oral texts adapted into French without the originals: *Kaïdara* in the 1978 prose version in French; *Njeddo Dewal* (1985), the unpublished Fula original of which is mentioned in the catalogue of the Bâ collection (Sow, 1970:25);
- *L'étrange destin de Wangrin* (1973), a novel written directly in French that is obviously by Hampâté Bâ alone; and the autobiography that appeared in the year of his death, *Amkoullel, l'enfant peul* (1991);
- Essays adapted from conference papers: *Aspects de la civilisation africaine* (1972)[Aspects of African civilization]; *Jésus vu par un Musulman* (1976) [Jesus as seen by a Muslim];
- A theological and historical essay, *Vie et enseignement de Tierno Bokar, le sage de Bandiagara* (1980) [The life and teachings of Tierno Bokar], which constitutes a new edition of the 1957 publication, carried two signatures, that of M. Cardaire and of A. Hampâté Bâ.

Thus a division is established between scholarly writing inscribed in the critical apparatus of authority-granting institutions, and literary writing proper, which does however retain certain traits of scholarly writing, such as the use of notes in *Wangrin* or in the autobiography, *Amkoullel*. A passageway is thus established between memory and knowledge, and supposedly scientific documents: in the first two text types, Hampâté Bâ is either a local researcher within the context of colonial ethnography (who is obliged to authenticate his discourse by having professional researchers from France present at his side), or the interpreter and the medium of a tradition that is condemned to become a museum object through lack of a public other than that of ethnologists and professional linguists. And yet, during the first two decades of independence there was a definite movement to reappropriate the discourse, demonstrated by the new edition of *Vie et enseignement de Tierno Bokar* (1980), by Fula texts published directly in French and by the recently published English edition (1999) of *The Fortunes of Wangrin*, with an insightful introduction by Abiola Irele. He considers that Hampâté Bâ's exploration

> may well appear summary in some important respects, but [that] it is sufficient to establish Wangrin as the quintessential marginal man, burdened with an ambiguity grounded in his existential condition. (Irele in Hampâté Bâ, 1999: xi)

This movement took place through the mother tongue: French was initially a type of metalanguage used to record the old knowledge of which Hampâté Bâ was the depositary. The author went from writing down historical investigations to the notation of texts of which he was the reporter; he then translated and annotated these texts, and, lastly, submitted them to the reader in French. He is acutely conscious of the fact that preserving tradition is a scientific practice and that a standard spelling as well as a language of reference is needed – what Marcel Diki-Kidiri aptly calls 'double distancing'. Hampâté Bâ then uses his language to practise a type of 'scientific ventriloquism', similar to Wande Abimbola's treatment of the corpus of Yoruba sacred texts, the *fa*. The researcher is already the depositary of the texts that he has produced, but he does not sign them; he assigns them to tradition. Hampâté Bâ goes one step further: French is not only a scientific metalanguage used to record and analyse texts: it becomes the language in which a vision of the world, marked by the colonial experience, may be expressed. This language is that of autobiographical expression, the narrative of one person's adventures in the historical context of the century. The writer does not share this experience with us in Fula. This does not imply that the era of the Fula novelistic narrative will never come, but simply that for the moment there is no tradition of writing about personal, non-lyrical experiences, nor of 'scientific' writing, in the absence of appropriate instruments of reference such as a unilingual dictionary.

The final outcome of this reappropriation of speech, of signing in one's own name, (as indicated by his use of novelistic narratives and by the new edition of his theological essays), may be the wider use of Fula as the theoretical language of linguistics, theology and politics and as the language in which personal experiences are expressed without recourse to the codes of lyrical poetry. This trajectory, tending towards the recovery of a personal text and of individual speech, shows Amadou Hampâté Bâ to be an authentic writer, despite his efforts at disguising himself. His oeuvre concludes with an autobiography full of charm and vivacity, as though, after such a long and full life, he had to give some unity to a corpus of texts that may have seemed disparate, through this childhood narrative. As though it were necessary to specify that narrative fiction should not be considered as truth, note 42 in the book (attributed to the author's 'representative', Bâ, 1991) warns that Wangrin has nothing to do with Amkoullel. And yet, I believe that the story of the swindler-interpreter, the roguish little boy and the mischievous, wise old man are complementary: fiction provides scientific truth in that it proclaims the interpreter to be nothing but a traitor – to which one may add Jean-Paul Sartre's insight, that treason is also literature's point of departure.

Okot p'Bitek (1931–82): Satirizing Tradition

With the exception of Ngugi since he began to write in Gikuyu, examples of writers who are known for their production in a European as well as an African language are indeed few and far between. For reasons indicated above – and which, in Anglophone Africa, are related to the greater importance of African languages in education – there was no obvious reason for writing in two languages. Examples such as that of Kagame, Hampâté Bâ or Rabearivelo are exceptional cases because of the quality of their production. They nevertheless follow an implicit hierarchy: in the end, French is what matters, that is the means by which the writer will be recognized. Each in its own way, the objectives of Kagame's Bantu Catholicism, Hampâté Bâ's black Islam and Rabearivelo's literary cult of the elders are all ultimately French recognition. The objective in English is similar: and yet, by allowing a wider margin for indigenous education, by insisting that the communities take charge of their education themselves, there has been room for the development of Islamic creation in Hausa, for example, or encouragement for a new production in Kiswahili. The fecund ambiguity of the three writers' works, discussed above, is rare in non-Francophone domains. However, it is worth taking a closer look, for the situation in Anglophone Africa is more nuanced than one would have thought.

For instance, there was no hesitation on the part of the Gold Coast's intellectual elite in choosing English, despite a few demonstrations to preserve the honour of Fanti. In East Africa, the first generations of intellectuals acted in a similar way: Jomo Kenyatta wrote his autobiography, *Facing Mount Kenya* (1938) in English, but the political pamphlets intended for his countrymen were always in Gikuyu. Swahili literature developed during the 'fifties on the shores of the Indian Ocean: and yet the greatest Kenyan essayist, Ali Mazrui, came from Mombasa. One of his central arguments was that social stratification in colonial Africa was founded on the mastery of English: he understood a system that he had trouble controlling, as he has told us (Mazrui, 1972; Mazrui, Ali A. & Alamin, 1998). Thus two of the region's and the continent's most eminent thinkers made a conscious choice to write in English.

This rationale was not obvious to everybody and in particular not to a member of the Acoli minority from Northern Uganda. At the beginning of the 'fifties Okot p'Bitek wrote *Lak Tar* (*White Teeth*), the first novel in Acoli, the central dialect of the Luo country. He was very young at the time and his idea was to defend and to illustrate his mother tongue. Thirty years later, his widow wrote that *White Teeth* was the first and only novel written by the late professor, whose reputation was made by the novel. This was during the colonial era and publications in African languages were limited to religion (p'Bitek, 1989a:1). The 1953 text, Okot's first publication, was translated on his return to Uganda in 1981, shortly before his death. Here, we are far removed from the edifying literature produced in other African languages to which we are accustomed. P'Bitek's hero is no Bunyan-inspired pilgrim, but a young man from the north who is forced to go and look for work in the southern plantations to save up enough dowry payment for the parents of his future wife. He works hard, and is exposed to all sorts of insults and prejudices. The descriptions of labour conditions on the plantation, relations between the workers and ethnic tensions are lively and precise, making the novel pleasurable and interesting to read. Okot p'Bitek enjoys the story of these young people and their adventurous spirit; moreover, because he writes in Acoli, he can refer to his people's oral poetry. In situations of conflict, the characters flaunt their *mwoc*, their motto, to give them courage; Okot composes songs to punctuate times of difficulty (1989a:105). The writer was no intellectual or solitary artist; he participated in all aspects of his people's popular culture. He was also something of a sportsman, a member of the 1958 Ugandan football team that was invited to England. He chose to stay on and obtained a degree in social anthropology from Oxford with a study of Acoli and Lango oral literature. Put in charge of adult training in Gulu in the north, he wrote the Acoli version of *Song of Lawino* between 1964 and 1966, which he translated into English and which was published in Nairobi in that latter year. It was very successful as a poem; later, he brought out the (hitherto unpublished) Acoli text in 1969.

His criticisms of various politicians resulted in his expulsion from Uganda. That same year, he became professor at the University of Nairobi, posted in Kisumu on Lake Victoria in the Luo country. He continued his work by publishing a series of songs – *Songs of Ocol* (1970); *Two Songs: Song of Prisoner, Song of Malaya* (1971) and some anthropological studies on religion (p'Bitek, 1980). In addition, he published more Acoli poetry anthologized, translated and annotated (p'Bitek, 1974) with this proviso:

> It is important to stress that these are my own translations and I believe that there can be other versions. It is for this reason that the vernacular had to be included, to give other translators and scholars the opportunity to criticise my translations and also to attempt their own.... I learnt many of these songs as I grew up.... From the elder generation of poets and musicians, the late Yona Ocwaa, Omal Adok, Too, Goya and Oryema Erenayo, I learnt the older songs, and they deserve special thanks. From 1960 to 1963 I carried out research among the Acoli and Lango. (Okot p'Bitek, 1974:164)

Whether playing football, directing the company of Uganda's cultural centre or following a university career, Okot p'Bitek never cut himself off from young people's culture, their songs and dances; nor did he distance himself from Northern Uganda's popular culture, either in his research or his other activities. This enterprise as an organizer of cultural life was expressed in Acoli as well as in English. He defended the right of the 'minority' languages (such as Acoli) to exist in the face of English and Kiswahili. He also understood, unlike many others, that the best way to defend a language was to create quality works in the field of fiction as well as in lyric poetry. He did not restrict himself to making a contribution as an anthropologist: with *Song of Lawino* he created a text that is a wonderful illustration of the ambiguity of a production in African languages, as regards means and discourse:

> All but a very few lines of *Song of Lawino* were written in Acoli originally and later translated into English. For most parts of the poem, the translation was an after-

thought. When Okot was trying to publish the Acoli version, he translated a small extract for a writer's conference in Nairobi. The enthusiastic reception of this persuaded him to translate the whole poem..... Okot's songs are not songs in any literal sense. You cannot sing them. They are not simply a written version of Acoli songs. Acoli songs do not grow to book length. They are one of two verses repeated with musical accompaniment. They are not written down under one person's authorship. They are sung and adapted by singer after singer, and each singer is free to create in his own way and change the song to fit current events or refer to his own girl friend. They do not use rhyme or the regular rhythm used in *Wer pa Lawino*.

So it is possible to exaggerate the influence of Acoli tradition on Okot's poems. From Western tradition he takes the idea of individual authorship, of spoken verse, of rhyme, of division into chapters, of the printed word.... Okot has adapted a traditional form to new conditions of performance, rather than created a new form. The writer chose to make a very literal translation of *Song of Lawino*. The main differences between the two versions are the rearrangement of the order of certain sections within the chapters, the filling out of some descriptions of things unfamiliar to readers of the English version, and the dropping from the English version of some details which are in the Acoli original. (Héron, in Okot p'Bitek, 1972:8)

On the pretext that the original is in Acoli, it would thus be a mistake to claim that this song reveals a traditional work; yet the paradox is that the discourse of the central character, who speaks in her own name, Lawino, sounds incontestably traditionalist. The ambiguity is complete: Okot p'Bitek writes in Acoli in a pseudo-traditional form, translating into English a text that exalts the traditional values of the Acoli women. Above all, he gives a precise and biting satire of the customs of the new Westernized generation:

Listen Ocol, my old friend/ the ways of your ancestors/are good,/Their customs are solid/And not hollow/They are not thin, not easily breakable/They cannot be blown away/By the winds/Because their roots reach deep into the soil.

I do not understand/The ways of foreigners/But I do not despise their customs/ Why should you despise yours? (Okot p'Bitek, 1972:41)

Lawino, the abandoned wife, wittily takes it out on her rival, Clementine, but it is Ocol, her husband, who provokes her anger. Lawino is the daughter of a chief, she comes from a prestigious lineage; if Ocol wants to take another wife, he may do so: why does he need to insult Lawino?

My husband rejects me/Because, he says/I have no Christian name....

My husband has read at Makerere University/He has read deeply and widely,/But if you ask him a question/He says ...

Even if he tried/To answer my questions/I would not understand/What he was saying/Because the language he speaks/Is different from mine/So that even if he/Spoke to me in Acoli/I would still need an interpreter/My husband says/Some of the answers/Cannot be given in Acoli/Which is a primitive language/And is not rich enough/To express his deep wisdom./He says the Acoli language/Has very few words/It is not like the white man's language/Which is rich and very beautiful/A language fitted for discussing deep thoughts. (Okot p'Bitek, 1972:87–8)

Lawino's inability to speak another language than Acoli marks her inferiority:

And I cannot tune the radio/Because I do not hear/Swahili or Luganda (Okot p'Bitek, 1972:49)

Lawino is hurt and humiliated; she does not contest her husband's rights, but she refuses to be insulted; she may even accept being abandoned. She is the incarnation of a certain form of dignity, which probably earned the text its popularity. She does not scorn what she does not understand, but asks not to be despised in turn. This attitude enables her to note with some irony the contrast between Ocol's preaching about national construction through inclusive tribal union and his refusal to enter his own brother's house. Political speeches incite her to lucid irony: 'The stomach seems to be/A powerful force/For joining political parties' (1970:108). Lawino is opposed to accelerated assimilation, which produces individuals who despise villagers, are unsure of themselves and incapable of practising what they preach. Lawino's message does not go beyond this satire; her wit is well served by the type of 'Acolized' English that p'Bitek was able to invent without lapsing into hermeticism, even if the text is sometimes only fully comprehensible to the Acoli people.

Okot p'Bitek the satirical poet creates characters who criticize the times they live in, while illustrating them with lively wit. Lawino is the prototype of a new kind of heroine who, during the independence era, embodied the main African cultural and moral claim: dignity. What is more, she does so from a woman's perspective, a 'minor within society' among the Acoli-Luo as among so many others, as an illiterate woman – which does not mean that she is uneducated, as many of Ocol's emulators seem to forget. A new version of the Acoli song translated by Taban lo Liyong was published in 2001 under the title *The Defence of Lawino*. What he calls 'Submission thirteen' is a good summary of Lawino's predicament: 'If my husband permits me to scour away the film of forgetfulness, the afflictions from apemanship; allows me to display the beauty of African culture before him and apologizes to the ancestors, he may become whole again' (2001:vi).

The songs that came after *Lawino* were neither written nor published in Acoli, but directly in English: the songs of Ocol, Malaya (the prostitute), the prisoner and lastly the soldier (unpublished). Although Okot p'Bitek's oeuvre was born in colonial Uganda, it embodied a claim to dignity that was welcomed by the whole of Africa, thanks to his skilful play on the obvious weaknesses of the new intellectuals. Like Sidi, Soyinka's heroine in *The Lion and the Jewel*, Lawino refuses to be taken in by pseudo-modern zealots. A quarter of a century later, we can only pay tribute to her lucidity!

Translating One's Culture: Jomo Kenyatta (1893–1978)

Okot p'Bitek's intellectual aim was not explicitly to create a mixed literature: it was rather to use Acoli and the central Luo culture as a point of departure for the presentation of the English version of an African culture. In an essay entitled 'African Aesthetics, the Acoli Example' (1986), Okot p'Bitek uses Acoli concepts to elaborate a vision of the world in English, one that is founded solely on these Acoli categories. In his opinion, the translation effort is part of a larger system of explanations and adaptations into English of the Acoli world conception:

> Now who can, then, judge such creative works? Who can meaningfully, announce the phrase *myel ma ber*, good dance, *wer ma mit*, sweet song; *ot ma ber*, good house? Who is the critic of the expressive works of the man of traditions? (Okot p'Bitek, 1986:37)

During the 'sixties Okot's oeuvre took on a militant tone and a rather controversial emphasis; and yet few writers studied oral literature as thoroughly as he did. English helped him to present his people's ethical and aesthetic conceptions. Okot p'Bitek never turned the language of his ancestors into a fetish; he used it up to a certain point and then left it behind. The important thing was not to relinquish the Luo-Acoli conception of the world. This form of ethnic nationalism, expressed with some extremism in assertions such as: 'It is only the participants in a culture who can pass judgement on it' (p'Bitek 1986:37), does not, however, bring into question his writings in English. His contradictions are insoluble, because of a cultural essentialism that the former anthropologist would maybe not have supported theoretically to its most absurd conclusion: how does one express the essence of Acoli culture in English? Why not admit that he had created another culture?

Translating his culture rather than his language was what Jomo Kenyatta attempted in *Facing Mount Kenya* (1938), less than a generation before Okot p'Bitek's first text.

> As a Gikuyu myself, I have carried them in my head for many years, since people who have no written records to rely on learn to make a retentive memory do the work of libraries. (Kenyatta, 1938:xvi)
>
> Following the tribal custom, I had to pass through the several stages of initiation along with my age group, *kehiomwere*, and can therefore speak from personal experience of the rites and ceremonies. (Kenyatta, 1938:xix)
>
> I can therefore speak as a representative of my people with personal experience of many different aspects of their life. (Kenyatta, 1938:xx)

By participating in the rites of his age group with his comrades, Jomo Kenyatta is also a witness: he speaks from experience about what he knows and yet he distances himself from this experience. He is talking about *their* life, not about his own. This ambiguity is marked by the permanent recourse to Gikuyu, into which language each reference is translated: Mount Kenya, *Kere Nyaga* ... Jomo Kenyatta seems not to be able to decide whether he is an anthropologist dealing with Mount Kenya or a Gikuyu narrating the myths around the sacred mountain called *Kere Nyaga*.

> If language is what enables self-definition and each language contains within it a self-contained *'lieu'* of the untranslatable idiom, Jomo Kenyatta would seem to be occupying at least two places at once with his constant movement between English and Gikuyu. This occupation of two *'lieus'* [sic] at once leads to a confusion of the autobiographic subject. Kenyatta seems to be attempting to describe the Kikuyu self in English but in using both Kenyatta is constantly reinscribing himself within the sites of Gikuyu even as he writes in English. (Wiley, 1991:8)

This precise analysis of a text from the 'thirties highlights the difficulty of posing the problem of the language of cultural creation: while English is the metalanguage of cultural analysis, and although the text is written in English, the reader is incessantly referred back to Gikuyu. Could this book have been written in Gikuyu? Probably not, and for the very reasons that complicated Ngugi's task forty years later: the absence of a reference dictionary to translate the concepts used by the author, and the absence of a narrative prose tradition other than that of the Bible. This autobiographical essay hesitates between two languages, but without ever mentioning the possibility of writing in Gikuyu. Later, during the political struggle, Jomo Kenyatta would write in Gikuyu, but initially he did not think about his political role in that language. These hesitations are fascinating; the language division takes place in a functional way and we are asked to accept it as such. Linguistic consciousness must be of a pragmatic nature. Any type of audience or text imposes its own language. And yet, this well-ordered functionality is contrary to everything that has just been said: an author who no longer writes in his language, no longer translates it, wants to translate his culture or even retreat into it, while detaching himself from it at the same time. How can two languages make themselves heard in one text? Which brings us back to Rabearivelo's problem....

Amos Tutuola's Linguistic Unconsciousness (1923–97)

Texts that are a little too carefully written in Africanized English, such as Gabriel Okara's *The Voice* (1965) do not gather general support. There is probably a need for strange texts that refer back to what I have called the total opacity of linguistic consciousness, in which the text itself appears to be the result of a language mixture and not the result of an elaborated reflection: what may be called an inspired makeshift job.

Such is the case of Amos Tutuola. When *The Palm Wine Drinkard* appeared in 1952, it marked the birth of Nigerian literature as well as the start of a long debate on Tutuola's language, and finally on the place he was supposed to occupy in this literature. Today, the case has been heard, while its originality was confirmed by the work of the authors who followed in his wake. Another Acoli writer, Taban lo Liyong (whose imaginative style has often been compared to Tutuola), describes it with some precision as a calculated result: 'Is he ungrammatical? Yes. But James Joyce is more ungrammatical than Tutuola' (Taban lo Liyong in Lindfors, 1975:115)

How were critics supposed to react to the syntax of a text that could be described as grammatically incorrect or acrobatic or simply faulty, by comparison to school norms? Reject it in the name of a more pedagogical vision of literature? Approve of it, with the understanding that this personal dialect might be a literary innovation, the written transposition of a certain Nigerian or even Yoruba way of speaking English? For a long time, Nigerian critics were of the first opinion:

> From the 'portrayal' it is clear that the author is not an academic man and therefore I submit that it is not a high literary standard that has attracted so many European and American readers. But I think there is another reason. Most Englishmen, and perhaps Frenchmen, are pleased to believe all sorts of fantastic tales about Africa, a continent of which they are profoundly ignorant. The 'extraordinary books' of Mr Tutuola (which most undoubtedly contain some of the unbelievable things in our folklores) will just suit the temper of his European readers as they seem to confirm their concepts of Africa. (Afolayan 1971, quoted in Lindfors, 1975:41)

Hostility became less intense in the face of the concerted offensive by literary critics and especially writers (in contrast to the academics) and support from the linguists. For critics like Gerald Moore and Taban lo Liyong, the essential element was the originality of the proposed verbal universe. In this sense Tutuola is truly extraordinary: his drunkard's quest for his palm wine tapster is a marvellous journey, filled with unusual situations and encounters that are closely related to the oral narrative, while being very far removed from its conditions of reconstruction: Tutuola's hero speaks in the first person, which the storyteller almost never does. Only the Sotho warrior speaks in his own name to sing his own praises; the storyteller, especially when taking us on fantastic adventures, does not often mention his own name. Tutuola's narrator amuses and interests us by staging himself in adventures worthy of Hellzapoppin. Moreover, he uses an odd language, the syntax of which sometimes escapes us, and which should not serve as a model for schoolchildren. A. Afolayan's (1971) essay provides a convincing demonstration of the Yoruba characteristics of Tutuola's English: syntactic or lexical *calques*, the adaptation of the English word order into Yoruba, and so many other elements that lead us to conclude that Tutuola's English represents the language of Yoruba speakers and can even be situated at a specific competence level:

> Tutuola's English is Yoruba English in the sense that it is representative of the English of the Yoruba users at a point on a scale of bilingualism.... His English is that of the Yoruba user, not of the average educated user but of generally the user with post-primary education at approximately the level of present-day Secondary Class Four (Afolayan 1971 in Lindfors, 1975:198)

Critics are well aware of the bitty, unsatisfactory nature of this sort of response to the question. Style is not a simple matter of language level, and language use has to be studied in the context of the Yoruba village in today's world. It is exactly this mixture of borrowings from folklore and totally contemporary elements (such as vinyl records or planes) that lends something magical and fantastical to the work of this author who makes light of the limits attributed to each domain. His world (like his language and like the tales he borrows from the Yoruba tradition) is a makeshift one.

> A lot of the vigour and freshness Gerald Moore and others see in Tutuola's language derives from his original Yoruba and the subsequent interplay between the two languages, Yoruba and English and not so much from Tutuola's refusal 'to be merely correct'. One may even suggest that Tutuola thinks he is correct when he writes. (Afolayan 1971, in Lindfors, 1975:206)

This is the definition of the opaque naïvety of linguistic consciousness: Tutuola thinks that his writing is correct. He is correct because Anglophones, whether they are mother-tongue or second-language speakers, understand him: in fact, he is only adapting the field of the norm to the new frontiers set down by his own texts. Today (as I indicated above) the case has been heard: Ben Okri, the 1991 Booker Prize winner for *The Famished Road*, is described as Tutuola's descendant (Felgine, 1992). Tutuola cannot write in Yoruba: as he told me himself, his rare attempts to do so ended in total failure for himself and for the handful of readers of the texts in question. What is more, he has nothing to say about his method or his literary aim: he finds himself in that uncertain space where the identity of a new Africa and especially Nigeria is still being played out. More and more artists and intellectuals are joining him, incessantly swelling the numbers of those who admire his success but are unable to explain it!

Conclusion

Jean-Joseph Rabearivelo wanted to write in Malagasy and French at the same time, to unite the two languages; both would have maintained their individual nature, but each would have consisted of the other's substance. The fusion would however have been to the advantage of French. Alexis Kagame and Okot p'Bitek wrote in their own languages while trying to translate their beauty into European languages. Okot p'Bitek finally gave up trying to write in his own language, but continued to translate it, as illustrated by the belated translation of his novel in 1981. Alexis Kagame never stopped writing in Kinyarwanda and tried to render its beauty in French. The same can be said of Hampâté Bâ, a collector of Fula literature, but also a poet who translated his own texts. Such works are truly 'digraphic': they provide us with two texts, enabling us to appreciate the translation effort. Other works are also situated at the threshold between cultures, but produce only one text, punctuated at times by references to another subterranean or unconscious text. Such is the case of Jomo Kenyatta's 'autobiographical' essay. Tutuola's case is stranger and more innovatory: without attempting to do so, he invented a new language, a type of Nigerian English modelled on Yoruba, which anticipated the translations of Okot p'Bitek and recalled those of Rabearivelo. Literary creation depends intimately on the plasticity of European languages and on their malleable capacity to give an account of the African cultural experience: this was the central question asked by Jean-Joseph Rabearivelo and of all the authors referred to in this chapter, whether consciously or not. This question is at the centre of African literary creation: Africans can always borrow from other languages, but they must create new language forms. As regards contemporary poetry and theatre, the question remains. In fiction, Tutuola showed one of the possible ways to create a personal language, all the more felicitously as there was nothing systematic in an attempt directed by the power of unconsciousness!

7
Towards a New Poetic Discourse?

Poetic consciousness is first and foremost linguistic consciousness: the keenest consciousness of the language situation must be sought within poetry. Plausible as this statement may seem, it is not the case in every language; one may even say that it almost never happens in French, except in the case of Senghor. His devotees and imitators have either forgotten his words or take them for granted: a case of double recklessness. The result is a strange, but interesting difference between African poetry in French and African poetry in English on this particular theme of the linguistic consciousness, intrinsic as it is to the writer's entire poetic conception.

> Within the major genres of literature, the poetic genre has perhaps been the most problematic for our writers, given the peculiar historical and cultural factors which determined the emergence and course of development of modern African Literature. It seems that within the specific genre of poetry, all the problems of a literature which arose from the womb of colonial society and is still struggling to free itself from the ambiguous legacies of its origins, achieve the most concentrated form. This is not the place to go into these problems. The essential point is that for each individual writer and incidentally for our collective literary development, the colonial legacy and its most problematic manifestation – the umbilical ties to metropolitan European traditions – must be transcended by the forging of a distinctive voice and a demonstrable rootedness in our own realities and experience. (Jeyifo, Introduction to Osundare's *Songs of the Marketplace,* 1987, 2nd edition:viii)

The Music of Conversation

Within the literary institution, written poetry occupies a central position, and yet poets are not accorded public success. In our world, the true poet is not a public figure. The writer is attracted to this discrete, demanding genre by the direct contact between language and experience. But expression and self-expression are not enough: means are also important, as well as avoiding the pitfalls of repetition, platitude and rhetoric. African poetry written in European languages was born in the twentieth century and started developing in the 'thirties, but cannot seem to free itself from what poetry has become. Octavio Paz expresses it very well:

> I still believe that the confusion between poetry and prose is a fatal one.... Prose is the written word and poetry is rhythmic speech. Discourse is the most perfect prose expression, which is why the militant and ideological poetry of our time was and still is discourse. It is a written literature that, although often populist, is not popular at all. Poetry does not feed on written prose, but on the rhythms of daily speech or, to quote Eliot, on the music of conversation. (Paz, 1987:385)

This text, based on an analysis of the differences between oral and written forms so frequently encountered in works on African literature, merits careful consideration. Prose is the written word: the written narrative may stem from its oral counterpart; the novel would be yet another elaboration. Contrary to the superficial point of view, discourse – the type used on a platform – is often a written genre: its reconstruction is oral, while its composition is written. Militancy and ideology are metalinguistic constructions calling for concepts (book-based by definition) that have been elaborated into a system. And yet, the rhythms of daily speech are those of interpersonal exchange, whether of conversation, secrets, quarrels or prayers. That is what should be set to music: poetry feeds on this verbal substance. It does not transcribe it in the manner of an ethnologist, but seeks to give it rhythm, to distinguish it from everyday speech by specific signs. Every line requires that one catches one's breath and allows the text to breathe. The graphic disposition is not just for decoration, but also has a rhythmic use. Assonances and alliterations may create rhythms out of phonic matter. The poet's task is to play on the entire keyboard of possibilities in the knowledge that he can no longer use formulae from past centuries (fixed metres, rhymes) except in parody or for archaic effect. Poets are all well aware of this; but what about the poet whose 'daily speech' occurs in a language that differs from his poetic speech, and who composes poetry in English, French or Portuguese? Octavio Paz and T.S. Eliot's minimal (but profoundly true) definition of poetic speech in terms of conversation highlights some of the difficulties peculiar to poetic speech in Africa today.

> The extent to which we regard poetry as tied to this kind of intimacy depends on our conception of poetry. It does certainly seem to be true that deep and intimate feelings connect us, throughout our lives, to childhood and family interactions, and at the present time in most parts of Africa this takes us back to the primary socialization of the mother tongue.... In other words, if there is a viable way of composing poetry in a second language it is likely to be one which employs practical linguistic experience in other texts current in that society. (Haynes, 1987:115)

Which 'other texts' are current in society? Haynes (1987:114) observes that: 'At the present time, in many Anglophone African countries, there are relatively few current English texts available to the majority of the people; and this is a definite limitation from the point of view of composition in English.' We are thus faced with a multilingual situation as one of the fundamental determining factors of poetic communication in Africa on the level of the creator as well as that of the reader.

We know that we are dealing here with a situation of 'diglossia' – of differentiated language distribution according to the situation of social communication. This distribution involves organizing functions into a hierarchy. A division takes place between noble functions (education, culture) and the most trivial of functions (commerce, work), between public and private domains. Numerous cases come to mind, but it should be noted that the practice of European languages is firstly an urban one (Ngalasso, 1988) and that situations may vary considerably, according to whether it is French, English or Portuguese competing with an important lingua franca, such as Lingala in Kinshasa, Hausa in Kano, or the multitude of languages spoken in Abidjan or Libreville. And yet, like electric music, written poetry is an urban genre. Yoruba songs are sung in Lagos, Lingala songs are sung in Kinshasa, while similar productions in African languages are harder to find in Abidjan, Libreville or Lomé. Written poetry cannot be unaware of these situations or these other texts – poets know this better than anybody else! Wole Soyinka knows that poetry can be appreciated in translation, even though he questions the mechanism of the mysterious 'black box' that manages to reconstruct this experience. He is pleased about the opportunity to use a great language of communication:

> If however what comes out is in English it means I am very much at home in that language. It's not an effort and so it comes out, it's written down in English. It comes out in English, alright. There is also that political condition in which we find ourselves in Africa having been heirs to more than one language and I think we should absolutely celebrate in our work even this very heritage of dual, triple, no matter how many languages. I think many, many, many Nigerian and African writers poets feel the same. We have many national languages in Africa, I might be cut off from the poets of Ghana, from Kofi Awoonor, even from the poetry of Garuba who mostly speaks Hausa. I enjoyed the lyrics of poetry of the Yoruba writers, the very densely textured poetic prose of Fagunwa, which I have translated in English also. How do I communicate with a Mozambican, should I not share his most intimate experiences, the passionate expression which have received such concision in that tight medium we call poetry? (Wole Soyinka, in conversation with AR, Abeokuta, July 1989)

When it comes to imported languages, the dominating attitude is a pragmatic one: multilingualism is accepted, or even surpassed, as it is considered an opportunity. Tchicaya U'Tamsi shares this view:

> I've got no complex about writing in French, but in the end I cannot deny that there is a cultural problem. I've said that writing in French is not the result of an inner choice, but the product of an external obligation. I'm assuming an environment. I tell myself that the rift is a real one. I keep my revolt for other tragedies. (Tchicaya U'Tamsi, in Maunick, 1975:135)

Thus, contemporary poetry in written form is usually composed in European languages and the prevailing attitude of linguistic consciousness is a pragmatic one. It is left to the writer's skills to make the new language obey his command. Nonetheless, the relation between the poet and his society is laid down in terms of a break, which is still true today:

> The language of the school was irrevocably European, the African language was a vernacular (in the Latin sense of the word: slave tongue). Uncountable penalties awaited vernacular speakers, ranging from a dozen strokes of the cane, to a forced memorization of large portions of the Bible, to in the case of 'perpetual offenders' suspension from school. (In the present writer's school, a student was once punished for whistling in Yoruba.) Our writer therefore grew up not only unable to speak his mother tongue but intensely ashamed of it. He spoke English, French, or Portuguese in an affected European accent and relished his inability to pronounce African names correctly. When a writer cannot write his name in his language, how can one expect him to write a book in it so his people can hear his voice? (Osundare, 1986:16)

Do all the resources that the creator is unable to find in his own language or community exist in another language or culture? How does one give new shape to an experience at the outset of literature in an adopted language? The first attempts may come across as rather clumsy:

> There is a charge often raised against African poets, that of aping other models, particularly the European. This charge is of course frequently true, even to the extent of outright plagiarism, and covers the entire spectrum of stylistic development: twenty years ago it was still possible to read poems of serious intent which began 'Gather ye hibiscus while ye may', while today we are more commonly inundated with re-creations of Waste Lands of tropical humidity. Dadaisms abound both in their founding innocence and in the revivalist adaptations hallowed by the 'beat' generation of America. Even the perverse phase of European decadence has not failed to diffuse its 'poisonous ecstasy' through situations clearly shaped in a far different clime, nurtured in the perpetual season of revolution. (Soyinka, 1975:14)

One may take pleasure from the instrument to which one has access without knowing how to draw new sounds and meanings from it. The pragmatism of linguistic consciousness is no guarantee of lucid poetic consciousness. This is an important point: the essential difference between the poets and language 'go-betweens' under discussion is exactly this totally new notion of pragmatism: the linguistic rift is no longer experienced in an intense or even tragic way, but simply accepted. Jean-Joseph Rabearivelo, Alexis Kagame and Amadou Hampâté Bâ used most of their creative energy to organize language encounters through translation – a painful enterprise, as they surely knew that the survival of their oeuvre depended on its Francophone part. Creation used to be a dialogue between two languages. It is no longer the case for the poets we are dealing with here: sometimes we don't even know what their mother tongue is. Which African language did Tchicaya U'Tamsi speak, for example? The creative project is no longer the encounter of two languages, but the mastering of a European language. They share this ambition with all the other poets, but many have neither their talent nor their cultural resources.

> [Lastly] something should be said about the concept of the modern in African poetry. In a recent essay Lewis Nkosi has written interestingly on this topic, and specifically on many of the poets included here. His conclusions are very close to those which have guided us in excluding the 'pioneers poets' of Anglophone Africa (Dei Anang, Armattoe, Osadebay, Vilakazi, Dhlomo, etc.), whilst including many Francophone poets of the same generation. Nkosi writes: 'Under the heading of the moderns, we shall, therefore, be discussing a variety of African poets, with a heterogeneity of styles and techniques: in the end what seems to unite them, and equally what seems to separate them from the 'pioneer poets' is a fundamental preoccupation with technique as important both in itself as well as providing the essential means for expressing a radically transformed cultural and political situation. In contrast what seems to have absorbed all the energies of the 'pioneer poets' were certain themes they regarded as urgent, method was left to look after itself.... Lack of fresh and original approach made the verse dull and uninspired.' A major concern with craft is inseparable from real achievement in poetry. A poet writing in a European language, even if he wishes to make a counter statement against the nation which brought it, must at least be aware of the current state of poetic form and diction in that language. The African poets of negritude displayed such an awareness of the state of French poetry (including that of such black poets as Damas and Césaire) as well as being more aware of Langston Hughes and the Harlem poets than their Anglophone contemporaries were. Hence they were able to find an authentic voice for their poetry. (Moore & Beier 1984:23)

There is no better description of and introduction to comparative studies of poetry in European languages. The Anglophone production proposes a convenient division of historical moments. The works of some of these forgotten pioneers will be examined successively, before studying the output of the innovators from the 'sixties who declared the autonomy of poetic language in their creations, without any speeches. Lastly, we will mention the present generation, which has appealed for renewed political solidarity, based on a re-reading of its tradition and a considerable extension of its literary references since the end of the 'seventies. On the other hand, it is much more difficult, if not impossible, to classify the periods within the Francophone domain with some clarity, because of Senghor's dominating influence on poetry for the past half century. He imposed a theory and a practice of poetic creation and gave poetry a status that greatly influenced French production until the present day. Only Tchicaya U'Tamsi's work offers another model and challenges L.S. Senghor's theoretical framework, without attempting to impose something other than the individualism of a creator who shows solidarity with his people instead of posing as their guide.

The Pioneers of Anglophone Poetry

The important emphasis on publications in the African languages made Anglophone fiction and poetry a rare occurrence before the 'fifties. South Africa's H.I.E. Dhlomo and S.T. Plaatje and the Gold Coast's J.E. Casely-Hayford are the only names that spring to mind. Before the 1952 publication of Amos Tutuola's *Palm Wine Drinkard*, which naturally reflected on the disaster of his compatriots' language prowess, no Nigerian published any book of English poetry or fiction. Journalism and politics absorbed all the available energy: the two important writers were Nkrumah and Kenyatta. In South Africa, the only poem representing black Anglophone poetry was Herbert Dhlomo's forty-page oeuvre, 'The Valley of a Thousand Hills'. For the first time, Bantu mythology was given its rightful place. The poetry of the other ethnic groups did not distinguish itself as African, even though, within African languages, poetry is one of the major genres. In South Africa, Vilakazi or Jolobe's works bear witness to the creation of a poetry tormented by issues of imitation and the difficulties of finding one's own language. How should one go about inventing written poetry? What is written poetry? Should one set oneself a metric framework? Invent prosodic rules, possibly borrowed from English poetry? Should one not 'versify' in African languages? The debate also raged amongst the pioneers of poetry in English. J.P. Clark-Bekederemo, a collector and the translator of *Ozidi's Saga* (1977), as well as an excellent poet and a penetrating critic, analysed the case of one of these African pioneers, Dennis Osadebay, using the example of *Africa Sings* (1962), one of the first anthologies of poetry published in Nigeria. It consists of some one hundred texts previously published in newspapers, and thus known to and often appreciated by the educated public. According to Clark, the choice of words creating an antique feel for the readers, the supposedly poetic inversions, the hackneyed images, the catch-all epithets were supposed to be the obvious signs of poetic style. This communication with the public was also based on the cult of common sense and honest moderation, the supreme values of this educated class; the poet confesses that he 'isn't looking for wealth, pomp or worldly power' and that his only aspiration is to 'breathe the gift of God's air' while able to 'take shelter from the elements' (Clark in Ricard, 1975a:102).

> Thus, when Africans began to write poetry in the English language, they had before them as models the hymnal verses of Christian worship, with their traditional sentiments, standard rhymes, and regular rhythms, as well as the poetry of English Romanticism. The determining impact of a conditioning to this kind of literary fare is well illustrated by the productions of the first generation of English-speaking West African poets in the years before the Second World War and in its immediate aftermath; in the poems of writers such as Raphael Armattoe, Gladys Caseley-Hayford, and Michael Dei-Anang in Ghana, Abioseh Nicol in Sierra Leone, and Denis Osadebay and Mabel Imoukhuede in Nigeria. (Irele, 2001:171)

These traits can also be found in other poets of that period. For instance, in his only anthology, *Deep Down the Blackman's Mind* (1954), Raphael Armattoe (1913–53), an Anglophone poet and a nationalist politician from Togo, tells us about his childhood dreams and, while appealing to black intellectuals, entrusts us with the secret that man is not ungrateful. Moreover, many of his texts have French titles: *'Les vieux colons'* ['The old colonists'] and *'Grandeur d'âme d'un noir'* ['A black man's generosity of spirit'], which does not suggest anything poetically original! Armattoe has certainly been freed of the straitjacket of strict versification and at times knows how to give up grouping into stanzas, but there is a great reduction in formal inventiveness. This type of 'poetry with a message' seems outmoded, despite a few successful evocations of old Togo and of Palimé, the poet's birthplace.

The most outdated oeuvre is probably that of Michael Dei-Anang (1959). *Africa Speaks*, with a preface by Nkrumah, was republished several times up to 1964. The banality of Dei-Anang's only work is rather distressing. It is divided into four sections according to theme, ranging from national, personal, or general to epitaphs. The titles to the texts are obvious enough: words from the national anthem, 'The Star of Ghana', 'My Race', 'Africa Speaks'. It also contains an essay on poetry in Africa, an attempt at analysing the condition of the poet in a bilingual situation and comparing Anglophones to Francophones.

> The African writer of today must be prepared to make a stand in the face of two vital and conflicting issues. He should either develop his powers of expression through traditional modes with their natural advantages of freedom and sincerity – a freedom that of course brings with it the double risks of parochialism and economic constraint. Alternatively he should develop his powers of expression in a foreign language to the point where his 'African-ness' dissolves into the penetrating but essentially foreign atmosphere of the stranger's way of thought. French African poets seem to have achieved this with little effort. It is odd however that today they appear to be reacting quite violently against its effects, and in so doing, reveal to us the impermanent and unnatural situation in which they find themselves. One suspects, indeed, that the ability to speak or write a foreign language better than one's own is not so soul-satisfying as it at first appears. It may well be therefore that the achievement of perfection in a foreign language, even where it is feasible, does not in itself satisfy the truly creative or native genius. (Dei Anang 1959:xii)

This text, which reveals the 'essentialist' vision of being African, is related to Senghor's conception of there being some untranslatable contents, while at the same time displaying feelings of inferiority when it comes to mastering a foreign language and creating a poetic language. These old formulae have run out of steam: in 1964, the same year as the third edition of this text, *Rediscovery*, the first book of a young Ghanaian poet, George Awoonor-Williams (1935–), was published in Ibadan. 'African-ness' is seen as a living process; the foreign language is mastered rather than appropriated for expressing experiences that echo the themes of Ewe poetry, which Kofi Awoonor (his new name) knows so well. A new type of Anglophone poetry has been born; the autonomous practice of poetry has begun to establish itself in Ibadan, and this movement will have a profound impact on all literature in English. The naïve idea that expression in French comes effortlessly to Francophone poets now gives way to the conviction that the production of literature is the condition of freedom of expression, and that the dialogue with universal poetry is one of the conditions of being successful.

In 1957, Ulli Beier founded the journal *Black Orpheus*; 1958 saw the creation of *The Horn*, a new revue directed by J.P. Clark-Bekederemo and Abiola Irele. Mbari published translations by Tchicaya U'Tamsi and Rabearivelo, the first books of Dennis Brutus and Christopher Okigbo, and Wole Soyinka's first plays. At the beginning of the 'sixties, the generation that had studied at Ibadan University set about establishing a Nigerian literature and original poetry in English in Nigeria and in Africa.

In his introduction to J.P. Clark-Bekederemo's *Collected Plays and Poems, 1958–1988* (1991:xv), Abiole Irele (former co-editor on the board of *New Horn*) gives us an in-depth historical perspective on this turning point:

> Clark-Bekederemo's work stands out in this respect. What is more, it can be said to have assumed a specific historic significance in the evolution of Nigerian, and indeed, African poetry in English, for it is indisputable that his early efforts were central to both the thematic reorientation and profound transformation of idiom that led to the decisive advance that the new poetry came to represent. (Irele 1991, in Irele, 2001:172)

Asserting Autonomous Poetry

Christopher Okigbo

The dominant trait of the new poets, especially Wole Soyinka and Christopher Okigbo (1932–67), is their search for a specific poetic language through which they can translate their experience (Udoyeop, 1973:134). Some thought they had found it in the mythologization of their physical and moral environment. Christopher Okigbo attempts to combine Catholic rites and Igbo ceremonies, while Wole Soyinka invents a mythological Yoruba site and a whole new poetic ceremony for *Idanre*. This meticulous research resulted in erudite, even hermetic poetry that distanced itself from the poetic rhetoric of previous public versifiers. Few of them expressed themselves as plainly as Christopher Okigbo who, according to Ali Mazrui, declared at Makerere University: 'I don't read my poems to non-poets' (Mazrui, 1971:69). A new generation started gathering around *Black Orpheus* and Ibadan's Mbari club. What they had in common was a university education and a need to establish themselves in the field of poetry written in English. They had read T. S. Eliot and Ezra Pound; they knew that the language of poetry had to be at once mythical and universal. Mythology and ritual provided them with the means to transform their own experience. However, the uninitiated reader of Christopher Okigbo may find his poetry something of an ordeal. The pastoral simplicity of 'Song of the Forest, Based on Virgil', one of the first poems published in *Four Canzones* (1961) is quite far removed from the work in 'Fragments out of the Deluge' taken from *Limits* (1964), which brings in Sumerian and Egyptian mythologies. The poet chooses a deliberately inventive language; metric regularity is replaced by breathing pace, lending the poem a natural rhythm. It is conceived as a progression along the lines of Wordsworth's '*Prelude*' or the works of Ezra Pound, from whom Okigbo borrows a certain poetic diction as well as some imagery. Like Pound, he needs a whole arsenal of mythical material to embody his specific experience, to make his expressions universal. Like Ezra Pound's *She*, the Idoto mermaid in *Heavensgate* (1962) incarnates eternal female beauty. Okigbo also borrowed Pound's idea that the poet must remain independent of political power (Udoyeop, 1973:134), which did not prevent him from enlisting in the Biafran army. Okigbo's last texts (he died in 1967) were poems anthologized as *Path of Thunder* (1968) that help us understand the background to his commitment:

> O mother mother Earth, unbind me; let this be
> my last testament; let this be
> The ram's hidden wish to the sword the sword's
> secret prayer to the scabbard – ('Elegy for Alto', Okigbo, 1986:99)

His personal experience merges with national events and government failures that led to civil war at the beginning of 1967. The texts are elegies with great emotional strength in their direct and unpretentious wording, uncluttered by the numerous classical references of previous texts. Okigbo exerted a lot of influence on Anglophone poetry, especially with his consideration of poetry as a vocation: he lived only for poetry, and did a number of jobs before becoming an officer in Biafra. He does not envisage his own death in his texts: rather, this is sensed as a tragic outcome, a presentiment of the 'road of thunder' taken by Nigerian history. In his texts, the poet intervenes in the third person in an effort to create a type of universal speech that calls up all cultural heritages. The reader may have difficulty in grasping what the poet is attempting to achieve, but his rigour commands admiration, and has provided young writers with an example that today, more than ever (and far beyond Nigeria's borders), serves as a guiding light. Ali Mazrui's novel, *The Trial of Christopher Okigbo* (1971) gives us ample evidence of that: Okigbo's trial recounts the betrayal of a scribe turned soldier, a man who gave up his poetic vocation for the sword. A volume of collected tributes, *Don't Let Him Die* (1977) bears witness to Okigbo's influence.

Wole Soyinka

Based on his own personal reinterpretation of the ceremonies associated with a very ancient Yoruba religious site on the Eastern boundaries of the country, Wole Soyinka represents political events in Nigeria in his own way. 'Wole

Soyinka's poetic oeuvre is considered obscure: it's a crowded world that one does not enter without being intellectually and sensitively prepared.' (E. Galle, in Soyinka 1987:6) Along with Christopher Okigbo, this abstruseness has made him the target of a new generation of Nigerian critics who attribute this taste for hermeticism to the influence of 'modernist' poetry, in particular that of T.S. Eliot's first period, of *The Waste Land* and not of the *Quartets*, which are truly the 'music of conversation'. In fact, they have criticized this new, national poetry for being nothing but an Africanized version of the Anglo-American poet's mythologizing tendencies. The pervading religiosity and mix of references (Yoruba, but also Christian and Greek) impede accessibility. The language of myth is used to mediate between text and reader; poetic expression is no longer confidences shared or conversation heard, but a construction, the key to which can no longer be discovered in the relationship between voice and listener or reader. Fortunately, Soyinka's first poetry was not restricted to this type. One of his best-known poems, 'Telephone Conversation' (1962), is the satirical narrative of a racist telephone experience. The first anthology (1967) also contains texts inspired by contemporary politics (the Teigel massacres, Ikeja), personal events (the death of his friend Segun Awolowo) or a road accident he witnessed ('Death in the Dawn').

More distinctively he produced a love poem, 'Psalm', and another dedicated to a 'Black singer', in which Wole Soyinka portrays himself in the same agonizing way as in the aptly termed '*prisonnettes*', written during his eighteen-month-long captivity, and which also appear in *A Shuttle in the Crypt* (1972). This last experience gave a whole new resonance to mythical constructions such as *Idanre*, which, in certain poems ('For Fajuyi', 'For Segun Awolowo'), drowns 'in a cacophony of mythmaking and impenetrable idiom' according to Niyi Osundare (1986:26). The formal inventiveness, which turns the poem upon itself and into a self-contained object, leaves the reader with the impression of an obtrusive attempt at literary distinction. The poet's intention is to make a convincing break with his predecessors' militant or naïvely lyrical discourse, while also making a rather antic display of his linguistic powers and the extent of his literary knowledge. In a way, he was rewarded for his pains: prefaced by L.S. Senghor, *Idanre* was one of the first poetry collections from Anglophone Africa to be translated into French (1982).

Poets of the 'sixties and 'seventies
The history of this first decade of independence, interrupted by the Nigerian civil war, can be couched in terms of quest and conquest of literary legitimacy through imitation, followed by an appropriation of the language of the English poetic masters. However, in the Africa of the 'sixties, poetry could not continue to be an erudite game: tragedy was waiting in the wings and would strike Okigbo, who died in the war, as well as changing Soyinka, who was imprisoned for a long time. These years also saw the emergence of a black South African discourse, although no longer in the regular metre of H.I.E. Dhlomo's verse, in African English poetry. The Ibadan edition of Dennis Brutus's first book, *Sirens and Knuckle Boots* (1963), gave us a new voice, one that at times is intensely lyrical, expressing intimacy and love, as in the beautiful 'Night Song', while simultaneously conveying sentiments of revolt and oppression. Is it a coincidence that Brutus, a coloured Rhodesian, whose mother-tongue was

English, and who was raised in the city of Athol Fugard, Port Elizabeth, should be the first black Anglophone writer in South Africa to find the right words to express intimacy, particularly in the moving *Letters to Martha* (1968)? The first poems by Oswald Mtshali (1940), *Sounds of a Cowhide Drum* (1972), appeared at the same time with resounding success. Mtshali first wrote in Zulu, frequently translating his own texts, which then appealed to the fringe of the English-speaking white population who read poetry and were moved by his writing. His first anthology of poems, with a preface by Nadine Gordimer, sold more than 16,000 copies in one year which, for poetry, is prodigious (Alvarez Pereire, 1979:336). He succeeded in creating an original 'township' language in English, by mixing classical and popular styles, English and Afrikaans words. His slang comes from Soweto as well as the United States. Africa voices its anger in street English through his poems. Many fine texts were published during these years: Arthur Nortje's (1942–70) *Dead Roots* (1973), Mongane Wally Serote's (1944–) *Yakhal Inkomo* (1972), Sipho Sidney Sepamla's (1932–) *Hurry Up to It* (1975).

All the above-mentioned South Africans could not afford the luxury of producing an intellectual, academic poetry, concerned as it is with the creation of a pure, beautiful object; they had to speak for the masses that apartheid politics wanted to reduce to silence. Probably influenced by South African poetry, the third period of Nigerian poetry was dominated by a confrontation with social reality.

New Ethics in Poetry

At the end of the 'seventies and in the early 'eighties, the University of Ibadan was still the meeting-place of this new generation of Nigerian poets, who, today, are considered to be Nigeria's third wave of English poets. The new era corresponded with the publication of a text that became a beacon light for its poetry: Odia Ofeimun's *The Poet Lied* (1989). The second series of the *Opon Ifa* review (signifying the tray of palm kernels presented by the *fa* priest) was published the same year in Ibadan to commemorate the return to civilian power and the birth of the second Republic. A fresh start in political life, petroleum revenues at their peak, but also the birth of a new crisis: 'kleptocracy' had seized power and would hold onto it for four years, causing serious damage to the country's economy and its moral state.

Founded in Ibadan in 1976 under the editorship of Femi Osofisan, *Opon Ifa* was presented as the 'Ibadan Poetry Chapbooks'. The first issue offered an interview with Odia Ofeimum while the third contained a poem by Wole Soyinka entitled *Ogun Abibiman*. This was an important event because, in Osofisan's words: 'In his recent works, notably *Death and the King's Horseman*, and now *Ogun Abibiman,* the initiatory process is complete, the apprentice has turned master-craftsman' (Osofisan in *Opon Ifa*, I, 3:76). Soyinka no longer needed to take refuge in the hermeticism of his early works, especially that of the *Idanre* anthology. In 1980, *Opon Ifa* offered a collection of texts entitled 'Life in the Second Republic' (written 'life in di 2nd republik'), a collective speech act, a manifesto of this new poetry. What do we read on the Ifa oracle's tray?

We hear
Rumours of discontent, that felons breed across
The land. In an age rich in contracts and imported rice
An age billowing with billions of development plans,
Our voters are so ungrateful. They write poems
Against our government.... (*Opon Ifa*, I, 2, 1980:2)

Niyi Osundare echoes the villagers' protestations in 'A Villager's Protest':

They come
armed with sweet words
inflated promises...

We'll build schools
We'll build hospitals
We'll bring water
To every backyard...

We'll turn every footpath
Into a motorway...

Another rain will fall
(its clouds already gathering)
and the distant wayfarer
will come seeking shelter
in huts long neglected
(Osundare in *Opon Ifa*, I, 2, 1980:6–7 reprinted 1984:47)

The protagonists in this new movement provided the following texts: Odia Ofeimun wrote *The Poet Lied* in 1980; Harry Garuba, *Shadow and Dream* in 1982 and Niyi Osundare, *Songs of the Market Place* in 1983; Niyi Osundare, *Village Voices* and Femi Fatoba, *Petals of Thought* in 1984.

These volumes can be supplemented with a whole series of critical articles, thus assigning to the texts the group status of Nigerian literature's *avant-garde*. Official recognition came in 1986 when the *Guardian*'s literary supplement published two articles by Harry Garuba on Odia Ofeimun and Femi Fatoba (Garuba 1988a:269). These poets were all present in *Opon Ifa* in 1980, and had been friends and neighbours for a long time. Niyi Osundare, Harry Garuba and Femi Fatoba taught in Ibadan, where Odia Ofeimun completed his thesis in political science while acting as Awolowo's private secretary. Funso Ayejina taught in neighbouring Ife. Garuba and Osundare's first volumes were published in Ibadan by the New Horn Press, a small publishing house specializing in literature and directed from Ibadan by Abiola Irele who, during the 'sixties, governed *The Horn*'s destinies.

The texts distance the reader from what Osundare calls Okigbo's 'poetic exclusivism'; the book titles are evocative in a lyrical rather than erudite sense. *Letters to Lynda* reminds one of Dennis Brutus's *Letters to Martha*; Femi Fatoba's *Petals of Thought* echo Ngugi's *Petals of Blood*, inspired in turn by a text by Derek Walcott. As for Niyi Osundare's *Village Voices*, they are heard from Greenwich Village as well as from Ikere-Ekiti. Okigbo is one of the movement's true guiding lights – one 1980 edition of *Opon Ifa* was devoted to him – but the review itself was not bound by the influence of Pound and Eliot. Osundare or Ofeimun's references can be found in Neruda, quoted by Osundare in an epigraph to his first collection of poems: 'the people will rediscover their voice in my songs'. Brecht and Neto's poems are quoted abundantly in *Opon Ifa*, thus depicting the poet as a social figure who stands in solidarity with his people's political struggles. In a bizarre way, the fact that Okigbo died while fighting for Biafra was to his credit: his writing was certainly obscure and difficult to access, but he did not shirk when put to the test. These poets undertook a critical re-reading of tradition. Below is what can be considered a definition of the group's *modus operandi,* written by Garuba, with great acuity:

> A literary tradition ... includes all the essays, opinions, debates, and the special orientations of consciousness stimulated by all those activities of thought and imagination which we vaguely refer to as literary. Traditions are more often created by the influence of the latter than by any 'intrinsic' merit of the former. This I suppose, is the reason why younger writers in every literary tradition attempt to create a space for themselves by fostering different orientations of consciousness which will focus attention on their works; whether this effort leads to rancorous posturing (as between James Baldwin and Richard Wright) or not (as between a Femi Osofisan, or a Niyi Osundare and a Wole Soyinka), the outcome is on the whole the healthier growth of the tradition. And this is why it is important to understand the relationships between our writers within that imaginative dialectic of images and ideas we call Literature. (Garuba, 1988a:269).

It could not have been expressed any better! This was truly a new generation of poets who no longer apologized for writing in English or demonstrating their skill, even by dint of obscurity, as in the case of the previous one. The poet no longer used the words of everyday speech; his work was a mythical construction and its relation to history was hidden by ritual elaboration. This was the dominant tone of *Heavensgate* or *Idanre*. However, it was certainly no longer the case in *Village Voices* or *The Poet Lied*. The masters with whom these writers identified, whether Neruda or Neto, never isolated themselves from political action, but their voices remained personal, even lyrical and that, together with commitment, is the interesting aspect of Nigerian poetry.

The first generation did not reject elitism nor even esotericism in the name of populism. Popular poetry in English exists in Nigeria and is published in the newspapers: General Vasta (who was shot in 1987 for having plotted against the government) was its most distinguished representative, with eighteen volumes to his credit ranging from nursery rhymes to militant martial poems. In the case of the Ibadan poets, commitment is never separated from considerations of form. But the latter does not lead to a re-evaluation of the continuous production of pidgin poetry.

> Pidgin poetry, or most of it, begins to falter where very serious issues are raised and no comic effects are intended. Like most pidgin poems, the themes of the poems here [by Tunde Fatunde] are social and political and in most instances the effects are comical.... These poems exemplify the triumphs and tribulations of pidgin poetry, the capacity to render experience in a language accessible to the common man and the less fortunate cathartic effect of blunting his anger by eliciting the unsolicited laugh. (Garuba 1988b:xxv)

Osundare's (1981) investigation into the relation between orality and writing enables us to phrase the question on poetry somewhat differently. It is no longer a case of translating the mythical Igbo and Yoruba constructions into English by connecting them to Christian rituals. The poet is seeking the direct presence of an Anglophone listening public; he no longer needs to distinguish his texts from those of a native speaker. This movement of direct poetic presence recalls the explorations in American poetry, especially those of the Black Mountain group, with such poets as Charles Olson and Denise Levertov (Roubaud 1980:20). One cannot distinguish experiments with form and political commitment from the personal presence of the textual voice in their work. Before it becomes an intellectual construction, poetry is an existential attitude: Valéry and Eliot are poets of the past.

The contemporary Nigerian poets are intellectuals and university lecturers, and do not apologize for writing in the language they teach. They are the third generation of Nigerian poets writing in English. The first generation progressed no further than Victorian rhetoric; poetry was a discourse intended for grandiloquent demonstrations of African intellectuals, politicians and journalists' mastery of English. The second generation consisted of a brilliant group of university lecturers aspiring to equal Eliot and Pound at the risk of becoming pedantic and ostentatious, but clearly indicating that poetry was being taken very seriously. For the Latinist Okigbo, poetry was a separate language destined for the *happy few*: the problem of political consciousness only consisted of mastering the codes particular to that language. For Wole Soyinka, poetry is also a distinct language and not the proper space for displaying the type of Yoruba eloquence that comes out in his plays. The poetic text is closed and no longer converses with the mother tongue. The third generation of poets appropriated English, but could not refrain from reflection on the links between poetic and linguistic consciousness. These writers do not need to feel self-conscious any longer: English is now the language of the Nigerian elite who have adopted Wole Soyinka's pragmatic attitude towards language practice. They do not want their poetry to be no more than an intellectual exercise and they want it to shed any academic connotations. They have to turn to reflecting on the languages of the people and the relation between their poetry and popular culture. A few writers thought that the best way of reaching the people would be to write in their language: Chinua Achebe became a poet in the Igbo language, and he greeted Christopher Okigbo in that language in the 1977 volume of collected tributes. However, his Igbo texts were not written in the standard dialect; his conflicts with Nigerian linguists probably prompted him to abandon the experiment, as mentioned above. There is nothing inflexible about the new generation's works; they are not claiming a systematic Africanization of the English text. The rule is liberty; collage is frequently employed, enabling the poet to indicate the text's origin and to launch into the relationship between text and music. Through his many public poetry readings, Niyi Osundare went furthest in this type of experiment: he wanted to re-oralize his poetry, to inspire it with an indigenous breath in its dictions. He went in search of the means and found it in a collage of Yoruba texts along with his own. When the 1986 Commonwealth Prize and the 1990 Noma Award both went to Niyi Osundare this confirmed the success of his method and prompted us to revisit the example of Senghor, who seems not to have dated!

Francophone Poetry: the Senghor Century

For more than thirty years, from *Chants d'ombre* (1945) [Songs of Shadow] and
Hosties noires (1948) [Black victims] to *Elégies majeures* (1979) [Major elegies],
by way of *Ethiopiques* (1956) and *Nocturnes* (1961), L.S. Senghor's poetry has
dominated Francophone African literature and continues to do so, as
illustrated by a recent (and final) edition of his poems, prepared by the author
himself and containing numerous previously unpublished poems. This
astonishing success was achieved in a number of ways. Firstly, thanks to
popular success in the schools: African schoolchildren all read Birago Diop and
L.S. Senghor, who are now quoted in French schoolbooks. Those who enjoy
reciting poetry have all added 'Femme noire' ['Black woman'] (1990:16) to their
repertoire. Its literary success is supported by an essay on poetry that has
become the Francophone poets' bible. It is be found essentially in two texts: the
postscript of *Ethiophiques:* 'As manatees go to drink from the spring' (1954)
and in the 'Dialogues on Francophone poetry' that appear at the end of *Elégies
majeures*. 'The things and beings evoked here are almost all from my canton',
says L.S. Senghor, speaking about these poems: 'Then why write in French?' He
provides a clear answer that, for many people, is also a valid one:

> Because culturally we are of mixed race, because although we feel ourselves to be
> black, we express ourselves in French, because French is an international language of
> address. (1979:166)

In the poetry of his village, he understood the essence of all poetry, but he
could only transmit this knowledge and these emotions in French.

L.S. Senghor's oeuvre rests on a paradoxical dialogue with a mute Africa.
The 'Dialogues' contain a condensed version of all his ideas on poetry and, in
particular, several translations from his mother tongue. Serer poetry embodies
'virtues' and not qualities, 'because it has a regard for the power of melody and
rhythm' of Negro-African languages, demonstrated by a short Bambara poem
'translated' by L.S. Senghor. To strengthen his argument, he also provides us
with his translation of a longer 'Bantu poem'. The reader may rightly question
the text's origin (seeing as 'Bantu' is not a language), as well as L.S. Senghor's
unusual polyglot abilities, which enable him to translate from 'Bantu' and
Bambara with equal ease. Moreover, his use of translation is rather peculiar: it
is used to validate the virtues of *African* languages. L.S. Senghor ascribes the
traits found in his own poetry to Negro-African poetry. All the demonstrations
concerning rhythm, based on the repetition of assonances and alliterations
without a fixed form and far too well arranged to serve the purpose of the
theorist, seem very artificial. Senghor's power and acuity lay in his suggestion
for accompaniments for his texts: for 'jazz orchestra', for 'koras, balafons and
tomtoms', for 'symphonic orchestra and organ', 'Negro-African, Chinese and
Indian instruments'. Actually these accompaniments give far too general
instructions: should 'jazz' be Armstrong or Charlie Parker? Does 'symphonic
orchestra' mean Beethoven or Mahler? The suggestions serve rather to define
'atmospheres': vaguely metaphoric relations are established between text and
music that are musically and prosodically not related to the possible links, say,
between a tonal language and talking drums. The notion of a text's musical

accompaniment can have a very precise meaning in Yoruba; the text may be written in staves because of the language's tones. L.S. Senghor shrewdly creates a musical setting for the text, but it is certainly not a transposition of the African rhythm and musicality he would like to rediscover in French. The music is supposed to transport Africa into French and to eliminate any translation difficulties: poetic and linguistic conscience dissolve into a musical conscience belonging not to the order of reason but to that of emotion.

Senghor's poetry had a great impact: the masterful, poetic utterance, the breath of the verses, the absence of syntactical embellishments and the metaphorical accompaniment of Negro-African music are not easily equalled. Younger poets were distracted from reflecting on translation and exempted from any form of linguistic consciousness, as though every problem had been solved. As regards Togolese poets influenced by Senghor's example, Jean-Louis Joubert observes that they

> fail to impose the authority of their poetry in French because they show too much confidence in the French language. They think it is enough to give the words free rein. But words are lazy; they follow the rut if they are not forced into new arrangements. (Joubert 1991a:198)

L.S. Senghor could use words without resorting to force: he modulated his poetic voice to the tones of Claudel's versification; the public figure and the politician are present in his poetry, mastering prayer and intimate discourse with equal confidence. His great success was to discover the byways of personal lyricism in French, which he expressed with great economy of means. At the heart of his work lay his desire for cultural *métissage*, which he translated in linguistic terms through an Africanization that was as tentative as it was flexible, notably in its use of repetitions. The Africanization of syntax calls for rhythmic references that he considers unique to Africa, (while this is obviously the basis of all poetic discourse). Vocabulary is similarly Africanized by a judicious choice of words from indigenous languages that evoke the realities of the South, in some sort of lexical backdrop. L.S. Senghor was the first poet to put these techniques into practice: he experienced linguistic consciousness not as a rift, but on the contrary as a musical fusion in French. His theory was that *métissage* had to be consciously taken over, and that poets had to claim back practical usage of this European language, to master its poetic voice.

Soyinka can be given the last word to summarize the Senghor century:

> No successful attempt can be made to gloss over the dilemma posed by Senghor, poet of peace and conciliator, so let us summarize it thus: articulating or celebrating memory, yet attempting to remain beyond its present impositions, is a feat that is possible only for a poet and priest, a contradiction that finds resolution in that elusive virtue that defines Senghor's 'quality of mercy'. It is of a different temper from that of Martin Luther King, whose quality of mercy is arbitrated with the rigour, not the catholicity of 'love'. Perverse though it seemed at the time – and is still thus regarded, to many of his critics and admirers – it is Senghor's, however, that now finds a prophetic resonance in the politics of post-Apartheid South Africa – a case of the poet yet again vindicating his role as one of the 'unacknowledged legislators of the world'. (Soyinka 1999:139)

The legacy of Senghor

To assess his influence, one need only read the 1948 *Anthology of new Black and Malagasy Poetry in French*, preceded by Jean-Paul Sartre's *Black Orpheus*. The African poets present in the *Anthology* make up just over a third of those selected: three Senegalese and three Malagasy poets among the sixteen in all. Apart from Rabearivelo – who would have been quite surprised to be introduced as a 'black' poet! – and Senghor, there is Birago Diop, the talented adapter of *The Tales of Amadou Koumba*, and David Diop (1927–60). Birago Diop is an elegant, talented poet whose few poems, often published as annexes to the stories, appear in all the anthologies, especially 'Souffles': 'Listen more often/To things than to people/The voice of the fire can be heard/Listen to the voice of the water...' (Diop, in Senghor 1948:144). Three previously unpublished poems by David Diop also appear in the *Anthology*. In 1960 his promising career was brought to an abrupt end and his slim output published posthumously (1973). His writing is at odds with the accommodating ease of an L.S. Senghor: David Diop denounces racism and colonialism; the militant tone that made his reputation seems rather outmoded today. He is also the poet of nostalgia and love, particularly in the beautiful tribute to 'Rama Khan, the Black Beauty': 'I like your wild look/and your mango-tasting mouth/Rhama Kan/your body is the black spice/whipping up my senses' (1973:53). Rabearivelo's heirs, the two Malagasy poets J.J. Rabemananjara (1913) and Flavien Ranaivo (1914), produced more classically crafted texts. J.J. Rabemananjara's oeuvre, often weighed down by rhetoric, conveys the emotion of a militant of Malagasy culture and identity, won over to the cause of Africa and the French-speaking world: 'The sail of his dhow haunted by the regret of distant geneses' (Rabemananjara in Kadima-Nzuji 1981:25) did not drive him towards the Orient.

Several worthy poets followed in Senghor's footsteps and placed themselves directly under his patronage. Such is the case of the generous Mauritian poet Edouard Maunick (1931), who may be considered an intermediary between Anglophone and Francophone Africa, between the African continent and its islands, between Africa and Asia (*Les manèges de la mer*, 1964, *Mascaret*, 1966, *Fusillez-moi*, 1970, *Ensoleillé vif*, 1976, *Paroles pour solder la mer*, 1988). 'Black by choice', he likes to define his texts as being moved by 'nobly ensavaged ideas, civilized by instinct, screened by Creole patois and by imagery bursting at the metaphoric seams' (Maunick 1975:109). His whole oeuvre revolves around the themes of the sea, women and love of the French language that, in its popular, Creole form, is the truly national language of Mauritius. Through his refined and parsimonious use of Creole, sustained by a flamboyant lyricism, Maunick succeeds in inventing an original, poetic language that is at once colourful and sensual and that cannot be equalled by an Africa that lacks the same linguistic resources and cannot draw inspiration from the same Creole wells.

Creolization, Métissage

The setting for Africa's other great Francophone poetic tradition is that of the 'French' Congo: Tchicaya U'Tamsi (1931–88) is as violent and as baroque as L.S. Senghor is classical and pacified. The first collections of poems (*Mauvais sang*, 1955, *Feu de brousse*, 1957 [*Brush Fire*, 1964], *A triche coeur*, 1958) are those of a rebel who is still under Rimbaud's influence, capable of composing musical poems in stanza form, expressing individual rage, and still out of touch with Africa. The experience of his return to the Congo, his stay in the 'Belgian' Congo, his brief association with Patrice Lumumba in his capacity as journalist, gave *Epitomé* (the collection that followed) a completely different tone. Revolt has its specific targets, even when it is an individual revolt: 'I know, I know, don't mention it/my brains have become clay/trampled on by headings/ bawling out my headaches: Boothead/skilfully studded boots/skilfully pernicious boots' (1962:23).

The poetic discourse may be disjointed, but remains intensely personal: the poet calls himself 'I', puts himself in the action; if he speaks of religion it is only by railing at Christ, not by inventing new poetic rituals. For a long time his existence was filled by these violently passionate and lyrical poems, fuelled by the Congolese civil war. In 1978 he published 'Le conga des mutins', a text written in 1960, in the collection of poems entitled *Le ventre*. The 'conga' pointed the way to a beautiful, poetic work called *Le bal de Ndinga*, which triumphed in Paris in 1986. He gave free rein to his sense of music and dance with rhythms borrowed from *Kin la violente* (Kin is the truncated form of Kinshasa). At last, Congolese music and poetry could meet on Tchicaya U'Tamsi's pages: 'Lumumba/like rumba, conga/Lumumba/like rumba, Congo...' (1978:125–131). *Le ventre* (1978) was his last collection of some importance, before he devoted himself entirely to theatre and the novel with his trilogy: *Les cancrelats* (1980), *Les méduses* (1982) and *Les phalènes* (1984). The salient aspects of his writing, the carnality of his texts, 'that origin is far too visceral', the blood, the wine, the musicality of the diction – all the heightened consciousness of a physically experienced injustice and suffering, fill his pages in vivid force. The collection ends with a sort of multi-voiced poem in which the characters herald the author's theatrical writings and represent the different voices expressed in his writing: the soothsayer, the surveyor, the soldier, the geometrician and the poet. As in his previous collections of poems, much attention was paid to composition in *Le ventre*; the order of the poems is very important. Although nothing is left to chance in Tchicaya U'Tamsi's oeuvre, he has no message to deliver and, unlike Senghor, prepared no theoretical manual to be read alongside it.

The crisis in Tchicaya U'Tamsi's poetic consciousness came from within the French language, not between French and a mother tongue. His ever-generous (although sometimes chaotic) outpourings represented renewal for Francophone Congolese poetry, which explains why translations and praise followed almost immediately. A less calculating, more generous and spontaneous poet than the Nigerian colleagues of his generation, he became outraged through his participation in the larger historical events of his country, resulting in his disillusionment. His goal was not to be the poets' poet, and he had no use for university campuses. During the 'seventies, he gave up publishing poetry and found another outlet for his anger: the theatre. To sum up (for the lover of parallelisms), Tchicaya U'Tamsi represents the second generation of Francophone poets, anxious to preserve the autonomy of their art, and who consider the literary ostentation of their Nigerian colleagues Okigbo and Soyinka excessive.

Although opposed to L.S. Senghor in mode of expression, U'Tamsi nevertheless shared the essential premise that the new African poetry would be written in French; French belonged to those who used it. His linguistic consciousness was essentially a pragmatic one when it laid claim to French. Taking this stand was common to the young generation of 'seventies Congolese poets such as Maxime Ndebeka or Sony Labou Tansi, who also positioned their poetic discourse directly in French. Their oeuvre is truly in the tradition of Tchicaya U'Tamsi: in contrast to L.S. Senghor's fluent, limpid speech, they prefer violent discourse and uneven syntax. But assaulting the French language and proclaiming oneself a revolutionary does not make one a poet. It is precisely for this reason that Tchicaya U'Tamsi's descendants run the risk, (as did Senghor's followers), finding that loss of impetus in a poetic discourse results from an over-simplistic use of old literary recipes without bothering to develop a new approach to the poet's situation in Francophone Africa.

The poetry genre is largely pursued by young writers beguiled by L.S. Senghor's success. It seems easy to put one's complaints, insights and anger down in writing, but how does one extract a new sound? 'You have to read yourself from a distance; one hears better that way', says Jean-Baptiste Tati-Loutard (1939–) in his *Extraits de la vie poétique* (1970:64), and he is right: 'First we imitate; from then on our work is based on rejection' (1985:61). In the Congo, guilty conscience plays no part in the deployment of poetic speech. The Congo is sub-Saharan Africa's most Francophone state, where the question of linguistic *métissage* is thought to be solved: French is the language of Africa. 'What poet has never, even for one day, thought of using his people's spirit as a writing tablet; I'm even thinking of those who support a hieratic language...' (1985:58). Tati-Loutard reflects on the poetic condition, but without revealing his mother tongue, and to tell the truth, his 'hieratic language' may even be French, which is a mother tongue in the nourishing sense of the word. His oeuvre (*Poèmes de la mer*, 1968a, *L'envers du soleil*, 1970, *Les normes du temps*, 1974, *Les feux de la planète*, 1977, *Le dialogue des plateaux*, 1982, *La tradition du songe*, 1985) conjures up rivers, love and the ocean in a language that is less profuse than that of Senghor: he prefers the clear-cut, less rhetorical technique of the verse to the couplet. His public responsibilities (he served as a minister for almost ten years) did not overcome the poet's assured voice. Unlike L.S. Senghor, he does not try to saturate his text with a web of words for African-ness; one would even be hard put to find traces of Brazzaville's urban speech in his writings. The world and nature make up the true material of his lyrical discourse. He rejects ethnology as well as mythology in favour of a lyrical individualism – which might seem haughty, if it were not for the sincere simplicity of his discourse and his fluid lyricisms which places him more as one of Senghor's heirs. In 1988, he won the first Okigbo Prize for poetry, awarded by the Nigerian Writers Association, for his collection *La tradition du songe*. This well-read, lyrical poet, who shows solidarity with his people, is devoid of rhetoric and concerns himself with the mechanisms of poetic creation, may be considered the Francophone prototype of the third literary generation of poets.

The fact that Congolese poetry is flourishing, is probably due in large part to the spread of French language teaching, the result of decades of pedagogical socialism (failing other successes).

With a French-speaking population estimated at 68.6 per cent of the total population (persons older than 15), the Congo is the first and only African country where more than half the population is French-speaking. (Queffelec & Niangiouna, 1990:40)

In the 'eighties, the Congo already had the largest concentration of French-speakers, along with Gabon; two decades later, the situation is more or less unchanged.

It would be difficult to assume such facts in the rest of French-speaking Africa, where the problem of bilingualism is posed differently, particularly in Senegal where the practice of Wolof is widespread, or in Kinshasa, where Lingala is also' very much in use. The aims of L.S. Senghor, Tchicaya U'Tamsi, J.B. Tati-Loutard and Edouard Maunick are admirable for poets who have mastered the French language after years of study and an extended stay in France, and who live in a country or a city where French is spoken. Those who do not have these assets and who consider the issue of the relation between their texts and the popular poetry of their city or country, or those who believe that poetry cannot be an expatriate genre, may wonder about the ways and means of this process of Africanization. The answer may lie partly in changing the status of poetry within French-speaking countries. Despite denials from authors like Tchicaya U'Tamsi, textual authority seems to be linked to that of the author, who is often a public figure; texts are often read as derivations of this form of authority. This political contamination of the poetic discourse, which is similar to that observed in the first generation of Anglophone poets, has had very negative effects on the imitators of the poets under discussion. Poetic practice seems to be permanently linked to a form of political rhetoric and an ostentatious use of French, as if demonstrating one's mastery of poetry necessarily resulted in social promotion.

African poetry in Portuguese is known principally through the oeuvre of Agostinho Neto (1922–79), an Angolan poet and resistance fighter. Apart from his militant political discourse, the reader is intrigued by his search for a new mode of speech reflecting crossed cultures. This is perfectly displayed in the originality of texts such as *Karingana ua Karingana* (1974) by the Mozambican author José Craveirinha (1922–). His work achieves a

linguistic contamination, which is also a form of poetic reshaping: using forms and terms that have been borrowed from the Mozambican mother tongue, a peculiar use of Portuguese.... In the end, his poems are poised between two languages: Portuguese and Ronga.... José Craveirinha impregnates the Portuguese language with poetic, linguistic, Mozambican semen and tries, musically, to create a new speech resulting from the partial transformation of two language systems. (Leite, 1985:378–9)

Will the path of Creolization (or 'Creolity' as it is also called), championed by the disciples of Edouard Glissant (also Bernabé, Chamoiseau & Confiant, 1993), run parallel to that of Portuguese *métissage*? I can only hope that these insular, Lusophone issues will impregnate the Francophone poetry of sub-Saharan Africa!

Conclusion

Léopold Senghor is the incarnation of the three periods of African poetry, which we differentiated through the example of Anglophone poetry: he was the pre-independence poet, Africa's moderate militant, the bard of *métissage*; he was already an academic poet, that is, language technician, the holder of an *agrégation* [degree] in grammar, knowledgeable enough about mythology to know that he had to leave it behind, before Christopher Okigbo or Wole Soyinka started writing erudite poetry. For Senghor, Paul Eluard and Paul Claudel played the roles that T.S. Eliot and Ezra Pound did for the young Nigerians. What is quite surprising is his presence in poetry's third period, when efforts were made to rediscover a less affected diction and a more intimate form of speech. Senghor never needed Soyinka's ritual or verbal machinery to express his feelings; he was simply a lyrical poet who knew how to speak to the beloved woman with tenderness, a rare occurrence in African poetry before the 'eighties.

Lastly, he remains a model for the young generation, because in cultural terms the *métissage* that was his point of departure is also the path of the future. One may very well be Nigerian or Yoruba and write poems in English. Niyi Osundare, Femi Osofisan and Okinba Launko are aware of this novelty, but their linguistic consciousness is totally pragmatic: today, there is actually a public for poetry in English in Nigeria. This public wants to hear Nigerian voices, and does not confuse a political message with communication through poetry. The 'eighties gave Senghor's oeuvre a new lease of life. Freed from its faded political glow after the poet's departure from the corridors of power and with its theoretical verbiage about *négritude* almost forgotten, his work can now be read and appreciated for what it is. The pages of critical praise dedicated to it in *Opon Ifa* bear witness to this new reading.

In a totally different register, but still in pursuit of the same goal – an 'authentic' expression of a lyrical 'African' subject – the writings of Dambudzo Marechera indicate a new course, combining the experience of township violence, of Southern Africa's black cities, with a supremely refined knowledge of European poetry. His breathlessness and his warm, husky voice search for ways of expressing love:

> I think that in a very macho society, to display feelings of love is actually to display weakness, that it is not male, that it is not a sign of strength to in any way emotionally rely on another person, and also that virility, male sexuality is not dependent on mutual understanding but on the conquest.... (Marechera in Veit-Wild & Schade, 1988:32)

For Marechera (and in this specific sense he embodies a new linguistic and poetic consciousness), writing means distilling language until it expresses what the poet wants to say.

> Writing in English which is of course a second language, means that one is always very conscious of the language one is using. And I find the only way I can express myself in English is by abusing the English language in such a way that it says what I want to say.... (Marechera in Veit-Wild & Schade, 1988:34)

However, while the recognition of Marechera's voice and the success of Osundare and Ofeimun's texts seems to indicate that Anglophone poetry has found its path, Francophone poetry is still hesitant. The success of the older generation screens out the newcomers. Unfortunately, the exacerbated lyricism of N.X. Ebony (1944–86) in *Déjà vu* (1983) or that of Véronique Tadjo (1950–) in *Laterite* (1984) was not taken up by others. Francophone poetry seems to suffer from a double handicap, a theoretical as well as political one. The political handicap stems from the poets' institutional position; a constant struggle is needed to get out from under the official position conferred by Francophone institutions. The poet is not a lawgiver on language; this attitude wreaks havoc amongst the young poets. The authors' lack of originality in national anthologies such as those of Benin and Togo results in dismaying reading matter. The collapse of numerous regimes and the organization of national conferences in the French language seemed to have allowed the expansion of the space of public speech and increased the poet's margin of liberty. The chaos ensuing has not produced any results as yet. Is it the condition of the Francophone poet to be condemned to exile and a diasporic community?

Still, the poet should not give up theoretical reflection nor imagine that Senghor has spoken the last word on the practice of poetry in Africa's Francophone countries. Theoretical texts by poets are scarce, while reflections on poetry are practically non-existent: while Senghor's form of *métissage* has finally arrived, while French has established itself in numerous African capitals, it is still not the time for poetry to become a field of debate on form and practice. What about the issues on writing in French alongside African languages? What of the contribution of Rabearivelo, Kagame, Hampâté Bâ and others? How does one proceed from the art of general considerations, of which Senghor was past master, to specific studies on the relation between the mother tongues? New roots have to be put down that will allow a new, creative appropriation of the French language – using Africa as the point of departure, not Paris, as has all too often happened before. The illustrious history of African French was written by linguists and grammarians; the post-Senghor poets need to rewrite it all over for themselves. Senghor was buried in Normandy in 2001: is that where all our poets should go, to live and die?

8 Inventing Theatre

Theatre as a social or aesthetic practice is peculiar to societies devoid of a sacred aura. (I am distinguishing it here from the verbal drama genre.) Such theatre is sustained by actors interpreting a role for pleasure or out of economic necessity, but certainly not for ritual motivations. It creates a space where actors tell stories through an established text, which paradoxically allows for improvisation. As I attempted to show in my book, *L'invention du théâtre* (1986b) [Inventing theatre], a fundamental break once took place between masked dances, ritual representations and theatre plays.

Linguistic & Collective Consciousness

Drama is the one genre where speech becomes entertainment: does this mean that it has been freed from all strictures in writing? Probably not, even if many authors would have us believe it. In its oral form, theatre is supposed to be closer to traditional orality and thus to popular speech, which, presumably, is expressed 'naturally' in African languages. It is assumed that theatre is spontaneously produced within the African village community, implying that this form of expression manifests a type of communal 'collective consciousness'. This line of thought further concludes that the problem of linguistic consciousness is resolved by the expression of collective consciousness through theatre – the community art *par excellence:*

> Drama in pre-colonial Kenya was not, then, an isolated event: it was part and parcel of the rhythm of daily and seasonal life of the community. It was an activity among other activities, often drawing its energy from those other activities. It was also entertainment in the sense of involved enjoyment; it was moral instruction; it was also a strict matter of life and death and communal survival. This drama was not performed in special buildings set aside for the purpose. It could take place anywhere – wherever there was an empty space, to borrow the phrase from Peter Brook. 'The empty space', among the people, was part of that tradition .... (Ngugi, 1986:37)

Clearly and eloquently, Ngugi expresses ideas that can be found in most of the critical literature on Africa and its theatre published during the past fifty years. Bakary Traoré's pioneering book, *Black African Theatre and its Social Functions* (1958, 1972) made the same claims when defining theatre as all forms of ritual and festive activity within the African village community. Before Africa's colonization, theatre was the community's way of staging expression. The vision of a pre-colonial Africa united in elaborate village rituals, almost outside of history, was a very successful one, as illustrated by its renewed articulation by Ngugi. However, it leaves no room for a critical description of the constraints that may weigh down on the creator (who is associated here with a collective subject). I leave it to the Swahili dramatist Ebrahim Hussein to criticize this theory:

> In his last work [*Decolonising the Mind*] Ngugi writes this: 'Drama has origins in human struggles with nature and with others. In pre-colonial Kenya the peasants in the various nationalities cleared forests, planted crops, tended them to ripeness and harvest....'
>
> He goes on: 'So there were rites to bless the magic power of tools. There were other mysteries: of cows and goats and other animals and birds mating – like human beings – and out came life that helped sustain human life....' But my concern in this brief essay is not so much with magic and poetry but with theatre. It does not need emphasizing to say that one finds rites and rituals in the mosque. And both Muslims and Christians do not particularly relish to refer to these rites and to these rituals as theatre as such. In this regard theatre art shows itself to be more selective than Ngugi presents it. It does not recognize every rite and ritual found in African tradition as theatre as such. The position held by Ngugi is analogous to that held by a number of African writers during the 60s. The writers asserted or assumed that there was theatre in Africa and that this theatre was in the course of time injured by colonialism.... (Hussein, 1988b)

For Hussein, theatre is an artistic practice and not a rite; the Tanzanian writer rejects the confusion between social and religious life and theatre: there is religion and politics on the one hand, theatre on the other. He criticizes Ngugi in the name of an independent conception of artistic practice and proposes an analysis of Aristotle's categories of poetics as applied to theatre. Obviously, this concern to differentiate between theatre and other social practices does not mean that Hussein neglects the multiple types of performance that Africa offers. As he formulated it in his thesis,

> It is necessary to distinguish between dramatic elements in rituals and fully fledged theatre which has detached itself from any ritual function and has become a specific aesthetic event. (Hussein, 1974:8)

Theatre is not necessarily communal or consensual art; the breach, which Ngugi attributes to the event of colonialism and which for him translates into the dislocation of this harmonious universe, may be analysed in different ways (as Wole Soyinka has shown in his article 'Towards a True Theatre' (1962)). The dramatist faces a dilemma: he has to acknowledge the independence of his art as a creative practice, and thus theorize about the breach between the ancient rites and theatre, of which the use of new languages is merely one of the signs. He also has to establish theatre within the representational modes accepted in African cultures and in particular create forms in which gestures, texts and music are combined; he must not cut himself off from popular culture, as one of its expressions is precisely the song form in an African language, or dancing. The dramatist must not succumb to the illusion of community, which is still very much alive in its different ideological guises today. However, the dramatist cannot turn his back on his community completely, making drama a totally independent art without social attachments. Artists who succeed in such theatre are able to combine these constraints without relinquishing any of the contradictory demands mentioned above. Today, verbal language is often made up of foreign words: what happens when this projected synthesis between text, gestures and music, specific to drama, must be invented from further scattered elements of culture that are not easily linked to ancient sounds and gestures? (I must add that this development is hardly a Western or European monopoly, as my definition also covers Chinese opera or Noh theatre.)

Orality & the Stage: Theories on the Origins of Drama

By their confusion on this issue, those who insist on interpreting African rites and liturgies as a form of theatre prevent others from seeing the true originality of the new African dramatic literature. By using theatre as a particular mechanism in *L'invention du théâtre* (Ricard 1986b), I emphasized its technical elements, notably the gap between actor and role, or the distance between author and text. That book examined the possibility of bringing critical consciousness into this space and linked dramatic art to this alienation from rite. I even suggested it was a theatrical prerequisite, basing my argument on the possibility of a 'script' and the use of the written word, which, unlike oral improvisation, allows for repetition and control.

Confronted by people for whom this type of art is merely a cultural heritage, my aim was to appeal to an understanding of the actor's and the dramatist's art. Theatre rightly belongs to poetics (as constructive, organized and creative thinking) and not to anthropology (as a cultural given). Defenders of the dramatic qualities of 'African cultures' refuse to recognize that the problems of distance, critical consciousness and art also have to be posed when it comes to tradition. In Africa, as is the case elsewhere, a 'holistic' conception of culture is a fundamental obstacle to creative thought. It is true that dramatic elements such as speech, image and gestures are all present, but they are distributed differently, for another purpose, originating in a different truth. The staging mechanics do not function as in the Western tradition. The storyteller will not dance, and the dancer will not tell stories.

In the narrative *récit,* time eats up the storyteller; time is his true master, while the stage is first and foremost ruled by space. The question of the 'I' telling the story takes centre stage. The novel text, like the drama text, is not an oral account; the novel's hero says 'I'. He is not a storyteller, and he can appropriate the space all by himself. For the narrator, concrete space is no help to him at all, whereas the space on stage is one where two characters can say *I* at the same time. Two characters can confront one another without a third coming on to put an end to the argument. This opposition probably gives birth to tragedy while narrative poetry or the epic are deployed within the time of discourse. Tragedy may be a dramatic genre because of the presence of these two conflicting desires, which no third party reconciles in an opportune way. Here, the space occupied by this co-presence creates a purely antagonistic, new dimension of which tragedy is the verbal form, as illustrated by Wole Soyinka's admirable play, *Death and the King's Horseman.*

In his hermeneutics of speech, Sory Camara insists (quite rightly) on the notion of time; the reader will have gathered by now that I prefer to stress the notion of space. Drama as we know it, with its particular mechanisms that have been in existence since ancient Greece, or what Sory Camara (1991:19) calls an 'organized and inhabited microcosm', is in fact the spatializing of speech – precisely everything that an oral culture refuses to do. In theatre, masks and statues move and speak. Speech acquires density and corporeity: it can no longer fly off to mysterious lands, conquering both space and time, but must take responsibility for its carrier. Wole Soyinka considers the staging of a play to be a type of sculpture, which, in his case, is further enhanced by magnificent Yoruba statues. It is true that the history of Yoruba theatre, in which speech and dance have broken all ties with the sacred, provides us with some food for thought. And yet, Yoruba theatre was the dance of the masks, called the *Egungun*, supposedly representing the ancestors during special ceremonies. In time, the *Egungun* dance companies became entertainment groups, and performance became pure show. Cut off from its founding text, theatre abandoned the 'gnostic ways' 'and chose the 'paths of entertainment' (Camara 1991:55). But it also opened up new routes that Yoruba men of the theatre could follow, and marked the birth of a new type of theatre within that culture. I have tried to retrace the origins of this theatre, coming into being precisely when speech and image are combined. This combination is not in the first instance an interior one, even if that were to be the dramatist's ultimate intention. In other words, other civilizations (especially those who invent theatre mechanisms) substitute the slow drift of discourse time that Mandinka civilization grants itself, with an attempt to master time and to link it to a space where digression will be impossible! Talking masks, masks that speak to one another: that is what theatre was in the beginning. Suddenly the community of men makes a concrete show of being a community of discourse, instead of having their access to the secret of the masks denied. As R.P. Armstrong puts it in his beautiful book, *The Affecting Presence* (1971), the silent mask absorbs our attention in order to lead it onto mysterious paths; the playful theatre mask gives us access to what can only be a human truth – the masquerade, the group of masks. By saying 'I', the mask establishes a presence that designates otherness, shattering the homogeneity of original speech.

All cultures produce signs, and thus engrave their social existence on objects. Cultures possess writing, even if the writing is without letters. One can emphasize the dynamic nature of this creative activity or, in contrast, the tangible results of it. In the first case, the purely interior activity is originally that of memory, of perpetual creation, while in the second case material substances are used to preserve and to circulate these signs of creation. Thus memorization is opposed to materialization: the first manipulates discourse (in time); the second uses signs, objects (in space). Obviously, creation based on the second category depends on visual support. A culture that has the economic means available for the visual recording of speech will tend to emphasize the spatial (therefore visual) dimension of the signs it produces. To my mind, this spatialization of discourse cannot be separated from the invention of theatre. When discourse that starts out as the music of time becomes the rhythm of space, masks begin to talk, storytellers start gesticulating and the actor, doubling as a storyteller and a dancer, steps forth. He does not delegate speech: on the contrary, he says 'I' in order all the better to serve the author who has put him on stage. Thus theatre is only possible where there is a rejection of the holistic conception of culture. Certain African theorists have attempted this by devoting themselves to a new exploration of their own mythology.

In his article 'Towards a True Theatre' (1962), Wole Soyinka observed that the architecture of theatre was not just about building, but also about one of the variables of 'the dubious art to which it must give birth'; and he added: 'How can one fail to grasp that it is no use employing mud-mixers and carpenters to design media which must eventually control or influence the creative act?' (Soyinka, 1962)

He endorsed the idea that authentic dances had to undergo a 'necessary transition' before being used in the 'conscious' art form of theatre. Theatre is in front of us, not behind us; it will be created by conscious artists.

The role of Ogun

For Wole Soyinka, the creator of theatre is Ogun, 'the first suffering deity, first creative energy, the first challenger, and conqueror of transition' who should be understood as a synthesis between Dionysos and Apollo, and who will eventually resemble Prometheus, who gave man the first knowledge for civilization. Ogun plunged into chaos, but he emerged from it to reach the stage of aesthetic joy. Possessed as was Dionysos, Ogun regains his senses and is able to compose and even to create like Apollo and Prometheus. Possession is not a shamanic journey but, on the contrary, a state of creative exaltation allowing the mastering of an art form. Ogun, the emblem of the actor, is the one who conquers possession, i.e. who can be possessed and consequently dispossessed of the powers that inhabit him. Mastering the transition from consciousness to unconsciousness describes the art of the acting master or the actor. It is left to the latter to put into practice that sequence originating in Ogun, the passage from 'enthusiasm' to control.

Ogun's act has ludic and aesthetic value and, according to Wole Soyinka, metaphysical value as well: he proclaims the unity of life and death, and victory over life, in the consciousness of death.

> Only one who has himself undergone the experience of disintegration, whose spirit has been tested and whose psychic resources laid under stress by the forces most inimical to individual assertion, only he can understand and be the force of fusion between the two contradictions. The resulting sensibility is also the sensibility of the artist, and he is a profound artist only to the degree to which he comprehends and expresses this principle of destruction and re-creation. (Soyinka 1976:150)

Why are the theories of J.A. Adedeji (Soyinka's successor as director of Ibadan University's School of Drama), for which the *fa* corpus texts represent the historical birth of theatre, and those of Wole Soyinka so important for my argument? Precisely because the notion of a dated breach, engraved in history at a time when myth and history meet, may signal *one* invention of theatre. Theatre starts when the techniques of possession and the incarnation of cultural beings are put into use as action and narrative. The poet has to textualize these techniques, organizing them into a narrative representation. In effect he has do what Euripides did for *The Bacchantes*. It is no coincidence, perhaps, that when Wole Soyinka was freed from prison at the end of the Nigerian civil war this was exactly the text he adapted in 1973, thus celebrating another victory for life, and thus for theatre, in his own way.

The acting tradition

Theatre starts with the birth of actors, who are the specialists in play. The first actors were either Esa Ogbin, of the lineage of Obatala, and the masked dancers celebrating the ancestral cult, the *Egungun*, if we accept J.A. Adedeji's exegesis of the *fa*, or the violent god Ogun, who first conquered transition, if we agree with Wole Soyinka's claim. They have both made their mark on Yoruba history. Wole Soyinka and J.A. Adedeji have elaborated a theory based on a phenomenon obvious to the observer, that of the present vitality of theatre in Yoruba country. Paradoxically, the theory of indigenous origins of theatre that start with a break in history allows Wole Soyinka to conceive a dramatic work in English. The idea of an 'ethnic' Yoruba collective consciousness is very foreign to him. If he had to characterize his culture, he would probably choose its capacity to appropriate foreign forms, its syncretic force. He rejoices in the possibility of creating in several languages and considers it to be an asset for Africa: his linguistic consciousness is dominated by pragmatism. That popular theatre is so alive amongst the Yoruba, proves he has a strong argument.

Popular Theatre

In 1980, the Association of Professional Nigerian Drama Companies, with Hubert Ogunde as its president, boasted more than a hundred members. During the mid-'thirties, he was one of the first people to stage productions on behalf of the church. The basis of these was musical, while biblical scenes provided the content. Thus it was a true case of the *kantata*, which Minister Baeta from the Keta Evangelical Church would introduce soon afterwards in Togo and not just an evening of choral singing, as the term derived from 'cantata' might suggest. During the Second World War, Ogunde's talent would blossom within this dramatic tradition. The titles of his first plays, *The Garden of Eden* and *God's Throne* (1944), *God and Africa* (1944), *Israel in Egypt, The Reign of Nebuchadenezzar* and *Balthazar's Feast* (1945) suffice to show the importance of the Bible in them (Clark, 1979:3).

Biblical influence alone is not enough to provide dramatic form. Ogunde's youth was marked by contact with the *fa* priests; he was initiated into their cult. He knew what a trance was, but he was also a member of a *Egungun apidan* group – those who play tricks – in a type of masked theatre from Ibadan, which was still in existence in 1976. He tells us that he shared their life for six months; he saw 'how the masks got dressed up' (Clark, 1979:25). He was experienced in a formalized theatrical process dependent on the actors' capacity to represent characters from everyday life, but with masks. Hubert Ogunde was familiar with the Gold Coast's 'concert party' productions, featuring 'companies of actors working from a framework, from a story told by one of them to create a production in which everyone invents his own lines: the actors of this genre use numerous devices and techniques, but in particular one may mention wordplay and frequent mixing of languages' (Zinsou, 1987a:5). In these productions, spoken language takes centre stage. Recognition of the multi-lingualism of society and its dramatic resources was an essential element in Ogunde's work.

According to Ebun Clark, Ogunde was the first theatre professional to go on the stage among the Yoruba without a mask (Clark, 1979:25). This is an important observation: the *Egungun apidan* were professionals actors but always appeared masked. It was Ogunde who broke the link between representation and traditional religion. He aligned himself with entertainment, even though his first productions took place in African churches, and he used *Apidan* theatre techniques to serve biblical narratives. Kacke Götrick's extremely detailed analysis (1984) of the productions she saw in Ibadan in 1976 applies structural models that highlight Ogunde's use of a repertoire of elements within a series of sequences all similarly structured. *Apidan* theatre still functions within the oral tradition, still repeats and even overworks the same models. Ogunde freed himself from this tradition in order to create Nigerian theatre. The implications of what he achieved have probably not been fully realized. The depth of his originality should not be measured simply by his use of the Yoruba language in his productions, but also by his creation of a form capable of providing an account of the social and political situation in his country. He managed to insert himself in the anti-colonialist struggle without cutting ties with older forms of expression. As early as 1945, he saw one of his plays suppressed by the colonial regime: it was produced in support of a miners' strike. He had reacted by composing new narratives based on the miners' situation, demonstrating his freedom from the framework of traditional narrativity, condemned to repeat tired schematic, over-familiar concert shows or *Apidan* theatre. Acting as observed and understood by Ogunde mutually reinforces biblical narratives that can be adapted to the purposes of anti-colonialist liberation rhetoric; this is precisely and clearly indicated. During the performance of the dramatic text, the historic subject erupts on stage.

> I understood some time later [after 1945] that success depended on the use of the term 'concert': the plays were in Yoruba, but to please the audience, titles had to be given in English. Today we mostly give Yoruba titles. Anyway, what we are doing is not a concert, but theatre: we are now the Ogunde Theatre Party. Here we perform in Yoruba, with some parts in pidgin. (Ogunde, in Ricard 1975b:28)

The show is no longer by a group or a church society, but by Ogunde, himself, someone with an artistic and political vision. Freeing oneself from the masks also means liberating oneself from the collective subject and confronting history in one's own name, with all implied contradictions, including the linguistic. This break had a domino effect, imposing a whole new shape on Yoruba theatre. For example, Ogunde's theatre is the only one that employs actresses. Even today, the *Apidan* companies are still exclusively composed of men, even though a few women may be hired as singers, and the concert party companies prefer to give the female roles to transvestites. Ogunde once told an audience how women joined his company in 1945:

> My first advert I advertised: Actors and Actresses Wanted, Apply in Person to Hubert Ogunde so, so and so ... (Laughter, clapping). Nobody answered my advert. (Prolonged laughter). No one, not even one. Then I decided to do something else, I decided on another trick.... I put out another advert: Lady Clerks Wanted, Apply in Person to Hubert Ogunde, and so on ... (Laughter). The next day, my house was full. Then my problem was how to tell them that they would not be 'lady clerks' or clerks, but

actresses and actors. But I said this and some went away and some stayed behind. But my problem was still money. After the first and second shows, all of them went away. Now I was able to get some boys, but I was unlucky with the girls. And so, as the chairman (of the lecture) mentioned, I decided.... I remembered the tradition back home: polygamy is the answer! So, I had to keep on the girls as wives in order to keep the group on the stage. (Ogunde in Jeyifo, 1981:211–12)

Ogunde was the first person to have managed a mixed company (men and women on stage) in West Africa. The 'conjugal' relation – admittedly in a polygamous context – intervenes on a stage that is no longer occupied by masks and transvestites. The dynamics of sexual difference, the assertion of an historical subject and the recognition of linguistic pluralism qualify Ogunde's company as a truly indigenous theatrical enterprise, born and developed within the Nigerian context, the prototype of hundreds of other groups. It is the former adept of the *fa*, the touring companion of the *Apidan*, the choirmaster of Lagos's Church of Christ who invented theatre in Nigeria, because he invented a professionalism with an open face. Hubert Ogunde, who was neither a sectarian traditionalist, nor a foreign zealot, brought us to understand the positive aspects of syncretism. It was in an urban and educated context that Ogunde's theatre cast aside the masks and the *Apidan* transvestites. He set the figure of the comic actor on the boards, freed from the weight of tradition, ready to play his role within the new African 'cultural fair'. As demonstrated recently by Karin Barber (2000), popular theatre played a central part in the self-definition of Yoruba consciousness and history.

The Model: Soyinka

Wole Soyinka's plays and in particular his first great play of mythological-historical inspiration *A Dance of the Forests* (1963) contain an entire theory of theatre.

Soyinka's theses on the origins of theatre in Africa throw some light on this dense, almost unperformable work. Too markedly iconoclastic, the play – commissioned for Nigeria's October 1960 independence ceremonies – was withdrawn from the official programme, but was nevertheless staged. We are told that on the occasion of a tribal assembly, the city's inhabitants invite a few illustrious ancestors. However, these ghosts do not honour the city dwellers, who eventually chase them away: the real celebration will take place in the presence of the forest inhabitants. The forest becomes a magic space *par excellence*, where past and future coexist, where dance and theatre may happen all at once. The drama text is a representation that takes the shape of a dance of possession; the text's real ambition is to show the moment of transition, that of Ogun, the first actor. Demoke, Ogun's disciple, is the hero of the play.

How can a theatre born when possession is brought under control, fit into the history of a new state? Theatre breaks down the closed universe of ethnic pantheons, forcing the writer to question himself and come up with new answers. It is no coincidence that the main character is Demoke, artist, poet and sculptor. Wole Soyinka writes plays; he is not preparing a ceremony. The dramatic text is constructed in confrontation with religious practices involving masks and trances, confirming ritual effectiveness (in particular those rituals employing the techniques of representational arts). What we have here is a discourse on history that has been built of a montage of reinterpreted dances and ceremonies. It is an attempt to make theatre happen using ceremony as a point of departure, one that has not yet found its own language. All the same, the central question is well put. To create a work for such a new dawn – the independence of Nigeria, the jewel in the British Empire's African crown – also means questioning the dayspring of the art itself. A national theatre cannot be inaugurated without examining the foundations of Nigerian dramatic art. This is not a rhetorical question, but a practical one, as illustrated by the attempt to textualize ritual practices, linked to examining the historic relations between Africa and Europe and the future of the great state whose birth is being celebrated. The language used is poetic prose, 'a type of stylized diction, neutral English without any roots', apparently inherited from English translations of Greek tragedians, seeing as 'verisimilitude must yield to tragic intention' (Bardolph, 1989:50). And yet the character of the 'dead man' provides us with echoes of Yoruba poetry, of which Eshu, the evil genie character, makes full use, thus already illustrating the scope of Soyinka's talents in this first play. The debates at the king's court also provide the author with an opportunity to give free rein to his satirical eloquence.

In 1959, Wole Soyinka was also the first Nigerian author to be staged at Ibadan's new school for theatre with *The Lion and the Jewel* (1963b). Today, this play is probably the best-known and most frequently performed of Wole Soyinka's works. A lucid, ironic vision of the relations between generations and social classes in the new state is served by extraordinary linguistic and dramatic virtuosity. A teacher, Lakunle, wants to marry Sidi, a village beauty, but refuses to pay the dowry to her parents. Sidi arouses the desires of the village chief, Baroka, an inveterate polygamist, who gets his way by making the young woman believe that he is impotent. Lakunle thinks that he can play the saviour and so avoid paying Sidi's dowry, calculating that she will be only too glad to get married after her public mishap with Baroka. However, Sidi rejects this arrangement, preferring to remain with Baroka and to join his cohort of wives! The play is written in free verse, thus imposing a linguistic stylization that allows for its basic convention: the Yoruba villagers speak in English. The teacher's mouth is full of big words; the old chief (the lion) weaves his discourse from words and images originating in Yoruba. Like the villagers, like his first wife, he knows all about the tricks of false speech. Confronted with these two types of discourse, the lovely Sidi must acknowledge that the words of the old chief strike more chords with her than the teacher's overblown declarations. The play's success was surprising: in this type of village situation, only the schoolteacher would normally speak English. By exaggerating the formality of this character's discourse, by making his pedantry unbearable, the author provides a linguistic translation of the difference between English and Yoruba. Similarly, through his capacity to copy the language of Yoruba tradition, he succeeds in making the gap felt between the language of the old chief and that of the other villagers. The text functions according to a detailed, subtle system of transposition delicately put in place.

A play like *Death and the King's Horseman* (1975) gives free rein to Wole Soyinka's linguistic virtuosity. It is based on an incident that actually happened in the 'forties: according to custom, when an *oba* (a Yoruba chief) dies, his horseman must join him in the hereafter by committing suicide of his own free will. In his efforts to have this barbarian practice abolished, a zealous and progressive British administrator succeeds in preventing a horseman's suicide. The scandal provokes an unexpected response: the horseman's son, a brilliant young medical student who has just returned from England, takes his father's place and, being a worthy eldest son, perpetuates the tradition that the administrator hoped to destroy. The play is a long meditation on death and sacrifice, served by language of superb variety and richness. The *griot* drones out Yoruba stylistic devices, the horseman holds his own and delivers a speech that sounds as though it was translated from Yoruba poetry, while the market women express themselves with the eloquence and rawness found in popular song. In this case, the successions of praise epithets, proverbs and images borrowed from the *oriki*, one of the pinnacles of Yoruba verbal art, are reproduced in English. It is also the first of Wole Soyinka's plays in which the mother tongue of two characters (the administrator and his wife) is English. For the first time, his dialogue is supposedly performed in its standard form. The different characters thus represent the play's social and linguistic stratification concretely: the English speak English; the military speak pidgin. The villagers, the horseman and the *griot* speak an artificial language that supposedly recreates Yoruba language-levels in English: the profound, poetic Yoruba of the *griot* and the satiric Yoruba of the market. The whole range of Western Nigerian language production has been restored to us in a work while serving a tragic conception. Each world speaks its own language, but the administrator's world cannot understand that of the horseman: the political cant of humanitarian goodwill is opposed to the subtle, condensed words of the horseman and his *griot*, who express the central values of a culture of solidarity and sacrifice, which administrative philanthropy is unable to grasp. Here, tragic conscience is served by linguistic consciousness. The art of this man of the theatre, Wole Soyinka, has reached its peak.

> He was one of the first people to establish this place, the department of theatre arts. Unfortunately, he didn't stay long before he was imprisoned by the government, then when he came out he didn't stay long either before leaving for exile. The Gowon government had put him in prison during the Nigerian civil war. But the little time he did spend here, he was able to leave some landmarks from which we have benefited, his approach to directing people who normally speak Yoruba, for example, farmers from the interior and rural areas. How do you put them on stage speaking English? To do this and to make it convincing Soyinka worked out a style which has become the paradigm, has become the model, which we have all been using since. So that's one sense of structure of the place, which we have benefited from; there are also the whole mechanics of staging, the music; dance, spectacle, the use of our own folklore; the world of our fables which he has also been able to exploit. (Osofisan, interview with AR, 1989)

Femi Osofisan went straight to the point in this interview. (He is a disciple of Soyinka and heir to his successes on the Nigerian stage and in Ibadan literary life.) As far as language is concerned, there is a Soyinka model, a 'paradigm' of dramatic style. Its effectiveness is the result of a clever mix of several elements. Wole Soyinka knows how to combine free verse or the poetic prose of literary

English theatre with a biblical style straight from the Anglican ministers; he knows how to mix the Nigerian English of the half-literate members of the population with the pidgin of the coach station barkers; he can repeat empty political slogans and match them with the satirical eloquence of songs in the style of Brecht or Joan Littlewood. It is worth noting that he produced a record with his own version of satirical songs about the 'kleptocrat' regime at the beginning of the 'eighties. This would be a remarkable feat for an English writer, but this author is Nigerian and Yoruba. His background is revealed in his translations of Yoruba poetry, from the way he copies idiomatic expressions and obviously from the Yoruba songs he composes for his own productions. In this case, the concept of linguistic consciousness is fully justified: acute consciousness of multilingualism and of the different levels within each language is expressed in markedly efficient dramatic speech, a clever fabrication that echoes the speech of the Nigerian populace. Such exceptional acuteness of linguistic consciousness is the achievement of a poet who has explored the ways of autonomous poetic language, and put them to admirable use for his dramatic conceptions. Wole Soyinka's mastery is outstanding; no other Nigerian dramatist comes close to him except maybe Femi Osofisan, at his best.

Anglophone Theatre

The question of linguistic realism in the theatre inspired Ngugi wa Thiong'o to critical reflection, resulting in the following analysis of his own method, which draws a very clear distinction between himself and Wole Soyinka:

> In all three plays, *The Black Hermit, This Time Tomorrow,* and *The Trial of Dedan Kimathi,* there were obvious contradictions though these were more apparent on the stage than in the script. In the opening line of *The Black Hermit,* the peasant mother is made to speak in a poetic language reminiscent in tone of T.S. Eliot. The elders from a rural outpost come to town for their son, the black hermit, and speak in impeccable English. So does Kimaathi, in *The Trial of Dedan Kimathi,* even when addressing his guerrilla army or the peasants and workers in court. Admittedly it is understood that the characters are speaking an African language. But this is only an illusion, since they are conceived in English and they speak directly in English. There are other contradictions too: these characters speak English but when it comes to singing they quite happily and naturally fall back into their languages. So they *do* know African languages! The illusion that in speaking English they were really speaking an African language is broken. The realism in theatre collides with the historical reality it is trying to reflect. It is only petty-bourgeois characters – those who have been to schools and universities – who normally and quite freely mix English with African languages in the same sentence or speech.... (Ngugi 1986:43)

Should African peasants speak English on stage? Nowadays Ngugi challenges the practice that he once espoused, finding it odd. But should one component of theatre – verbal language – be allowed to take precedence over everything else? The important task is to use a wide range of means to obtain the desired effect. If one of the mechanisms is the use of English, there is no reason to exclude it in the name of a limited conception of dramatic realism. Stage language is always artificial: is theatrical Gikuyu or Yoruba less so than theatrical English? In the case of Kiswahili, for example, Ebrahim Hussein has produced a dramatic oeuvre that is as good as the best, but his theatrical Kiswahili is also an artificial language that he is anxious to keep close to the new standard language, *Sanifu Kiswahili*, while not losing its ability to express the colourful and elliptical imagery of the poetic mind. Language is therefore poetic as well as normative, if that is not deemed incompatible. Contrary to Ngugi's ideas, speaking an African language on stage is not in itself a guarantee of authenticity, coming from the people. Theatre is a literary construction and not an anthropological or linguistic given.

> I had not properly argued out the case until early 1976 when I gave a public lecture at Kenyatta University College entitled 'Return to the roots: the Language Basis for a Kenyan National Literature', in which I called on Kenyan writers to return to the sources of their beings in the languages of their peasant mothers and fathers, to thoroughly immerse themselves in the rural community life of our people and to seek inspiration from the daily rhythms of life and problems of the peasants. (Ngugi 1981:182)

This return to the land is a drama theory, initially implemented in *The Trial of Dedan Kimathi* (1976), in which the peasants sing in Gikuyu and Kiswahili, the soldiers speak a rudimentary Kiswahili and the other characters speak English. It is because Ngugi realized the limitations of this practice that he decided to write in Gikuyu, resulting in a play that was co-written with Limuru peasants, *Ngaahika Ndeenda* [I Will Marry When I Want] (1982) and intended to be a partly collective work. Jacqueline Bardolph (1991:51) considers it to be a play that challenges the domain of literary criticism. These texts probably belong to the 'agit prop' tradition, with its different forms of development theatre devoted to educational work in many East and Southern African countries. These forms are known to us because of their English translations, including songs in African languages. Populist speeches about authentic collective creation aside, these works bear the mark of their authors. Their circulation outside the group that created them finds precedent in the work of Wole Soyinka, although they do not match his virtuosity. The aim of Femi Osofisan's theatre is also to lead to political awareness. It is written in English with songs in Yoruba, on which he comments:

> For the sake of productions for non-Yoruba audiences, the songs, incantations, etc., may need to be translated into the language of the new locale. To facilitate such a transference, I have thought it helpful to provide the following approximate renderings in English of some of the songs.... Dirges, for instance, normally possess their own specificity and, like proverbs or sayings, never really translate well: so that, in fact, it is better to make substitutions rather than translate them.... (Osofisan 1980:74)

Another playwright, John Ruganda (1941–) has written two plays, *The Floods* (1980) and *Echoes of Silence* (1986), in which he presents theatre in English; in these, he believes the language problem has been solved. His characters are actors or intellectuals who speak contemporary, urban English without a trace of an African context. The author is not trying to create popular or realistic theatre. On the contrary, he uses the verbal resources of dramaturgy to create metaphors for certain social situations within his discourse: floods signify the soldiery's arrival; silent echoes represent the weight of the past, or the prejudices that create barriers between his characters. In *Echoes of Silence*, the people of the lake are contrasted with the people of the forest; the history of the region can be summarized as the misunderstanding between these two ecologies. The lake people, the first ones to be 'civilized', are smooth talkers; the forest and mountain people are grasping, rebellious peasants. The spectator experiences this metaphor of the tensions between Kenya's two main ethnic groups, the Luo and the Gikuyu, via the intense and brilliant dialogue of two protagonists in a Nairobi villa. John Ruganda sets aside the issue of linguistic interpretations of Kenya's social injustices, for he writes as if English were the only language of the country. His success is indisputable, although this type of theatre runs the risk of losing its roots and (paradoxically) of finding itself unrecognized outside Kenya: Ruganda may be said to have mastered the formal codes of American psychological theatre and the style of Tennessee Williams too well, without attempting to recreate the symbolic (or even mythical) dimension potentially contributed by African languages (and which, for Ngugi, became the essence of dramatic writing). Ruganda's dramas, which can be defined as theatre for the Anglophone elite, contrast with Ngugi's aggressive populism. And yet, his elegant metaphors also speak clearly about contemporary Kenya. By 'neutralizing' the linguistic dimension in the phonological sense of the term, John Ruganda fully exploits the operation of dramatic language as a collection of conventions, without links to its milieu of origin. Does the reason for this lie in the fact that he is a Ugandan exile, and that his language choice implies constraint, as in the case of another exile, the erudite, cosmopolitan and polyglot novelist from Somalia, Nuruddin Farah?

At the beginning of the 'sixties, lack of understanding of the complexities of the situation, rendered the student theatre of Sarif Easmon, Ama Ata Aidoo and Henshaw equally indifferent to the language question. The language found in the texts produced by the École Normale William Ponty was dull and flavourless. Ruganda gives a brilliant rendition of the language spoken by Nairobi's new urban elite: in a way, this international English is just as experimental as Ngugi's Gikuyu.

Athol Fugard

> [T]o compare Fugard's reductive dramas with the large casts and expansive universe of Wole Soyinka, Africa's other playwright of world stature, is, metaphorically speaking, to move from an enclosed claustrophobic space, say a prison cell or a private hospital ward, to the bustle of West Africa's open-air markets. (Jeyifo 1985:99)

The plays of Athol Fugard (1932–) may be termed a series of dialogues between characters who are the prisoners of their surroundings and their hovels in the coloured ghetto, as in the case of the brothers in *The Blood Knot* (1974) or the tramps in *Boesman and Lena* (1974). The outside world enters this closed universe unexpectedly: by means of a letter in *The Blood Knot* or by the appearance of an African character muttering away in Xhosa (without actually taking part in the conversation) in *Boesman and Lena*. According to Biodun Jeyifo, the characters' improvised role playing is another way for the outside world to break in, shattering what might have become a suffocating *tête à tête*: Zacharias imagines himself married to his mysterious penfriend while Lena loses herself in dreams. The characters are also held prisoner by language, by the Afrikaans spoken by Coloureds and borrowed from the Whites. Fugard's characters speak English to escape the Afrikaans ghetto created by apartheid. English allows their voice to be heard by the international public whose democratic conscience contributed to the fall of the regime. And yet, Fugard's English is well and truly a language of the theatre, forever bound to Afrikaans when retranslating the realities of the country and of institutionalized racism. The closed universe of his theatre presents a metaphor for the vast system of controls and prohibitions that limited individual movement. The Afrikaans language often intrudes into the English discourse. It is the language of childhood, of social reality and of oppression. Fugard's writing is rooted in this creative tension: the glossary at the back of the Port Elizabeth plays contains more than 200 Afrikaans terms!

> An important element in my own writing is this question of 'translating' from Afrikaans to English. I was particularly conscious of it this time with *Boesman and Lena*. To begin with, so much of it was in Afrikaans and many phrases still seem to defy translation into an English equivalent that would have the same texture or give off the same feeling.... (Fugard 1974:xix)

Fugard's linguistic consciousness is a tragic one: for his testimony to be heard, it has to be spoken in English, but he can only talk about his country in the language of its construction, Afrikaans, which was also, in a sense, its death-trap. Such tensions are responsible for the roughness and bitterness of his texts, as indispensable to the playwright as Yoruba poetry is for withstanding the English administrator's discourse on progress in *Death and the King's Horseman*. Fugard's theatrical consciousness *is* a linguistic awareness, thus explaining (at least in part) the strength of his texts.

In South Africa, the language question was indeed a central one, particularly as regards theatre, due to the institutional separations of the public: from 1964 onwards, racially mixed casts were prohibited, and authorization was needed for actors to perform in front of communities of which they were not originally members. To cross these barriers, English seemed the obvious choice: it was also a means of communication with the rest of the world. During the 'forties and 'fifties, the efforts of other early black dramatists, such as H.I.E. Dhlomo (the author of *Moshoeshoe*, published only in 1985), were considered too rustic and traditional for urban tastes (Coplan 1992:309). The playwrights centred on the Bantu Dramatic Society: despite their enlightened humanism, they remained far removed from the new black experience in the 'townships' – those artificial cities created by the apartheid system where blacks were allowed to rent government-built houses. At the beginning of the 'sixties, Gibson Kente's productions from English scripts became the symbol of a desire to move beyond ethnic divisions and a small-town mentality. Gibson Kente succeeded in inventing a particular style by mixing jazz, gospel and local music in productions of a 'high moral standard', well focused on the problems of black townships (Coplan 1992:316). Like his Nigerian colleague, Hubert Ogunde, he used theatre to deliver a message that in his case was based on a moralistic interpretation of Christianity. By the end of the 'seventies, the new generation of black writers was still choosing English, while distinctively borrowing from (or resorting to) lengthy quotations from (especially oral) poetry in the African languages, as in the case of Fatima Dike (1948–) or Zakes Mda (1948–).

The dismantling of apartheid and the toppling of its coercive administrative restrictions on theatre activity will probably give rise to new 'interferences' in South Africa; theatre will certainly be one of the genres most sensitive to the future politics of language and education. The collective dynamics of the language communities and their more open society are changing language awareness in an unprecedented way, compared with the rest of Africa. At this point in time it is extremely difficult to say what tomorrow will bring.

Francophone Theatre

The works of Bakary Traoré (1958), Robert Cornevin (1975) and Bernard Mouralis (1984) stimulated interest in the theatre of the École Normale William Ponty, which gathered together French West Africa's best pupils. From the viewpoint of dramatic art, their chosen form is a very interesting one: the dramatization of traditional narratives, enlivened by songs and dances. At the 1937 Paris Exhibition, the students presented *Les Prétendants rivaux* [The Rival Suitors] and *Sokamé* (published in 1944 in *Présence africaine*). The Ponty *normaliens* (students at an École Normale Supérieure), known as *pontins*, who came from the four corners of West Africa, went home equipped with theatrical practice and a conception of dramatic art that continues to influence Francophone African productions today. The text is in French, while the songs are in an African language; this was the main attraction for the European public of 1937 (and not only for them). For Senghor (1964:66), their 'replicas' are written in a language that is 'dull and flavourless': it is a successful classroom exercise, but goes no further. More than the actual productions (which constitute a sort of *patronage* theatre on a grand scale), it is the 'Pontins' themselves who make this theatre interesting – figures such as Bernard Dadié or Bakary Traoré, who wrote the first study on Francophone theatre (1958) in which he reserved special mention for his 'alma mater'. The success of these productions is probably due to the fact that they offered an opportunity to satisfy the pupils' two key desires: to speak French in public and to present the song and dance folklore of their countries – an apparent contradiction that all of a sudden revealed how complementary it could be.

In 1938, Coffi Gadeau and Amon D'Aby created the Théâtre Indigène de Côte d'Ivoire and adopted the same formula. During the 'fifties, French West African cultural centres were set up; drama competitions were organized within and between the states, reflecting the same concern for French pedagogy through theatre. The method was so successful that problems concerning theatre itself tended to fall by the wayside. Within the French educational tradition, these issues belong to the academy or *conservatoire*, and not the school or university. Africa was reduced to folklore: theatre was reduced to Francophone speeches with African songs and dances tacked on. Some effort was made to copy expressions translated from African languages, but these examples of local colour did not go beyond the limits dictated by classical drama theory.

This may explain why two innovative works in this history of theatre did not attract the attention they deserved: L.S. Senghor's *Chaka* (1956) and Keita Fodeba's *African Sunrise* (1965). *Chaka,* a multi-voiced dramatic poem with tom-tom accompaniment, is part of the *Éthiopiques* collection. It is a short little play with chorus, experimenting in an original way with the fusion of African music and the French language. *African Sunrise* is one of the first productions where music, song and dance merge in a venture that is both aesthetic and political. During the 'sixties, these two poets began to explore ways of inventing a new dramatic art: they wanted to innovate by integrating spoken language into a dramatic whole. Few would follow their example: independence signalled the victory of school theatre, exceeding the hopes of even the most enthusiastic 'Pontins'.

In the course of his extended 1966 study tour, Jacques Scherer, director of the Sorbonne's Theatre Studies Institute, presented the full picture of African theatre (Scherer 1967): he saw 139 plays in six months and met several of the authors. However, such abundance did not hide the lack of original, creative drama, which had been stifled by school demands. According to Scherer, in most of the productions, declamations and musical dances alternate; the text, which is spoken in French, does not fit in well with the rhythm of the song and dance scenes. It is 'not only the sentence, but the whole play that should find its rhythm'. This concerns dramatic form as a whole and the conception of relations between the verbal and the non-verbal, as well as the text's dynamic organization. It is a problem of drama technique, one not to be solved by a mere application of classroom theatre solutions that alternate declamation and songs in a dance-punctuated *ensemble.*

Most of the texts dating from the first two post-independence decades can be grouped into two categories: comedy of manners set in a village or an urban office, and historical drama. These two subject-defined groups nonetheless match two types of writing, both characterized by their aesthetic conception and origin in the classroom.

More than twenty years after its first production, the best example of the village comedy of manners remains that of Guillaume Oyono (1939–). *Trois prétendants, un mari* (1964) [*Three Suitors: One Husband*] (1968) was already, in 1985, in its fourteenth edition. Many African companies have staged it, with well-deserved success. Oyono's writing is light and humorous, and his play contains all the necessary ingredients to appeal to pupils and students whose 'progressive' point of view it espouses. One might regret the fact that it does not display the same dramatic inventiveness with which Wole Soyinka was treating a similar theme at the same time, finding a diametrically opposite solution to the problem in *The Lion and the Jewel.* Guy Menga (1935–) wrote *The Oracle,* a Molièresque satire about fetishistic healers, and another of the above-mentioned, widely circulated texts. These plays are often written by students or teachers, almost always interpreted by pupils or students for a public made up of the same social strata, celebrating the same communal cult of progress via city and school. Satires on the new urban, bureaucratic bourgeoisie have appeared in quick succession: Jean Pliya (1931–) wrote *La secrétaire particulière* (1970) [The private secretary], Bernard Dadié (1916–) was the author of *Monsieur Thôgô-gnini* (1970), while one of the most recent plays by S.A. Zinsou (1946–), *Le Club* (1984), enhances the list. These texts have all been written as realistic comedies (in spite of a few bouts of fantasy in *Le Club*): the aim is entertainment through education. As a rule, there is no reflection on history or precise political and social contextualization. The 'classicism' of the language adapts to the so-called universality of the comments, yet, more than twenty years after publication, are school worship and the mockery of traditional medicine still fitting subjects? In today's world, it might be said that the contents of these texts has become just as obsolete as its writing.

Political considerations find refuge in national, historical dramas, a genre that showed exceptional growth between 1960 and 1975: *La mort de Shaka* by Seydou Badian (Mali, 1961); *Kondo le requin* by Jean Pliya (Dahomey, 1966); *L'exil d'Albouri* by Cheikh Ndao (Senegal, 1967); *Le trône d'or* by Raphaël Atta Koffi (Côte d'Ivoire, 1969); *Sikasso*, by D.T. Niane (Guinea, 1976); and *Tanimoune* by André Salifou (Niger, 1974).

One of the more interesting works is Bernard Dadié's *Béatrice du Congo* (1970). The erstwhile 'Pontin' and coordinator of Côte d'Ivoire's Centre for Culture and Folklore probably felt that he had reached the thematic and aesthetic limits of the form he had been practising for thirty years. Béatrice-Antigone appears against the backdrop of a Congo put to fire and the sword. His text was one of only a few African plays from that period performed at the 1971 Avignon Festival in a Jean-Marie Serreau production.

The dominating themes of these plays are death, exile and the end of the world; they are often performed in their respective countries and have appeared on the bill of recent foreign festivals. Unfortunately, their artistic success seldom measures up to their political ambition: who is interested in staging them today? The authors are often politicians or history teachers who are preoccupied with ideological contents rather than with dramatic form. There is rarely a balance between the historical dialogue and the song and dance sequences. The textual language, generally limited to the high register, reminds one of political speech making. There has been no effort to experiment with language: in *Tanimoune*, for example, the *griot* declaims genealogies in Hausa, but because there is no translation, the effect of the linguistic collage is one of local colour rather than a poetic enrichment of the text, contrary to the *griot*'s interventions in *Death and the King's Horseman*. This noble, neutral language (which can even be called classroom or administrative French) is the language of nationalism. The attempt to 'disavow' French by assuming true linguistic pluralism, by attempting to convert it to a system of stage conventions where certain characters speak a certain version of it, while others deal in pidgin French, and still others a translation from African languages with different expression levels, could have been a means of renewal and innovation for this type of theatre, but it was not to be. Tchicaya U'Tamsi's earthiness determined to rattle this theatre's linguistic cage with his 'henormous' satire of the local despot, *Le destin glorieux du Maréchal Nnikon Nniku prince qu'on sort* (1979). The effect of a poet bursting onto the theatre scene must have had a beneficial effect on many young dramatists, especially Sony Labou Tansi (1947–). Issues about a new dramaturgy persist, demonstrated by the surprising absence of theoretical texts on this subject authored by dramatists themselves.

After this all too brief survey, I would like to focus on a few of the factors standing in the way of a definition of autonomous drama creation. Instituting national theatres in almost all of the Francophone countries has not always been a bonus for playwrights. Rather, the foundation of such companies in and around the 'seventies expressed state aspiration to a politics of culture: it often translated as control over cultural life. Although this resulted in the professionalization of the theatrical world, it was in the shape of state employment. In the end it was the semi-professional groups (in the sporting sense of the word!) like Sony Labou Tansi's Rocado Zulu, Bottey Zadi Zaourou's Didiga Company or Werewere Liking's (1950–) Ki-Yi Mbock who tried and often succeeded in reconciling research, innovation and self-sufficiency while hoping to avoid the various forms of censorship. The problem of aesthetics remains: how does one successfully combine foreign words, gestures and rhythms to be carried and experienced in a corporal way? How does one establish communication between this synthesis and the citizens of the new African states? How does one address one's fellow citizens as well as the entire universe? To put it simply, how does one create theatre? For some, the language of the (French-speaking) people should be used on the stage: S. Bemba tries to give an account of popular speech in *Un foutu monde pour un blanchisseur trop honnête* (1979). For others who remain true to Scherer's recommendations, the future lies in opera and musical comedy. Since the enormous success of *On joue la comédie* (1975), S.A. Zinsou probably shares this view. This is how he describes the early stages of his life as a man of the theatre and the origins of his 'calling':

> My father's shows were a mixture of spoken text, songs, dances and music and that's what I have tried to do. In fact, my father was influenced by a certain artistic culture, that of the *kantata*, a type of theatre that was born in the 'forties. In Togo, the incontestable master of the *kantata* was Moorhouse Apedoh Amah, a choir master and composer of religious songs. (Zinsou 1989:24)

Written and published in 1972, the play was not performed for several years. It was the first example of dramatic art modelled on the folk theatre of the biblical cantata and on the concert party, similar to the productions of Hubert Ogunde. It is a dramatic universe quite separated from declamatory theatre; it is composed of burlesque litanies in pidgin, rhetorical interventions from the Bible, songs punctuated by a series of 'amens' as in Pentecostal ceremonies, poetic parodies, and the use of transvestites. The same inventiveness of form is found in *La tortue qui chante* (1987b), an original attempt to adapt the wonderful universe of fairy tales for the stage. It tells the story of a hunter, Asho Kpanzo, who leaves the forest empty-handed and encounters a tortoise. The tortoise can sing and becomes involved in the struggle to become king. However, the refrain hummed by the tortoise, 'Evil doesn't provoke man, it's man that provokes evil' is worth it: the tortoise does not sing if the listener is not considered deserving. In a parodic way, the court jester, who is allowed to say anything and proclaims, 'Truth belongs to the king', defends the logic of power. The hunter retorts that truth belongs to his tortoise. The fool understands fully, and provides the moral of the story: 'To each his own tortoise, Majesty: the difference is that villains can no longer hear their tortoise's song' (Ricard 1986a:102).

Since *On joue la comédie*, classroom-type declamation has disappeared from Zinsou's light and didactic writing, as fairy tales are wont to be. Ewe songs and music are inserted into a text that manages to retain the flow of the narrative. Werewere Liking's present successes and puppet theatre draw from the same source, that of folk art, which she manages to translate visually rather than verbally (*Dieu Chose*, 1985). The same can be said of Gabriel Garran's production based on the poetry of Tchicaya U'Tamsi, *Le bal de Ndinga* (1985), in which the warm presence of Congolese music can be heard – an essential vehicle of emotions in a large part of Black Africa.

Another creative route would have been unequivocally political theatre, except that in many countries the road was closed. In many countries, staging a 'classic' like *Ubu Roi* was unthinkable: on a Bangui or a Kinshasa stage, Mother Ubu and the King of Poland's madness would have triggered too many comparisons with social reality. The fact of having to conceal one's intentions probably partly explains the number of plays about Soweto or about the student situation in South Africa, as pointed out by Pius Ngandu, with special reference to Zaïre (1982:58–76). Struggles for liberty are indivisible; the tyranny of apartheid can never justify the absence of liberty in other countries, but it is always more convenient to denounce oppression somewhere else, leaving it to the public to understand the true meaning, should they be so inclined. And so South Africa remained a symbolic place as regards African politics: from the emblematic figure of the politician and his 'hubris' (Shaka) to the world of Soweto, a source of metaphors of oppression of young people and intellectuals by tyrannical regimes, decipherable to the north and south of the Limpopo. For many dramatists living in small countries devoid of any liberty of expression, the South African scene offered the ideal image of their own situation. For the pupils at least, the validity of the equation 'Botha equals Bokassa' was obvious. When speech became freer in a number of Francophone countries at the beginning of the 'nineties, vast new spaces opened up to poets and dramatists. What will they do with these opportunities? Will they be able to invent new forms to express new times or will they be content to make speeches? The work done by Sony Labou Tansi's company, from the first plays like *Conscience de tracteur* (1979) and *La parenthèse de sang* (1981) to *La double résurrection rouge et blanche de Romeo et Juliette* (1990, based on Shakespeare), shows a way forward for theatre that draws on the heritage of Tchicaya U'Tamsi's flamboyant writing, oriented towards the decree of a generous, universalist humanism. The question remains whether the young generation of writers will make the most of the following powerful words by Sony Labou Tansi, a writer who was able to free his own discourse from the constraints of schoolroom theatre through a vigorous verbal expansion:

> Frankly, I believe one needs specific words to express each and every thing, every situation. You can't use the same words to express and describe two situations. It's very difficult. To talk in terms of discharge, there are words that cannot contain all the strength, all the power of a thought. Either the word explodes, or the thought is compressed. Great effort is needed, a lot of language skill. Whether he wants to or not, a writer is someone who enters the forest of language and who starts clearing the undergrowth, the landscape, the space where he's going to plant. It's a metaphor I got from my parents. (Sony Labou Tansi in Malanda 1983:149)

By way of conclusion, I want to reflect on a paradox and propose a hypothesis for comparative research. Why is theatre still the poor relation of Francophone African literature, while Soyinka's output (and that of a few others) has become the crown jewel of Anglophone literature? This paradox is even more surprising in view of the international recognition of Francophone

African cinema (as opposed to Nigerian cinema, for example). Theatre and cinema are cousins, they are variants of one and the same artistic form: interaction constantly takes place between the two means of expression. From the start, Francophone African cinema was in contact with the New Wave *avant-garde* who took to filming with limited means, natural scenery and unknown actors whose faces would speak for themselves. It is worth remembering that in 1959 Jean-Luc Godard greeted Jean Rouch's film, *Moi, un Noir* as a cinematographic revolution. The film's actor used his own words – the pidgin French (of an Abidjan docker) seldom heard on a Francophone stage before the shows of the Ivoirian Koteba company which, unfortunately, toned down the subversiveness of the caricature. Nigerian cinema wanted to copy Hollywood, and it failed. Anglophone theatre was not as linguistically prudish, nor as timid. Towards the end of the 'fifties, London was theatre's *avant-garde* capital. Peter Brook was staging Genet and Georges Devine was lecturing on Brecht at the Royal Court Theatre, where a young Nigerian dramatist, Wole Soyinka, was receiving his training. He was soon to return to his country where he would teach what he had understood. In short the Orient-inspired *avant-garde* was not defending a narrow, Western concept of theatre, but theatre in general, a type of expression where aesthetics and politics could not be dissociated, where verbal language was only a part of the musical, gestural whole. That is what the new generation of Francophone dramatists, the generation of Zinsou, Zadi Zaourou, Sony Labou Tansi and Werewere Liking had finally understood: in theatre, words must also be invented.

9 Narrative Fiction

THE SANDS OF BABEL

If writers consider poetry their prime genre, the reading public is more familiar with literature through the novel. It is the genre that attracts the most readers; it is also the form that enables the writer to recompose the world or, on the contrary, to illustrate its decomposition. A multilingual, multicultural Africa provides the ideal subject matter for a great polyphonic novel in which history will be expressed in all its incoherence and complexity through a vast chorus of voices. Writing a novel means daring to pose the two questions on history and language: 'Which options should one take from the different possibilities with which History compels the writer to signify literature?' (Barthes, 1953:10). This question has particular relevance for the colonial situation – the African context for the greater part of the nineteenth century. Many novelists resolved (or thought they had resolved) this problem by writing in their own language. By setting down the story of the Zulu, Shaka, in Sesotho, Thomas Mofolo revealed his distant admiration for the man whose panegyric he quoted in Zulu. By collecting hunters' tales in Yoruba, D.O. Fagunwa restored the memory of his tradition while offering a model to pupils. The fact that E. Kezilahabi expressed his concern for the future of the young Tanzanian generations in Kiswahili also contributed to the construction of that country's future. To create in an African language means to put a strain on it, to force it to be equal to a history that might otherwise get written elsewhere. Can one avoid questions about writing and aesthetic choices in general in the process? I think not, and Ngugi's example is a clear indication that the issues around language and history cannot be resolved solely by an author's choice of his own language as vehicle. African novelists are all too conscious of this responsibility. They want to change the subordinate status given to their writing, and they know that this will only be made possible by escaping their language's dependent and peripheral status, thus taking their history in their own hands.

Initially, the pioneers of novel writing in the European languages were daunted by the sheer scope of the undertaking and the limitations of their writing. This soon becomes apparent when one looks at the Onitsha novelists or the works of Félix Couchoro. This probably explains the phenomenon of 'tutelage' or even 'assisted' writing, which was common during the early days of Francophone literature in Africa and which, to me, seems a curious example of linguistic thoughtlessness. At a time when African countries were attaining independence, writing models were developed that in many cases still operate today: the 'classical' Mongo Beti novel and Chinua Achebe's 'Igbo' novels with their various formulae for obtaining a balance between language and history have not exhausted all their resources and still have their followers. And yet, the long silence of authors like Achebe (in the period after the start of the Nigerian civil war) and Mongo Beti (during the 'sixties) indicated that this means of expression was beginning to lose momentum by the end of the first decade of the 'suns of independence' (to quote the title of a book discussed below). This type of writing would be revitalized later in the 'seventies and would culminate in Achebe's return to fiction with the publication of *Anthills of the Savannah* (1987).

Similarly, Sony Labou Tansi (1947–) drew strength for his novels from the legacy of Tchicaya U'Tamsi, speaking with the same generous voice and inspired by the latter's great theatrical experience. Such representational writing, which is principally concerned with its link with reality, now coexists with a type of enunciated writing that puts the emphasis on a stream of personal expression. The revitalization of classical writing, which took place during the last two decades of the twentieth century, accompanied more radical efforts to modify the textual link between language and history. In 1968, Ahmadou Kourouma (1927–2003), a writer from Côte d'Ivoire, produced a text of extraordinary originality entitled *Les soleils des indépendances* [*The Suns of Independence*], which seemed to give birth to a new language. In a different context and with different means, it may be considered the French equivalent of Tutuola's oeuvre. The latter still poses a problem, especially as far as translations are concerned; it has its followers, as exemplified by Ken Saro-Wiwa's (1941–95) powerful novel on the Nigerian civil war, entitled *Sozaboy* (1985). Such productivity is commendable and probably stems from a positioning of the subject within the text like that found in the work of the Portuguese writer, Luandino Vieira (1935–). The text does not separate languages for the sake of some clear linguistic consciousness; on the contrary, its discourse arises out of a whole collection of languages: the act of utterance itself is a translation of the plurality of social voices. The reader hears several languages within the same text; the disciples of Turito, that little prophet who is Vieira's protagonist, have drawn a line in the 'sands of Babel' beyond which only innovators and poets dare to tread (Trigo, 1981:29). It is up to them to keep showing us the way.

Pioneers of the Novel

Ethiopia Unbound (1911) is considered the first fictional text in English by an African writer: J.E. Casely-Hayford (1866–1930), a Gold Coast lawyer and politician. The anonymous author of *Marita: or the Folly of Love*, published in 1885–88, has yet to be identified, while Liberian writer Joseph J. Walters's *Guanya Pau*, published in Lincoln (USA) in 1891, was discovered only recently. *Ethiopia Unbound* is a strange text, even incoherent to some; at any rate, it is difficult to follow as the plot unfolds on several levels. It tells the story of Kwamankra and his friend Whitely who, at the beginning at the novel, are busy having discussions in London and who meet again in Gold Coast at the end of the novel. One is a famous lawyer with nationalistic convictions and the other is a chaplain in the colonial government. The story does not play itself out in a linear way: we are taken on an excursion to paradise where Kwamankra rediscovers his wife; we leave for the United States in the company of the hero, and we hear the speeches and debates that punctuate his travels there. The backdrop of the novel is an often sarcastic depiction of colonial society through the discourse of its principal representatives. The narration is livened up (and sometimes interrupted) by songs, fables and narratives. Songs in Fanti and poems written in Victorian English are also added to the at times confusing mix. The chief aim of the book is to defend the cause of the Ethiopians whose country, it is suggested, is the cradle of Christianity. However, this illustrious heritage does not lead the author to a didactic attitude or to proselytize: on the contrary, he is very critical of a religion dominated by whites although it originated with blacks. Being a lawyer and a politician, J.E. Casely-Hayford can sustain a powerful rhetoric. Inspired by the masters of what was to become the Black Renaissance (E. Blyden, W.E.B. du Bois), the book is primarily demonstrative and polemical. And yet, the strictly political intention of this piece of fiction is enriched by its use of the marvellous and of caricature. The book is filled with driving passion and the debate is never clumsy, even if the same cannot be said for the overall construction.

Another Gold Coast novel, *Eighteen Pence* (1941) by R.E. Obeng (1868–1951) the father of Anglophone fiction, is still regarded as the 'the first true novel to be published by a Gold Coaster' (Obeng, 1998: xi, in the new manuscript-based edition by Kari Dako). It tells the story of Akrofi, an insolvent debtor, who pawns himself to his creditor. He is wrongly accused of rape by his master's wife and brought to justice. Akrofi's (female) accuser insists on a colonial instead of an indigenous court. The novelist spares us none of the accusations and defences: the hero is acquitted and proceeds to lead a very successful life, all the while keeping us fully informed of his ideas, which are set out in long, moralizing speeches. The text belongs to the older period in the history of the African novel, that of the pioneers. The author is the Anglophone equivalent of Félix Couchoro, showing the same devoted respect for academic rules of correct language, the same pedagogical concern, but also some of the fantasy of Couchoro's characterizations.

An essay from the same period as Caseley-Hayford's novel eludes classification as an allegory through its precise analysis and its descriptive accuracy. *Native Life in South Africa* (1916) by the South African author Sol T. Plaatje (1876–1932) was published mid-war to mobilize British and American opinion against the 1913 Land Act. Unfortunately, this timing was ill-chosen and the campaign had no effect on the white government's determination to pursue the Act's implementation. During this period, Plaatje wrote a novel, *Mhudi*, which lay unpublished for almost fifteen years before it came out in 1930 from the missionary Lovedale Press. Plaatje was an experienced writer and a journalist; his *Mafeking Diary, a Black Man's View of a White Man's War* (1989), published almost a century after it was written, is still a fascinating account. *Mhudi* is probably the first novel written in English by a black South African and is equally worth reading today. It tells of the meeting and the subsequent relationship between the eponymous heroine and Ra Thaga, the courageous Tswana hunter who saves her from a lion's claws in a country devastated by Zulus. Upon returning to his clan, Ra Thaga marries Mhudi and befriends a Boer, regardless of the hostility of the rest of the white nomadic community (or 'trekkers'). The characters of Mhudi, her husband Ra Thaga, Phil the good Boer and Mzilikazi the Zulu chief are well drawn and allow for the emergence of a coherent historical vision. The story takes place in a society in the process of transformation: the old world is collapsing under Boer pressure and Zulu attacks. The only way to confront the Boers would be to unite the 'Kaffir' tribes, to preserve Tswana clan independence, but this seems difficult to accomplish. The Boers' Great Trek is certainly not presented as a central event in Southern African history, but just another tribal migration, involving many dangers. Plaatje writes in the language of the 'fish eaters', the English, while his heroes speak 'Dutch' or 'Rolong' (Setswana). In the end, the 'fish eaters' are Plaatje's only hope for resistance to the Boers' exorbitant claims, which will be translated into reality by the Land Act of 1913.

His impassioned eloquence combines with a feeling for nature inherited from the English romantics. His profound knowledge of Shakespeare (whom he would translate into Setswana) lends archaic charm to a slightly old-fashioned prose, redeemed by the strength of his ideas and by his grasp of the situation, so far removed from the concerns of fiction writing in England.

The great author associated with Africa, who dominates all English fiction and not only its 'colonial' writing, is Joseph Conrad. There is no equivalent figure in France's colonial literature, out of which the African novel in French was born (even if it challenged many of that genre's prejudices).

The beginnings of fictional literature in French are situated between the two world wars. No criticism is levelled at the colonial power; rather, it is naïvely exalted, as in the novel *Force-Bonté* (1926) by Bakary Diallo (1892–1979). Indigenous culture is depicted and defended in *L'esclave* (1929) by Félix Couchoro (1900–1968) or placed under the beneficent tutelage of France as in *Karim* (1935) by Ousmane Socé Diop (1922–73) or in *Doguicimi* (1938) by Paul Hazoumé (1890–1980). In the Belgian Congo, the names of Stefano Kaoze (1885–1951), the first Congolese priest and author of ethnographic articles, and of Thadée Badibanga, the presumed author (never identified with any certainty) of a collection of short stories, *L'éléphant qui marche sur les oeufs* (1931), do not really suggest the dawn of a great literature. According to Mukala Kadima-Nzuji (1984:13), the next noteworthy period did not arrive till the 'sixties, with the notable exception in fiction of Paul Lomami-Tshibamba's *Ngando* (1948).

There is little doubt that *Force-Bonté* exemplifies a supervised literature in which the author is actually a man of straw. From the moment it was published, critics expressed their doubts about the extent of Bakary Diallo's contribution. In his preface to the new edition (1985), M. Kane does not help to allay suspicions:

> It is evident that from 1911 to 1926 Bakary Diallo could not have learnt enough French to be able to write a novel, seeing that from 1911 to 1918 he was developing his military career, waging war and, later, treating his wounds. We know, too, that the army is not the best school for learning about language and literature. (Kane, in Diallo, 1985:viii)

Kane suggests that the work in its entirety could not have been produced by its 'author' and that it must have been checked and corrected by the publishing director, the writer Jean-Richard Bloch: 'Bakary must have provided the raw material, the first attempt' (Kane, in Diallo, 1987:viii). The text develops a number of themes – departure, the difficulties of living in Europe, etcetera – that will reappear in later novels, but this thematic similarity is not enough to arouse the reader's interest in a text that is, linguistically speaking, too good to be true. Except for rare instances of attention to local colour, the former *tirailleur* does not always take careful aim as a writer. However, a recent re-evaluation of the text (Riesz, 1996) provides a convincing defence of its literary quality and authenticity, and claims that both are the result of the author's personal experience.

Félix Couchoro's *L'esclave* [The Slave], which was curiously absent from literary history books until the beginning of the 'seventies, is a real novel, clearly from the outset in the tradition of colonial literature. The author's intention is the rehabilitation of black people: 'We shall see that passion is not at all the prerogative of a particular race having reached a certain degree of civilization. To be awakened, passion needs only the heart of man' (Couchoro, 1929:8). The latter quote was taken from the novel's preface, an interesting text because of its testimony to the author's linguistic awareness, rare in Francophone Africa at the time:

> We have tried to convey the words and ideas of our heroes in a cultivated foreign language. The reader should not be too surprised! In our countries, we have our own education, polite forms of language, intellectual culture, a code of conventions, and ceremonies where grandiloquence is equal only to the desire to be polite and to please. In our idioms, we have an earthy form of language, a style for good company as well as for the sublime. Our hearts are capable of noble sentiments; our spirits radiate with elevated thoughts. (Couchoro, 1929:9)

The author does not pretend that writing in French comes naturally to him: in his novel, he sets out to try and restore the African mode of expression, the result of which may come as a surprise. He avoids dwelling on the transition from oral style to written language by emphasizing the difficulty of rendering the different levels in a foreign language. He has understood that one of the central problems of writing in another language is maintaining a smooth transition between language levels within the discourse. In order to avoid *tirailleur* Diallo's awkward, starchy style, an author must be able to master the different registers, which is a question of practice rather than perfect grammar. In his initial texts Couchoro perfected the Africanization techniques that served as situation cues: the cries of the market women, ritual invocations during fetishist ceremonies, greetings between friends. Alas, Couchoro's novelistic talents do not match the standard of his theoretical clarity, as I tried to illustrate in my book devoted to this pioneer, who was a militant in his own way (Ricard, 1987). Despite these difficulties, Couchoro continued writing in French and debating on the validity of colonial literature. In his second novel, *Amour de féticheuse* [The Love of a Fetish Priestess], he defended Africa in his own way:

> The key idea guiding the pens of some of the kings of colonial literature, is that as soon as the evolved black man returns to his own environment he falls back into the rut from which civilization tried to extract him. And they try their utmost to prove it. The abundant number of books following this line of thinking are read with interest. It's an opinion. If we may be allowed to say so, the idea is questionable. The heroes of this novel will prove it.... (Couchoro, 1941:iv)

The fiction output of the first Francophone writers must be seen within the framework of colonial literature: they believe they can improve on the work of the colonial authors, or give a more authentic rendition, because as Africans they have inside knowledge of their world. *Karim* (1935), a Senegalese novel by Ousmane Socé Diop, recounts the lives of a well-to-do class of 'Muslim bourgeois' with just enough borrowings from Wolof to add some local colour. Paul Hazoumé's novel, *Doguicimi* (1938), is a more ambitious project, yet set within the same frame of reference.

> The spelling of some indigenous names and the use of expressions that might appear unusual to the reader represent an accurate rendering of local pronunciation and a faithful translation of the picturesque speech of the Dahomeans. We are convinced that this solemn manner of speaking will, by virtue of its rootedness in the land, succeed in imparting a seal of authenticity and exoticism to our documentation, for that is the constant concern of a true regionalist writer. (Hazoumé, 1938: 14)

When dealing with regional customs, Paul Hazoumé is on solid ground: shortly before writing his novel, he completed a dissertation on *Le pacte de sang au Dahomey* (1937) at the Ethnographical Institute of the University of Paris. The regionalist African novel is a type of colonial novel written by 'regionals' or natives, not from Provence or Gascony, but from Dahomey. *Doguicimi* is an important work: it is a text of more than 500 pages, including numerous notes demonstrating his ethnographic competence. He tells the story of a Dahomean princess at the beginning of the nineteenth century who, true to custom and conjugal love, chose to follow her royal spouse to the grave. The novel succeeds in combining understanding of ancient Africa, its order and ceremonies, with eulogy of colonisation. It is not surprising that development of the anti-colonialist novel during the post-war years eclipsed references to this text. Moreover, the princess's heroic decision does not result in struggle, but in suicide. Identification with such a heroine is problematic at a time when the political stage is occupied by the themes of national reconstruction. Ultimately, in our view, Paul Hazoumé does not succeed in exploiting the situation's tragic virtues in the way that Wole Soyinka was able to do in the similar situation staged in *Death and the King's Horseman*. Doguicimi is completely a creature of her time, representing a world of cruelty and grandeur that fascinated Paul Hazoumé, and she takes it with her to the grave. The density and complexity of Wole Soyinka's play are absent here. This linear quality, added to the novel's sometimes didactic nature, prevents the book from becoming a feat of historical reconstitution, in the manner of Flaubert's *Salammbô*. In a sense, it suffers even more acutely from the same defect: the drama is buried under a pile of stage-sets.

New editions of these pioneering works, praised upon publication and then forgotten, only came to be published decades later: *Ethiopia Unbound* in 1969, *Mhudi* in 1975, *Doguicimi* in 1978, *L'esclave* in 1983 and *Force-Bonté* in 1985. There is thus a linguistic as well as an historical break between the texts written before 1945 and those of the post-war years. The first authors of fiction were on the fringe of society; often unknown to their targeted public and unsuccessful in imposing themselves as novelists. The colonial world had no room for fiction that challenged its very existence through its realistic depiction of the social situation. Ethiopia would only be 'unbound' during the course of the twentieth century; Mhudi, like Doguicimi, is a heroine from the past. However, Karim and the other characters in *L'esclave* are more at ease in a world that is contemporary with the publication date of these other two titles. The colonial world, which both tried to paint in African colours, succeeded only in turning Mhudi and Doguicimi into artificial and outdated ciphers, thus revealing the basic conditions of fiction writing that must always be kept in mind behind any analysis.

Local Fiction

In Africa, fiction writing in European languages started after the war, when improved schooling developed a larger reading public. Numerous locally published works contributed to shaping public expectations. In West Africa, the field of local publications is called 'market literature', and more specifically 'Onitsha' literature (the name of Nigeria's biggest market), but it can be found in many other regions and is similar to so-called 'hawker's litera-ture' in the French tradition. I can vouch for the fact that, at the beginning of the 'seventies, these booklets could still be bought at markets or coach stations. They provided the linguistic context for fiction writing: the French or the English written in Africa is modelled on these texts, and writers began by situating themselves in relation to this context. Such literature dealt with politics, racial conflicts and the whole tumult around independence, which was often absent from the first African novels published in Europe. The following lines from Thomas Iguh's *The Last Days of Lumumba, the Late Lion of the Congo, a Drama*, by one of the most prolific Onitsha authors (1961: 13–1), are a case in point:

> 1st citizen: Kill every Belgian: Lumumba will be our king....
>
> *At this stage, shouts of War! War! can be heard from the crowd.*
>
> 1st citizen: Let us match [sic] to the battle field for this is the hour.
> 2nd citizen: I shall wash my hands with the blood of a Belgian tomorrow.
> 3rd citizen: I must carry home the head of a Belgian....
>
> *At this stage a Belgian millionaire with his family can be seen approaching the market square in his expensive car:*
>
> 1st citizen: There comes the enemy.
> Lumumba: Kill him! Let him be an example, for the tree of liberty must be watered by the blood of the tyrants.
>
> *At this stage the angry crowd surges onto the road and stops the car. They drag the occupants out and slash them to pieces. They march home singing war songs while parts of the bodies of the butchered Belgians are conspicuously displayed at the front of the unruly parade.* (Iguh, 1961:15)

Racial violence has seldom been portrayed in such a crude manner in African literature. This quotation is not an isolated one; numerous other lines display the same taste for expressing violence. This extract can be compared with other detailed descriptions of rapes and abortions, as in Speedy Eric's *Mabel, the Sweet Honey That Poured Away* (quoted in Obiechina, 1972:110). No details are spared:

> She swallowed handfuls of contraceptives. The next day what was bound to happen, happened. The abortion happened in the middle of the day, and a torrent of blood

flowed out.... Inside the lavatory our seventeen-year-old sweet honey was pouring away.... (Speedy Eric, in Obiechina, 1972:110)

These novels offer extremely evocative details of sex and violence, two themes rarely mentioned in fiction before the end of the 'sixties. One remembers the scandal caused by *Le devoir de violence* [*Bound to Violence*] by Yambo Ouologuem (1940–), which initiated the reader into the bonds between sex and violence. 'Local' writing labels all that is 'without a name' in the formal African literature of its time. We need only think of the prudishness of some Nigerian authors (like Onitsha writers, they are often of Igbo origin): the first that springs to mind is Chinua Achebe. At best, this type of writing transgresses the 'literary' norm imposed by educational institutions and creates a new language on sex and racial violence, which will obviously shock academic critics. While on this point, it is noteworthy that publications on these texts (notably by Obiechina, 1972) make no mention of what critics less concerned about pedagogy would call their pornographic aspect: in a nutshell, their treatment of taboo subjects. Added to this first transgression is the second, just as serious: writers expressing themselves in an unacceptable way. Onitsha writing is defined in relation to the academic norm and is on its margin: its exponents do not write in a pidgin language, but in a generally correct English characterized by a particular fondness for neologisms, surprising metaphors and borrowings from various specialized technical languages: sport, journalism, using a mixture of language levels. Once captured in print, what is tolerated in spoken language changes in relation to written norms and consequently becomes a reprehensible deviation in a country where access to printed matter, at the time, conferred a certain moral authority.

Errors in grammar (especially errors in good taste by mixing language levels), added to other moral 'errors' such as violence and pornography, may define a sector of Onitsha literature as beyond the pale, but it is nonetheless, writing:

> The pleasure of reading obviously comes from certain ruptures (or certain collisions): codes of unpleasantness (the noble and the trivial, for example) come into contact, pompous and derisory neologisms are created. (Barthes, 1973:14)

These texts are interesting in many ways: they provide us with information on the level of English written by the pupils and the new literate of a given region; they give a glimpse of the readers' need to communicate, their desire to get away from it all, as well as their predilection for historical characters. Apart from being a literary phenomenon and offering a cheap read, these texts express the desire to appropriate a European language and illustrate their numerous (sometimes surprising) capacities to reach this objective. A literary phenomenon such as the work of Amos Tutuola is incomprehensible without reference to the example set by these creators, who suffered no cultural complexes and were left to their own devices, to their limited knowledge and boundless imagination. Like Tutuola, they assert their right to invention and fantasy.

The pioneer writer Félix Couchoro, who was published in Paris in 1929, was also a local writer of stature, and his works deserve to be considered as such. He published two novels in Dahomey (*Amour de féticheuse* 1941, *Drame d'amour à Anecho*, 1950) followed by a steady stream of serials in Togo from 1962 to 1968 (Ricard, 1987). His oeuvre, composed of more than twenty novels, describes the life of the *évolués* along the Benin coast. Félix Couchoro had the talent and luck to move the public and to keep up a dialogue with them. Not only was he one of the first African novelists, but he even found new readers in the 'sixties. He made his mark as a writer through his capacity to play around with the French language. In his early works he was more concerned with displaying his competence, but in the Togolese books he succeeded in showing what he could do with the French language by 'Togolizing' it. His readers were doubtless sensitive to this nationalist dimension of his oeuvre. His intuitive linguistic awareness (as expressed by the surprising preface to *L'esclave*), his continuous development of his work, which included rewriting certain texts and using recurring themes and sometimes characters, show a high degree of linguistic consciousness. Unfortunately, he remained the prisoner of a restricted environment that is still riddled with age-old class prejudices. His attitude towards French was that of a writer and not of a teacher: he created a whole world in his language and was the only believer in the actual possibility of the world he depicted. However, the 'evolved' population of Togo and Dahomey's Beninese coast could not really create a small Francophone, bourgeois republic for themselves, cut off from the rest of the continent!

Congolese fiction

In the Belgian Congo of 1948, Paul Lomami-Tshibamba wrote *Ngando*, a clever combination of mythology and life in the townships. In its geographical context, this was a truly fundamental work and was recognized as such in Zaïre (the name adopted in 1971 by the former Belgian colony and present Democratic Republic of Congo). It was reprinted in 1982, but has remained on the fringe of Francophone literature (Kadima-Nzuji, 1984). The same applies to the Zaïrean novelist Zamenga Batukezanga, who writes in the French style of the local press and has sold hundreds of thousands of copies of his works (Mata, 1993). He represents a veritable literary phenomenon and bears witness to the possibilities of a local literature and publishing industry. The author can deal with the ethical problems of daily life in polished and yet colloquial language, akin to newspaper talk, but refined enough to appear in book form. Félix Couchoro's success in writing edifying novels for a non-existent middle class, for readers who are slightly more cultivated than those attracted to Onitsha productions – which have been taken over today by multinational publishing firms, according to Coulon (1987) – can also occur elsewhere in Africa. The economic crisis does not signify the end of local publishing firms: authors are legion, and the readers are fond of books in which they can rediscover their everyday environment.

Establishing a Body of Reference

According to Kole Omotoso (1994:34), André Brink commented

> that in multilingual societies, social, political and other reasons might direct a writer
> to write in one or other of the many languages in the society. Somehow African

intellectuals, often supposedly left-leaning African intellectuals, seem to be incapable of grasping this reasonable situation, thus making it impossible for them to use all the options available to them.

This is what happened in South Africa with many writers; the situation holds true for the rest of the continent as I have tried to show in previous chapters.

In an essay on the literature of sub-Saharan Africa, Nadine Gordimer does not hesitate to hand out compliments: for her, Senghor is the greatest poet, Soyinka the best dramatist and Achebe the only novelist in the 'world literature' class (Gordimer 1973). Thirty years later, we still think her assessments are justified, at least for poetry and drama. Her only omission was not to consider the South African writers as Africans. The international success of Peter Abrahams's novel, *Mine Boy* (1946), preceded his exile and relegated him to the fringes of South African literature. Today we can reread him as an African writer and reflect on the prophetic nature of his text about power in Africa, *A Wreath for Udomo*. In the end, Nadine Gordimer's triumph is that of a novelist who refused to leave her country, reflecting on ethical and practical implications of such a choice (for example, *July's People*, 1981), and who maintained a dialogue without condescension or compromise with writers from the rest of the continent.

Establishing a novelistic tradition of reference in French requires first a series of memory lapses: forgetting the pioneers, the local writers (Félix Couchoro, again!), and a few exceptions (Paul Hazoumé, Paul Lomami-Tshibamba). Thus, the African novel starts with the works of Camara Laye (1928–1981): *L'enfant noir* (1953) [*Dark Child*] and *Le regard du roi* (1954) [*The Radiance of the King*], contemporary with *Cruel City*, the first novel by Mongo Beti (1932–), which appeared under the pseudonym Eza Boto. Camara Laye's two texts were relatively successful: *Dark Child* gives an idyllic vision of rural Africa, totally in keeping with the impressions the reader gets from Senghor's *Chants d'ombre*. *The Radiance of the King* is an ambitious and successful search into the meaning of the African experience for a European. The text is a strange one, offering a metaphysical vision of Africa somewhat removed from the anti-colonial preoccupations of its era. And yet, from their date of publication until the present day, these two texts have been accused of lacking authenticity. Camara Laye, who worked in a car factory, was no more 'able' to write these novels than Bakary Diallo, the Senegalese *tirailleur* was deemed capable of an autobiography. In Camara Laye's case, there were no precise elements to support such misgivings. In fact, the issue centred on his unlikely ability to write texts in good French of such length *at all*. The only acceptable African writer is one who, like Hazoumé or Senghor, can present the proofs of academic legitimacy, which a simple 'black' worker cannot. This recurrent 'forgery' theme is truly indicative of a profoundly ambiguous attitude towards language appropriation: if the language of a text is correct or even elegant while the author is not a recognized intellectual, it can only be attributed to foreign – French – intervention!

> Why didn't he appeal to the law when he saw that he was being maligned? It's because he thought that he would not be believed: a double inferiority complex due to race and social position.... (Sembène, 1957b:72)

The first novel by Sembène Ousmane (1923–) *Le docker noir* (1957) [*Black Docker*], is a narrative about the lives of dockers, as well as a tale of literary plagiarism in which an African writer discovers himself to be a French author's involuntary ghostwriter. A black docker could not have written the beautiful pages of *The Slaveship Sirius*, the award-winning novel (mis)appropriated in manuscript by the French woman writer who was supposed to have published it. Contrary to what could have happened to Bakary Diallo, Sembène Ousmane's hero, the compromised ghostwriter, is a reticent man who does not accept the theft of his manuscript at first and whose eventual violent punishment of the thief causes her death. 'This monster pretends to be the author of *The Slaveship Sirius*! This insult to our literature is also a criminal offence...' (Sembène, 1957b:69).

Le docker noir 'not only describes a case of plagiarism, it has itself become the object of an accusation of plagiarism' (Riesz, 1995:95). According to Riesz, these insinuations are part of a strategy of exclusion aimed at African authors (Riesz, 1998) thus 'denying Africans access to higher education and to the literary market' (Riesz, 1995:95). *Le docker noir* exorcises the suspicion surrounding the self-taught black writer: he followed *O pays, mon beau peuple* (1957a) with his most successful novel, *Les bouts de bois de Dieu* (1960) [*God's Bits of Wood*], the story of a successful strike on an international scale. Yet, once he had addressed the French and other Europeans in an attempt to show the reality of the anti-colonial struggle, Sembène Ousmane felt the need to speak to his own people and chose the cinema to do so (*La Noire de*, 1966, *Mandabi*, 1968, *Xala*, 1974), while continuing to write short stories (*Voltaïques*, 1962, *Vehi Ciosane*, 1965).

Francophone Africa was fundamentally transformed during the period from 1956 to 1960: the colonial regime was succeeded by the Community, which in turn was followed by the independent states; the political situation was simultaneously fluid and volatile. In France as well as in Africa, the context encouraged freedom of expression, producing a series of very successful novels, which have to be read against the background of the intimate nature of Franco-African political destinies during those years. The intellectual elite of the French-speaking world was a reality before becoming a political movement. Their fictional output is part of the framework of French literature, earning its place with comic masterpieces such as Ferdinand Oyono's *Une vie de boy* (1956a) [*Houseboy*], *Le vieux nègre et la médaille* (1956b) [*The Old Man and the Medal*] or Mongo Beti's *Le pauvre Christ de Bomba* (1956) [*The Poor Christ of Bomba*] and *Mission terminée* (1957) [*Mission to Kala*]. Using a boy's diary, as in *Houseboy* or *The Poor Christ of Bomba*, is a very effective device for portraying colonial Africa through a naïve consciousness, thus revealing the often absurd and frequently odious nature of events. The figure of the administrator and the missionary are the victims of this springcleaning process; more than two generations later, the attitudes denounced by these Voltaire-like novelists are still an issue. Their efforts at linguistic awareness were made to fit into the French literary world as effectively as possible. Mongo Beti became a teacher with an *agrégation* [highly competitive teaching diploma] in Humanities in a French secondary school: he waited twenty years before writing another novel and only returned to his country forty years later. The texts of Oyono and Beti, as well as Cheikh Hamidou Kane's novel, *L'aventure ambiguë* (1928) [*Ambiguous Adventure*] – an admirable meditation on the significance of encountering different cultures and religions – were aimed at participating in the universalist discourse on colonization, which, at that stage, could only take place in France. They contributed a discourse that was certainly African, but first and foremost 'leftist', to use Mongo Beti's own terms (Mouralis, 1981:17). This may have been opposed to authority, but it nonetheless took place – or was trapped? – within the French political and intellectual debate. These authors bear witness to a rare, fleeting moment when a small group of African intelligentsia spoke in France in their own name, and were listened to. The linguistic consciousness of these writers contributed to the democratic universalism contained in the anti-colonial projects of the *Loi cadre* or 'Enabling Act' (1956) and the Act of Community (1958). It was expressed in 'political' and no longer in 'ethnological' terms, as Bernard Mouralis so aptly remarks (1981:17). For want of other horizons, it was a Francophone awareness. It took a decade of independence for these dreams to evaporate, during which period a new political and cultural movement, founded at the Niamey Conference in 1970 in the presence of André Malraux, was claimed for a French-speaking universe that had become less apparent with the passing years. The 'decolonization' of sub-Saharan Africa could not be allowed to fail, as had happened elsewhere. Since the terms of the debate had been defined by France and its intellectual elite, the cooperation of Black African intellectuals was essential (in spite of their reluctance) and necessarily obtained. But, once it had been accomplished, other issues attracted the African writers' attention and they looked for another public, at times unsuccessfully so, or they turned to other activities, even abandoning their early dreams. Ferdinand Oyono and Cheikh Hamidou Kane gave up trying to get their books published; Sembène Ousmane concentrated on the cinema, while Mongo Beti stayed silent for a long time before producing an essay denouncing the relations established between France and 'decolonized' Cameroon (*Main basse sur le Cameroun*, 1972). He took up his pen again for a work of fiction reflecting on his country's history (*Remember Ruben*, 1974a) and a satire on contemporary African power, *Lament for an African Pol* (1980). Upon his return to Cameroon, Mongo Beti went back to publishing with new-found verve, inspired by his return to Africa, and kept working until his death (*Trop de soleil tue l'amour*, 1999, *Branle-bas en noir et blanc*, 2000).

Masters of Representative Writing

When *Things Fall Apart* appeared in 1958, the only well-known Nigerian writer was the eccentric Amos Tutuola. The artistry of Chinua Achebe (1930–), still flourishing today, is of another order, demonstrating African writers' successful formula in appropriating English language and literature. This first novel became an international bestseller, inaugurating Heinemann's African Writers' Series. Achebe became the editor of the series, which has published every Nigerian and African author of any importance. As for Achebe, *Things Fall Apart* was followed by *No Longer at Ease* (1960), *Arrow of God* (1964), *A Man of the People* (1966) and then, after a long silence except for the publication of poems, essays and short stories, the admirable *Anthills of the Savannah*

(1987). This novel is dominated by a reflection on the African writer's language: English is the logical choice for a Nigerian confronted with a multitude of languages and who, on top of everything, is Igbo-speaking, a language devoid of a long written literary tradition. It is thus quite fitting to adapt English to one's own purposes. Within the context of literature written in English, Chinua Achebe's literary project may be considered the anti-novel about Africa: he wants to demonstrate that Africa's fictional material has not been exhausted by Joseph Conrad's *Heart of Darkness* (1902) or Joyce Cary's *Mister Johnson* (1939), contrary to what people might conclude from the lengthy silence of African novelists up to Tutuola (Casely-Hayford and Obeng notwithstanding).

The first four Achebe novels form a cycle about the end of village society and the chaotic beginnings of the new State. In *Things Fall Apart*, Okonkwo, the hero, has been driven from his village after an accidental murder. On his return he finds that everything has changed: the missionaries have arrived and the villagers have welcomed them with open arms. Bitterly disappointed, he kills the administrator's messenger. When he realizes that the clan no longer supports him, he commits suicide. The old world has gone and he has stayed behind, possessed by the strong spirit within him (his *chi).* He struggles against it but is eventually defeated. In *No Longer at Ease*, Okonkwo's grandson (whose village paid for his studies in England) is given an administrative post on his return, but is easily corrupted and ends up in prison. *Arrow of God* once again takes us to the village: Ezeulu, the priest of the serpent, realizes that the world has changed and sends his son to the missionary school. He quarrels with the clan when his son is caught in the act of killing a sacred python and Ezeulu is imprisoned by the administrator. Upon his release, the priest provokes the villagers' anger by refusing to perform the new yam rites. He thus causes his own downfall, as well as that of his priesthood and of his cult. The last novel of this quartet, *A Man of the People*, takes us into the world of politics. Odili, the hero, seduces Minister Nanga's girlfriend. The Minister, a corrupt, crafty and vulgar character, wins the elections by fraudulent practice on a grand scale. The novel ends with a military takeover and the arrest of all politicians, a conclusion that anticipated the events in Nigeria of 1966 and the situation depicted twenty years later in the opening paragraphs of *Anthills of the Savannah*. Achebe's stylistic power comes from the skilful and always pertinent use of proverbs, treated as fragments of ethical discourse inherited from the oral tradition that are translated and embedded either in the characters' speech or in the author's discourse.

> Achebe's literary talents are clearly revealed in his use of proverbs. One can observe his mastery of the English language, his skill in choosing the right words to convey his ideas, his keen sense of what is in character and what is not, his instinct for appropriate metaphor and symbol, and his ability to present a thoroughly African world in thoroughly African terms. (Lindfors, 1972:92)

Chinua Achebe renders the characters' supposed Igbo discourse in English: he excels in reproducing their turns of phrase, their use of proverbs and their set formulas, and in representing the world of the village in a way that is equally as acceptable to Nigerian and non-Nigerian readers. He is a master of characterization through dialogue; in this respect the words and speeches of Minister Nanga, the man of the people, have become favourite extracts for anthologies.

Moreover, it is truly surprising that when Achebe caricatures Anglophone characters, he rediscovers the burlesque eloquence of some of the Onitsha texts, whose authors are past masters at parodying political speeches!

After the civil war (during which he was briefly in charge of Biafran propaganda), Chinua Achebe stopped writing novels: he composed poems in English and in Igbo, published short stories and a pamphlet entitled *The Trouble with Nigeria* (1983). Pre-civil war texts attempted to give form and significance to the colonial experience, showing the educated elite's moral and intellectual bankruptcy. It took Achebe twenty years to produce a new metaphor of his country's history and a new relationship between language and history, in *Anthills of the Savannah*. In this 'eighties novel, the political staff is no longer the one that served in *A Man of the People*: the head of state graduated from Sandhurst (the English equivalent of France's Saint-Cyr or the USA's West Point) and is anything but an illiterate drunkard; the ministers are university graduates, and one of the characters is a famous writer. Post-colonial society is the result of an 'absurd raffle-draw' (p.183); one of the characters ends up working as a houseboy while his brother is a minister. Because of this chaotic cohabitation, the characters' verbal characterization is even more pertinent: their speech expresses their social condition. We are in Lagos: the waiters and taxi-drivers speak pidgin; Beatrice, a senior civil servant and the novel's heroine, is the first woman to have received a 'first class honours' in English (p. 75). Two types of set formulae are found in the novel: proverbs originating in the Igbo tradition, and the sloganizing of politicians and communications advisors. Thus the rawness of popular speech is pitted against the political cant of the state apparatus. The author reflects on this taste for proverbs and traces it back to his father, an early pathfinder in the language jungle (p.109). He can still remember his favourite saying: '*Procrastination is a lazy man's apology*' (p.109), a 'mixed breed' maxim, Achebe tells us, the product of a misalliance between teacher triteness and Latinist pomp. This reflection on language is personified in Beatrice, a brilliant intellectual, who comes to understand the condition of the subordinate classes through her efforts to help outlawed politicians. At the end of the novel, students, servants and soldiers meet again at a christening ceremony, and it is through the language of the English Bible as well as through pidgin that their hopes for change are expressed. The writer is murdered, the minister dismissed from his post converses with the students, while Beatrice herself speaks to the young and the poor, praying with them. The reader can judge the significance of these various connections, through the way that the author voices each distinctive character. So, this polyphonic object of language, the novel, concludes with a utopian meeting between characters speaking in different voices. The author's linguistic representation of his society is highly convincing.

Through his mastery of language and the clarity of his political vision, Achebe has exerted tremendous influence on Anglophone African literature. The organization of Ngugi's cycle of novels probably owes a lot to the example of his Nigerian predecessor. His first novel (although not the first one to be published), *The River Between* (1965), is 'like *Things Fall Apart*, an almost mythical reconstitution that borrows from a situation described by the elders and experienced two generations earlier' (Bardolph 1991:36). Two young people are in love; they live on two hills facing each other. The hero respects his ancestors' religion as well as the missionaries' teachings. Everyone will reject him for wanting to marry the catechist's daughter, who has not been circumcized. *Weep Not, Child* (1964) is the story of Njoroge who wants to get away from his father's day labourer situation by excelling at school; the novel develops against the background of a state of emergency. Kenyatta's arrest is the sign that the country's fate will also shatter the hero's future, dragging both into civil war. *Grain of Wheat* (1967) is a more complex text, situated during the period leading up to independence, in 1963. Ngugi successfully manages a narrative based on the lives of five characters, one of whom is an English administrator, and another a Mau Mau pseudo-hero who is in fact a traitor. *Petals of Blood* (1977) is Ngugi's most ambitious work and his last novel written in English. It is probably also one of the longest African novels. As in the previous text, the story is related from the viewpoints of various characters. The author breaks the chronological order with numerous flashbacks retelling the story of the village of Ilmorog before the opening incident – a fire in a brothel that belongs to a former prostitute by the name of Wanja. The whole story of contemporary Kenya is reconstituted through the mobilization of Ilmorog's peasants and other inhabitants against construction operations linked to a trans-African highway. On the highlands, land is scarce and expensive and the Gikuyu politicians are on the lookout for profitable ventures. Ngugi's target is the public auctioning off of the land to the big foreign or multinational companies, with the complicity of a corrupt political class. He gives voice to the people by inserting various songs in English, Gikuyu or even Kiswahili. He also reproduces extracts from speeches and does not spare us a certain amount of political sermonizing, which is detrimental to the narrative flow.

Unlike Achebe's, Ngugi's characters are not characterized by their means of expression: 'The question of their educational or social background is irrelevant. Whether educated or uneducated, Ngugi's characters speak meticulous English; the language of the author' (Ngara, 1982:97) – even if a few Swahili words do crop up from time to time. The material used in the creation of the novel is quite other than some reworked oral discourse. Characters use all kinds of references, including biblical quotations and extracts from reports that are almost journalistic in style, while the translated songs express the collective voice of a people who become the essential material of his two latest novels. The book exudes an epic spirit, energized by deep resources that he draws up from history. The petals of blood become the flames of sacrifice, but also the blaze of purification; it is the burning of alcohol and of the sex of the female (Bardolph, 1991:46), especially in the form of the protagonist Wanja, the prostitute. To put his universe of people even more firmly centre-stage, Ngugi has used the theatre of social intervention: his play *Ngaahika Ndeenda* (1980) certainly had political impact, for it was banned. Its reader is not won over by the tedious use of slogans and revolutionary chants, though these might fill a spectator (or rather a participant) with enthusiasm. Ngugi probably finds himself restricted by fictional forms, but does not quite know what to put in its place. According to numerous press accounts, he would like to become a film director like Sembène Ousmane, one of the writers he admires and who has succeeded in portraying his people in both fiction and film.

The language situation is a product of socio-historical development: it is not a closed entity within an intangible ethnic identity. And yet, Ngugi's descriptions of Gikuyu society – especially in his works for the theatre, as we saw in the preceding chapter – create the impression of a universe that is closed to any form of historicity, and embodies an immutable identity. Gikuyu identity has indeed experienced change: in his admirable *Facing Mount Kenya,* Kenyatta was the first to bear witness to a mutation that had started back in the 'thirties. For him, writing an autobiography in English certainly did not mean rejecting the Gikuyu language, which, later, he did use:

> The politics of language in colonial Africa [not in the French colonies, AR] have a second dimension which Ngugi omits: the African appropriation of the European idiom did not necessarily imply a negation of the mother tongue as an instrument of nationalism. (Gikandi, 1992:142)

Introducing the novel into written Gikuyu does not mean liberating the Gikuyu language, but rather participating in its mutation by producing words, concepts and stylistic devices. Popular Gikuyu theatre is close to Brecht: when Ngugi writes a novel in Gikuyu, he cannot omit parts of his own literary culture, even if he wanted to:

> To appreciate *Devil on the Cross* (1982), one has to remember the influence of theatre and particularly of Brecht, that of the great Protestant preachings in the spirit of the revivalist movement and especially the oral tradition to which the author refers explicitly. (Bardolph, 1991:52)

This formal eclecticism is certainly an innovation in his writing, which rejects the realistic novel and aims at the creation of a new form.

> His decision to write in Gikuyu provided an escape from this dilemma, for it enabled him to reject realism without renouncing it, and to experiment with modernist and postmodernist forms without acknowledging their legitimacy. (Gikandi, 1992:139)

Simon Gikandi aptly observes that the materialistic and communicational conception of language emerging from all Ngugi's essays on the question (Ngugi, 1986) are in contrast to his own aesthetic theories on Gikuyu art and culture, which are all heavily influenced by an essentialist and religious conception of culture.

> He recognizes that the crucial question in the search for an African narrative is 'not that of the racial, national, and class origins of the novel, but that of its development and the uses to which it is continually being put'. But he also believes that literature can be an agent of decolonizing the African mind only if its languages can be shown to possess innate liberating qualities well beyond its pragmatic function. (Gikandi, 1992:143)

The logical conclusion of linguistic and materialistic theories is of a truly pragmatic kind: it is not language itself that is important, but its cultural and ideological uses. Ngugi is wrong to think that it is enough to write in Gikuyu to escape European influence. The fundamental question is one of exchange, of *métissage,* of mutual appropriation. The Kenyan government's underhand tyranny forced Ngugi into exile, leading to a hardening of the writer's intellectual position, which distances him from Kenya's socio-linguistic realities. In

Anthills of the Savannah, one of Achebe's characters refuses to go into exile –
but the intellectual does not always have a choice: he does not want to leave
for Europe to 'Go into exile and drink a lot of booze in European capitals and
sleep with a lot of white girls after delivering revolutionary lectures to admiring
audiences seven worlds away from where my problem is ...' (Achebe, 1987:
118). The contradiction between Ngugi's political and linguistic theories
probably results from this lack of home contact.

One may choose exile in the name of a cosmopolitan vision of literature that
is both eclectic and liberating. Such is probably the case of Nuruddin Farah
(1945–), a Somali writer who, since leaving his country, has led a nomadic
existence on the African continent. His first novel, *From a Crooked Rib* (1970),
was well received by the critics, but while he was preparing its publication as
a serial in his own language, it was prohibited, driving him into exile and
reinforcing his choice of English as his language of expression. His following
novels form a trilogy on the subject of African dictatorship: *Sweet and Sour
Milk* (1979), *Sardines* (1981) and *Close Sesame* (1983). Writing in English
opens new horizons for him, although the presence of Somali oral literature
makes itself felt in his works through the use of certain allegorical devices. Like
all Somali poets, he considers woman to be the country's symbol. The rigorous
narrative construction and the Islamic literary presence lend an absolutely
original tone to an oeuvre in which the choice of English is not a form of
colonial heritage, but the expression of a certain modernity. It is an overture to
the world via Anglophone Africa, a world to which Somalia does not belong.

Words in Action: the Sands of Babel

Literature gives meaning to historical experience: such has been its essential
function in Africa during the course of the last century. Only literature can
express the experiences, dreams and illusions of the intellectual class. This
capacity of giving form to human experience, however tragic it may be (as in
Anthills of the Savannah) is a sign of strength. As Henri Godard so excellently
put it, 'by linking certain aspects of the world with the things and the human
beings he evokes, in his use of language and forms of writing' (1990:170), the
writer should be able to impress enough coherence on the work for it to remain
a sign of recognition for the reader, despite the metamorphosis. 'For the oeuvre
to remain lively, not only must this coherence have done battle with the power
of dispersion, but it must also have prevailed' (Godard, 1990:170). Language
consciousness is the designated realm of confrontation between the forces of
dispersion and of coherence. Wole Soyinka's admirable autobiographical texts,
such as *The Man Died* (1972) and *Ake* (1984) illustrate this control of history
through the painful mastery of the language. Important works do not seek to
deny their origin, to slip silently into the mould of European literatures, but
show the extent of the struggle that have been waged. These few observations
illustrate the importance of those works that allow questions about the relation
between language and history to be posed in terms that no longer exactly
belong to the classical tradition, as with Mongo Beti or Chinua Achebe. They
establish the growing autonomy of language in a piece of writing diverging
from its purely representational function. Within this perspective, Chinua

Achebe's return to the novel certainly indicates an evolution that probably took him further along this road than Mongo Beti, whose satirical talent is backed by more traditional narrative and stylistic forms.

When Ahmadou Kourouma (1927–2003) published *Les soleils des indépendances* [*The Suns of Independence*] in Paris in 1970, the same year that a Francophone movement was organized during the Niamey Conference, it was an 'event' in more than one respect. To start with, the text was well received in Quebec – after having been refused by all the French publishers – and awarded the prize of the *Études françaises* review, which had been created to reward original French writing. It was so original, in fact, that Parisian publishers were put off and only came round to publishing it two years later. And yet, thirty years after its publication, this text is one of Seuil's most successful novels (it has sold more than a hundred thousand copies). As far as literature is concerned, Ahmadou Kourouma was a self-taught man. A former *tirailleur* turned actuary, he was one of Francophone Africa's most successful insurance specialists; the novelist's remote view of social reality is a source of humour. His vision of independence, projected through the aging chief Fama and his wife Salimata, is a rather reactionary one. Fama abhors the new world in which he has neither power nor status. His resentment makes him perceptive and his criticism of independence becomes increasingly topical as the new rulers begin to fail in their task: 'At the time we thought, naïvely, that independence would solve all our problems' (Kourouma, 1970:6). Not only does he denounce the illusions of those who thought that independence was a sort of panacea, but he also questions French writing in Africa:

> The French language is the object of deep devotion and of a type of sterile fetishism that, until recently, set little store by the work of non-French writers, while constituting their sole means of expression.... The style that is attributed to me results from the fact that I don't try to contain the flood of African wordplay, but to channel it. (Kourouma, 1970:6)

The Mandinka words that come to the textual surface at key moments are projected into the French discourse, resulting in particularly clever verbal inventions (Houis, 1977:68–9). Moreover, as Jean Derive observed, 'Ahmadou Kourouma's originality lies in the fact that he attributed an ambiguous status to the emergence of traditional myth in the novel, when compared to his real-life experience of Mandinka culture' (Derive, 1990:84). Mandinka words are not used as mere idiomatic expressions, but as a codified form of speech. His second novel, *Monnè, outrages et défis* (1990), published twenty years later, confirms Kourouma's command of the writer's art, despite the misgivings of the many readers who considered *Les soleils des indépendances* to be a one-off achievement, similar to Amos Tutuola's *The Palm Wine Drinkard* – this author's six other novels are often forgotten. The entire colonial history is re-read in a humorous and eloquent way. The reader observes significant changes in the way the lexicon is Africanized in *Monnè, outrages et défis*:

> The move away from lexical re-codification in the Francophone novel can be observed not only in the general evolution from early ethnological concerns to present-day neo-informationalism, but also in the artistic itinerary of a single writer. In Kourouma's second novel, *Monnè, outrages et défis*, the twin methods of accommodating and

contextualizing clearly outweigh recodification, which was more instrumental in *Les soleils des indépendances*. This shift of priorities is readily observable in the titles, since *'Soleils'* as we remarked in Chapter 4, is recodified 'tele' or rather 'tele lu' in its plural form, [*suns or days*] and 'Monnè' is cushioned with its two French tags [*'outrages et défis'*, AR] denoting flagrant insult and defiance. (Zabus, 1991: 171)

African words crop up here and there: Kourouma still uses translations, which can be completed by adding explanatory terms. Ultimately, the author leaves it to one of the French characters to explain the language's inability to interpret all the nuances of the Mandinka languages. The period has passed during which somewhat naïve pioneers like Félix Couchoro sought approval from the guarantors of the norm. West African literature can now look forward to the rehabilitation of the mother tongue. What could its form be? Will others follow Ngugi's example?

For reasons related to ideology, Angolan literature was faced with this problem from the very beginning:

> *Vôvô Bartolomeu* is the first experiment in fictional form in which a representation of the Angolan reality, which is radically at odds with colonial reality, may be observed. The handling of social and human ingredients takes place in a language that already contains signs of transgressing the norm within the characters' discourse, the recourse to linguistic *métissage*, the awareness of different language levels, not to mention the use of irony by way of the metalinguistic function. (Ferreira in Jacinto, 1979:13)

The African appropriation of the Portuguese language ran parallel to the national movement of liberation; the *métissage* theme is central to this history and literature, illusions and all. The dialectal plasticity of Portuguese, a language already split between a vast country like Brazil and its small European seat, resulted in a permeability to Bantu languages, at least in lexical terms. Linguistic and political consciousness are inseparable within Portuguese-speaking African countries. Admittedly, this is also the case elsewhere in Africa, but it seems to me that from the outset of the struggle, militants of the liberation process in these countries had a clear idea of the situation, unlike the *négritude* poets, to quote one example. In Francophone countries, *Les soleils des indépendances* had a positive effect on many writers: French could bend to the rhythm of an African language; they were seduced by the freedom of its tone. The six novels by Sony Labou Tansi (1947–) offer another form of writing, a lyrical outpouring rather than a representation of the world. 'J'écris par étourderie,' comments the author in the foreword to his first novel, *La vie et demie* (1979): 'This book takes place entirely within myself: let none of today's politicians or human beings come and interfere with it' (Labou Tansi, 1979:10). His writing is pure utterance, which is linked to a form of 'absent-minded' thoughtlessness – a wise precaution for a writer wanting to remain in his country, the People's Republic of Congo, but who was able to impose himself to such an extent that he was able to make the following observation in the foreword to his fifth novel, *Les sept solitudes de Lorsa Lopez* (1985):

> In this book I demand another centre to the world, other apologies to list and name. Because nowadays, being a poet means wanting with all one's might, with all of one's

soul, with the whole of one's flesh, in the face of guns, in the face of money that also becomes a gun and above all in the face of received truth on which we poets have the right to piss, that none of the faces of human reality be covered by the silence of history.... (Labou Tansi, 1985:6)

Somewhere between writing because of 'absent-mindedness' and responsibility in the face of 'the silence of history' stands the figure of an author trying to voice his world, and take responsibility for it: during all those years of conflict, Sony Labou Tansi remained in the Congo, where he directed a theatre company. His third novel, *L'anté-peuple,* tells the story of a virtuous civil servant who eventually becomes a *maquisard* [underground fighter] and assassinates the chief of police. It is a good example of the lyrical warmth of a writer who is attentive to popular Congolese Francophone speech. Most of the population is concentrated in Brazzaville, making the Congo Africa's most Francophone country, as indicated above. Sony Labou Tansi's eloquence feeds on the particular language spoken by pupils and students. In Brazzaville, Lingala and Kikongo are also spoken (Queffelec & Niangouna, 1990), as can be heard in quotations from the songs of Congolese singer Tabu Ley or in his use of fishermen's tunes. And yet, this speaking 'in the language', is not the object of the process of transformation. Calques and attempts at lexical recodification are still discrete activities. Although Sony Labou Tansi fully accepted French as a world language, he did not go so far as to sing the praises of a language that for him was always just an instrument. He did not claim to defend French; he tried to appropriate it for himself.

The terrible Congolese civil war and his premature death lend a tragic dimension to his literary aims:

> Sony envisions the complete erasure of the effects of colonial history. But this desire to liberate one's people from the weight of a tortured historical past proves as impossible as escaping from the deadly consequences of sexual promiscuity in *Le commencement des douleurs.* Just as Sony seeks to escape history by retreating to the realm of ethical absolutes, the pattern of repetition reasserts itself. (Clark, 2000:62)

Sony Labou Tansi's absent-mindedness is shared by Amos Tutuola, who has gained quite a following. Here is a local writer who has achieved success! His first book, a collection of unlikely stories, best described as dreams illustrated with the photographs of ghosts, did the rounds of the Lagos publishers, but nobody was interested. It is not surprising that a somewhat eccentric English publisher, specializing in books on photography, took an interest in the text without publishing it either. Such was the adventure of a Nigerian messenger at the end of the 'forties. Tutuola persisted, and we know that he eventually succeeded. What is more important, his example is still relevant. As I have tried to illustrate, these texts surprise the reader as much by their imaginative intentions and by the author's direct implication in these ramblings, as by his use of a strange language, 'with asides, interminably repeated words, parentheses' (Dussoutour-Hammer, 1976:16). Tutuola poses a literary problem in the Francophone as well as Anglophone domain, especially when considering the 1953 translation: did Raymond Queneau's mischievousness include giving Sally Mara a Nigerian brother, the messenger-poet Tutuola? For the theorist, the novel *The Palm Wine Drinkard,* translated from 'Nigerian English' into French, was published at exactly the right moment, the same year that Roland Barthes' *Le degré zéro de l'écriture* [*Writing Degree Zero*] brought 'literature [back] to a problem of language' and praised Queneau, who had shown that 'the spoken contamination of written discourse was possible in all its parts' (Barthes, 1953:23). This Tutuola was just too good to be true! And yet, more than forty years later, Tutuola was still around: the messenger became a storeman, a departmental manager and finally a radio producer. A few years ago he lived in a huge villa in Ibadan, retired, respected and appreciated by his fellow-countrymen. The translator of *My Life in the Bush of Ghosts* (1954, 1988) understood that even if Tutuola wrote English badly, 'he used it well' (Dussoutour-Hammer, 1976:19). Following in Queneau's footsteps, she was fully aware that her translation was somewhat outrageous. The text was even adapted for the stage and continues to meet with some reluctance when performed in Francophone countries. Mongo Beti's neo-classical fiction ideals of syntactic clarity are mutilated in these burlesque creations, and yet the author successfully achieves his aims, transporting us into the mysterious world of the bush ghosts. He even has some disciples. The last one to date survived the Nigerian civil war only to be executed in 1995 for his activism on behalf of the Delta people. Ken Saro-Wiwa narrated the war in his own way:

> *Sozaboy*'s language is what I call 'rotten English', a mixture of Nigerian pidgin English, broken English and occasional flashes of good, even idiomatic English. This language is disordered and disorderly. Born of a mediocre education and severely limited opportunities, it borrows words, patterns and images freely from the mother-tongue and finds expression in a very limited English vocabulary. To its speakers, it has the advantage of having no rules and no syntax. It thrives on lawlessness, and is part of the dislocated and discordant society in which Sozaboy must live, move and have not his being.
>
> Whether it throbs vibrantly enough and communicates effectively is my experiment. (Saro-Wiwa, 1985, Foreword)

Sozaboy's epic journey – the word means 'soldier boy' in pidgin – is that of a young man from Eastern Nigeria who only joins the Biafran army to have a nice uniform, is related in 'rotten English'. Sozaboy wants to impress Agnes, his pretty young wife; he has no idea what he is fighting for. Stationed in a mangrove swamp, he never sees the enemy, and will only see action when his companions shoot their officer in the back for having forced a soldier to drink his urine as a punishment. After this military exploit, Sozaboy deserts and is made prisoner by the Federals, who use him as a chauffeur. He steals a truck to return to his village, where he discovers that Agnes and his mother are dead and that he has to flee as soon as possible. The few surviving villagers take him for a ghost and want to send him back to where he belongs, to the land of the dead ... Sozaboy has become Sozaman: the naïve hero has learnt the value of life through contact with the dead. He is no ghost and no longer has any dreams. 'But now, if anybody say anything about war or even fight, I will just run and run and run and run and run. Believe me yours sincerely ...' (Saro-Wiwa, 1985:181).

Sozaboy was surprisingly successful: its 'rotten' language reflects the hero's chaotic and incoherent universe. Pidgin is the language of chauffeurs, bus station barkers and everyone living on the edge of urban society; here it has been transformed into a literary language. Saro-Wiwa's novel is a successful experiment that illustrates the fluidity of the language situation as well as the rich materials available to the writer. Recounting the absurdity of war probably required this poignantly assembled speech. This voice of the people has provided the most convincing representation of civil war I have ever read, a sort of 'journey into night', waiting for another Céline to translate it. Elsewhere, the experience of war is also contributing to a literary revival, as in the case of José Luandino Vieira's Angolan Portuguese oeuvre: although he has been silent for the past twenty years, he provided a reconciled country with an imaginary form.

> [It] inaugurates words of wandering, a search for what lies beyond the text, i.e. the text before Babel, the text that has not yet been divided on the sands of Babel (*areia babelica*). I mean that the voyage of writing to the unknown planet of Tetembuatubia also means the desire to put an end to Babel's borders and to the belligerent sands (*areia bellica*), to the war that killed all understanding between those languages and cultures present in Angola.... (Trigo, 1981:615)

The central character, Turito, is the leader of a small group of boys playing on the sandy ground of the shanty towns at the city's edge. They amuse themselves with water and birds until one day, when they play with a naked girl who willingly participates in their undertakings. Turito, who makes all the decisions, has become a prophet, an inventor of words ever since the apparition of a 'French angel' (a girl) while he was lying sick. When Turito draws a line on the sand to call his followers to him, the narrator is with him, with those who invent things. The grains of sand on the ground represent the multitude of languages that Turito leaves behind when he invents his own language.

This is what writing fiction means: one must go beyond the multiple languages spoken on the ground, beyond the sands of Babel, and always invent one's own writing, find one's own voice, and sound out the multiple voices of society. The linguistic consciousness is aware of the fact that Babel left its mark; it is also conscious that one must always draw the line on the ground from which one invents, even if it is the 'illiterate writings' of orality. War, city, sex: a mixed language in Luandino Vieira's creolized, kimbundized, anglicized, gallicized Portuguese. 'We were almost bilingual' he tells us (Trigo, 1981:46): the text always comes back to the river grasses and the shores of childhood. The text's very movement lies in this cacophony of Babel. In a way, all novelists and all writers hail from Makusulu, or are Sozaboys in their own right: perpetually naïve descendants of the ante-people, lost in the bush of ghosts....

Bibliography

Abdalla, A. 1973. *Sauti ya Dhiki.* Nairobi: Oxford University Press.
Abdulaziz, M.H. 1979. *Muyaka, 19th Century Swahili Popular Poetry.* Nairobi: Literature Bureau.
Abdulkadir, D. 1974. *The Poetry, Life and Opinions of Sa'adu Zungur.* Zaria: Northern Nigerian Publishing Corporation, 109 p.
Abdullah, M.S. 1960. *Mzimu wa watu wa kale.* Arusha: Eastern Africa Publications, 80 p.
Abimbola, W. (ed.) 1975. *Yoruba Oral Tradition, Selections from the Papers Presented at the Seminar on Yoruba Oral Tradition, Poetry, Music, Dance, Drama.* Ife: Department of African Languages and Literatures, 1093 p.
— 1975. *Sixteen Great Poems of Ifa.* Lagos: Unesco, 468 p.
— 1976. *Ifa. An Exposition of Ifa Literary Corpus.* Ibadan: Oxford University Press, 256 p.
Abrahams, P. 1946. *Mine Boy.* London: Crisp, 183 p.
— 1956. *A Wreath for Udomo.* London: Faber, 309 p.
Achebe, C. 1958. *Things Fall Apart.* London: Heinemann, 185 p.
— 1960. *No Longer at Ease.* London: Heinemann, 170 p.
— 1964. *Arrow of God.* London: Heinemann.
— 1966. *A Man of the People.* London: Heinemann, 166 p.
— 1972. *Beware Soul Brother, Poems.* Ibadan: Heinemann Educational Books, 68 p.
— 1983. *The Trouble with Nigeria.* Enugu: Fourth Dimension, 68 p.
— 1984. 'Editorial and Linguistic Problems in Aka Weta, a Comment', *Uwa Ndi Igbo* 1, 94–5.
— 1987. *Anthills of the Savannah.* London: Heinemann, 233 p.
— and Okafor, D. (eds) 1978. *Don't Let Him Die: An Anthology of Memorial Poems for Christopher Okigbo (1932–1967).* Enugu: Fourth Dimension.
Adam, A.S. 1978. *Kasri ya Mwinyi Fuad.* Dar es Salaam: Tanzania Publishing House, 162 p.
Adedeji, J. 1975. 'Le concert-party au Nigéria et les débuts d'Hubert Ogunde', *Revue d'Histoire du Théâtre* 27, 21–5.
Ade Ajayi, J.F. 1966. 'How Yoruba Was Reduced to Writing', *Odu* 8, 49–58.
Adejunmobi, M. 1996. *J.-J. Rabearivelo, Literature and Lingua Franca in Colonial Madagascar.* New York: Peter Lang.
— 1998. 'Translation and Postcolonial identity: African Writing and European Languages', *The Translator, Translation and Minority* 4 (2), 163–81.
Ademola, F. (ed.) 1962. *Reflections, Nigerian Prose and Verse.* Lagos: African Universities Press, 119 p.
Afigbo, A.E. 1975. 'The Place of Igbo Language in Our Schools, a Historical Explanation', in F.C. Ogbalu and E.N. Emenanjo (eds), *Igbo Language and Culture*, pp. 70–84. Ibadan: Oxford University Press.
Afolayan, A. (ed.) 1982. *Yoruba Language and Literature.* Ife/Lagos: University of Ife Press/University Press, 316 p.
Aig-Imoukhuede, F. 1982. *Pidgin Stew and Sufferhead.* Ibadan: Heinemann Educational Books, 57 p.
Akinlade, E.K. 1975. *Alosi Ologo.* Ibadan: Longman, 176 p.
— 1976. *Owo Eje.* Ibadan: Onibonoje Press, 121 p.
Alexander, N. 1990. 'The Language Question', in Schire (ed.), *Critical Choices for South Africa*, pp. 126–46. Cape Town: Oxford University Press.
Alexandre, P. 1967. *Langues et langage en Afrique noire.* Paris: Payot, 171 p.
— 1981. 'Les langues bantu, tableau d'ensemble', in J. Perrot (ed.), *Les langues dans le monde ancien et moderne, Afrique sub-saharienne, pidgins et créoles* 1, pp. 352–75. Paris: Editions du CNRS.
Aliyu, A. 1976. *Fasaha Akiliya.* Zaria: Northern Nigerian Publishing Corporation, 80 p.
Allen, J. de V. 1993. *Swahili Origins: Swahili Culture and the Shungwaya Phenomenon.* London: James Currey.
Alvarez-Pereire, J. 1979. *Les guetteurs de l'aube, poésie et apartheid.* Grenoble: Presses de l'Université.
Amarteifio, V. 1962. *Bediako.* Accra: Waterville Publishing House, 165 p.
— 1965. *Bediako, the Adventurer.* Accra: Waterville Publishing House, 161 p.
Amegbleame, S. 1975. *Le livre ewe, essai de bibliographie.* Talence: Centre d'études d'Afrique

noire, 80 p.

Anati, E. 1997. *L'art rupestre dans le monde imaginaire de la préhistoire*. Paris: Larousse.

Andoh-Kumi, K. 1985. 'Some Aspects of Literary Works in the Akan Language', *Bulletin de l'AELIA* 8, 91–102.

Andrzejewski, B.W., Pilaszewicz, S. and Tyloch, S. (eds) 1985. *Literature in African Languages*. Cambridge/Warsaw: University Press/Wiedza Powszechna, 672 p.

Arbousset, T. 1842. *Relation d'un voyage d'exploration au nord est de la colonie du Cap de Bonne Espérance*. Paris: Société des missions évangéliques, 642 p.

— 1991. *Missionary Excursion*, trans. from French manuscript and edited by D. Ambrose and A. Brustch. Morija/Nairobi: Morija Archives/CREDU, 219 p.

— 2000. *Excursion missionnaire dans les montagnes bleues suivi de la notice sur les Zoulas*. Introduction by A. Ricard, pp. 5–68. Paris/Johannesburg: Karthala/IFAS.

Armattoe, R.E.G. 1954. *Deep Down the Blackman's Mind*. Elms Court/Ilfracombe: A. Stockwell, 112 p.

Armstrong, R.G. 1967. *The Study of West African Languages. An Inaugural Lecture*. Ibadan: Ibadan University Press, 74 p.

Armstrong, R.P. 1971. *The Affecting Presence. An Essay in Humanistic Anthropology*. Urbana/Chicago: University of Illinois Press, 213 p.

Arnold, R. 1977. *Afrikanische Literature und Nationale Befreiung*. Berlin: Akademie verlag.

Arnold, S.H. 1980. 'Popular Literature in Tanzania, Its Background and Relation to East African Literature', *Présence africaine* 115, 156–77.

Assefa, T. 1989. 'The Post-Revolutionary Amharic Novel', *Proceedings of the Eighth International Conference of Ethiopian Studies*, pp. 591–606. Addis Ababa: Institute of Ethiopian Studies.

Atta Koffi, R. 1969. *Le trône d'or*. Paris: ORTF/DAEC, 109 p.

Awoniyi, T.A. 1978. *Yoruba Language in Education*. Ibadan: Oxford University Press, 182 p.

Awoonor, K. 1974. *Guardians of the Sacred Word, Ewe Poetry*. New York: Nok Publishers, 104 p.

Awoonor-Williams, G. 1964. *Rediscovery and Other Poems*. Ibadan: Mbari publications, 36 p.

Azuonye, C. 1992, 'The Development of Written Igbo Literature', in A.E. Afigbo (ed.), *Groundwork of Igbo History*. New York: Nok Publishers.

Bâ, A.H. 1972. *Aspects de la civilisation africaine*. Paris: Présence africaine, 141 p.

— 1973. *L'étrange destin de Wangrin*. Paris: UGE, 445 p. (*The Fortunes of Wangrin*, Ibadan: New Horn Press 1987; 2nd edition Bloomington: Indiana University Press, 1999).

— 1976. *Jésus vu par un Musulman*. Abidjan/Dakar: Nouvelles éditions africaines, 62 p.

— 1978. *Kaydara*. Abidjan/Dakar: Nouvelles éditions africaines, 112 p. (*Kaïdara*, Washington DC: Three Continents Press, 1988).

— 1980. *Vie et enseignement de Tierno Bokar, le sage de Bandiagara*. Paris: Le Seuil, 256 p.

— 1985. *Njeddo Dewal, mère de la calamité, conte initiatique peul*. Abidjan/Dakar/Lomé: Nouvelles éditions africaines, 158 p.

— 1991. *Amkoullel, l'enfant peul, mémoires*. Arles: Actes sud, 412 p.

— and Cardaire, M. 1957. *Tierno Bokar, le sage de Bandiagara*. Paris: Présence africaine, 125 p.

— and Daget, J. 1962, 1965. *L'empire peul du Macina*. Paris/La Haye: Mouton, 309 p. (vol. 1); 306 p. (vol. 2).

— and Dieterlen, G. 1961. *Koumen, texte initiatique des pasteurs peuls*. Paris/La Haye: Mouton, 196 p.

— and Kesteloot, L. (eds) 1969. *Kaïdara, récit initiatique peul*. Paris: Julliard (Les classiques africains).

—, Kesteloot, L., Seydou, C. and Sow, A.I. 1974. *L'éclat de la grande étoile*, suivi de *Bain rituel*. Paris: Armand Colin (Les classiques africains), 151 p.

Babalola, A. 1968. *The Content and Form of Yoruba Ijala*. Oxford: Clarendon Press, 395 p.

Badibanga, T. 1931. *L'éléphant qui marche sur des œufs*. Brussels: Éditions L'Églantine, 90 p.

Badian, S. 1961. *La mort de Chaka*. Paris: Présence africaine, 61 p.

Bakhtin, M. 1981. *The Dialogic Imagination*. Austin: University of Texas Press.

Baldi, S. 1977. *Systematic Hausa Bibliography*. Rome: Istituto Italo-Africano/Collana di Studi Africani 3, 145 p.

Balisidya, N. 1975. *Shida*. Nairobi: Foundations Books, 86 p.

Bamgbose, A. 1974. *The Novels of D.O. Fagunwa*. Benin City: Ethiope, 132 p.

— (ed.) 1976. *Mother Tongue in Education*. London/Paris: Hodder and Stoughton/Unesco, 153 p.

— 1982. 'Constituents of Yoruba Studies' in Afolayan (ed.), *Yoruba Language and Literature*, pp. 1–12.

Baratte, E.-B. T., Chauveau-Rabut, J. and Kadima-Nzuji, M. 1979. *Bibliographie des auteurs africains de langue française*. Paris: Nathan, 245 p.

Barber, K. 1983. 'Style and Ideology', in Fagunwa and Okediji (eds), *Ife Monographs on Literature and Criticism*. Department of Literature in English/University of Ife, 38 p.

— 1991. *I Could Speak Until Tomorrow: Oriki, Women and the Past in a Yoruba Town*. Edinburgh: Edinburgh University Press.

— 1995. 'African Language Literature and Postcolonial Criticism', *Research in African Literatures* 26 (4), 3–30.

— 2000. *The Generation of Plays, Yoruba Popular Life in Theater.* Bloomington/ Indianapolis: Indiana University Press.

— and De Moraes, F.P.F. (eds) 1989. *Discourse and its Disguises: the Interpretation of African Oral Texts.* Birmingham University/African Studies Series 1, 209 p.

Bardey, A. 1981. *Barr Adjam, souvenirs d'Afrique orientale, 1880–1887.* Paris: Éditions du CNRS, 389 p.

Bardolph, J. 1989. 'Language and Voices in *A Dance of the Forests*', *Commonwealth* 1, 49–58.

— 1991. *Ngugi Wa Thiong'o, l'homme et l'œuvre.* Paris: Présence africaine, 184 p.

Barthes, R. 1953. *Le degré zéro de l'écriture.* Paris: Le Seuil, 65 p. (*Writing Degree Zero,* London: Cape 1967)

— 1973. *Le plaisir du texte.* Paris: Le Seuil, 108 p. (*The Pleasure of the Text,* New York: Hill and Wang 1975)

Bascom, W. 1969. *Ifa Divination, Communication between Gods and Men in West Africa.* Bloomington: Indiana University Press, 624 p.

Batukezanga, Z. 1983. *Souvenirs du village.* Kinshasa: Éditions Saint-Paul Afrique, 111 p.

Beik, J. 1984. 'National Development as Theme in Current Hausa Drama in Niger', *Research in African Literature* 15, 1–24.

Bemba, S. 1979. *Un foutu monde pour un blanchisseur trop honnête.* Yaounde: CLE, 48 p.

Bérenger-Féraud, L.J.B. 1885. *Recueil de contes populaires de la Sénégambie.* Paris: Editions Larousse.

Bernabé, J., Chamoiseau, P. and Confiant, R. 1993. *Eloge de la créolité.* Paris: Gallimard.

Bertoncini, E. 1984. *Profilo della letteratura swahili.* Naples: Istituto Universitario Orientale, 310 p.

— 1989. *Outline of Swahili Literature.* Leiden: E.J. Brill.

Beti, M. 1956. *Le pauvre Christ de Bomba.* Paris: Robert Laffont, 370 p. (*The Poor Christ of Bomba,* London: Heinemann, 1971)

— 1957. *Mission terminée.* Paris: Buchet Chastel, 254 p. (*Mission to Kala,* London: Heinemann Educational, 1964)

— 1972. *Main basse sur le Cameroun.* Paris: Maspero, 219 p.

— 1974a. *Remember Ruben.* Paris: UGE, 313 p.

— 1974b. *Perpétue et l'habitude du malheur.* Paris: Buchet Chastel, 303 p. (*Perpetua and the Habit of Unhappiness,* London: Heinemann Educational, 1978)

— 1979. *La ruine presque cocasse d'un polichinelle.* Paris: Éditions des peuples noirs, 320 p. (*Lament for an African Pol,* Washington DC: Three Continents, 1980)

— 1999. *Trop de soleil tue l'amour.* Paris: Julliard, 251 p.

— 2000. *Branle-bas en noir et blanc.* Paris: Julliard.

Biebuyck, D. 1978. *Hero and Chief, Epic Literature from the Banyanga (Zaïre Republic).* Berkeley/Los Angeles: University of California Press, 320 p.

Bierksteter, A. 1996. *Kujibizana: Questions of Language and Power in 19th and 20th Century Poetry in Kiswahili.* East Lansing: Michigan State University Press.

Birnie, J.R. and Ansre, G. (eds) 1969. *The Study of Ghanaian Languages.* Legon/Accra: Institute of African Studies/Ghana Publishing Corporation.

Bivar, A.D.H. and Hiskett, M. 1962. 'The Arabic Literature of Nigeria to 1804: a Provisional Account', *Bulletin of the School of Oriental and African Studies* 25 (1), 104–8.

Bleek, W.H.I. 1864. *Reynard the Fox in South Africa, or Hottentot Fables and Tales.* London: Trübner.

Boelaert, E. 1949. *Nsong'a Lianga, l'épopée nationale des Nkundo.* Anvers: De Sikkel.

Bontinck, F. 1974. *L'autobiographie de Hamed Ben Mohammed el Murjebi Tippo Tip,* trans. from Kiswahili and annotated with K. Janssen. Brussels: Académie royale des sciences d'outre-mer, 274 p.

— 1978. *Le catéchisme kikongo de 1624,* D. Ndembe Nsasi (ed.), Brussels: Académie royale des sciences d'outre-mer.

Boto, E. (pseud. M. Beti) 1954. *Ville cruelle.* Paris: Présence africaine, 214 p.

Boyce, W.A. 1834. *A Grammar of the Kaffir Language.* Grahamstown: Wesleyan Mission Press.

Bradlow, F.R. 1987. *Printing for Africa, The Story of Robert Moffat and the Kuruman Press.* Kuruman: Kuruman Moffat Mission Trust.

Brutus, D. 1963. *Sirens, Knuckles, Boots.* Ibadan: Mbari Publications, 36 p.

— 1968. *Letters to Martha and Other Poems from a South African Prison.* London: Heinemann, 57 p.

Bureau of Ghana Languages 1967. *Bibliography of Works in Ghana Languages.* Accra: Bureau of Ghana Languages, 161 p.

Bureau, J. 1987. *Éthiopie, un drame impérial et rouge.* Paris: Ramsay, 317 p.

Burns-Ncamashe 1961. *Masibaliselane.* Cape Town: Oxford University Press, 121 p.

— 1979. *Izibongo zakwaSesile.* Grahamstown: Institute of Social and Economic Research, Rhodes University, Xhosa Texts 4.

Calame-Griaule, G. 1987. *Ethnologie et langage* (2nd edn). Paris: Gallimard.
Camara Laye. 1953. *L'enfant noir*. Paris: Plon, 256 p. (*The Dark Child*, New York: Noonday Press, 1954)
— 1954. *Le regard du roi*. Paris: Plon, 255 p. (*The Radiance of the King*, London: Collins 1965).
— 1978. *Le maître de la parole, Kouma Lafolo Kouma*. Paris: Plon, 314 p. (*The Guardian of the Word*, New York: Vintage Books 1980).
Camara, S. 1975. *Gens de la parole*. La Haye/Paris: Mouton (2nd edn 1992, Karthala), 358 p.
— 1982. *Paroles très anciennes*. Grenoble: La pensée sauvage, 221 p.
— 1994. *Grain de vision*, Afrique noire: Drame et liturgie. Bordeaux: Travaux et documents du CEAN 42.
— 2001. *Les vergers de l'aube*. Bordeaux: Confluences.
Capo, H.C. 1983. 'Le Gbe est une langue unique', *Africa* 53 (2), 47–57.
Caron, B. and Amfani, H.A. 1997. *Dictionnaire français-haoussa, suivi d'un index haoussa-français*. Paris: Karthala/IFRA.
Cary, J. 1939. *Mister Johnson*. London: Carfax Edition.
Casalis, E. 1841. *Études sur la langue séchuana, précédées d'une introduction sur l'origine et les progrès de la mission chez les Bassoutos*. Paris: Imprimerie royale, 104 p.
Casely-Hayford, J.E. (1st edn 1911) 1969. *Ethiopia Unbound, Studies in Race Emancipation*. London: F. Cass, 215 p.
Cawl, F.M.J. 1982. *Ignorance is the Enemy of Love*, trans. from Somali by B.W. Andrzejewski. London: Zed Books, 104 p.
Cerulli, E. 1958. *Scritti teologici etiopici dei secoli XVI–XVII*, vol. 1, *Tre opusculi dei Micaeliti*, Citta dei Vaticano.
— 1961. *Storia della letteratura etiopica*. Milano: Nuova Academia Editrice, 280 p.
Chakaipa, P. (5th edn 1980) 1961. *Rubo Ibofu*. Gwelo: Mambo Press, 96 p.
Chevrier, J. (1st edn 1974) 1984. *Littérature nègre*. Paris: Armand Colin (Revised edn), 272 p.
— 1986. *L'arbre à palabre, Essai sur les contes et récits traditionnels d'Afrique noire*. Paris: Hatier, 336 p.
Chidyausiku, P. 1962. *Nyadzi dzinokunda rufu*. Cape Town: Oxford University Press/Southern Rhodesia African Literature Bureau, 49 p.
Chiwome, E.M. 1996. *A Social History of the Shona Novel*. Harare: Juta Zimbabwe.
Chrétien, J.-P 1981. 'Vrais et faux nègres', *Le Monde*, 28 June, p. x.
Chum, H. 1962. *Utenzi wa vita vya Uhud. The Epic of the Battle of Uhud*. Dar es Salaam: East Africa Literature Bureau, 97 p.
Cissé, Y.T. and Kamissoko, W. (eds) 1988. *La grande geste du Mali, des origines à la fondation de l'empire*. Paris: Karthala/Arsan, 427 p.
Clark, E. 1979. *Hubert Ogunde and the Making of Nigerian Theatre*. Oxford: Oxford University Press, 170 p.
Clark, P. 2000. 'Passionate Engagements: a Reading of Sony Labou Tansi's Private Ancestral Shrine', *Research in African Literatures* 39 (3), 39–68.
Clark-Bekederemo, J.P. 1970. *The Example of Shakespeare*. Evanston: Northwestern University Press.
— 1964. *Three Plays, Song of a Goat, the Masquerade, the Raft*. London/Ibadan: Oxford University Press, 134 p.
— 1966. *Ozidi*. London/Ibadan: Oxford University Press, 121 p.
— 1977. *The Ozidi Saga, Collected and Translated from the Ijo of Okabou Ojobolo*. Ibadan: Ibadan University Press/Oxford University Press, 408 p.
— 1978. *The Hero as a Villain*. Lagos: University of Lagos Press, 20 p.
— 1991. *Collected Plays and Poems*, introduction by A. Irele. Washington DC: Howard University Press.
Coldham, G. 1966. *A Bibliography of Scriptures in African Languages*. London: British and Foreign Bible Society, xi + 848 p (2 vols.).
Cole, C. 2001. *Ghana's Concert Party Theatre*. Bloomington/Indianapolis: Indiana University Press.
Colin, R. 1957. *Les contes noirs de l'ouest africain*. Paris: Présence Africaine.
Comba, P. 1958. 'Bref aperçu sur les débuts de la littérature de langue amharique et sur ses tendances actuelles', *Ethiopian Observer*, II.
Conrad, D. and Franck, B. 1995. *Status and Identity in West Africa: Nyamakalaw of Mande*. Bloomington: Indiana University Press, 204 p.
Conrad, J. 1902. *Heart of Darkness*. London.
Conteh-Morgan, J. 1994. *Theatre and Drama in Francophone Africa*. Cambridge: Cambridge University Press.
Cope, T. 1968 (2nd edn 1988 with a note, UNISA). *Izibongo, Zulu Praise Poems*. Oxford: Oxford University Press/Oxford Library of African Literature.
Coplan, D. 1985. *In Township Tonight! South Africa's Black City Music and Theatre*. New York: Longman.

— 1994. *In the Time of Cannibals*. Chicago: Chicago University Press.
Cornevin, R. 1970. *Le théâtre en Afrique noire et à Madagascar*. Paris: Le livre africain, 335 p.
— 1975. *Littératures d'Afrique noire de langue française*. Paris: Presses universitaires de France, 273 p.
Couchoro, F. 1929. *L'esclave*. Paris: La dépêche africaine, 304 p.
— 1941. *Amour de féticheuse*. Ouidah: Imp. d'Almeida, 74 p.
— 1950. *Drame d'amour à Anecho*. Ouidah: Imp. d'Almeida, 168 p.
Coulmas, F. (ed.) 1986. *Direct and Indirect Speech*. New York: Mouton.
Coulon, V. 1987. 'Onitsha Goes National: Nigerian Writing in Macmillan's Pacesetters Series', *Reserach in African Literatures* 18 (3), 304–19.
— 1994. *Bibliographie francophone de littérature africaine*. Vanves: EDICEF, 143 p.
Coussy, D. 1988. *Le roman nigérian anglophone*. Paris: Silex, 527 p.
— , Bardolph, J., Durix, J.-P., and Sevry, J. 1983. *Anthologie critique de la littérature africaine anglophone*. Paris: UGE, 479 p.
Couzens, T. 1985. *The New African: a Study of the Life and Work of H.I.E. Dhlomo*. Johannesburg: Ravan Press, 382 p.
Craveirinha, J. 1974. *Karingana ua Karingana*. Lourenço Marques: Ed. da Academica, 145 p.
Creissels, D. 1989. *Aperçu sur les structures phonologiques des langues négro-africaines*. Grenoble: Ellus, 287 p.
Dadié, B. 1970. *Monsieur Thôgô-gnini*. Paris: Présence africaine.
— 1970. *Béatrice du Congo*. Paris: Présence africaine.
Dalby, D. 1986. *L'Afrique et la lettre*. Lagos/Paris: Centre culturel français/Fête de la lettre, 32 p.
— (ed.). 1970. *Language and History in Africa*. London: Frank Cass.
Damane, M. and Sanders, P.B. (eds) 1974. *Lithoko, Sotho Praise Poems*. Oxford: Oxford University Press/Oxford Library of African Literature, reproduced by UNISA, 1983.
Danquah, J.B. 1941. *Nyankonsem*. London: Longman Green, 56 p.
— 1943. *The Third Woman*. London/Redhill: United Society for Christian Literature, 151 p.
David, M.V. 1965. *Le débat sur les écritures et l'hiéroglyphe au XVIIe et XVIIIe siècles et l'application de la notion de déchiffrement aux écritures mortes*. Paris: SEVPEN, 169 p.
Davies, W.V. 1987. *Reading the Past: Egyptian Hieroglyphs*. London: British Museum Publications, 64 p.
De Francis, J. 1989. *Visible Speech: The Diverse Oneness of Writing Systems*. Honolulu: University of Hawaii Press.
Dei-Anang, M. 1959. *Africa Speaks*. Accra: State Publishing Company, 104 p.
Derive, J. 1975. *Collecte et traductions des littératures orales, un exemple négro-africain, les contes ngbaka-ma'bo de RCA*. Paris: SELAF, 256 p.
— 1990. 'L'oralité africaine ou la littérature en kit', in J. Riesz and A. Ricard (eds), *Semper aliquid novi*, pp. 215–26.
Dhlomo, H.I.E. 1985. *Collected Works*. T. Couzens and N. Visser (eds). Johannesburg: Ravan Press, 500 p.
Dhlomo, R.R.R. 1928. *An African Tragedy (a Novel in English by a Zulu Writer)*. Lovedale: Lovedale Press, 40 p.
— 1936. *UDingane Ka Senzangakhona*. Pietermaritzburg: Shuter and Shooter, 198 p.
— 1937. *UShaka*. Pietermaritzburg: Shuter and Shooter, 191 p.
— 1938. *UMpande ka Senzangakhona*. Pietermaritzburg: Shuter and Shooter, 142 p.
Diabaté, M.M. 1970. *Kala Kata*. Bamako: Éditions populaires, 96 p.
— 1975. *L'aigle et l'épervier suivi de la geste de Sunjata*. Paris: P.J. Oswald/L'Harmattan, 90 p.
— 1986. *Le lion à l'arc, récit épique*. Paris: Hatier, 128 p.
Diallo, B. 1926 (new edn 1985). *Force-Bonté*. Paris: Rieder, 208 p.
Dike, F. 1971. 'The Sacrifice of Kreli', in S. Gray (ed.), *Theatre One, New South African Drama*, pp. 34–73. Johannesburg: Donker.
Dion, G.-M. 1967. 'Répertoire bibliographique de Monsieur l'Abbé Alexis Kagame'. Manuscript, 32 p.
Diop, B. 1947. *Les contes d'Amadou Koumba*. Paris: Fasquelle, 191 p. (*Tales of Ahmadou Koumba*, London: Oxford University Press, 1966).
— 1958. *Les nouveaux contes d'Amadou Koumba*. Paris: Présence africaine, 173 p.
— 1977. *L'os de Mor Lam*. Dakar/Abidjan: Nouvelles éditions africaines, 73 p.
Diop, C.A. 1965. *Nations nègres et culture*. Paris: Présence africaine, 534 p. (*The African Origin of Civilization: Myth or Reality*, New York: Lawrence Hill, 1974)
— 1974. *Les fondements économiques et culturels d'un État fédéral d'Afrique noire*. Paris: Présence africaine, 126 p. (*Black Africa: the Economic and Cultural Basis for a Federated State*, Westport, Conn.: Lawrence Hill, 1978).
— 1979. *Nations nègres et culture, De l'antiquité nègre égyptienne aux problèmes culturels de l'Afrique noire aujourd'hui*. Paris: Présence africaine, 3rd edn (*The Cultural Unity of Negro Africa: the Domains of Patriarchy and of Matriarchy in Classical Antiquity*, London: Karnak House, 1989).

— 1988. *Nouvelles recherches sur l'égyptien ancien et les langues négro-africaines modernes.* Paris: Présence africaine, 221 p.

Diop, D. 1973. *Coup de pilon.* Paris: Présence africaine, 62 p.

Dogbe, Y.-E. (ed.). 1980. *Anthologie de la poésie togolaise.* Condé-sur-Noireau: Éditions Akpagnon, 223 p.

Döhne, J.L. (Rev.) 1857. *A Zulu Kaffir Dictionary and an Introduction on the Zulu Kaffir Language.* Cape Town: CPM, 407 p.

Doke, C.M. 1935. 'Early Bantu literature', *Bantu Studies* 9 (1), 87–114.

— 1936. 'Bantu Language Pioneers of the Nineteenth Century', *Bantu Studies* (10) 3, 207–46.

— 1948. *Zulu–English Dictionary*, B.W. Vilakazi (ed.). Johannesburg: Witwatersrand University Press.

Dolezel, L. 1973. *Narrative Modes in Czech Literature.* Toronto: University of Toronto Press.

Domenichini Ramiaramanana, B. 1983. *Du ohabolana au hain teny, Langue littéraire et politique à Madagascar.* Paris: Karthala, 665 p.

Doring, T. 1996. *Chinua Achebe und Joyce Cary. Ein postkoloniales Rewriting Englischer Afrika–Fiktionen.* Pfaffenweiler: Centaurius Verlag Gesellschaft, 231 p.

Dube, J.L. 1933. *Insila Ka Tshaka.* Marianhill: Mission Press, 80 p.

— 1951. *Jeqe, the Bodyservant of King Tshaka*, trans. from Zulu by J. Boxwell. Lovedale: Lovedale Press, 84 p.

Duggan, J.J. (ed.) 1975. *Oral Literature.* Edinburgh/London: Scottish University Press, 107 p.

Dussoutour-Hammer, M. 1976. *Amos Tutuola, Tradition orale et écriture du conte.* Paris: Présence africaine, 158 p.

Duthie, A.S. and Vlaardingerbroek, R.K. (eds) 1981. *Bibliography of Gbe (ewe, gen, aja, xwala, fon gun, etc.): Publications on and in the Language.* Basel: Basler Afrika Bibliographie, 229 p.

Ebony, N.X. 1983. *Déja vu, suivi de Chutes.* Paris: Éd. Ouskokata, 192 p.

Edgar, F. 1911–1913. *Litafi Na Tatsuniyoyi Na Hausa.* Belfast: W. Erskine Mayne, *Litafi na Farko*, 435 p; *Litafi na Biyu*, 463 p; *Litafi na Uju*, 384 p.

Emenanjo, E.N. 1984. 'After the Blackout, Editorial and Linguistic Problems in Aka Weta', *Uwa Ndi Igbo* 1, 89–93.

Emenyonu, E. 1978. *The Rise of the Igbo Novel.* Ibadan: Oxford University Press, 212 p.

— 1988. 'The Rise and Development of Igbo Literature', in Y. Ogunbiyi (ed.), *Perspectives on Nigerian Literature* 1, 33–8.

Equilbecq, F.V. (1st edn 1913) 1972. *Contes populaires d'Afrique occidentale.* Paris: Maisonneuve et Larose, 520 p.

Etherton, M. 1982. *The Development of African Drama.* London: Hutchinson, 368 p.

Evita, L. (1st edn 1953) 1996. *Cuando los Combes Luchaban.* Madrid: Centro Cultural Hispano-Guineano.

Fagerberg-Diallo, S. 1995. 'Milk and Honey: Developing Written Literature in Pulaar', *Yearbook of General and Comparative Literature* 43, 67–83.

Fagunwa, D.O. 1938. *Ogboju Ode ninu Igbo Irunmale.* Lagos: CMS, 102 p.

— 1958. 'Teaching of Vernacular Languages', *Teachers Monthly* 4 (9), 7.

— 1960. 'Writing a Novel', *Teachers Monthly* 6 (9), 12.

— 1961. *Adiitu Olodumare.* Edinburgh/London: Nelson, 148 p. ('Adiitu Olodumare', London: SOAS, ms 1961)

— 1968. *The Forest of a Thousand Daemons*, trans. from Yoruba by W. Soyinka. London: Nelson, 140 p.

Faïk-Nzuji, C. 1970. *Énigmes luba, nshinga, étude structurale.* Kinshasa: Éditions de l'Université Lovanium, 169 p.

— 1974. *Kasala, chant héroïque luba.* Lubumbashi: Presses de l'Unaza, 252 p.

— 1976. *Lenga et autres contes d'inspiration traditionnelle.* Lubumbashi: Imprimerie Saint-Paul, 78 p.

— 1992. *Symboles graphiques en Afrique noire.* Paris/Louvain: Karthala/Ciltade, 190 p.

Farah, N. 1970. *From a Crooked Rib.* London: Heinemann, 182 p.

— 1979. *Sweet and Sour Milk.* London: Allison and Busby, 237 p.

— 1981. *Sardines.* London: Allison and Busby, 237 p.

— 1983. *Close Sesame.* London: Allison and Busby, 252 p.

Fatoba, F. 1984. *Petals of Thought.* London: New Beacon Books, 55 p.

Fatunde, T. 1986. *Oga Na Tief-Man, a Play.* Benin City: Adena Publishers, 57 p.

Federal Ministry of Education, Science and Technology 1985. *National Curriculum for Junior Secondary Schools*, Vol. 3, *Nigerian Languages, Hausa, Igbo, Yoruba.* Ibadan: Heineman Educational Books, 191 p.

Felgine, O. 1992. 'Réalisme magique au Nigeria', *Le Monde diplomatique* 4, 27.

Ferenc, A. 1985. 'Writing and Literature in Classical Ethiopic (Giiz)', in B.W. Andrzejewski, S. Pilaszewicz and S. Tyloch (eds), *Literatures in African Languages*, pp. 255–300.

Fiawoo, F.K. 1937. 'Toko Atolia', *Mitteilungen der Ausland-Hochschule an der Universität Berlin*, Afrikanische Studien 3, 1–53.

— 1943. *The Fifth Landing Stage*, trans. from Ewe by the author. London: Longmans, 88 p.
— 1973. *Tuinese, Fia Yi Dziehe, Two Plays in Ewe and English*. Marburg: Marburger Studien zur Afrika und Asienkunde, series A, vol. 3, 295 p.
Fodeba, K. 1965. *Aube africaine*. Paris: Seghers, 80 p.
Fugard, A. 1974. *Three Port Elizabeth Plays: The Blood Knot, Hello and Goodbye, Boesman and Lena*. London/Cape Town: Oxford University Press, 227 p.
Furniss, G. 1984. 'Hausa Literature', in B. Lindfors (ed.), *Research Priorities in African Literatures*, pp. 62–75. London/New York/Paris: Zell/Saur, 338 p.
— 1985. 'Réflexions sur l'histoire récente de la littérature haoussa', *Bulletin de l'AELIA* 8, 123–9.
— 1986a. 'Standards in Speech, Spelling and Style, the Hausa Case'. Mayence: J. Gutemberg Universität, International Symposium on Language Standardization in Africa, manuscript, 14 p.
— 1986b. 'Social Problems in Kano, a Poet's Eye View'. Madison: University of Wisconsin, African Studies Association Conference, manuscript.
— 1991. *De la fantaisie à la réalité dans la littérature haoussa en prose*. Bordeaux: Travaux et documents du CEAN 31.
— 1996. *Poetry, Prose and Popular Culture in Hausa*. London: Edinburgh University Press/ International African Institute.
— and Gunner, L. (eds) 1995. *Power, Marginality and African Oral Literature*. Cambridge: Cambridge University Press, 285 p.
Fusella, L., Tedeschi, S., and Tubiana, J. 1984. *Trois essais sur la littérature éthiopienne*. Antibes: ARESAE (Bibliothèque Peiresc).
Fuze, M. (1st edn 1922) 1998. *The Black People and Whence They Came*. T. Cope (ed.), trans. from Zulu by H.C. Lugg. Pietermaritzburg/Durban: University of Natal Press/Killie Campbell Africana Library.
Gaakara wa Wanjau. 1983. *Mwandiki wa Mau-Mau Ithaamirio-ini*. Nairobi: Heinemann Educational Books, 189 p.
Gabre-Medhin, T. 1965. *Oda-Oak Oracle*. London: Oxford University Press.
Gagare, B. 1982. *Karshen Alewa Kasa*. Lagos: Nigeria Magazine.
Garlake, P. 1982. *Great Zimbabwe Described and Explained*. Harare: Zimbabwe Publishing House, 64 p.
Garuba, H. 1982. *Shadows and Dream*. Ibadan: New Horn Press.
— 1988a. 'Odia Ofeimun and Femi Fatoba', in Y. Ogunbiyi (ed.). *Perspectives on Nigerian Literature* 2, 269–76.
— 1988b. (ed.) *Voices from the Fringe, an ANA Anthology of New Nigerian Poetry*. Lagos: Malthouse Press, 205 p.
Geary, C. 1994. *King Njoya's Gift: A Beaded Sculpture from the Bamum Kingdom Cameroon in the National Museum of African Art*. Washington: National Museum of African Art.
Gérard, A. 1966. 'Antoine Roger Bolamba ou la révolution subreptice', *La revue nouvelle* 46 (10), 286–98.
— 1971. *Four African Literatures: Xhosa, Sotho, Zulu, Amharic*. Berkeley/Los Angeles: University of California Press, 458 p.
— 1981. *African Language Literatures*. London/Washington DC: Longman/Three Continents, 348 p.
— (ed.). 1982. *Comparative Literature and African Languages*. Goodwood: Via Afrika, 116 p.
— 1984. *Essais d'histoire littéraire africaine*. Paris/Sherbrooke: ACCT/ Naaman, 248 p.
— (ed.). 1986. *European-Language Writing in Sub-Saharan Africa*, vols 1, 2 in *A Comparative History of Literatures in European Languages*. Budapest: Akademiai Kiado, International Comparative Literature Association, 1289 p.
Gerhardt, L. 1995. 'The Place of Carl Meinhof in African Linguistics', *Afrika and Übersee* 78 (2), 163–75.
Gibbe, A.G. 1980. *Shaaban Robert Mshairi*. Dar es Salaam: Tanzania Publishing House, 133 p.
Gikandi, S. 1987. *Reading the African Novel*. London/Nairobi/Portsmouth: Heinemann/ James Currey, 172 p.
— 1992. 'Ngugi's Conversion, Writing and the Politics of Language', *Research in African Literatures* 23 (1), 131–44.
Glissant, E. 1981. 'Langue, multilinguisme', in *Le discours antillais*, pp. 316–24. Paris: Le Seuil.
Godard, H. 1990. *L'autre face de la littérature: essai sur André Malraux et la littérature*. Paris: Gallimard.
Gomez, K. 1982. *Opération Marigot*. Lomé/Dakar/Abidjan: Nouvelles éditions africaines.
Goody, J. (ed.). 1968. *Literacy in Traditional Societies*. Cambridge: Cambridge University Press.
— 1971. 'The Impact of Islamic Writing on the Oral Cultures of West Africa', *Cahiers d'études africaines* 21 (3), 455–66.
— 1993. *The Interface Between the Written and the Oral*. Cambridge: Cambridge University Press.

— and Gandah, S.W.D.K. 1980. *Une récitation du Bagré*. Paris: Armand Colin (Les classiques africains).

Gordimer, N. 1973. *The Black Interpreters*. Johannesburg: Ravan Press, 76 p.

— 1981. *July's People*. New York: Viking Press, 160 p.

Götrick, K . 1984. *Apidan Theatre and Modern Drama, a Study in Traditional Yoruba Theatre and its Influence on Modern Drama by Yoruba Playwrights*. Goteborg: Almquist and Wiksell International, 271 p.

Greenberg, J. 1953. 'Hausa Verse Prosody', *Journal of the American Oriental Society* 79 (3), 125–35.

— 1963. *The Languages of Africa*. La Haye: Mouton, 104 p.

Griaule, M. and Dieterlen, G. 1951. *Signes graphiques soudanais*. Paris: Hermann, 86 p.

Gromov, M. 1996. 'The Linguistic Situation and the Rise of Anglophone Literature in Tanzania', in E. Breitinger (ed.), *Defining New Idioms and Alternative Forms of Expression*, ASNEL papers, Cross Cultures 23.

Guma, S.M. 1967. *The Form, Content and Technique of Traditional Literature in Southern Sotho*. Pretoria: J.L.Van Schaik, 215 p.

Gunner, E. (Liz) 1988. 'Power House, Prison House: an Oral Genre and its Use in Isaiah Shembe's Nazareth Baptist Church', *Journal of Southern African Studies* 14 (2), 204–7.

— 2000. 'Hidden Stones and the Light of the New Day: a Zulu Manuscript and its Place in South African Writing Now', *Research in African Literatures* 31 (2), 1–16.

— and Gwala, M. (eds and translators) 1991. *Musho, Zulu Popular Praises*. East Lansing: Michigan State University Press, 237 p.

Ha, M.-P. 2000. *Figuring the East*. Albany: SUNY Press.

Hagège, C. 1985. *L'homme de paroles*. Paris: Fayard, 314 p.

Hair, P. 1964. 'Early Vernacular Printing in Africa', *Sierra Leone Language Review* 3, 47–52.

Haji, H.G. 1994. *Kimbunga, Tungo za visiwani*. Collected by T.S.Y. Sengo. Dar es Salaam: TUKI, 45 p.

— 1999. *Utenzi wa visa vya nabii Suleiman bi daudi*. Zanzibar: Al Khayria Press, 90 p.

Haring, L. 1994. 'Introduction: The Search for Grounds in African Oral Tradition', *African Oral Traditions/Oral Tradition* 9 (1), 3–22.

Harries, L. 1962. *Swahili Poetry*. Oxford: Clarendon Press.

Harries, P. 1994. *Work, Culture, and Identity*. Portsmouth NH/Johannesburg/London: Heinemann/Witwatersrand University Press/James Currey, 305 p.

Hartwig, C.M. and Gerald, W. 1972. 'Aniceti Kitereza, a Kerebe novelist', *Research in African Literature* 3 (2), 162–70.

Hausser, M. 1988. *Pour une poétique de la négritude*. Paris: Silex, 408 p.

Havelock E. 1976. *Origins of Western Literacy*. Toronto: The Ontario Institute for Studies in Education.

— 1982. *The Literate Revolution in Greece and its Cultural Consequences*. Princeton: Princeton University Press, 362 p.

Haynes, J. 1987. *African Poetry and the English Language*. London: Macmillan, 165 p.

Hazoumé, P. 1937. *Le pacte de sang au Dahomey*. Paris: Institut d'ethnologie, 170 p.

— 1938. *Doguicimi*. Paris: Larose (English trans. 1990, Washington: Three Continents Press).

Herdeck, D.E. 1974. *African Authors: a Companion to Black African Writing 1300–1973*. Washington: Inscape.

Hiskett, M. 1975. *A History of Hausa Islamic Verse*. London: School of Oriental and African Studies, 274 p.

Hodgkin, T. 1966. 'The Islamic Literary Traditions in Ghana', in I. Lewis (ed.), *Islam in Tropical Africa*, pp. 76–97. Cambridge: Cambridge University Press.

Homburger, L. 1941. *Les langues négro-africaines et les peuples qui les parlent*. Paris: Payot, 350 p.

Horne, K.M. 1970. *Language Typology: 19th and 20th Century Views*. Washington: Georgetown University, School of Language and Linguistics, 46 p.

Houis, M. 1971. *Anthropologie linguistique de l'Afrique noire*. Paris: PUF, 220 p.

— 1977. 'Les niveaux de signification dans *Les soleils des indépendances*', *Recherche, pédagogie et culture* 28, 68–9.

— 1980. 'Égyptien pharaonique et langues africaines, un dossier ouvert', *Afrique et langage* 13, 69–79.

Hove, C. 1986. *Masimba Avanhu*. Gweru: Mambo Press, 95 p.

— 1988. *Bones*. Harare: Baobab Books, 135 p.

Hulstaert, G. (ed.) 1972. *Poèmes mongo modernes*. Brussels: Académie royale des sciences d'outre-mer, 237 p.

Hussein, E. 1969. *Kinjeketile*. Dar es Salaam/Nairobi: Oxford University Press, 49 p. (*Kinjeketile*, trans. from Kiswahili by the author, Dar es Salaam: Oxford University Press, 1970).

— 1970. *Michezo ya kuigiza*. Nairobi/Dar es Salaam/Kampala: East African Publishing House, 64 p.

— 1971. *Mashetani*. Nairobi: Oxford University Press, 57 p.

— 1974. 'On the Development of Theatre in East Africa'. D. Phil thesis, Berlin: Humboldt University, 180 p.
— 1976. *Jogoo kijijini, Ngao ya jadi*. Nairobi: Oxford University Press, 50 p.
— 1980. *Arusi*. Nairobi: Oxford University Press, 50 p.
— 1988a. *Kwenye ukingo wa Thym*. Nairobi: Oxford University Press, 56 p. (*At the Edge of the Thim*, Nairobi: Oxford University Press, 2000).
— 1988b. Lecture on Ngugi. Nairobi: CREDU, manuscript.
— 1991. *Comment écrire pour le théâtre en suivant Aristote?* trans. from Kiswahili by K. Tumbwe. Nairobi: CREDU, 12 p.
Hyman, L.M. 1975. *Phonology, Theory, and Analysis*. New York: Holt, Rinehart and Winston, 275 p.
Iguh, T. 1965. *The Struggles and Trial of Jomo Kenyatta*. Onitsha: Academy Nigerian Bookshop, 56 p.
— 1961. *The Last Days of Lumumba, the Late Lion of Congo*. Onitsha: A. Onwudiwe & Sons.
Ikiddeh, I. (ed.). 1982. 'Ozidi, the Film, the Saga, and the Play in S.O. Asein', *Comparative Approaches to Modern African Literature*, pp. 46–64. Ibadan: Department of English.
Imam, A. (1st edn 1935) 1966. *Ruwan Bagaja*. Zaria: Northern Nigerian Publishing Corporation, 44 p.
— (1st edn 1937) 1980. *Magana jari Ce*. Zaria: Northern Nigerian Publishing Corporation, 556 p.
Iniesta, F. 1989. *Antiguo Egipto: La nación negra*. Barcelona: Sendai, 218 p.
Innes, G. 1975. *Sundiata: Three Mandinka Versions*. London: School of Oriental and African Studies, 326 p.
Irele, A. 1981. *The African Experience in Literature and Ideology*. London/Ibadan/ Nairobi: Heinemann, 216 p.
— 1989. 'Éloge de l'aliénation', *Notre librairie* 98, 46–58.
— 1992. 'The Crisis of Legitimacy in Africa', *Dissent*, Summer, 296–302.
— 1993a. 'Is African Music Possible?' *Transition* 81, 56–71.
— 1993b. 'In Praise of Alienation', in V. Mudimbe (ed.), *Surreptitious Speech:* Présence Africaine *and the Politics of Otherness*. Chicago: University of Chicago Press.
— 2001. *The African Imagination, Literature in Africa and the Black Diaspora*. Oxford/New York: Oxford University Press.
Isola, A. 1970. *Efunsetan Aniwura*. Ibadan: Oxford University Press, 82 p.
— 1988. 'Contemporary Yoruba Literary Tradition', in Y. Ogunbiyi (ed.), *Perspectives on Nigerian Literature* 1, 73.
Jabavu, D.D.T. 1923. *Bantu Literature, Classification and Reviews*. Lovedale: Book Department, 27 p.
— 1943. *The Influence of English on Bantu Literature*. Lovedale: Lovedale Press, 26 p.
Jacinto, A. 1979. *Vôvô Bartolomeu*, Preface M. Ferreira. Lisbon: Ediçoes, 70 p.
Jacottet, E. 1899. *Études sur les langues du Haut-Zambèze*, Textes Soubiya, 2nd section. Paris: Ernest Leroux.
— 1909. *Litsomo Tsa Basotho*. Morija: Morija Sesuto Book Depot.
Jahn, J. 1968. *Neo-African Literature; a History of Black Writing*. New York: Grove Press 1968, 301 p.
— and Dressler, C.P. 1971. *Bibliography of Creative African Writing*. Nendeln (Liechtenstein): Kraus Thomson, 446 p.
Jeyifo, B. 1981. 'Interview with G.T. Onimole', in *The Yoruba Professional Itinerant Theatre*, Oral Documentation, pp. 153–74. Lagos: Federal Ministry of Culture.
— 1985. *The Truthful Lie: Essays in a Sociology of African Drama*. London/Port of Spain: New Beacon, 122 p.
— 1992. 'Literature in Post-colonial Africa', *Dissent*, Summer, 353–60.
Jolobe, J.J.R. 1936. *Umyezo*. Johannesburg: Witwatersrand University Press, 94 p.
— 1946. *Poems of an African*, trans. from Xhosa by the author. Lovedale: Lovedale Press, 34 p.
Jordan, A.C. 1940. *Ingqumbo yeminyanya*. Lovedale: Lovedale Press, 250 p. (*The Wrath of the Ancestors*, trans. from Xhosa by the author Lovedale: Lovedale Press, 1980).
— 1973. *Towards an African Literature, the Emergence of Literary Form in Xhosa*. Berkeley/Los Angeles: University of California Press, 116 p.
Joubert, J.-L. 1991a. 'La poésie togolaise en langue française', in J. Riesz and A. Ricard (eds), *Le champ littéraire togolais*, pp. 189–201. Bayreuth: African Studies Series 23.
— 1991b. *Littératures de l'océan Indien: Histoire littéraire de la francophonie*. Paris: Edicef, 304 p.
Juma Bhalo, A.N.bin. 1966. *Poems from Kenya: Gnomic Verses in Swahili*, ed. L. Harries. Madison: University of Wisonsin Press.
Kadima-Nzuji, M. 1981. *Jacques Rabemananjara, l'homme et l'œuvre*. Paris: Présence africaine, 186 p.
— 1984. *La littérature zaïroise de langue française*. Paris: Karthala/ACCT, 345 p.

Kagabo, J. 1986. 'Alexis Kagame', in *L'école de la tradition*, pp. 31–48. Paris: Radio France Internationale.

Kagame, A. 1949–1951. *Isoko Y'amajyambera*. Kabgayi: Éditions royales, 3 vols: 72, 101 et 103 p.

— 1949. *Indyohesha-birayi*. Kabgayi: Éditions royales, 60 p.

— 1952a. *La divine pastorale*, French translation, by the author, of an epic written in Rwandese. Brussels: Éditions du marais, 109 p.

— 1952b. *Le code des institutions politiques du Rwanda précolonial*. Brussels: Institut royal colonial belge, 136 p.

— 1952c. *Umulirimbiyi wa nyili-ibiremwa*. Kabgayi: Éditions royales, 64 p.

— 1955a. *La naissance de l'univers, deuxième veillée de la divine pastorale:* Brussels, Éditions du marais, 85 p.

— 1955b. *La philosophie bantu-rwandaise de l'être*. Brussels: Académie royale des sciences coloniales, 64 p.

— 1961. *Histoire des armées bovines dans l'ancien Rwanda*. Brussels: Académie royale des sciences d'outre-mer, 147 p.

— 1963. *Les milices du Rwanda précolonial*. Brussels: Académie royale des sciences d'outre-mer, 196 p.

— 1967. 'Curriculum-vitae', manuscript, 5 p.

— 1976. *La philosophie bantu comparée*. Paris: Présence africaine, 334 p.

Kagara, B. (1st edn 1934) 1966. *Gandoki*. Zaria: Gaskiya Corporation, 73 p.

Kahari, G. 1972. *The Novels of Patrick Chakaipa*. Salisbury: Longman Rhodesia, 110 p.

— 1975. *The Imaginative Writings of Paul Chidyausiku*. Gwelo: Mambo Press, 175 p.

— 1982. 'Realism and the Contemporary Shona Novel'. Harare: University of Zimbabwe, manuscript, 27 p.

— 1990a. *The Rise of the Shona Novel*. Harare: Mambo Press, 407 p.

— 1990b. *Plots and Characters in Shona Fiction*. Harare: Mambo Press, 309 p.

Kane, C.H. 1961. *L'aventure ambiguë*. Paris: Juillard, 207 p. (*Ambiguous Adventure*, New York: Walker 1963)

Kane, M. (1st edn 1967) 1981. *Essai sur les contes d'Amadou Koumba, du conte traditionnel au conte moderne d'expression française*. Dakar: NEA, 249 p.

Karama, S. and Khan, K. 1980. *Kusoma na kufahamu mashairi*. Nairobi: Longman, 120 p.

Kaschula, R. 1991. 'Mandela Comes Home, the Poet's Perspective', *Journal of Ethnic Studies* 19 (1), 15–18.

Kati ben El-Hadj El-Motaoukkel Kati, Mahmoud. 1913–14. *Tarikh el Fettach*. 1981 French trans. by O. Houdas and M. Delafosse. Paris: Librairie d'Amerique et d'Orient/Adrien Maisonneuve.

Katsina, S.I. 1982. *Turmin Danya*. Lagos: Nigeria Magazine, 129 p.

Kellman, S. 2000. *The Translingual Imagination*. Lincoln: University of Nebraska Press.

Kenyatta, J. 1938. *Facing Mount Kenya*. London: Martin Secker and Warburg, 339 p.

Kesteloot, L. (1st edn 1964) 1977. *Les écrivains noirs de langue française, naissance d'une littérature*. Brussels: Éditions de l'Université libre, 344 p.

— 2001. *Histoire de la littérature négro-africaine*. Paris: Karthala/AUF, 386 p.

— and Dieng, B. 1997. *Les épopées d'Afrique noire*. Paris: Karthala/UNESCO, 626 p.

Kezilahabi, E. 1974. *Kichwa maji*. Dar es Salaam: East African Publishing House, 218 p.

— (1st edn 1971) 1981a. *Rosa Mistika*. Arusha: Eastern Africa Publications, 119 p.

— 1981b. *Dunia uwanja wa Fujo*. Arusha: Eastern Africa Publications, 190 p.

— 1987. *Sofferenza*, trans. from Kiswahili (Kichomi) by E. Bertoncini. Naples: Plural, 100 p.

— 1988. *Karibu ndani*. Dar es Salaam: Dar es Salaam University Press, 45 p.

Khaketla, B.M. 1960. *Mosali a nkohola*. Johannesburg: APB, 195 p.

Kitereza, A. 1980. *Bwana Myombekere na bibi Bugonoka na Ntulanalwo na Nulihwali*. Dar es Salaam: Tanzania Publishing House, 617 p.

— 2002. *Mr Myombekere and his Wife Bugonoka, their Son Ntulanalwo and Daughter Bulihwali: The Story of an Ancient African Community*, trans. from Kikerewe by G. Ruhumbika. Dar es Salaam: Mkuki na Nyota Publishers, 687 p.

Klima, V., Ruzicka, K.F., and Zima, P. 1976. *Black African Literature and Language*. Dordrecht/Boston: D. Reidel Publishing Company, 310 p.

Knappert, J. 1962–3. 'In memoriam, Shaaban Robert', *Swahili*, Journal of the East African Swahili Institute, 10.

— selected and trans. by, 1972. *A Choice of Flowers: Swahili Songs of Love and Passion*, [*Chaguo la maua*]. London: Heinemann, 202 p.

Kofoworola, Z. and Lateef, Y. 1987. *Hausa Performing Arts and Music*. Lagos: Nigeria Magazine, 330 p.

Kom, A. *Dictionnaire des œuvres littéraires négro-africaines de langue française, des origines à 1978*. Paris/Sherbrooke: ACCT/Naarnan, 671 p.

Konka, R. 1983. *Histoire de la littérature camerounaise*. Ablon: author's home, 173 p.

Kourouma, A. 1970 (1st edn 1968). *Les soleils des indépendances*. Paris: Le Seuil, 208 p. (*The*

Suns of Independence, New York: Africana Publishing Corporation 1981).
— 1990. *Monnè, outrages et défis*. Paris: Le Seuil, 290 p. (*Monnew, a Novel*, San Francisco: Mercury House, 1993).
— 1998. *En attendant le vote des bêtes sauvages*. Paris: Le Seuil, 357 p. (*Waiting for the Vote of the Wild Animals*, Charlottesville: University Press of Virginia 2001).
Kunene, D. and Kirsh, R. 1967. *The Beginning of South African Vernacular Literature*. Los Angeles: African Studies Center, UCLA, 55 p.
— 1971. *Heroic Poetry of the Basotho*. Oxford: Oxford University Press, 203 p.
— 1978. *Pirates Have Become Our Kings*. Nairobi: East African Publishing House, 91 p.
— 1989. *Thomas Mofolo and the Emergence of Written Sesotho Prose*. Johannesburg: Ravan Press, 251 p.
Kunene, R.M. 1979. *Emperor Shaka the Great*. London: Heinemann, 438 p.
Labouret, H. and Rivet, P. 1929. *Le royaume d'Arda et son évangélisation au XVIIe siècle*. Paris: Institut d'ethnologie, pp. 31–62.
Labou Tansi, S. 1979. *La vie et demie*. Paris: Le Seuil, 197 p.
— 1983. *L'anté-peuple*. Paris: Le Seuil, 188 p. (*The Antipeople, a Novel*, London/New York: M. Boyars 1988)
— 1985. *Les sept solitudes de Lorsa Lopez*. Paris: Le Seuil, 201 p. (*The Seven Solitudes of Lorsa Lopez*, Oxford/Portsmouth, NH: Heinemann 1995).
— 1990. 'La résurrection rouge et blanche de Roméo et Juliette', after Shakespeare, supplement to *Acteurs*, no. 83, 32 p.
Lacroix, P.-F. (ed.) 1965. *Poésies peules de l'Adamawa*. Paris: Armand Colin (Les classiques africains), 2 vols, 647 p.
Ladipo, D. 1964. *Three Yoruba Plays*, adapted by U. Beier. Ibadan: Mbari Publications, 75 p.
— 1972. *Oba Ko So*, trans. from Yoruba by R.G. Armstrong. Ibadan: Institute of African Studies, 70 p.
Larousse, P. (ed.) 1875. *Grand dictionnaire universel du XIXème siècle*. Paris.
Leclant, J. 1980. *Leçon inaugurale, Chaire d'égyptologie*. Paris: Collège de France, 29 p.
Leite, A.M. 1985. 'Permanência e transformação das formas tradicionais na poesia de J. Craveirinha', in *Les littératures africaines de langue portugaise*, pp. 377–84. Paris: Fondation Gulbenkian.
Lemma, M. 1970. *The Mariage of Unequals, a Comedy*, trans. from Amharic by the author. London: MacMillan.
Lenake, J.M. 1984. *The Poetry of K.E. Ntsane*. Pretoria: J.L. Van Schaik, 176 p.
Lerotholi, G. 1962. *Lithoko tsa Morena e moholo Seeiso Griffith*. Morija: Morija Sesuto Book Depot, 32 p.
— 1964. *Lithoko tsa Motlotlehi Moshoeshoe II*. Morija: Morija Sesuto Book Depot.
Leroy, J. 1973. *L'Ethiopie, archéologie et culture*. Bruges: Desclée de Brouwer, 276 p.
Lindfors, B. 1972. 'An Interview with Okot p'Bitek', *World Literature Written in English* 16 (2), 281–99.
— 1973. *Folklore in Nigerian Literature*. New York: Africana Publishing Corporation, 178 p.
— (ed.). 1975. *Critical Perspectives on Amos Tutuola*. Washington: Three Continents Press, 318 p.
— 1986. 'Interview with Njabulo Ndebele', *Kulankula*, Bayreuth African Studies Series 14.
— 1994. *Comparative Approaches to African Literatures*. Amsterdam: Rodopi, 160 p.
Livre d'or de la mission du Lessouto, 1912, Paris: Société des missions évangéliques.
Liyong, T. 2001. 'On Translating the "Untranslatable": Chapter 14 of *Wer Pa Lawino* by Okot p'Bitek', *Research in African Literatures* 24 (3), 87–92.
Lomami-Tshibamba, P. 1948. *Ngando (le crocodile)*, G.D. Périer (ed.). Brussels: Éd. Georges A. Deny, 119 p.
— 1972. *La récompense de la cruauté, suivi de N'Gobila des Mswata*. Éditions du monde noir, 91 p.
Lord, A.B. 1960. *The Singer of Tales*. Cambridge (Mass.): Harvard University Press, 308 p.
Lordereau, P. (ed.) 1984. *Littératures africaines à la Bibliothèque nationale, 1973–1983*. Paris: Bibliothèque nationale, 209 p.
— (ed.) 1991. *Littératures africaines à la Bibliothèque nationale, 1920–1972*. Paris: Bibliothèque nationale, 235 p.
Machobane, J.J. 1946. *Mahaheng a matso*. Morija: Morija Sesuto Book Depot, 38 p.
— 1947. *Mphtlalatsane*. Morija: Morija Sesuto Book Depot, 107 p.
— 1954. *Senate shoeshoe a Moshoeshoe*. Morija: Morija Sesuto Book Depot, 38 p.
Maillu, D.G. 1976. *The Kommon Man*, Part 3. Nairobi: Comb Books, 259 p.
Malanda, A.S. 1983. 'Le projet littéraire de Sony Labou Tansi', *Le mois en Afrique* 205–206, 145–152.
Manessy, G. 1981, 'Les langues de l'Afrique noire', in J. Perrot (ed.), *Les langues dans le monde ancien et moderne, Afrique subsaharienne, pidgins et créoles* 1, 1. Paris: Éditions du CNRS,
Mangoaela, Z.D. 1988. *Lithoko tsa marena a Basotho*. Morija: Morija Sesuto Book Depot (13th

edn, first edn 1921), 247 p.
Mann, M. and Dalby, D. 1987. *A Classified and Annotated Inventory of the Spoken Languages of Africa, with an Appendix on their Written Representation*. London/New York/Paris: Hans Zell/Butterworths, 325 p.
Mantel-Niecko, J. 1985. 'Ethiopian Literature in Amharic', in B.W. Andrzejewski, S. Pilaszewicz and S. Tyloch, (eds), *Literatures in African languages*, pp. 301–36.
Marechera, D. 1988. *Pictures, Poems, Prose, Tributes*. Compiled and edited by F. Veit-Wild and E. Schade. Harare: Baobab Books, 36 p.
— 1990. *The Black Insider*. Harare: Baobab Books, 128 p.
— 1992. *Cemetery of Mind*. Harare: Baobab Books.
Masolo, D.A. 1986. 'Alexis Kagame and African socio-linguistics', in G. Floistad (ed.), *Contemporary Philosophy*, vol. V, *African Philosophy*, pp. 181–205. La Haye: Martinus Nijhoff.
— 1994. *African Philosophy in Search of Identity*. Bloomington/Edinburgh: Indiana University Press/Edinburgh University Press (for the International African Institute).
Mata Masala, C. 1993. 'Anatomie d'un succès populaire: Zamenga Batukezanga et son œuvre'. Doctoral thesis: Université de la Sorbonne nouvelle, 2 vols, 650 p.
Mateso, L. 1986. *La littérature africaine et sa critique*. Paris: ACCT/Karthala, 399 p.
Maunick, E.J. 1964. *Les manèges de la mer*. Paris: Présence africaine, 101 p.
— 1966. *Mascaret ou le livre de la mer et de la mort*. Paris: Présence africaine, 141 p.
— 1970. *Fusillez-moi*. Paris: Présence africaine, 59 p.
— (ed.) 1975. *De tous les lieux du français*. Hautvillers: Fondation d'Hautvillers pour le dialogue des cultures, 152 p.
— 1976. *Ensoleillé vif*. Paris: Éditions Saint-Germain-des Prés/Nouvelles éditions africaines, 115 p.
— 1988. *Paroles pour solder la mer*. Paris: Gallimard, 81 p.
Maupoil, B. 1943. *La géomancie à l'ancienne côte des esclaves*. Paris: Institut d'ethnologie (Travaux et mémoires 38), 690 p.
Mazrui, Ali A. 1971. *The Trial of Christopher Okigbo*. London: Heinemann, 145 p.
— 1972. *Cultural Engineering and Nation Building in East Africa*. Evanston: Northwestern University Press, 301 p.
— 1974. *World Culture and Black Experience*. Seattle/London: University of Washington Press, 111 p.
— 1975. *The Political Sociology of the English language, an African Perspective*. Paris/La Haye: Mouton, 231 p.
— 1984. 'The Semitic Impact on Black Africa, Arab and Jewish Cultural Influences', *Issue* XIII, 3–8.
— 1980. *The African Condition, the Reith Lectures 1979*. London: Heinemann, 123 p.
— 1986. *The Africans, a Triple Heritage*. London: BBC, 336 p.
— and Mazrui, Alamin 1995. *Swahili State and Society, the Political Economy of an African Language*. Nairobi/London: East African Educational Publishers/James Currey, 171 p.
— and Mazrui, Alamin 1998. *The Power of Babel, Language and Governance in the African Experience*. Oxford: James Currey, 228 p.
Mbaabu, I. 1985. *New Horizons in Kiswahili, a Synthesis in Developments, Research and Literature*. Nairobi: Kenya Literature Bureau, 229 p.
Mbot, J.-E. 1975. *Ebughi bifia, démonter les expressions; énonciation et situations sociales chez les Fang du Gabon*. Paris: Institut d'ethnologie, 150 p.
Mbughuni, P. 1978. 'The Politicization of Kiswahili Literature'. PhD thesis, Indiana University.
Mbutuma, M. 1977. *Isife somzi*. Grahamstown: Institute of Social and Economic Research, Rhodes University, Xhosa Texts 3.
Mda, Z. 1990. *The Plays of Zakes Mda*. Johannesburg: Ravan Press, 156 p.
Meillassoux, C. and Messiant, C. (eds). 1991. *Génie social et manipulation culturelles en Afrique du Sud*. Paris: Arcantère éditions, 314 p.
Meinhof, C. 1912. 'Die Urgeschichte im Lichte der Afrikanischen Linguistik', *Deutsche Literatur-Zeitung* 33, 2376, cited in D. Olderogge, 'The Hamitic Problem in Africanistics', *Soviet Ethnography*, 1949, 3, 156–70.
— 1915. *An Introduction to the Study of African Languages*, trans. by A. Werner. London/Toronto/New York: J.M. Dent/E.P. Dutton.
— 1936. *Die Entstehung Flektierender Sprachen*, Berlin, p. 22, cited in D. Olderogge, 'The Hamitic Problem in Africanistics', *Soviet Ethnography*, 1949, 3, 156–70.
Menga, G. *L'oracle*. Paris: ORTF-DAEC, 93 p.
Miller, C. 1986. 'Langues et intégration nationale au Soudan', *Politique africaine* 23, 29–41.
Milubi, N.A. 1997. *Aspects of Venda Poetry*. Pretoria: Van Schaik Publishers.
Mlacha, S.A.K. and Madumulla, J.S. 1991. *Riwaya ya Kiswahili*. Dar es Salaam: Dar es Salaam University Press, 80 p.
Mnyampala, M. 1965. *Diwani ya Mnyampala*. Nairobi: Kenya Literature Bureau, 156 p.

— 1995. *The Gogo, History, Customs and Traditions*. Trans. from Kiswahili, introduced and edited by G.H. Maddox. London/New York: M.E. Sharpe, 150 p.

Mofolo, T. 1907. *Moeti oa Bochabela*. Morija: Morija Sesuto Book Depot, 161 p.

— 1910. *Pitseng*. Morija: Morija Sesuto Book Depot, 433 p.

— 1925. *Chaka*. Morija: Morija Sesuto Book Depot, 288 p. (*Chaka, an Historical Romance*, trans. from Souto by F.H. Dutton, London: International African Institute/ Oxford University Press, 1931, 198 p.).

— 1934. *The Traveller to the East*, trans. from Sotho (*Moeti oa Bochabela*) by H. Aston. London: Society for Promoting Christian Knowledge, 125 p.

— 1940. *Chaka, une épopée bantoue*, trans. from Sotho by V. Ellenberger. Paris: Gallimard, 272 p.

— 1981. *Chaka, a new translation*, by D. Kunene. London: Heinemann, 168 p.

— 2003. '*L'Homme qui marchait vers le soleil levant*, trans. from Sotho (*Moeti oa Bochabela*) by P. Ellenberger, Bordeaux: Confluences.

Mohamed, S.A. 1980. *Dunia Mti Mkavu*. Nairobi: Longman.

Mohamed, S.M. 1972. *Kiu*. Dar es Salaam: East African Publishing House.

— 1976. *Nyota ya Rehema*. Nairobi: Oxford University Press.

— 1978. *Kicheko cha Ushindi*. Nairobi: Shungwaya Publishers.

Möhlig, W.J.G. 1991. 'D. Westermann pionnier de la recherche sur la culture ewe', in J. Riesz and A. Ricard (eds), *Le champ littéraire togolais*, pp. 67–82.

Moilwa, J. 1983. 'Monyaise as a Setswana Novelist, with Particular Reference to the Novel *Go sa baori*', *Pula, Botswana Journal of African Studies* III (2), 61–70.

Mokhtar, G. (ed.). 1981. *General History of Africa II*. Symposium on the Peopling of Ancient Egypt: Heinemann/California/Unesco, pp. 59–82.

Moletsane, R.I.M. and Matsoso, C.M. 1985. *Handbook on the Teaching of Southern Sesotho*. Maseru: FEP International, 179 p.

Moloi, A.J. 1975. *The Development of the Sotho Novel in the Sixties*. Austin: African Literature Association, 43 p.

Monteil, V. 1980. *L'islam noir, une religion à la conquête de l'Afrique*. Paris: Le Seuil (coll. Esprit, 2nd revised edn), 469 p.

Moore, G. and Beier, U. (eds). (2nd edn 1984) 1963. *The Penguin Book of Modern African Poetry*. Harmondsworth/New York/Ringwood: Penguin Book, 315 p..

Mopeli-Paulus, A.S. 1950. *Liretlo*. Bloemfontein: Via Afrika Bookstore, 72 p.

— in collaboration with Basner, M. 1956. *Turn to the Dark*. London: Cape, 287 p.

— and Lanham, P. 1953. *Blanket Boy's Moon*. New York: Crowell, 309 p.

Moser, G. and Ferreira, M. 1983. *Bibliografia das literaturas africanas de expressão portuguesa*. Lisbon: Impresa nacional, Casa da Moeda, 407 p.

Motlamelle, M.P. 1937. *Ngaka ea mosotho*. Morija: Morija Sesuto Book Depot, 119 p.

Mouralis, B. 1975. *Les contre-littératures*. Paris: PUF, 206 p.

— 1981. *Comprendre l'œuvre de Mongo Beti*. Issy-les-Moulineaux: Éditions Saint-Paul, 128 p.

— 1984. *Littérature et développement*. Paris: Silex/ACCT, 572 p.

— 1988. *V. Y. Mudimbe, ou le discours, l'écart et l'écriture*. Paris: Présence africaine, 143 p.

Mpotokwane, B.E. and Rasebotsa, N.L. 1990. 'Literature in Indigenous Languages, Problems and Progress in the Case of Botswana', ATOLL, Gaborone: *Conference on the Study and Analysis of Literature and Language for Development*, 17 p.

Mqhayi, S.E.K. 1929. *UDon Jadu*. Lovedale: Lovedale Press, 105 p.

— 1943. *Inzuzo, Xhosa Poems*. Johannesburg: Witwatersrand University Press.

Msimang, C.T. 1986. *Folktale Influence on the Zulu Novel*. Pretoria: Acacia Books.

— 1992. *African Language and Language Planning in South Africa: The Nhlapo Alexander Notion of Harmonisation Revisited*. Inaugural Address UNISA. Pretoria: Bard Publishing, 20 p.

Mtshali, O. 1971. *Sounds of a Cowhide Drum*. Johannesburg: Renoster Books.

Mudimbe, V.Y. 1988. *The Invention of Africa: Gnosis, Philosophy and the Order of Knowledge*. Bloomington/Indianapolis: Indiana University Press, 241 p.

— 1989. *Shaba Deux*. Paris: Présence africaine.

— 1991. *Parables and Fables, Exegesis, Textuality and Politics in Central Africa*. Madison: University of Wisconsin Press, 238 p.

— (ed.) 1992. *The Surreptitious Speech: Présence Africaine and the Politics of Otherness, 1947-1987*. Chicago/London: University of Chicago Press.

Muhando, P. 1972. *Hatia*. Nairobi: African Publishing House, 41 p.

— 1975. *Pamba*. Nairobi: Foundations Books, 56 p.

Mukama, I.M.E. 1988. *Un écrivain de langue swahili, Ndyanao Balisidya, Shida*, Université de Lille 3, Mémoire de maîtrise, 100 p.

Mulokozi, M.M. 1990. 'Kitereza: The Man and His Works', *Kiswahili* 57, 68–79.

— and Kahigi, K.K. 1979. *Kunga za ushairi na diwani yetu*. Dar es Salaam: Tanzania Publishing House.

— and Kahigi, K.K. 1995. *Malenga wa Bara*. Dar es Salaam: Dar es Salaam University Press

(East African Literature Bureau 1976), 93 p.
— and Sengo, T. 1995. *History of Kiswahili Poetry, AD 1000–2000*. Dar es Salaam: Institute of Kiswahili Research.
— (ed.) 1999. *Tenzi Tatu za Kale, Fumo Liyongo, Al Inkishafi, Mwana Kupona*. Dar es Salaam: TUKI, 140 p.
Mungoshi, C. 1980. *Inongova Njakenjake*. Harare: Longman, 68 p.
— 1970. *Makununu maodzamwoyo*. Harare: The College Press, 109 p.
— 1975. *Ndiko kupindana kwamazawa*. Gwelo: Mambo Press, 158 p.
— 1980. *Some Kinds of Wounds and Other Short Stories*. Gweru: Mambo Press, 179 p.
— 1980. *Inongora Njakenjake*. Harare: Longman Zimbabwe.
— 1981. *Waiting for the Rain*. Harare: Zimbabwe Publishing House, 180 p.
Mutswairo, S.M. 1956. *Feso*. Cape Town: Oxford University Press/Southern Rhodesia Literature Bureau, 84 p.
— 1974. *Zimbabwe, Prose and Poetry*, including *Feso*, trans. from Shona by the author and D. Herdeck. Washington: Three Continents Press, 275 p.
— 1983. *Mapondera, Soldier of Zimbabwe*. Harare: Longman, 116 p.
Nakhbany, Sheikh A. 1975, *The Ship of Lamu Island*. eds. G. Miehe and T.C. Schadeberg. Leiden: Afrika-Studiecentrum.
— 1995. *Umbuji wa Mnazi*, trans. by N. Brown. Stanford Honors Essays in Humanities xxxix. Stanford: Stanford University.
Namangi, A. 1972a. *Wakokin Imfiraji* (1–4). Zaria: Northern Nigeria Publishing Corporation, 52 p.
— 1972. *Wakokin Imfiraji* (5–9). Zaria: Northern Nigeria Publishing Corporation, 103 p.
Nassir, S.A.A. 1972. *Al Inkishafi, The Soul's Awakening*, trans. from Kiswahili and edited by W. Hickens. Nairobi: Oxford University Press, 190 p.
Ndao, C. 1967. *L'exil d'Albouri*. Paris: P.J. Oswald, 131 p.
Ndebele, N.S. 1989. 'Interview with B. Lindfors', in B. Lindfors (ed.), *Kulankula*, pp. 42–63. Bayreuth: African Studies Series 14.
— 1983. *Fools and Other Stories*. Johannesburg: Ravan Press, 280 p.
Ndulute, C.L. 1985. 'Politics in a Poetic Garb, the Literary Fortune of Mathias Mnyampala', *Kiswahili* 52 (1–2), 143–60.
— 1987. 'Shaaban Robert's Poetic Landscape, From Ethnicism to Nationalism', *Kiswahili* 54 (1–2), 92–116.
Newell, S. 2002. *Marita or the Folly of Love: a Novel by a Native*. Leiden/Boston/Cologne: Brill.
— 2002. *Literary Culture in Colonial Ghana*. Bloomington/Indianapolis: Indiana University Press.
Newman, P. 1980. *The Classification of Chadic Within Afroasiatic*. Leiden: Presses universitaires.
— 2002. *The Hausa Language, an Encyclopedic Reference Grammar*. New Haven/London: Yale University Press.
Ngalasso, M.M. 1985. 'Tableau d'ensemble sur les situations et politiques linguistiques dans les 46 États d'Afrique', *Définition d'une stratégie relative à la promotion des langues africaines*, documents of the meeting held in Conakry (Guinea) 21–25 September 1981, pp. 95–114. Paris: Unesco.
— 1988. 'Usages du français dans un milieu urbain african', *Présence francophone* 33, 105–20.
Ngandu Nkashama, P. 1979. *Comprendre la littérature africaine écrite*. Issy-les-Moulineaux: Éditions Saint-Paul, 165 p.
— 1982. 'Le théâtre et la dramaturgie du masque au Zaïre', *Culture française* 3–4, 58–76.
— 1992. *Littératures et écritures en langues africaines*. Paris: L'Harmattan, 407 p.
Ngara, E. 1982. *Stylistic Criticism and the African Novel*. London: Heinemann, 184 p.
Ngugi wa Thiong'o. 1964. *Weep Not Child*. London: Heinemann, 162 p.
— 1965. *The River Between*. London: Heinemann, 174 p.
— 1967. *Grain of Wheat*. London: Heinemann, 280 p.
— 1977. *Petals of Blood*. London: Heinemann, 352 p.
— 1981. *Detained, a Writer's Prison Diary*. London: Heinemann, 232 p.
— 1982a. *Caitani Mutharabaini*. Nairobi, Heinemann Educational Books, 234 p.
— 1982b. *Devil on the Cross*, trans. from Gikuyu (1982) by the author. London: Heinemann, 254 p.
— 1985. 'On writing in Gikuyu', *Research in African Literatures* 16 (2), 151–6.
— 1986. *Decolonising the Mind: the Politics of Language in African Literature*. London: James Currey, 114 p.
— 1987. *Tsango Yembeu* (Shona trans. by C. Mungoshi, *Grain of Wheat*). Harare: Zimbabwe Publishing House, 344 p.
— 1993. *Moving the Centre: The Struggle for Cultural Freedom*. London/Nairobi/Portsmouth: James Currey/East African Educational Publishers/Heinemann.

— and Mugo, M. 1976. *The Trial of Dedan Kimathi*. London: Heinemann.
— and Ngugi, W.M. 1980. *Ngaahika Ndeenda*, Nairobi, Heinemann Educational Books, 118 p.
— and Ngugi, W.M. 1982. *I Will Marry When I Want*, trans. from Gikuyu by the author, 1980. London: Heinemann Educational Books.
Niane, D.T. 1960. *Soundjata ou l'épopée mandingue*. Paris: Présence africaine, 154 p. (*Sundiata; An Epic of Old Mali*, London: Longmans, 1965)
— 1976. *Sikasso*. Paris: P.J. Oswald, 65 p.
Niangoran-Bouah, G. *L'univers akan des poids à peser l'or*. Abidjan: NEA.
Njogu, K. and Chimerah, R. 1999. *Ufundishaji wa Fasihi*. Nairobi: Jomo Kenyatta Foundation.
Nketia, J. 1952. *Anwmonsem, 1944–1949*. Cape Coast: Methodist Book Depot, 40 p.
— 1955. *Funeral Dirges of the Akan Peoples*. Achimota: University College of the Gold Coast, 296 p.
Nketia, J.H.K. 1974. *Ayan*. Accra: Ghana Publishing Corporation, 115 p.
Nortje, A. 1973. *Dead Roots*. London: Heinemann, 146 p.
Ntsane, K.E. 1946. *'Musa-pelo*. Morija: Morija Sesuto Book Depot, 76 p.
— 1961. *Mmusapelo*, book 2. Johannesburg/Cape Town: APB. 100 p.
Ntuli, D.B.Z. 1982. 'Zulu Literature in the Seventies', in A. Gérard (ed.), *Comparative Literature and African Languages*, pp. 66–70.
— 1984. *The Poetry of B.W. Vilakazi*. Pretoria: J.L.Van Schaik, 246 p.
— and Swanepoel, C.F. 1993. *Southern African Literature in African Languages: a Concise Historical Perspective*. Pretoria: Acacia, 165 p.
Nwachukwu-Agbado, J.O.J. 1997. 'Tradition and Innovation in the Igbo Novels of Tony Ubesie', *Research in African Literatures* 28 (1), 124–33.
Nwana, P. 1935. *Omenuko*. London: Atlantis Press, 67 p. (2nd edn, Longman, 1951; 3rd edn in official spelling, 1963, Ikeja, Longman).
Nyaigotti-Chacha, C. 1992. *Sauti ya Utetezi, Ushairi wa Abdilatif Abdalla*. Dar es Salaam: Dar es Salaam University Press, 146 p.
Nyembezi, C.L.S. 1958. *Izibongo Zamakhosi*. Pietermaritzburg: Shuter and Shooter, 158 p.
— 1961. *Inkinsela Yasemgungundlovu*. Pietermaritzburg: Shuter and Schooter, 200 p.
Nzabatinda, A. 1999. 'Traduttore, Traditore? Alexis Kagame's Transposition of Kinyarwanda Poetry into French', *Journal of African Cultural Studies* 12 (2), 203–10.
Obeng, R.E. 1941. *Eighteen Pence*. Ilfracombe/Devonshire: Stockwell, 180 p.
Obenga, T. 1980 (new edn 1998). *Pour une nouvelle histoire*. Paris: Présence africaine, 170 p.
— 1988. In C.A. Diop (ed.), *Nouvelles recherches sur l'égyptien ancien et les langues négro-africaines modernes*. Paris: Présence africaine.
Obianim, S.J. 1949. *Amegbetoa alo Agbezuge fe nutinya*, London: Macmillan, 139 p. (French translation *Amegbetoa ou les aventures d'Agbezuge*, Karthala, 1990).
Obiechina, E. (ed.). 1972. *Onitsha Market Literature*. New York: Africana Publishing Corporation, 182 p.
Ofeimun, O. 1980. *The Poet Lied and Other Poems*. Lagos: Update Communication, 176 p.
Ofosu-Appiah, L.H. 1975. *Joseph Ephraim Casely-Hayford, the Man of Vision and Faith*. Accra: the J.B. Danquah Memorial Lectures, Academy of Arts and Sciences, 31 p.
— 1976a. *Sophokles Antigone*, translation in Twi. Accra: Waterville Publishing House, 65 p.
— 1976b. *Sokrates Anoyi, Plato's Apology of Sokrates*, trans. in Twi. Accra: Waterville Publishing House, 61 p.
Ogbalu, F.C. and Emenanjo, E.N. (eds) 1975. *Igbo Language and Culture*. Ibadan: Oxford University Press, 216 p.
Ogunbiyi, Y. (ed.). 1981. *Drama and Theatre in Nigeria, a Critical Source Book*. Lagos: Nigeria Magazine, 522 p.
— (ed.). 1988a. *Perspectives on Nigerian Literature, 1700 to the Present*, vol. 1. Lagos: Guardian Books, 203 p.
— (ed.). 1988b. *Perspectives on Nigerian Literature, 1700 to the Present*, vol. 2, Lagos: Guardian Books, 359 p.
Ohly, R. 1981. *Aggressive Prose, a Case Study in Kiswahili Prose of the Seventies*. Dar es Salaam: Institute of Kiswahili Research, 151 p.
— 1982. *Swahili, the Diagram of Crises*. Vienna/Dar es Salaam: Afro-Pub, 175 p.
Okara, G. 1965. *The Voice*. London/Ibadan/Nairobi: Heinemann, 127 p.
Okediji, O. 1969. *Aja Lo Leru*. Ibadan: Longman, 160 p.
Okigbo, C. 1962. *Limits*. Ibadan: Mbari Publications, 12 p.
— 1986. *Collected Poems*. London: Heinemann, 99 p.
Okpewho, I. 1979. *The Epic in Africa: Towards a Poetic of Oral Performance*. New York: Columbia University Press, 288 p.
— 1992. *African Oral Literature: Background, Character and Continuity*. Bloomington: Indiana University Press, 392 p.
Olatunji, O. (ed.) 1982a. Ewi *Adebayo Faleti, 2* vols. Ibadan: Heinemann Educational Books, 87 p., 107 p.
— 1982b. *Adebayo Faleti: a Study of his Poems 1954–1964*. Ibadan: Heinemann Educational

Books, 182 p.
— 1984. *Features of Yoruba Oral Poetry*. Ibadan: University Press Limited, 267 p.
Olderogge, D.A. 1949. 'The Hamitic Problem in Africanistics', trans. from Russian by P.O. Dada, *Soviet Ethnography* 3, 156–170. Ibadan: Institute of African Studies, 25 p.
Omotoso, K. 1986. *The Form of the African Novel, a Critical Essay*. Ikeja: MacQuick Publishers, 87 p.
— 1994. *Season of Migration to the South*. Cape Town: Tafelberg.
Opland, J. 1983. *Xhosa Oral Poetry, Aspects of a Black South African Tradition*. Cambridge: Cambridge University Press, 303 p.
— 1997. 'The Drumbeat of the Cross: Christianity and Literature' in R. Elphick and R. Davenport (eds), *Christianity in South Africa*. Oxford/Cape Town: James Currey/David Philip.
— 1998. *Xhosa Poets and Poetry*. Cape Town: David Philip, 365 p.
— 2001. 'The Languages of South Africa', in P. France (ed.), *The Oxford Guide to Literature in English Translation*. Oxford: Oxford University Press.
Opon Ifa, 1980. Ibadan Poetry Chapbooks, 1 and 2, 28 p., 40 p.
Osofisan, F. 1978. *Who's Afraid of Solarin?* Ibadan: Scholars Press Ltd, 83 p.
— 1980. *Once Upon Four Robbers*. Ibadan: BIO Educational, 82 p.
— 1985. *Midnight Hotel*. Ibadan: Evans Brother Publishers, 65 p.
— 1986. *Two One-Act Plays, the Oriki of a Grasshopper and Altine's Wrath*. Ibadan: New Horn Press, 90 p.
— 1989. Interview with A. Ricard, July, Ibadan.
Osadebay, D.C. 1952. *Africa Sings*. Ilfracombe: Stockwell.
Osundare, N. 1981. 'From Oral to Written: Aspects of the Sociostylistic Repercussions of Transition', *Journal of African and Comparative Literature* (Ibadan) 1, 1–13.
— 1983 (2nd edn 1987). *Songs of the Marketplace*. Ibadan: New Horn Press, 90 p.
— 1984. *Village Voices*. Ibadan: Evans Brothers Limited, 71 p.
— 1986. The Writer as a Righter, *Ife Monographs on Literature and Criticism*. Ife: Department of Literature in English, University of Ife, 51 p.
— 1986. *A Nib in the Pond, Poems*. Ife: Department of Literature in English, University of Ife, 51 p.
— 1986. *The Eye of the Earth*. Ibadan: Heinemann Educational Books, 49 p.
— 1988. *Moonsongs*. Ibadan: Spectrum Books, 74 p.
Ouologuem, Y. 1968. *Le devoir de violence*. Paris: Le Seuil. (*Bound to Violence*, New York: Secker & Warburg, 1971).
Owolabi, O. (ed.). 1996. *Language in Nigeria: Essays in Honour of Ayo Bamgbose*. Lagos: Group Publishers.
Oyono, F. 1956a. *Une vie de boy*. Paris: Julliard, 183 p. (*Houseboy*, London: Heinemann, 1966).
— 1956b. *Le vieux nègre et la médaille*. Paris: Julliard, 211 p. (*The Old Man and the Medal*, London: Heinemann, 1967).
Oyono, G. 1964. *Trois prétendants, un mari*. Yaounde: CLE, 126 p. (*Three Suitors: One Husband* (and) *Until Further Notice*, London: Methuen, 1968).
Pageard, R. 1961. 'Soundiata Keita et la tradition orale', *Présence africaine* 31, 51–70.
Pankhurst, R. 1962, 'The Foundations of Education, Printing, Newspapers, Book Production, Libraries and Literacy in Ethiopia', *Ethiopian Observer* VI (3), 241–90.
Paulhan, J. 1938. *Les hain-tenys*. Paris: Gallimard, 216 p.
Paulme, D. 1976. *La mère dévorante*. Paris: Gallimard, 322 p.
Paz, O. 1987. *Sor Juana Inès de la Cruz ou les pièges de la foi*. Paris: Gallimard, 636 p.
p'Bitek, Okot 1953. *Lak Tar Miyo Kinyero Wi Lobo*. Kampala/Nairobi/Dar es Salaam: Eagle Press, 137 p.
— 1966 (1972, 3rd edn with preface). *Song of Lawino*. Nairobi: East African Publishing House, 216 p.
— 1969. *Wer pa Lawino*. Nairobi: East African Publishing House, 214 p. (*The Defence of Lawino*, Kampala: Fountain Publishers, 2001).
— 1970. *Song of Ocol*. Nairobi: East African Publishing House, 86 p.
— 1971. *Two Songs: Song of Prisoner, Song of Malaya*. Nairobi: East African Publishing House.
— 1974. *The Horn of My Love*. London/Nairobi/Ibadan: Heinemann, 182 p.
— 1980. *Religion of the Central Luo*. Kampala: Uganda Literature Bureau, 164 p.
— 1986. *Artist, the Ruler: Essays on Art, Culture and Values*. Nairobi: Heinemann Kenya, 134 p.
— 1989a. *White Teeth*. Nairobi: Heinemann (trans. of *Lak Tar*), 108 p.
— 1989b. *Song of Lawino, Song of Ocol*. Nairobi: Heinemann Kenya, 151 p.
— 2001. *The Defence of Lawino*, a new translation of *Wer pa Lawino* by Taban lo Liyong. Kampala: Fountain Publishers, 115 p.
Pedersten, K. 1989. 'The "Malke", an Ethiopian Prayer Form with Latin Origins', *Proceedings*

of the Eighth International Conference of Ethiopian Studies, pp. 547–60. Addis Ababa: Institute of Ethiopian Studies.

Peires, J.B. 1981. *The House of Phalo: a History of the Xhosa People in the Days of Their Independence*. Johannesburg: Ravan Press, 281 p.

Perrot, C.-H. 1963. 'Premières années de l'implantation du christianisme au Lesotho (1833–1847)', *Cahiers d'études africaines* 4 (1), 97–125.

Phillipson, D.W. 1985. *African Archaeology*. Cambridge: Cambridge University Press, 234 p.

Plaatje, S.T. 1975. *Mhudi*, with an introduction by T. Couzens. Johannesburg: Quagga Press, 165 p.

— (ed.). 1983 (1st edn 1916). *Native Life in South Africa*. B. Willan, London: Longman, 267 p.

— 1989. *Mafeking Diary, a Black Man's View of a White Man's War*, J. Comaroff (ed.). Johannesburg: Southern Book Publishers, 172 p.

Pliya, J. 1966. *Kondo le requin*. Cotonou: Éditions du Bénin, 106 p.

— 1970. *La secrétaire particulière*. Cotonou: ABM, 80 p.

Priese, K-H. 1997. 'La langue et l'écriture méroïtique', in *Soudan, Royaumes sur le Nil*, pp. 253–64. Paris: Flammarion/Institut du monde arabe.

Pugliese, C. 1994a. *Author, Publisher and Gikuyu Nationalist: the Life and Writings of Gakaara wa Wanjau*. Bayreuth: IFRA/Bayreuth African Studies 37, 270 p.

— 1994b. 'The Organic Intellectual in Kenya: Gakaara wa Wanjau'. *Research in African Literature* 25 (4) 177–87.

Quaghebeur, M. (under the direction of) 1992. *Papier blanc, encre noire, Cent ans de culture francophone en Afrique centrale*, E. Van Balberghe, N. Fettweis and A.Vilain (eds). Brussels: Labor, 2 vols, 690 p.

Queffelec, A. and Niangouna, A. 1990. *Le français au Congo*. Aix-en-Provence: Publications de l'Université de Provence, 335 p.

Rabearivelo, J.–J. 1924. *La coupe de cendres*. Antananarivo: Pitot de la Beaujardière, 39 p.

— 1935. *Traduit de la nuit*, transcribed from Hova. Tunis: Éditions des mirages, 69 p.

— 1980. *Vieilles chansons du pays d'Imerina*, trans. by the author. Antananarivo: Madprint, 53 p.

— 1988. *L'interférence, suivi de Un conte de la nuit*. Paris: Hatier, 189 p.

— 1990. *Poèmes*. Paris: Hatier, 224 p.

Ranger, T. 1985. *The Invention of Tribalism in Zimbabwe*. Gweru: Mambo Press, 20 p.

Raum, O. 1943. 'The African Chapter in the History of Writing'. *African Studies* 2, 178–92.

Ribeiro, E. 1967. *Muchadura*. Gweru: Mambo Press, 128 p.

Ricard, A. 1972. *Théâtre et nationalisme*. Paris: Présence africaine, 235 p. (*Theatre and Nationalism: Wole Soyinka and LeRoi Jones*, Ile-Ife, Nigeria: University of Ife Press, 1983).

— 1975a. *Livre et communication au Nigeria*. Paris: Présence africaine, 136 p.

— 1975b. 'Hubert Ogunde à Lomé', *Revue d'histoire du théâtre* 27, 26–30.

— 1986a. 'Au pays des tortues qui chantent', *Mélanges offerts à Jacques Schérer*, pp. 99–104. Paris: Nizet.

— 1986b. *L'invention du théâtre*. Paris/Lausanne: L'Age d'homme, 134 p.

— 1987. *Félix Couchoro, naissance du roman africain*. Paris: Présence africaine, 228 p.

— 1997. 'Traversées de l'Afrique', *Cahiers du centre régional des lettres d'Aquitaine* 2.

— 1998. *Ebrahim Hussein: Théâtre swahili et nationalisme tanzanien*. Paris: Karthala, 186 p. (*Ebrahim Hussein: Swahili Theatre and Individualism*, Dar es Salaam: Mkuki na Nyota Publishers 2000).

Richards, S. 1996. *Ancient Songs Set Ablaze: the Theatre of Femi Osofisan*. Washington DC: Howard University Press.

Riesz, J. 1995. 'Audible Gasps From the Audience: Accusations of Plagiarism against African Authors and Historical Contexts', *Yearbook of Comparative and General Literature* 43, 84–96.

— 1998. *Französisch in Afrika Herrschaft durch Sprache*. Frankfurt: IKO Verlag für Interkulturelle Kommunikation.

— and Ricard, A. (eds) 1990. *Semper Aliquid novi: Littérature comparée et littératures d'Afrique. Mélanges offerts à Albert Gérard*. Tübingen: Gunter Narr, 404 p.

— and Ricard, A. (eds) 1991. *Le champ littéraire togolais*. Bayreuth: African Studies 23, 200 p.

Riva, S. 2000. *Ruli di tam-tam dalla torre di Babele: Storia della litteratura del Congo Kinshasa*. Milan: LED.

Rive, R. and Couzens, T. (1993). *Seme, the Founder of the ANC*. Africa World Press, 91 p.

Robert, S. 1951. *Kusadikika*. Nairobi: Nelson, 67 p.

— 1959. *Insha na mashairi*. Dar es Salaam: Nelson, 106 p.

— (1st edn 1947) 1966. *Pambo la lugha*. Nairobi/Dar es Salaam: Oxford University Press, 50 p.

— 1967a. *Wasifu wa Siti binti Saad*. Nairobi: Nelson, 77 p.

— 1967b. *Kufikirika*. Nairobi: Oxford University Press, 60 p.

— 1967c. *Insha na Mashairi*. London/Nairobi/Dar es Salaam: Nelson, 106 p.

— 1968. *Utubora Mkulima*. London/Nairobi: Nelson, 91 p.

— (1st edn 1952) 1977. *Adili na Nduguze*. Nairobi: Oxford University Press.
— 1981. A. Joukov (ed.) *Izbranoe* (Selected Works). Trans. in Russian, 256 p.
— (1st edn 1949) 1991a. *Maisha yangu, na Baada ya miaka hamsini*. Dar es Salaam: Mkuki na Nyota, 130 p.
— (1st edn 1962) 1991b. *Kielezo cha Fasihi*. Dar es Salaam: Mkuki na Nyota.
Rollins, J.D. 1983. *A History of Swahili Prose: from Earliest Time to the End of the Nineteenth Century*. Leiden: E.J. Brill, 141 p.
Rouaud, A. 1982a. 'Pour une bibliographie des œuvres d'Afä Wärq Gabra Iyasus', *Bulletin des études africaines de l'INALCO* 2 (3), 123–36.
— 1982b. 'Contribution à l'histoire des impressions éthiopiennes', *Bulletin des études africaines de l'INALCO* 2 (4), 119–30.
— 1986. 'Quelques précisions sur les impressions et imprimeries éthiopiennes', *Bulletin des études africaines de l'INALCO* 6 (2), 131–46.
— 1989. 'Sur le genre voyage dans les débuts de la littérature imprimée amharique', *Proceedings of the Eighth International Conférence of Ethiopian Studies*, pp. 573–79. Addis Ababa: Institute of Ethiopian Studies.
— 1991. *Afä Wärq, 1868–1947, un intellectuel éthiopien témoin de son temps*. Paris: Éditions du CNRS, 363 p.
Roubaud, J. (ed. and trans.) 1980. Presentation, *Vingt poètes américains*. Paris: Gallimard, 487 p.
Ruganda, J. 1980. *The Floods*. Nairobi: East African Publishing House, 110 p.
— 1986. *Echoes of Silence*. Nairobi: Heinemann Educational Books, 104 p.
— 1992. *Telling the Truth Laughingly: the Politics of Francis Imbunga's Drama*. Nairobi: East African Educational Publishers.
Ruhumbika, G. 1981. 'The Role of Literary Translation in the Development of Swahili Literature', *Studies and Documents, Eacrotanal* 2, 35–44.
Rycroft, D. 1984. 'An 1842 Version of Dingana's Eulogies', *African Studies* 43 (2), 249–74.
— and Ngcobo, A.B. (eds) 1988. *The Praises of Dingana: Izibongo zika Dingana*. Durban/Pietermaritzburg: Killie Campbell Africana Library/University of Natal Press.
Sacleux, C. 1891. *Dictionnaire swahili-français*. Paris: Institut d'Ethnologie, 1939.
al-Sa'di 'Abd al-Rahman b. 'Abd Allah. 1656. *Tarikh es Sudan*. O. Houdas (ed. and revised trans. 1964). Paris: Maisonneuve et Larose, 540 p.
Salifou, A. 1974. *Tanimoune*. Paris: Présence africaine, 128 p.
Samb, A. 1972. *Essai sur la contribution du Sénégal à la littérature d'expression arabe*. Dakar: IFAN, 534 p.
Saro-Wiwa, K. 1985. *Sozaboy*. Port-Harcourt: Saros International, 186 p.
Satyo, S.C. 1982. 'Xhosa Literature', in A. Gérard (ed.), *Comparative Literature and African Languages*, pp. 70–91.
Schapera, I. 1965. *Praise Poems of the Tswana Chiefs*. Oxford: Oxford University Press, 255 p.
Scherer, J. 1967. 'Le théâtre en Afrique noire francophone', in *Le théâtre moderne dans le monde*, pp. 103–16. Paris: Éditions du CNRS.
Schön, J.F. 1885. *Magana Hausa, Native Literature or Proverbs, Tales, Fables and Historical Fragments in the Hausa Language, to which Is Added a Translation in English*. London: Society for the Promotion of Christian Knowledge, 288 p.
Segoete, E. 1982. *Monono ke moholi ke muoane*. Morija: Morija Sesuto Book Depot, 107 p.
— 1983. *Raphekeng*. Morija: Morija Sesuto Book Depot, 57 p.
Sembène, Ousmane 1957a. *Ô pays, mon beau peuple*. Paris: Le livre contemporain, 237 p.
— 1957b. *Le docker noir*. Paris: Debresse, 223 p. (*Black Docker*, London: Heinemann 1987)
— 1960. *Les bouts de bois de Dieu*. Paris: Le livre contemporain, 383 p. (*God's Bits of Wood*, Garden City, NY: Doubleday 1962)
— 1962. *Voltaïques*. Paris: Présence africaine, 207 p.
— 1965. *Vehi Ciosane ou Blanche genèse, suivi du Mandat*. Paris: Présence africaine, 221 p.
Senghor, L.S. 1945. *Chants d'ombre*. Paris: Le Seuil, 78 p.
— 1948. *Anthologie de la nouvelle poésie nègre et malgache de la langue française*. Paris: PUF.
— 1956. *Éthiopiques*. Paris: Le Seuil, 126 p.
— 1961. *Nocturnes*. Paris: Le Seuil, 93 p. (*Nocturnes*, London: Heinemann Educational, 1969).
— 1964. *Liberté 1, Negritude et humanisme*. Paris: Le Seuil, 444 p.
— 1979. *Élégies majeures, suivi de Dialogue sur la poésie francophone*. Paris: Le Seuil, 123 p.
— 1990. *Œuvre poétique*, 2nd edn Paris: Le Seuil, 438 p.
— 1991. *The Collected Poetry/Léopold Sédar Senghor*. Charlottesville: University Press of Virginia, xli+598 p.
Sengo, T.S.Y. 1992. *Shaaban Robert, Uhakiki wa Mwandishi yake*. Dar es Salaam: KAD Associates, 86 p.
Sepamla, S. 1975. *Hurry Up To It*. Johannesburg: A.D. Donker.
— 1977. *The Soweto I Love*. Cape Town: Rex Collings/David Philip, 53 p.

Serote, M.W. 1972. *Yakhal'Inkomo*. Johannesburg: Renoster Books, 52 p.
Setsoafia, B. 1968. *Mede Ablotsidela alo Esinam kple Dadzi*. Accra: Bureau of Ghana Languages, 104 p.
Seydou, C. (ed.). 1972. *Sillamaka et Poullori, récit épique peul raconté par Tinguidji*. Paris: Armand Colin (Les classiques africains), 278 p.
— 1973. 'Panorama de la littérature peule', *Bulletin de l'institut fondamental d'Afrique noire* 35 (1), 176–218.
— 1977. 'Bibliographie générale du monde peul', in *Études nigériennes* 43, Niamey: Institut de recherches en sciences humaines, 111 p.
Shakespeare, W. 1973. *Dintshontsho tsa bo-Juliuse Kesara*, Setswana trans. of *Julius Cesar* by S. Plaatje. Johannesburg: Witwatersrand University Press.
Shole, J.S. 1982. 'Setswana Literature', in A. Gérard (ed.), *Comparative Literature and African Languages*, pp. 97–105.
Sinxo, G.B. 1922. *UNomsa*. Lovedale: Lovedale Press, 63 p.
— 1956. *Isakhono sontfazi namanye amabalana*. Johannesburg: APB, 78 p.
Sipikin, M. 1971. *Tsofaffin Wakoki Da Sababbin Wakofi*. Zaria: Northern Nigeria Publishing Corporation, 119 p.
Sitas, A. 1994. 'Traditions of Poetry in Natal', in E. Gunner (ed.) *Politics and Performance: Theatre, Poetry and Song in Southern Africa*. Johannesburg: Witwaterstrand University Press, 293 p.
Sklar, R.L. 1960. 'Contribution of Tribalism to Nationalism in Nigeria', *Journal of Human Relations* 8 (3–4), 407–27.
Smit, J.A., Van Wyk, J., and Wade, J.P. 1996. *Rethinking South African Literary History*. Pietermaritzburg: Y Press.
Smith, P. 1975. *Le récit populaire au Rwanda*. Paris: Armand Colin (Les classiques africains), 432 p.
Socé Diop, O. 1935. *Karim, roman sénégalais*. Paris: Imp. Marcel Puyfourçat, 135 p.
— 1964. *Mirages de Paris*. Paris: Nouvelles éditions latines, 187 p.
Sow, A.I. (ed.). 1966. *La femme, la vache, la foi*. Paris: Armand Colin (Les classiques africains) 376 p.
— (ed.) 1970. *Inventaire du fonds Amadou Hampâté Ba*. Paris: Klincksieck, 83 p.
Soyinka, W. 1962. 'Towards a True Theatre', reprinted in Y. Ogunbiyi (ed.) 1981, *Drama and Theatre in Nigeria, a Critical Source Book*, pp. 457–61.
— 1963a. *A Dance of the Forests*. London/Ibadan: Oxford University Press, 89 p.
— 1963b. *The Lion and the Jewel*. London/Ibadan: Oxford University Press, 64 p.
— 1967. *Idanre and Other Poems*. London: Methuen, 88 p.
— 1972. *The Man Died*. London: Rex Collings, 315 p.
— 1973. *The Bacchae of Euripides*. London: Methuen, 97 p.
— 1975. *Death and the King's Horseman*. London: Heinemann.
— (ed.). 1975. *Poems of Black Africa*. London: Heinemann, 379 p.
— 1976. *Myth, Literature and the African World*. Cambridge: Cambridge University Press, 212 p.
— 1984. *Ake*. London: Rex Collings, 230 p.
— 1987. *Cycles sombres*. E. Galle (ed.). Paris: Silex, 194 p.
— 1999. *The Burden of Memory, the Muse of Forgiveness*. New York: Oxford University Press.
Sumner, C. 1976. *Ethiopian Philosophy*, vol. 2, *The Treatise of Zära Ya'acob and of Wäldä Haywat, Text and Authorship*. Addis Ababa: Central Printing Press, 367 p.
— 1978. *Ethiopian Philosophy*, vol. 3, *The Treatise of Zära Ya'acob and of Wälda Haywat, an Analysis*. Addis Ababa: Central Printing Press, 367 p.
— 1986. *The Source of African Philosophy: the Ethiopian Philosophy of Man*. Stuttgart: Steiner Verlag, 156 p.
Swanepoel, C.F. 1988. 'Oral and Written Poetry in Southern Sotho: Space and Boundaries', *Actes du XIIe Congrès de l'association internationale de littérature comparée*, Munich, Ivdicium, 4, 443–8.
— 1991. *Sotho Dithoko tsa Marena: Perspectives on Composition and Genre*. Pretoria: UNISA, 39 p.
— 1996. 'Merging African-Language Literature into South African Literary History', in J.A. Smith, J. Van Wyk, J.-P. Wade, *Rethinking South African Literary History*, 21–30.
— 1997. 'An Exploration of J.J. Moiloa's *Thesele, Nguana Mmamokgatjkane*, the Epic Tradition and the Oral-written Interface', *Research in African Literature* 28 (1), 112–22.
— 1998. 'Making South African Literary History in the 1990s: N.P. Maake's *Kweetsa ya Pelo ya Motho* (1995) – Narrative of Human Behaviour in Political Turmoil' in E. Lehmann, E. Reckwitz, and L. Vennarini (eds), *Constructing South African Literary History*, pp. 143–51. Essen: Die Blaue Eule.
Tadjo, V. 1984. *Latérite*. Paris: Hatier, 93 p.
Tafawa Balewa, A. (1st edn 1935) 1966. *Shaihu Umar*. Zaria: Northern Nigeria Publishing Corporation, 49 p.

Tati Loutard, J.-B. 1968a. *Poèmes de la mer*. Yaounde: CLE, 64 p.
— 1968b. *Les racines congolaises*, précédé de *La vie poétique*. Paris: P.J. Oswald, 77 p.
— 1970. *L'envers du soleil*, poèmes. Honfleur: P.J. Oswald, 68 p.
— 1974. *Les normes du temps*. Kinshasa/Lubumbashi: Éditions du mont noir, 67 p.
— 1977. *Les feux de la planète*. Dakar/Abidjan: Nouvelles éditions africaines, 47 p.
— 1982. *Le dialogue des plateaux*. Paris: Présence africaine, 60 p.
— 1985. *La tradition du songe*. Paris: Présence africaine, 63 p.
Tchicaya U'Tamsi, G.F. 1969. *Le mauvais sang* [1955], *suivi de Feu de brousse* [1957], *A triche cœur* [1958], Honfleur: P.J. Oswald, 137 p. (*Brush Fire*, Ibadan: Mbari Publications, 1964).
— 1978. *Le ventre, suivi de Le pain ou la cendre*. Paris: Présence africaine, 171 p.
— 1979. *Le destin glorieux du Maréchal Nnikon Nniku prince qu'on sort, suivi de Uwène le fondateur*. Paris: Présence africaine, 112 p.
— 1980. *Les cancrelats*. Paris: Albin Michel, 320 p.
— 1982. *Les méduses ou les orties de mer*. Paris: Albin Michel, 265 p.
— 1984. *Les phalènes*. Paris: Albin Michel, 250 p.
Thomas, I.B. 1930. *Iran Emi Segilola*. Lagos: CMS.
Tippu Tip 1974. *Maisha ya Hamed bin Muhammed el Murjebi yaani Tippu Tip kwa maneno yake mwenyewe*, W.H. Whiteley (ed. and trans. into English). Kampala/Nairobi/Dar es Salaam: East African Literature Bureau, 145 p.
Todorov, T. 1993. *On Human Diversity, Nationalism, Racism and Exoticism in French Thought*. Cambridge (Mass): Harvard University Press.
Traoré, B. 1958. *Le théâtre négro-africain et ses fonctions sociales*. Paris: Présence africaine, 159 p. (*The Black African Theatre and its Social Functions*, Ibadan: Ibadan University Press, 1972).
Trigo, S. 1981. *Luandino Vieira, O Logoteta*. Porto: Brasilia Editora, 647 p.
Tutuola, A. 1952. *The Palm Wine Drinkard and His Dead Palm Wine Tapster in the Dead's Town*. London: Faber and Faber, 125 p.
— 1954. *My Life in the Bush of Ghosts*. London: Faber and Faber, 174 p.
— 1980. *O Bebedor de vinho de palma*, Portuguese trans. of Tutuola, 1952. Lisbonne: Éditions 70, 92 p.
— 1982. *The Wild Hunter in the Bush of Ghosts*, reproduction of manuscript and intr. by B. Lindfors. Washington: Three Continents Press, 167 p.
Udoeyop, N.J. 1973. *Three Nigerian Poets*. Ibadan: Ibadan University Press, 166 p.
Vatsa, M. 1977. *Will Live Forever*. Uwani: Nwamife Publishers Limited, 35 p.
Veit-Wild, F. 1992a. *Teachers, Preachers, Non-believers, a Social History of Zimbabwean Literature*. London: Hans Zell Publishers.
— 1992b. *Survey of Zimbabwean Writers, Educational and Literary Careers*. Bayreuth: African Studies Series 27, 172 p.
— 1992c. *Dambuzo Marechera: a Source Book on His Life and Works*. London: Hans Zell Publishers.
Veit-Wild, F. & E. Schade (eds). 1988. *Dambudzo Marechera (4 June 1952–18 August 1987): Pictures, poems prose, tributes*. Harare: Baobab Books.
Verger, P. 1965. 'Grandeur et décadence du culte de Iyanu Osoronga (ma mère la sorcière) chez les Yorouba', *Journal de la Société des Africanistes*, pp. 141–243.
— 1972. 'Automatisme verbal et communication du savoir chez les Yorouba', *L'Homme* 12 (2), 5–46.
Verlet, M. 1986. 'Langue et pouvoir au Ghana sous N'Krumah', *Politique africaine* 23, 67–82.
Vidal, C. 1987. 'Alexis Kagame entre mémoire et histoire', Communication at colloquium: *Mémoire, Histoires, Identités*. Quebec: Université Laval, manuscript, 7 p.
— 1991. *Sociologie des passions: Côte d'Ivoire, Rwanda*. Paris: Karthala, 181 p.
Vieira, J.L. 1974. *No antigamente, na vida*. Lisbon: Éditions 70, 223 p.
— 1975. *Nós, os do Makusulu*. Lisbon: Sa'da Costa, 141 p.
Vilakazi, B.W. 1938. *Amal'ezulu*. Johannesburg: Witwatersrand University Press, 46 p.
— 1973. *Zulu Horizons*, adapted in English verse by F.L. Friedman. Johannesburg: Witwatersrand University Press, 144 p.
— (1st edn 1935) 1982. *Inkondlo ka Zulu*. Johannesburg: Witwatersrand University Press, 93 p.
Volney, C. 1787. *Voyages en Syrie et en Égypte*. Paris: Librairie Volland, 2 vols.
WAEC (West African Examinations Council) 1985–6. *Regulations and Syllabus for the Joint Examination for the School Certificate and General Certificate of Éducation (Ordinary Level) and the General Certificate of Education (Advanced Level)*, Lagos, WAEC, 384 p.
Wafula, R.M. 1999. *Uhakiki wa Tamthilia, Historia na Maendeleo Yake*. Nairobi: Jomo Kenyatta Foundation, 202 p.
Walters, J.J. 1994. *Guanya Pau, A Story of an African Princess*. Lincoln/London: University of Nebraska Press (1st edn 1891).
Warren, D.M. 1976. *Bibliography and Vocabulary of the Akan (Twi Fante) Language of Ghana*, Bloomington: Indiana University Publications, 266 p.

Wauthier, C. (1st edn, 1964) 1977. *L'Afrique des africains, inventaire de la négritude*. Paris: Seuil, 366 p. (*The Literature and Thought of Modern Africa: a Survey*, London: Pall Mall, 1966).
Weinrich, H. 1990. *Conscience linguistique et lectures littéraires*. Paris: Maison des sciences de l'homme, 355 p.
Westermann, D. 1907. *Grammatik der Ewe Sprache*. Berlin: Reimer, 16 + 158 p.
— and Bryan, M.A. 1970. *Languages of West Africa*. London: Dawsons of Pall Mall/ International African Institute, 277 p.
Whiteley, W. 1969. *Swahili, the Rise of a National Language*. London: Methuen, 150 p.
Wildung, D. (ed.) 1996. *Soudan, royaume sur le Nil*. Paris: Institut du monde arabe/ Flammarion, 428 p.
Wiley, B. 1991. 'Jomo Kenyatta, the Untenable Witness', *Passages* 2, 5–8. Evanston: North- western University.
Willan, B. 1984. *Sol T. Plaatje, South African Nationalist*, 1876–1932. London: Heinemann, 340 p.
Williams, D. (ed.) 1983. *The Journal and Selected Writings of the Reverend Tiyo Soga*. Cape Town: Balkema. Published for Rhodes University, Grahamstown, 221 p.
Williamson, K. 1984. *Practical Orthography in Nigeria*. Ibadan: Heinemann Educational Books, 70 p.
Wise, C. 1997. 'Resurrecting the Devil: Notes on Ngugi's Theory of the Oral-aural African Novel', *Research in African Literature* 28 (1), 134–140.
Xitu, U. (for de Carvalho, A.), 1979. *Maka na sazala*. Lisbon: Éditions 70, 147 p.
Yahaya, I.Y. 1988. 'The Development of Hausa Literature', in Y. Ogunbiyi (ed.), *Perspectives on Nigerian Literature* 1, 10–21.
— 'Aminu Kano', *Perspectives on Nigerian Literature* 2, 85–91.
— 1985. 'Trends in the Development of Creative Writing in Hausa', *Bulletin de l'AELIA* 8, 103–22.
Yali-Manisi, D.L.P. 1977. *Inkululeko, uzimele-gege e Transkayi*. Grahamstown: Institute of Social and Economic Research, Rhodes University, Xhosa Texts 1.
— 1952. *Izibongo zeenkosi zama-Xhosa*. Lovedale: Lovedale Press.
Zabus, C. 1991. *The African Palimpsest, Indigenization of Language in the West African Europhone Novel*. Amsterdam/Atlanta: Rodopi, 224 p.
Zell, H., Bundy, C. and Coulon, V. (eds). 1983. *A New Readers Guide to African Literature*. London: Heinemann, 553 p.
Zhukov, A. 1998. 'Shaaban Robert in the Russian Language', *AAP: Swahili Forum* 55, 185–9.
Zima, P. 1976. 'Literatures in West African Languages', in V. Klima, K.F. Ruzicka, and P. Zima, *Black Africa, Literature and Language*, pp. 140–80.
Zinsou, S.A. 1975. *On joue la comédie*. Paris: ORTF-DAEC, 114 p.
— 1984. *Le Club*. Lomé: Haho.
— 1987a. trans. and adaptation, *L'africaine de Paris par le Happy Star Concert Party*, Lome: Ministère de la jeunesse, des sports et de la culture, 62 p.
— 1987b. *La tortue qui chante*. Paris: Hatier, 127 p.
— 1989. 'Aux sources de la création', *Notre librairie* 98, 22–25.
Zumthor, P. 1983. *Introduction à la poésie orale*. Paris: Le Seuil, 319 p.
Zungur, S. 1968. *Wakokin Sa'adu Zungur*. Zaria: NNPC, 22 p.

Index

225